# OXFORD ENGLISH MONOGRAPHS

# Elizabethan Fictions

ESPIONAGE, COUNTER-ESPIONAGE,
AND THE DUPLICITY OF FICTION
IN EARLY ELIZABETHAN
PROSE NARRATIVES

R.W. MASLEN

CLARENDON PRESS · OXFORD
1997

Oxford University Press, Great Clarendon Street, Oxford OX2 6DP

Oxford New York

Athens Auckland Bangkok Bogota Bombay
Buenos Aires Calcutta Cape Town Dar es Salaam
Delhi Florence Hong Kong Istanbul Karachi
Kuala Lumpur Madras Madrid Melbourne
Mexico City Nairobi Paris Singapore
Taipei Tokyo Toronto

and associated companies in
Berlin Ibadan

Oxford is a trade mark of Oxford University Press

Published in the United States
by Oxford University Press Inc., New York

British Library Cataloguing in Publication Data

Data available

Library of Congress Cataloguing in Publication Data
Maslen, R. W. (Robert W.)
Elizabethan fictions: espionage, counter-espionage, and the
duplicity of fiction in early Elizabethan prose narratives/R.W. Maslen.
(Oxford English monographs)
Includes bibliographical references (p.  ) and index.
1. English fiction–Early modern, 1500–1700–History and criticism.  2. Spy stories, English–History and criticism.
3. English prose literature–Early modern, 1500–1700–History and criticism.  4. Intelligence service–Great
Britain–History–16th century–Historiography.  5. Great Britain–History–Elizabeth, 1558–1603–
Historiography.  6. Espionage, British–History–16th ccentury.  7. Espionage, British, in literature.  8. Spies
in literature.  I. Title.  II. Series.

PR839.S65M38  1997
823'.309–dc21  97–927
ISBN 0–19–811991–7

1 3 5 7 9 10 8 6 4 2

Typeset by Pure Tech India Limited, Pondicherry
Printed in Great Britain
on acid-free paper by
Biddles Ltd,
Guildford and Kings Lynn

# Acknowledgements

This book has been many years in the making, and I have accumulated more debts than I can count. My greatest debt is to the supervisor of my doctoral thesis, Dr Helen Cooper of University College, Oxford, for her endless patience, her encouragement, her meticulous criticism of each chapter as it emerged, sometimes with painful slowness, sometimes in a panic rush. Without her help and friendship this would never have been written.

My thanks too to Professor Anne Barton of Trinity College, Cambridge, for her stimulating supervision during my first year as a doctoral student; to Mrs Patricia Ingham of St Anne's College, Oxford, for introducing me to Elizabethan rhetoric and logic; and to Professor Ian McFarlane of Wadham College, for a term's intensive discussion of relations between England and the Continent in the sixteenth century. His wit and energy revived my pleasure in the subject when it was beginning to wilt. Professor Martin Dodsworth of Royal Holloway and Bedford New College and Dr David Margolies of Goldsmith's College gave me confidence at crucial moments. All these names mark vital stages in the book's development.

I owe immeasurable thanks to Mr Peter Conrad of Christ Church for the inspiration he has given me through his writing and conversation, for his unfailing kindness throughout my time at Oxford, and for giving me employment at a point when my funds were running out. Dr Michael Piret of Magdalen College, Oxford, helped to shape my mind over many years with his scholarship and wisdom. An extraordinary year at the School of English and American Studies at the University of Exeter helped to transform my thinking about criticism and theory; for this, my thanks to the whole school, especially to Dr Richard Bradbury, Dr Chris Brooks, Dr Gareth Roberts and Professor Michael Wood. My time at the University of Glasgow has consolidated this transformation. I owe particular debts of gratitude to Dr John Coyle, the subtlest critic I know of; to Professor Philip Hobsbaum; to Mr Paddy Lyons; and to Mr Stephen Johnson, who read part of the book in typescript and who altered my perception of history. If it had not been for these four, this book would have been a quite different one. As it stands, it does not do justice to what they have taught me.

The Very Revd Eric Heaton and Mrs Rachel Heaton of Christ Church, Oxford, and Mr Kenneth Palmer and Mrs Elizabeth Palmer of University College London, sustained me with their affection and scholarly interest.

My thanks to my family, like my other debts, could fill up volumes. My mother, Mrs Elizabeth Maslen of Queen Mary and Westfield College, London, has lived with this book throughout the many stages of its composition. My good luck in having unrestricted access to her critical sensitivity, her intellectual generosity, and her enthusiasm for literature cannot be measured.

Finally, my thanks are due to my wife Kirsty for refusing to marry me until the book was finished. She kept me alive in the latter stages of its writing, and brought discipline and delight to parts of my life where it was wanting. *Elizabethan Fictions* is dedicated to Kirsty, with love.

R. M.

# Contents

# Conventions Used in the Text and Notes

In quoted matter initial 'i' and 'v' have been amended in accordance with modern convention, and abbreviations have been expanded. In the titles of books, initial letters have been capitalized.

# Introduction
# Monstrous Imaginations

The Renaissance knew of strange manners of poisoning—poisoning by a helmet and a lighted torch, by an embroidered glove and a jewelled fan, by a gilded pomander and by an amber chain. Dorian Gray had been poisoned by a book.

(Oscar Wilde, *The Picture of Dorian Gray*)

[T]his phantasie may be resembled to a glasse . . . whereof there be many tempers and maner of makinges . . . for some be false glasses and shew thinges otherwise than they be in deede, neither fairer nor fouler, nor greater nor smaller. There be againe of these glasses that shew thinges exceeding faire and comely, others that shew figures very monstruous and illfavored. Even so is the phantasticall part of man (if it be not disordered) a representer of the best, most comely and bewtifull images or apparences of thinges to the soule and according to their very truth. If otherwise, then doth it breede *Chimeres* and monsters in mans imaginations, and not onely in his imaginations, but also in all his ordinarie actions and life which ensues.

(George Puttenham (?), *The Arte of English Poesie*)

At the heart of a labyrinthine library in Umberto Eco's novel *The Name of the Rose* a book lies hidden: a book that kills its readers, and that brings about the burning of the finest store of manuscripts in Christendom and of the fabulous treasury of ancient artefacts which is the abbey that housed it. The book derives its devastating destructive powers not so much from the inflammatory nature of its contents as from the context in which they are read. One of the monastic librarians, steeped in a theology that endorses the imposition of orthodoxy through violence, has convinced himself that the volume holds the key to the demolition of order itself, and has smeared its pages with venom in a futile bid to keep that key from others; but his private act of censorship results in the collapse of the very structures he has struggled to protect. For modern readers of Elizabethan prose fiction, Roger Ascham looks a little like Umberto Eco's murderous librarian: the self-appointed guardian of a reactionary morality, struggling to turn back the tide of imaginary heresies which is destined to drown the world he knew. Ascham's violent attack on Italian fiction stands out for its apparent unreasonableness in the midst of the sensible pedagogic programme he proposes in his famous treatise on teaching Latin, *The Scholemaster* (1570). Yet in exposing the dangers to English culture posed by the fashion for new Italian forms of narrative, Ascham spoke both for the advocates of censorship and for the writers of prose fiction themselves. Both the censors and the writers seem to have sensed that something strange and disturbing was going on in Elizabethan prose: something that threatened to transform the nature of fiction itself and to explode contemporary theories of its ideological function. But where the censors sought to stem this threatening tide, many of the younger English writers revelled in the rich abundance of exotic objects it carried to their shore, and chose to make the problems and perils of writing fiction the subject of their fictions.

The dangers of imaginative writing were well known by the time Ascham launched his attack on the Italian imagination. Plato banished poets from his ideal republic, the medieval church fathers charged them with contributing to the spread of paganism, and the sixteenth-century magician–satirist Cornelius Agrippa censured poetry as the vainest and most debilitating of the arts, 'the principall Author of lyes'.[1] Richard Rainolde summarizes the case against poetry in *The Foundacion of Rhetorike* (1563), where he argues that besides their 'monsterous lies against God, thei inventyng a genealogie of many Goddes procreated, where as there is but one God', poets are capable of overwhelming the art of communication itself with the astonishing fecundity of their productions: the ancient authors 'invented and forged folie upon folie, lye upon lye, as in the battaill of Troye, thei aggravate the dolour of the battaill, by pitifull and lamentable invencion' (sig. G). This assault on the sheer *quantity* of fictions manufactured by the poets is repeated time and again by the Elizabethan

---

[1] The chief charges against poetry were laid out in Boccaccio's *De Genealogia Deorum*, bk. 14, chs. 3, 4, and 5. For Plato's banishment of poets see *Republic*, 2; for early attacks on poetry, see E. K. Chambers, *The Medieval Stage*, 2 vols. (Oxford: Oxford University Press, 1903), i. 9 and 31, ii. 290; for Agrippa's characterization of poetry as the author of lies see *Of the Vanitie and Uncertaintie of Artes and Sciences*, trans. James San[d]ford (1569), fo. 11.

advocates of state censorship. Roger Ascham compares the destructive exuberance of Italian fiction to that of a river that has burst its banks, and Stephen Gosson conceives of the poetic imagination as a hothouse of erotic fantasies, whose unruly seed scatters itself throughout the orderly garden of the printed text and reduces its neat plots to trackless wildernesses.[2] Even the defenders of fiction (and Rainolde, in one of his other hats, was one of them) acknowledged its appalling potential for corrupting its readers.[3] Sir Philip Sidney confessed that 'Poesy may not only be abused, but that being abused, by the reason of his sweet charming force, it can do more hurt than any other army of words';[4] his choice of a military metaphor to articulate its potency implies that these destructive capabilities might constitute a material threat to the security of the Elizabethan state. George Puttenham, the putative author of *The Arte of English Poesie* (1589), warns the poets he addresses to keep a careful controlling eye on their verses, because the taking of excessive imaginative liberties might get them into serious trouble. The chief tool of the poet, he explains, is the figure of speech, and it would take very little to convert a rhetorical figure into a criminal act:

As figures be the instruments of ornament in every language, so be they also in a sorte abuses or rather trespasses in speach, because they passe the ordinary limits of common utterance, and be occupied of purpose to deceive the eare and also the minde, drawing it from plainnesse and simplicitie to a certaine doublenesse, whereby our talke is the more guilefull and abusing.[5]

The Greek lawgivers, he goes on, banned the use of metaphors in the courtroom, since they considered this kind of 'forraine and coulored talke' to inhibit the process of justice. Indeed, Puttenham is remarkably wary of encouraging poets to indulge in fiction at all; like their chief Elizabethan antagonist Stephen Gosson, he considers their primary function to consist in the versified retailing of historical events.[6]

---

[2] See my discussions of Gosson and Ascham in Ch. 1, ss. 3 and 4.

[3] Rainolde's defence of fiction occurs in the course of his 'Oracion by a fable', when he launches into a panegyric on the fables of Aesop: 'his fables in effect contain the mightie volumes and bookes of all philosophers in morall preceptes, and the infinite monumentes of lawes stablished'. *A Booke Called The Foundacion of Rhetorike*, sig. B[v].

[4] *An Apology for Poetry*, ed. Geoffrey Shepherd (London: Nelson, 1965), 125. All subsequent references are to this edition.

[5] *The Arte of English Poesie*, facsimile edn. (Menston: Scolar Press, 1968), 128. All subsequent references are to this edition.

[6] See ibid. 14–15, where Puttenham discusses the 'monstruous imaginations' engendered by the 'inventive parte of the minde' when it is wrongly used, as against the 'bewtifull visions' produced by the properly disciplined imaginative faculty. See also Ch. 2, s. 1 below.

Appeals to the imagination, such as metaphor and fable, can easily be taken for the guileful strategies of foreign infiltrators in the streets and houses of a beleaguered nation, cunning spies who aim to seduce the private citizen into the stupefied acceptance of alien ideologies by enmeshing them in a network of alluring lies. For the Protestant English writers who argued for and against the art of poetry in the 1570s and 1580s, at once the most seductive and the most destructive form of fiction was Catholicism. The college of Douai was founded in Flanders in 1568 with the specific purpose of training young English recruits for the dangerous task of reclaiming England from Protestantism; and throughout the two decades that followed—decades of intense debate about the respective functions of poetry, prose, and drama—the menace of continental Catholicism hung over both sides of the controversy, and lent it an urgency that it has rarely recovered since.

Ascham had every reason, then, to be alarmed at the flood of foreign prose fiction that was pouring into the country like the advance guard of a surreptitious invasion. The 1560s saw an unprecedented rise in the number of Italian texts being made available to English readers in translation, and Ascham runs rapidly through his multiplication tables in his efforts to express the damage done by even one of these ingratiating publications.[7] 'Ten Sermons at Paules Crosse', he calculates, 'do not so moch good for movyng men to trewe doctrine, as one of those bookes do harme, with inticing men to ill living'.[8] The richest fund of Italian fictions could be found in the story-collections of William Painter and Geoffrey Fenton, *The Palace of Pleasure* (1566–7) and *Certaine Tragicall Discourses* (1567): two inexhaustible treasure-chests of narratives which released into England a hoard of unfamiliar plots and dialogues that seems at once to have captivated the fantasies of the Elizabethan public. Painter advertises the innovative nature of his translations by describing them as 'novels', after the French and Italian words for pithy narratives in prose, and he explains in his prefatory notes that they were selected for their 'strangeness'—for their alluring foreignness, their calculated violation of the settled expectations of his sixteenth-century readers.[9] And the challenge these novels

---

[7] For a useful account of the influx of Italian translations into Elizabethan England see Violet M. Jeffery, *John Lyly and the Italian Renaissance* (Paris: Champion, 1929).

[8] *Roger Ascham: English Works*, ed. W. A. Wright (Cambridge: Cambridge University Press, 1904), 230. All references to Ascham's works are taken from this edition. For further discussion of Ascham see Ch. 1, s. 3 below.

[9] For my discussion of Painter, see Ch. 2, s. 2 below.

presented to the humanist curriculum was by no means a figment of Ascham's imagination. In the decade that followed the publication of *The Scholemaster*, English writers of prose fiction proceeded to ransack Painter's and Fenton's collections for concepts, situations, and sophisticated dialogues, and they made sure that their readers were well aware that their witty narratives had been thoroughly infected by corrupt Italian values. At the same time, they cast these narratives in the form of impudent responses to *The Scholemaster*, lifting words, phrases, arguments, even character-studies from Ascham's text to furnish themselves with raw material for their fictions. In the process the clever young writers of the 1570s worked hard to confirm every one of Ascham's fears about the debilitating effects of Italian fiction on the idle young: to insinuate, in fact, that an emerging generation of English intellectuals was being systematically depraved, tempted one by one into the rapidly expanding web of Catholic intrigue. In a number of ways, *The Scholemaster* may be said to have added fuel to the literary fire it was trying to quench.

The pedagogic system Ascham promoted in his treatise was designed to keep the young and sexually active members of the ruling classes firmly locked in the benevolent embrace of a ceaselessly vigilant pedagogue, from infancy to early middle age, when they would presumably be well established on the straight and narrow path to marriage, or a safe career, or both. The texts to which his pupils adhered were to be strictly monitored, and he provides a list of accredited authors in the second section of his treatise. It includes Cicero, bowdlerized versions of plays by Terence and Plautus, Caesar's *Commentaries*, and the orations of Titus Livius, 'such as be both longest and plainest' (238). Care must be taken to endear these authors to the youthful reader, since 'he, that can neither like *Aristotle* in Logicke and Philosophie, nor *Tullie* in Rhetoricke and Eloquence, will, from these steppes, likelie enough presume, by like pride, to mount hier, to the misliking of greater matters: that is either in Religion, to have a dissentious head, or in the common wealth, to have a factious hart' (243–4). The dangers presented by the wrong kind of reading, then, are very much more serious than the corruption of a few private citizens; and these dangers are peculiarly difficult to avert. Ascham's didactic method is based on the premiss that the most effective means of instructing the young is to make instruction pleasurable. But as his treatise unfolds it becomes increasingly clear that other, more potent pleasures are competing with the schoolmaster for the attentions of his adolescent charges. The most seductive of these rival pleasures is the kind his pupils derive from non-canonical texts; and the most alluring of these texts are fictions imported from Italy by the likes of Painter and Fenton. The perils of Italian books are manifold. In the first place, Ascham spends many pages of *The Scholemaster* warning parents of the deleterious effects of sending their children to complete their education abroad, where they will be subjected to the predatory charms of Italy. But Italian fiction renders travel unnecessary; it smuggles Italian sophistication, Italian libertarianism, and Italian religion into the very hearts of English households, without putting its impressionable readers to the trouble of leaving their firesides. And Ascham clearly fears that the lessons it inculcates are vastly more pleasurable than anything his own curriculum can afford.

As he sees them, the lessons taught by Italian fictions are these:

1. They take love as their subject, and so excite the adolescent hormones, which leads to intellectual confusion—and a loss of interest in Cicero.

2. They are sophisticated, and tempt their youthful readers to employ their intellects in the service of extra-curricular activities. By this means they destroy that unthinking adherence to a set of simple values which Ascham holds to be the best qualification for trustworthy servants of the state.

3. They occupy the same territory as pedagogic treatises. Ascham's method depends on an appeal to his pupils' wills; Italian fiction takes the will by storm. The metaphors he uses for the operations of these texts are derived from the schoolroom: they are peppered with perverted 'preceptes' (229), they teach 'old bawdes new schole poyntes' (231), they grace their poisonous contents with 'honest titles' (229), and they insinuate themselves into the system of patronage by which new texts are admitted into the catalogue of authorized literature, being 'dedicated over boldlie to vertuous and honorable personages, the easilier to begile simple and innocent wittes' (229–30). Finally, they are translations, and so participate in the processes of translation and imitation which he sets at the heart of his educational programme. It is therefore with some justification that he predicts, 'Suffer these bookes to be read, and they shall soone displace all bookes of goodly learning' (231).

4. They encourage freedom of speech. One of the dangers courted by English travellers who encounter Italian culture is that of learning

to discuss politics. Such travellers employ their learning in a free-
lance capacity, like the inhabitants of one of the disastrously liberal
Italian states. They transform themselves in fact into honorary Italians, as if they had been:

brought up in *Italie*, in some free Citie, as all Cities be there: where a man
may freelie discourse against what he will, against whom he lust: against
any Prince, agaynst any governement, yea against God him selfe, and his
whole Religion: where he must be, either *Guelphe* or *Gibiline*, either *French*
or *Spanish*: and alwayes compelled to be of some partie, or some faction, he
shall never be compelled to be of any Religion: And if he medle not over
much with Christes true Religion, he shall have free libertie to embrace all
Religions, and becum, if he lust at once, without any let or punishment, Jew-
ish, Turkish, Papish, and Devillish.(236)

Ascham's solution to this insidious transition from reader to heretic
and rebel is the same as the one advanced by Stephen Gosson: ceaseless
vigilance on the part of the authorities, and the tightening up of the
Elizabethan censorship system. Without these controls, the appalling
fertility of the Italian imagination will inexorably overrun the socio-
political structures of Protestant England; because Italian fictions,
like the over-sexed and under-disciplined youngsters who read
them, are capable of reproducing with the energy of rabbits.

The Elizabethan censors agreed with him about the power of the
printed text as a medium for distributing Catholic propaganda. The
close of the 1560s was a period of intense activity on the part of
the High Commission, the ecclesiastical body responsible for policing
printed texts under Elizabeth I. It was also a period of political turbulence, with outbreaks of Catholic conspiracy and rebellion, the long-
expected papal excommunication of the English queen, and signs of
disaffection from the radical wing of the Anglican church.[10] In
response to these events the Privy Council issued a succession of proclamations aimed at suppressing such 'Bookes, Billes and Writinges' as
could be construed as encouraging sedition. Ascham's assault on Italian
narratives identified them with the propagandistic documents pro-
scribed in these proclamations, and linked their authors by implication
both with the conspiracies of the 1560s and 1570s and with the young
English recusants who were being groomed for martyrdom at Douai.
One would think that there could not have been a better time for
admirers and imitators of Italian fiction to have stayed discreetly silent.

[10] See Ch. 1, s. 4.

Instead the 1570s witnessed an astonishing deluge of English narrat-ives which freely acknowledged their debts to Italian models. They range from the pseudo-Italian sections of George Gascoigne's poetic miscellanies, *A Hundreth Sundrie Flowres* (1573) and *The Posies* (1575), to George Whetstone's Italianate miscellany *The Rocke of Regard* (1576); from George Turberville's versifications of the stories of Boc-caccio and Bandello in his *Tragical Tales* (1576), to George Pettie's Anglo-Italian variations on Classical themes in *A Petite Pallace of Pettie his Pleasure* (1576); from John Lyly's Neapolitan romance *Euphues* (1578) to Stephen Gosson's Venetian morality tale *The Ephemerides of Phialo* (1579). The High Commission was quick to make its power felt in this new and troublesome literary scene, and the text that bore the brunt of its displeasure was George Gascoigne's brilliant little anti-romance *The Adventures of Master F.J.* (1573). The *Adventures* was only partly based on Italian patterns; it owes as much to a tradition of erotic narrative in English whose chief exponent was Chaucer, and it seems to have been suppressed because the censors read it as a piece of scandalous gossip about a noble family in the north of Eng-land.[11] But when Gascoigne reprinted it in his next miscellany he recast it as a translation from the Italian of an imaginary writer called Bartello, as if to acknowledge and explain the seditious nature of its contents.[12] This second version, like the first, was withdrawn from circulation by the censors; but the banning of Gascoigne's works seems only to have stimulated his admirers into imitating his provoc-ative texts with greater enthusiasm: nearly every prose fiction written in English over the next ten years pays homage in one way or another to F.J.'s scurrilous antics. The shadow of censorship hung, then, over the fictions of the 1570s, and the young writers who chose to show an

---

[11] But, as Andrew Hadfield points out, Chaucer was hardly the English purist he was taken for by commentators like E.K. in *The Shepheardes Calender*. Hadfield argues that 'when Chaucer was re-invented as the great English poet in the Renaissance, he ... actually had what he first started—the English adoption of Italian poetic forms—eventually defined against the use made of him by later writers'. *Literature, Politics and National Identity* (Cam-bridge: Cambridge University Press, 1994), 4. For my discussion of Gascoigne see Ch. 3 below.

[12] In *The Posies*, *The Adventures of Master F.J.* becomes 'The pleasant Fable of *Ferdinando Jeronimi and Leonora de Valasco*, translated out of the Italian riding tales of *Bartello*': *The Com-plete Works of George Gascoigne*, ed. John W. Cunliffe, 2 vols. (Cambridge: Cambridge Uni-versity Press, 1907), i. 383. Another narrative in the same collection, 'The fruite of fetters', which relates the adventures of the Green Knight, is also ascribed to Bartello (369), and a third narrative, 'Dan Bartholmew of Bathe', announces that its hero is the Green Knight under another name (136). In other words, Gascoigne's games with the question of author-ship are as giddily cross-referenced as Vladimir Nabokov's in *Pale Fire*.

interest in suspicious foreign and native texts must have been fully aware that they were playing with literary fire. They demonstrate this awareness by playful allusions to the dangers they were courting. Gascoigne's second miscellany incorporates an impudent address to the censors of the High Commission, Pettie's Italianate story-collection pretends, like Gascoigne's first miscellany, to have slipped into print by mistake, Lyly's *Euphues* books are full of allusions to the precarious status of foreign visitors and texts in a hostile country, and all the prose fictions of the decade refer repeatedly to the presence of malicious informers among their readers, who will fraudulently twist the most innocuous of phrases in their efforts to inculpate its guileless author. In Gascoigne's words, the prose fiction of the 1570s is the literature of 'petty treason', and its producers do not seem to have been afraid to lay themselves open to still more serious charges.[13]

In fact, to the suspicious mind these fictions would seem to be filled to bursting-point with the language of sedition. They are stuffed with acts of treachery, secret messages in code, cunning infiltrations of restricted areas, and the leaking of highly sensitive confidential documents. Their heroes and heroines are professional secret agents with all the accessories of a James Bond or a Mata Hari: an eye for fashion, an irresistible attraction for the opposite sex, an unnerving rapidity of response to unexpected situations, and a predilection for assuming exotic disguises at the drop of a hat. They watch one another like hawks, pass letters to and fro which can be read in a dozen different ways, hatch plots against their aristocratic hosts and patrons, and exhibit the geographical and social mobility of the late twentieth-century business executive. And the narrators of these fictions associate themselves with their protagonists at every opportunity, posing as unreliable operatives whose political affiliations are always suspect, and who have insinuated themselves by stealth into the world of the printed text. Most unsettlingly of all for devotees of Ascham, the sphere in which these Anglo-Italian operatives ply their devious trade is the private household: they specialize in breaking and entering the hearts and properties of the ruling classes. From one point of view,

---

[13] The phrase 'petty treason' is a legal term, meaning, in the words of the *OED*, 'treason against a subject, spec. the murder of one to whom the murderer owes allegiance'. Gascoigne uses it in *The Adventures of Master F.J.*, repr. in *An Anthology of Elizabethan Prose Fiction*, ed. Paul Salzman (Oxford: Oxford University Press, 1987), 80. For a recent discussion of Elizabethan conceptions of treason, see Lucy Baldwin Smith, *Treason in Tudor England* (London: Jonathan Cape, 1986).

the prose fictions of the 1570s can be read as spy-stories, written by aspiring spies for the delectation of the spymasters; and if the spheres in which they engage in their subtle practices—the beds and boards of their prospective patrons—seem petty enough to the twentieth-century reader, the censorship of Gascoigne's apparently frivolous narrative suggests that the Elizabethan authorities thought otherwise.

If the notion of prose fiction as the literary equivalent of espionage seems far-fetched, it is worth taking a look at the careers of its practitioners.[14] As is well known, these writers devoted much of their careers to the more or less successful pursuit of government employment.[15] Geoffrey Fenton, who eventually landed the coveted post of principal secretary of the Irish Council, had worked for years beforehand as a spy in Ireland, while George Gascoigne ended his life in the service of the Elizabethan spymaster Francis Walsingham.[16] John Lyly expended considerable pains in a futile bid to obtain the newly established position of Master of the Revels, the chief censor of plays and entertainments under Elizabeth I.[17] Failing this, he employed his talents in the service of the church, by writing a series of satirical ripostes to the Puritan polemical tracts of Martin Marprelate. The office of Master of the Revels fell to another author of prose fiction, Edmund Tilney, who produced in 1568 a little dialogue on marriage called *The Flower of Friendshippe*, which demonstrated his easy familiarity with the languages and customs of continental Europe.[18] William

[14] At this point I should explain that I do not intend to examine the practices of the Elizabethan spy service in this book. My concern is with the *idea* of espionage as it is exploited in the plots and recurring metaphors of Elizabethan prose fiction, rather than with espionage as such. The operations of the historical spy service are documented in Conyers Read, *Mr Secretary Walsingham and the Policy of Queen Elizabeth*, 3 vols. (Oxford: Clarendon Press, 1925). A fascinating recent study of espionage in the 1580s is John Bossy, *Giordano Bruno and the Embassy Affair* (New Haven: Yale University Press, 1991). John Michael Archer discusses links between Elizabethan literature and espionage in *Sovereignty and Intelligence: Spying and Court Culture in the English Renaissance* (Stanford, Ca.: Stanford University Press, 1993); and Charles Nicholl examines Marlowe's links with spies and spying in *The Reckoning* (London: Picador, 1993).

[15] For the relationship between Elizabethan literature and the careers of its practioners, see Richard Helgerson, *The Elizabethan Prodigals* (Berkeley, Ca.: University of California Press, 1976), and Lorna Hutson, *The Usurer's Daughter: Male Friendship and Fictions of Women in Sixteenth-Century England* (London: Routledge, 1994).

[16] For my discussion of Fenton, see Ch. 2, ss. 2 and 3.

[17] For accounts of Lyly's career, see Albert Feuillerat, *John Lyly: Contribution à l'histoire de la Renaissance en Angleterre* (Cambridge: Cambridge University Press, 1910), and G. K. Hunter, *John Lyly: The Humanist as Courtier* (London: Routledge & Kegan Paul, 1962).

[18] For an account of Tilney's life, see W. R. Streitberger, *Edmond Tyllney: Master of the Revels and Censor of Plays* (New York: AMS Press, 1986).

Painter worked as clerk of the ordnance at the Tower of London, John Grange seems to have been a lawyer, and the three Georges—Pettie, Whetstone, and Gascoigne—all served as soldiers in the Netherlands and France.[19] Writers of prose fiction, then, occupied, or planned to occupy, positions which gave them direct experience of the workings of Elizabethan foreign and domestic policy, and many of them were closely involved in matters relating to the security of the nation. In this there is little to distinguish them from contemporary practitioners of other kinds of imaginative writing. They wrote their fictions, for the most part, before they had got the jobs they wanted, and to an extent their sophisticated narratives can be read as rehearsals for a life of political action. But the choice of prose fiction as a means of advertising their untapped potential delivered a very mixed set of signals to prospective employers. On the one hand it marked them out as exceptionally clever young men, cunning in the uses of rhetoric, logic, sophistry, and fraud, knowledgeable about current affairs in Europe, sharp-eyed and wary when surrounded by enemies, and capable of setting down their observations in a prose that revealed a good deal more to the scrutiny of the well informed than it did to the casual reader. On the other hand it proclaimed their potential for corruption: the shakiness of their loyalties, the delight they took in putting themselves in danger, their interest in the doings of Catholic nations, and their mastery of the skills that would make them formidable undercover activists should the forces of the counter-Reformation manage to recruit them. Charles Nicholl has pointed out that many of the most effective of Walsingham's agents began their careers as Catholic sympathizers, and continued to be regarded with suspicion even while they were working for the Elizabethan government.[20] By flirting with traits that were associated with Catholicism, the young writers of the 1570s took the daring step of showing that they were uniquely qualified to act as double agents.

Throughout the sixteenth century, prose fiction seems consistently to have been regarded, by its authors as well as by its readers, as the most slippery of literary mediums. Its slipperiness lay partly in the difficulty of defining what it was. Prose fiction refused to conform to any

---

[19] Convenient accounts of the careers of Grange, Painter, Pettie, and Whetstone can be found in the *Dictionary of Literary Biography*, 2nd ser. cxxxvi: *Sixteenth-Century British Non-dramatic Writers*, ed. David A. Richardson (Detroit, Mich.: Bruccoli Clark Layman, 1994), 155–8, 259–63, 269–72, and 330–5.

[20] See Nicholl, *The Reckoning*, ch. 13.

of the generic categories by which contemporary textbooks charted the hegemony of what is written: tragedy, comedy, history, epic, satire, and the rest. It masquerades as anything but fiction. The *Tragicall Discourses* passes itself off as a collection of chronicle histories; *The Adventures of Master F.J.* poses as a piece of literary criticism; John Grange's *The Golden Aphroditis* (1577) cannot decide whether it is a cutting allegorical satire, a fluffy romance, a morsel of high-society gossip, or an extended exercise in plagiarism.[21] John Lyly's two *Euphues* books undergo a bewildering succession of changes into new and unexpected shapes. The first begins as an Italianate novel and ends as a series of letters, becoming an educational treatise and a theological dispute along the way; the second shifts from novel to fable to patriotic eulogy, and closes as a marriage guidance pamphlet.[22] And this resistance to classification had been a feature of prose fiction since the beginning of the century. More's *Utopia* (1516) casts itself as a less than reliable transcription of a traveller's observations; the anonymous story-collection *The Deceyte of Women* (*c.*1520) adopts the guise of a crude misogynistic tract; and the anti-Catholic satire *The Image of Idleness* (1556) poses both as a translation from the Cornish and as a bundle of comic letters, loosely flung together and published on a whim.[23] Sixteenth-century prose fiction could not be pinned down, and insinuated itself into places where it had no business and where it could cause the maximum disruption—political treatises, rhetorical handbooks, theological disputations, philosophical theses—while adapting its own infinitely malleable texture to accommodate each of these literary kinds. To the suspicious eye of the censor, its very heterogeneity may have seemed menacing.

From the beginning of the century, too, prose fiction had shown an unhealthy interest in questions of 'policy': of the cunning manipulation of words and circumstances to achieve a specific goal, the sort of political opportunism to which Machiavelli had given a bad name. *The Deceyte of Women* investigates the sly domestic policies of mistresses and wives in order to rescue its young male readers from the coils of feminine intrigue. In the process it demonstrates the

---

[21] See my article 'John Grange', *Dictionary of Literary Biography*, cxxxvi. 155–8.

[22] For my discussions of Lyly's *Euphues* books see Chs. 5 and 6 below.

[23] See 'The First English Epistolary Novel: *The Image of Idleness*. Text, Introduction and Notes', ed. Michael Flachmann, *Studies in Philology*, 87 (1990), 1–74. For the date of *The Image of Idleness* see Michael Pincombe, 'The Date of *The Image of Idleness*', *Notes and Queries*, 239 (NS 41 no. 1) (Mar. 1994), 24. For my discussion of *The Deceyte of Women* see Ch. 4, s. 1.

almost insurmountable difficulty of unmasking plots that are hatched in the home. *The Image of Idleness* records the efforts of its incompetent protagonist, Bawdin Bachelor, to worm his way by 'policy' (his favourite word) into the affections of a series of women, in an unsuccessful bid to find a wife. In the process it establishes his commitment to the culture of hypocrisy which is endorsed by the Catholic state under Mary I.[24] More's *Utopia* is, of course, the most politic prose fiction of them all, and one that casts its influence over all the sophisticated narratives of the century. It is narrated by the sailor Hythloday who is a devotee of 'simplicity'—the straight talking and plain dealing that induces trust—and it describes a nation that is founded on a similar reverence for simplicity: where there are no secrets, where laws are formulated in such a way that every citizen can understand them, and where double-dealing spies are the only enemies of the state who are subject to execution without mercy.[25] At the same time the Utopians themselves practise every kind of treachery, guile, and undercover intrigue to undermine their enemies, and *Utopia* itself is a brilliant exercise in duplicity, hiding its acerbic criticisms of Henry VIII's government beneath a naïvely comic mask.[26] *Utopia* and *The Image of Idleness* are hostile agents in disguise, secretly working against the policies of the regimes under which they were written. And their disguises have withstood the test of time. Scholars still argue vociferously over different readings of the first, while the second has simply been excluded from most discussions of early modern fiction.

The fictions of the 1570s, on the other hand, snatch off the disguises of their authors and protagonists at every opportunity. Both parties are endlessly assuming false identities and involving themselves in clandestine plots, and thus declaring their enthusiastic participation in the

[24] There are several indications that *The Image of Idleness* is (among other things) an anti-Catholic satire; from its dedication 'to the Lady Lust' (18), whose court (described in the preliminary epistle) is dominated by hypocrites, the chief of whom is one Friar Floysterer; to the presence in one of Bawdin Bachelor's letters of an 'image of alabaster' to which lovers go on pilgrimage and which gives them dubious counsel on sexual matters (35). The text was published by the Protestant printer William Seres, who was gaoled at the beginning of Mary's reign.

[25] More commends his friend Peter Giles for his 'prudent simplicity', but Hythloday covets the same compliment, as he explains to More's persona: 'if I would speak such things that be true I must needs speak such things; but as for to speak false things . . . truly it is not my part.' *Utopia*, trans. Ralph Robinson (1551), introd. Richard Marius (London: J. M. Dent, 1985), 14 and 48; all references are to this edition. For the lack of secrecy in Utopia see pp. 74 and 76; for utopian laws, see pp. 103–4; for the merciless treatment of spies, see p. 116.

[26] For utopian subterfuge in times of war, see *Utopia*, 108–17.

machinations of policy. *The Adventures of Master F.J.* presents itself, in the first version, as the work of two non-existent English writers, and in the second as a translation from the work of a non-existent Italian. *A Petite Pallace of Pettie his Pleasure* claims to have been written by Pettie's younger, wilder self, from whom he is divorced both by time and by his recent restoration to the path of moral probity.[27] F.J. and Euphues, like their inventors, have a mask for every occasion, a plausible excuse for every treacherous act. At the same time, both writers and protagonists are constantly laying themselves open to investigation, dropping hints about their 'real' identities and half-concealed agendas. Protagonists are always being analysed by narrators and by other fictional characters, their strengths and weaknesses probed, their slipperiness pinned down. Euphues' and F.J.'s excuses for their conduct are manifestly laboured, and they cannot help drawing attention to the ingenuity of their disguises. In the same way, authors are constantly signalling their responsibility for the unruly fictions they pretend to disown. Gascoigne connects himself with the *Adventures* by incorporating his name into the title of the second miscellany that contains it: *The Posies of George Gascoigne Esquire*. Pettie's collection makes the same arrogant declaration of its author's identity, blazoning his signature across its title-page in defiance of his dissociation of himself, in a preliminary epistle, from the irresponsible narratives of his youth. Packed though they are with secrets, each of these texts invites its readers to unveil the 'truth' behind the conspiracies it examines, the historical 'facts' behind its fictions. Critics have responded to this invitation by reading the narratives of the 1570s as autobiographical anecdotes, commentaries on incidents in their authors' private lives.[28] The Elizabethan censors responded by construing *The Adventures of Master F.J.* as a dangerous libel on the aristocracy, and ordering its suppression.

In other words, if the writers of Elizabethan prose fiction delight in manufacturing and accumulating secrets, they also seem unusually sus-

---

[27] For my discussion of Pettie, see Ch. 4.

[28] See e.g. C. T. Prouty, *George Gascoigne: Elizabethan Courtier, Soldier, and Poet* (New York: Columbia, 1942), 197–8: 'We can also see in the details of the story that the author, and therefore Gascoigne, is recounting his own adventures.' R. W. Bond similarly observes that in *Euphues* 'the probability of an autobiographical element is considerable': *The Complete Works of John Lyly*, 3 vols. (Oxford: Clarendon Press, 1902), i. 2. Autobiographical readings seem to have been practised from the moment these books were printed. Simon Forman, for instance—an astrologer who was Lyly's contemporary at Oxford—was convinced that *Euphues* was based on Lyly's amorous adventures with 'the mayor's daughter of Bracly'. See Feuillerat, *John Lyly*, 274–5 n.

ceptible to giving them away. They are vulnerable as well as devious, their cleverness can easily trick them into seeming acts of stupidity, and their verbal pyrotechnics repeatedly betray them into accidental self-exposure. At the same time their obsession with private policies makes them eminently suitable for exploitation by the cunning orchestrators of the better-organized and less penetrable policies of the state. And of course the same qualities make them equally eligible for recruitment by the state's opponents. The undirected energies of these writers exist in a state of suspension, hovering at the margins of political commitment, waiting to be appropriated either by the protectors of the Elizabethan Utopia—the devious defenders of the ideological simplicity that keeps a nation stable—or by the equally subtle enemies who seek to undermine the nation's unity. The confrontation between these two sides, the Catholic spy service and the Protestant forces of counter-espionage, is most openly articulated in Lyly's second *Euphues* book, which traces the wanderings of Greek and Italian strangers through a utopian England that baffles all their efforts to penetrate its secrets. But the two sides are also implicitly present in other prose fictions of the decade, battling for control of the intellectual resources of authors and protagonists alike. In *The Adventures of Master F.J.*, the clever and responsible Dame Frances contends with the clever but corrupt Dame Elinor for the mind and body of Gascoigne's hero. In *The Golden Aphroditis*, a jealous troublemaker aptly named I.I. seeks to convert the inoffensive eloquence of the hero and heroine into the rhetoric of treachery by persuading each of them that the other is a dangerous fraud.[29] The aged Eubulus struggles vainly with the brilliant Lucilla for the attention of Lyly's Euphues. And a similar struggle between transgression and conformity manifests itself in the language of the narrators, whose sympathies swing wildly from their misbehaving protagonists to the counsellors who labour to reform them. *A Petite Pallace of Pettie his Pleasure* offers a striking

---

[29] The hero N.O. insists on the innocence of his lover's rhetoric in a passage which is also a fine example of Grange's ebullient prose style: 'the buzzing bees whiche flew aboute *Platoes* mouth, sleeping in his cradle, have likewise left parte of their hony in thy mouth, whiche proveth rather it to pronounce the sweete wordes of *Naestor*, than the bitter talke of *Achilles*: whiche Bees likewise sitting upon the mouth of *Ambrose* being a childe without hurting him, I gather thereby, thy wordes proceeding of their relicte hony, pretendeth me no evill' (sig. H3). I.I. tries to persuade N.O. that his lover is untrustworthy by claiming that he himself has a monopoly on honesty: 'Hir sugered wordes perswadeth you not to beleve my penne: but *time trieth truth*, and therefore *trie and truste*' (sig. I3ᵛ). 'Time trieth truth' is the motto N.O. has adopted as his own.

instance of this conflict of loyalties on the part of the narrator. Pettie's persona, a master of improvised storytelling called G.P., seems quite incapable of deciding whether to cater for the tastes of his younger readers, who admire the witty deceitfulness of star-crossed lovers, or whether to throw his authorial weight behind the older generation, who strive to subject the talents of recalcitrant youngsters to the discipline of moral and religious reformation. The narrator never succeeds in making up his mind; but this carefully calculated failure on Pettie's part identifies his novels as a new kind of fiction, where the act of reading is itself the most exhilarating of adventures, a risky encounter with persuasive strangers who urgently call our attention to the splits and contradictions in our own personalities: conflicting desires, divided loyalties, mutually exclusive commitments, and alternative perceptions of the same events—conflicts which achieved their most exuberant expression in the dazzling stylistic dualisms that have come to be known as euphuism, after Lyly's Euphues, their most accomplished user. These were the contradictions that had been glossed over by the commentators on canonical texts and suppressed by the many authoritarian treatises of the time which demanded absolute submission from their readers.[30] Mid-Elizabethan writers of prose fiction wrenched these splits and contradictions into the open, placed them at the centre of their narratives, and, most radically of all, intimated that they had not been and perhaps never could be resolved, despite all the efforts of contemporary pedagogues and statesmen. In doing so they made a major contribution to the development of the sophisticated literature of the late sixteenth century; a contribution that until recently has been consistently devalued or ignored, and which continues to be referred to by commentators in tones of apology, as if the only function of mid-Elizabethan narratives were to serve as a somewhat dreary corridor which must be hurriedly negotiated in order to gain access to the brightly coloured chambers that accommodate their talented successors.[31]

This is of course a good enough reason for reading them. My own interest in the prose fiction of the 1570s arose from a wish to know more about Shakespeare's comedies: where did these astonishing

---

[30] See Ch. 1, s. 2.

[31] For instance, in her groundbreaking book *The Usurer's Daughter*, Lorna Hutson explains that she has 'no intention of refuting the charges of tedium regularly levelled against the prose fiction of this period' (88). She is, however, mostly concerned with Fenton, who is the nastiest and most verbose of early novel-writers.

games with language come from, and are there any of Shakespeare's predecessors whose awareness of rhetorical duplicity was remotely akin to his? Literary histories trace the roots of the comedies to his adolescence in the late 1570s, when some of the most brilliant pedagogues of the sixteenth century were either in print or in action, and when the Elizabethan reading public seems to have been fired with unprecedented enthusiasm for the arts of language they had learnt at school; an enthusiasm that was matched by the abundance of rhetorical and logical handbooks in English that sprang up in the latter part of the sixteenth century.[32] This was the decade which for C. S. Lewis heralded the passing of the 'drab age', and the inception of the 'golden age' of Elizabethan poetry;[33] when Spenser and Gabriel Harvey exchanged notes about their experiments in English versification;[34] when Spenser's *Shepheardes Calender* (1579) invested poetry in the vernacular with a new seriousness and a new ambivalence, which Sidney went on to analyse so acrobatically in his criticism. This was the decade that witnessed the first and most virulent attacks on the theatre by John Northbrooke and Stephen Gosson, who recognized, so the story goes, the new imaginative energy which was being generated by Elizabethan drama, and which had recently been given a local habitation and a name by the construction of the first purpose-built playhouse in England (the Theatre, built by Richard Burbage in 1576). But there is something missing from this busy picture. Most of the writers I have just mentioned began to produce their best-known work at the very *end* of the decade; and many of them chose to begin their careers not

[32] In the 1570s alone a number of handbooks were published; for example, Thomas Browne's translation of Sturmius on rhetoric, *A Ritch Storehouse or Treasurie for Nobilitie* (1570), the first edition of Henry Peacham's *The Garden of Eloquence* (1577), reprintings of Ralph Lever's *Arte of Reason* (1573), MacIlmaine's translation of Ramus' *Logike* (1574), and Abraham Fleming's instructions for writing letters, *A Panoplie of Epistles* (1576). Shakespeare's possible debts to such handbooks and to the pedagogues of his youth are traced by T. W. Baldwin, *William Shakespere's Small Latine and Lesse Greek* (Urbana, Ill.: University of Illinois Press, 1944); Sister Miriam Joseph, *Shakespeare's Use of the Arts of Language* (New York: Columbia University Press, 1947); and Jane Donawerth, *Shakespeare and the Sixteenth-Century Study of Language* (Urbana, Ill.: University of Illinois Press, 1984).

[33] Lewis explains the distinction between the drab age and the golden age, which still haunts the imagination of commentators, in *English Literature in the Sixteenth Century Excluding Drama* (Oxford: Oxford University Press, 1954), 64–5. He places the prose fictions of the 1570s in a category between the two which he calls 'transitional' (309–17).

[34] Gabriel Harvey published his correspondence with Spenser as *Three Proper and Wittie, Familiar Letters* and *Two Other Very Commendable Letters* in 1580. The two letters mentioned last were written before the first three, in 1579. They can be found in *The Works of Gabriel Harvey*, ed. Alexander B. Grosart, 3 vols. (London: Hazell, Watson & Viney, 1884), vol. i. Subsequent references are to this edition.

only with poems, plays, or narratives in prose but with contributions to an ongoing critical debate about fiction, a debate which they all acknowledge to have been raging in England for some time before they entered the arena. *The Shepheardes Calender* hurls itself into the fray with the weighty support of an accompanying commentary, ostensibly composed by the anonymous E.K., who takes it on himself to defend Spenser's archaic diction against the hostile but fascinated scrutiny of very different stylists, writers who privilege the imported vocabulary of 'straungers...and alienes' above the resources of 'their own mother tonge'.[35] Sidney's *Apology for Poetry* (1580–5) ends with a survey of the state of the art in England which recognizes, even as it dismisses, the diversity of literary experiment that was going on at the time of writing.[36] As with E.K., one of the principal targets of his criticism is the excessive straining after rhetorical inventiveness among his peers, which prompts them to seek out 'far-fetched'— that is, foreign or unfamiliar—words and phrases which 'must seem strangers, to any poor Englishman', together with the tendency among writers of prose to speak 'curiously' rather than 'truly'.[37] The writers of prose fiction earlier in the decade produced only a small proportion of the literary experiments to which E.K. and Sidney were alluding, but theirs were among the most significant contributions to the contemporary debate about the theory and practice of fiction, and without their sometimes ungainly quest for the strange and the curious, neither Spenser's nor Sidney's better-known experiments could have acquired the meticulously organized complexity for which they are famous.

But the prose fiction of the 1570s is not just a corridor to better things, nor is it merely a useful repository of plots and situations to be quarried by later dramatists. It is witty, and daring, and innovative, in ways that are not always obvious to the twentieth-century reader who is unaware of its context, and who has lost some of the rules of the literary and political games it plays. It marks out fiction as shifty, exploratory, perilous territory, which maintains (or fails to maintain) a precarious equilibrium between sustaining current orthodoxies and dallying with forbidden ideologies and novel notions; which refuses

[35] *The Complete Poetical Works of Edmund Spenser*, 3 vols. (Oxford: Clarendon Press, 1909–10), vol. i: *Minor Poems*, ed. Ernest de Selincourt, 6.

[36] I take the date limits of the *Apology for Poetry* from *Sir Philip Sidney*, ed. Katherine Duncan-Jones (Oxford: Oxford University Press, 1989), 371.

[37] *An Apology for Poetry*, 138 and 139.

every kind of closure; which helps, in fact, to make prose fiction the unruly and disruptive medium it has remained ever since. It lends new weight to the complex transactions between men and women which take place in the hitherto neglected regions of domestic space. It charts the multiple intersections between the micropolitics of the private household and the macropolitics of the state. It takes as its presiding metaphors the monsters, wildernesses, and labyrinths which are part of the lexicon of imaginative writing in the late twentieth century. And it demands and deserves closer investigation than it has so far received, even in the excellent discussions of the last two decades.[38] The intelligence of writers such as Gascoigne, Pettie, Gosson, and Lyly needs to be trusted; the enjoyment and suspicion they provoked among their peers need to be recognized; their ability to initiate and to produce inspired variations on contemporary rhetorical and intellectual fashions needs to be reiterated, as does their willingness to take calculated political risks. We need, in fact, to acknowledge that these writers were as serious as they were playful. Their emphasis on the lightning verbal reflexes of wit conceals a recognition of the danger as well as the delight of manufacturing fictions, the sometimes desperate gambles taken by the storyteller, the courtier, the chancer, the double-dealer, the spy. Without trying to understand what made them so alluring to their imitators and so odious to their detractors we run the risk ourselves of falsifying part of Elizabethan history, of dismissing what was important then in the interests of a sterile recapitulation of what we think important now. Perhaps we cannot hope to recover the excitement that Elizabethan readers may have felt as they opened the long-awaited second volume of *Euphues*; but we will be part of the way there if we begin to perceive that what they must have felt *was* excitement. These were texts that challenged their recipients on many different levels, and that explored with the wary alertness of colonists or adventurers the social, political, and linguistic subtleties that the late sixteenth-century reader had long experienced but had not yet seen so cunningly articulated. They take up the

[38] Important general discussions include: Helgerson, *The Elizabethan Prodigals*; David Margolies, *Novel and Society in Elizabethan England* (London: Croom Helm, 1985); Paul Salzman, *English Prose Fiction 1558–1700* (Oxford: Oxford University Press, 1985); Arthur F. Kinney, *Humanist Poetics: Thought, Rhetoric, and Fiction in Sixteenth-Century England* (Amherst, Mass.: University of Massachusetts Press, 1986); Caroline Lucas, *Writing for Women: The Example of Woman as Reader in Elizabethan Romance* (Milton Keynes: Open University Press, 1989). For a fuller bibliography see Reid Barbour, 'Recent Studies in Elizabethan Prose Fiction', *English Literary Renaissance*, 25 (1995), 248–76.

gauntlet thrown down by the sophisticated texts of the early huma-
nists—*Utopia*, *The Praise of Folly*, *Gargantua and Pantagruel*—and if
they cannot be said to match the achievements of these earlier texts,
they do not suffer from being compared with them. And if you are
looking for precursors of Shakespeare's comedies, or of Sidney's
prose epics, or of the satires of Marlowe and Nashe, or of Swift's, Sterne's or even Joyce's disruptions of conventional narrative forms, you
will not be disappointed if you look at the works of Gascoigne or of
Lyly.

I have taken as my focal point the two texts I discuss in the last two
chapters, Lyly's *Euphues: The Anatomy of Wit* (1578) and *Euphues and
his England* (1580). To my mind these are two of the cleverest fictions
of the century, and the number of editions they went through suggests
that the Elizabethans might have agreed with me. All the other texts
discussed in detail in this book, from William Baldwin's satirical
fable *Beware the Cat* (1570) to Stephen Gosson's mock-novella *The
Ephemerides of Phialo*, may well have been known to Lyly, and many
are mentioned by him, either directly or in the form of pastiche.

The book begins as this introduction does, with a discussion of
some of the educational and political theories to which the sixteenth-century novelists responded. These theories are woven into
the book as thoroughly as they are woven into Elizabethan fiction,
since Sir Thomas Elyot and Roger Ascham seem to have generated
as many imaginative variations on their themes as any of the fictions
that exploited their arguments.

The second chapter considers the impact on Elizabethan fiction of
the story-collections of William Painter, Geoffrey Fenton, and the lit-
tle-known fabulists who worked alongside them. The third, fourth,
fifth, and sixth chapters contain discussions of Elizabethan prose
fictions, their violations of current conventions, their impudent and
courageous mockery of contemporary platitudes, their oblique
acknowledgements of the potentially poisonous nature of their contents, their self-conscious stylishness, their subtlety. The recurring
topic of these chapters is the various kinds of fiction these narratives
explore: erotic fantasy, religious superstition, inflated self-esteem,
paranoia, propaganda, lies, and a hundred different varieties of castle
in the air. If the respect and affection I have conceived for these
often clumsy, often scintillating literary labyrinths make themselves
felt from time to time, this book will have done its job.

# The Fiction of Simplicity in the Sixteenth-Century Treatise

## 1. SIMPLICITY AND SUBTLETY

When reading sixteenth-century texts it is dangerous to make clear-cut distinctions between genres. Tragedy bursts its confines and invades the comic; philosophy and satire engage one another in dialogue; myth masquerades as history, and history blurs into fable. This generic elusiveness is especially marked in the fluid medium of prose. For a Tudor audience a theoretical treatise was as much an act of entertainment as a work of fiction, and fiction had the same serious political implications as a work of theory. Treatises are constantly breaking into narrative, just as narratives could, by a process like the one described in Richard Rainolde's *A Booke Called The Foundacion of Rhetorike*, be stripped down to their component theoretical parts.[1] In the middle of his political treatise *The Book Called The Governor* (1531) Sir Thomas Elyot abruptly breaks off to tell a story from the *Decameron*, which serves both to illustrate his argument and to give his jaded readers a well-earned rest: 'But now in the midst of my labour, as it were to pause and take breath, and also to recreate the readers, which, fatigued with long precepts, desire variety of matter, or some new pleasant fable or history, I will rehearse a right goodly example of friendship.'[2] Thomas Wilson's *The Arte of Rhetorique* (1553) unexpectedly plunges into a digression on laughter which is

[1] Rainolde demonstrates how a fable can be broken down into its component parts in the course of analysing 'An Oracion by a fable', *The Foundacion of Rhetorike*, sig. A4ᵛ ff. For a fine discussion of Rainolde's treatise see Marion Trousdale, *Shakespeare and the Rhetoricians* (London: Scolar Press, 1982), 3–7.

[2] *The Book Called The Governor*, ed. S. E. Lehmberg (London: J. M. Dent, 1962), 136. All references to *The Governor* are taken from this edition.

more funny than instructive;[3] and the end of George Puttenham's *The Arte of English Poesie* dissolves into a series of anecdotes designed both to explain the tricky concept of 'decorum' and to 'solace' the reader's 'eares'.[4] At the same time, treatises provided Elizabethan fictions of all kinds with an inexhaustible supply of subject-matter. From its use of the smallest units of speech to its investigations of the workings of contemporary culture, Elizabethan fiction proclaims its debt to the political and literary theorists who are the subject of this chapter.

For Tudor practitioners of rhetoric, whether pedagogues or story-tellers, politicians or professional clowns, the word was the most important brick in the fabric of society. Rhetorical handbooks repeatedly stress the link between the right use of the word and the stability of the state. In *A Treatise of Schemes and Tropes* (1550) Richard Sherry explains that 'The myghte and power of eloquucion consisteth in wordes considered by them selves, and when they be joyned together', and Thomas Wilson sees the art of eloquence as the power that shapes civilization itself, since it enables people to 'live together in fellowship of life, to maintaine cities, to deale truely, and willingly obey one another'.[5] One of the writers who most searchingly explored the political significance of the word in the Tudor state was the educational theorist Sir Thomas Elyot, a courtier in the turbulent time of Henry VIII and the author of the first Latin–English dictionary.[6] His treatise on the education of the ruling classes, *The Governor*, is the subtlest sixteenth-century defence of the concept of 'simplicity': the quality of preserving the agreed meaning of words, which humanist scholars strove to elucidate in so many far-from-simple texts.

*The Governor* might be described as an extended political dictionary, a study of the vocabulary of power. It begins with the definition of a Tudor state and proceeds to define, one by one, the words that allow such a state to function. In the opening chapter Elyot exposes the

[3] Thomas Wilson's account of different kinds of humour, 'Of delyting the hearers, and stirryng them to laughter', takes up twenty-two pages in the 1560 edition of *The Arte of Rhetorique*, beginning at sig. I4[v].

[4] 'This that I tell you is rather to solace your eares with pretie conceits after a sort of long scholasticall preceptes which may happen have doubled them, rather then for any other purpose of institution or doctrine.' *The Arte of English Poesie*, 231.

[5] Sherry, *A Treatise of Schemes and Tropes* (1550), sig. B[v]. Wilson, *The Arte of Rhetorique* (1560 edn.), sig. A7[v].

[6] *The Dictionary of Syr Thomas Eliot* (1538), rev. and enlarged as *Bibliotheca Eliotae*, (1542). For an account of Elyot's career and writings, see John N. Major, *Sir Thomas Elyot and Renaissance Humanism* (Lincoln, Nebr.: University of Nebraska Press, 1964).

extent to which he conceives of his society as a verbal construct by embarking on a lengthy discussion of the word he will use to denote the state as a whole. He explains that he has chosen to substitute the term 'public weal' for the more familiar 'common weal' because the latter term involves a misuse of the word 'common' that threatens to smash the conception of hierarchy on which the monarchic system is based. 'Weal' signifies wealth, he insists, and 'commonalty...signifieth only the multitude', so that to translate the Latin word for state (*respublica*) as 'commonwealth' would have the absurd implication that ultimate control of economic power lies not with the nobility but with the commoners (1–2). In fact the misuse of the word 'common' jeopardizes not only the dominant position of the ruling classes but also the communicative links between a kingdom and its heavenly ruler:

For as much as *Plebs* in Latin, and commoners in English, be words only made for the discrepance of degrees, whereof proceedeth order; which in things as well natural as supernatural hath ever had such a preeminence that thereby the incomprehensible majesty of God, as it were by a bright leam of a torch or candle, is declared to the blind inhabitants of this world. (2)

Elyot's imaginary public weal would seem to be a precariously fragile structure, ready to shatter at a verbal touch. Alter the proper meaning of a word and you risk demolishing the entire framework of the social order and losing touch with the source of monarchic authority, God. Chaos threatens to break loose with every sentence that is spoken; and even the word 'chaos' must be scrupulously defined if the integrity of discourse is to be preserved: 'Moreover take away order from all things', Elyot admonishes, 'what should then remain? Certes nothing finally, except some man would imagine eftsoons *Chaos*, which of some is expound a confuse mixture' (2). In this way he articulates a politician's sense of the terrifying volatility of words in the age of Reformation, when all the powers of Europe were fighting over custody of the scriptural Word. His contemporary Cranmer, who would die in the struggle, wrote in equally apocalyptic terms about the link between language and the social order. Disobedience to the king, he warned, would result in 'babylonical confusion': the unleashing of the curse of Babel, whereby the English language and people would be reduced to a state of defenceless incoherence.[7] For Elyot and his

[7] Quoted by Conrad Russell, *The Crisis of Parliaments* (Oxford: Oxford University Press, 1977), 106.

colleagues in the ruling classes, the policing of the English tongue was as much a matter of national security as the policing of the English coasts.

When words are this explosive, the role of the teacher, the custodian of words, assumes unparalleled political importance. The head teacher in Elyot's imaginary public weal is the head of state, the prince himself. In the course of defining 'nobility' Elyot argues that ideally the social hierarchy should correspond to the hierarchy of intelligence and virtue: the prince should possess the best intellect and the most unassailable morals as well as the highest office in the kingdom. Elyot supports this contention with an etymology of the word 'gentleman'. 'In the beginning', he alleges, 'private possessions and dignity were given by the consent of the people, who then had all things in common' (103–4). Later, by mutual consent, the people gave both wealth and power to 'him at whose virtue they marvelled' (104). In other words, 'nobility is not after the vulgar opinion of men, but is only the praise and surname of virtue; which the longer it continueth in a name or lineage, the more is nobility extolled and marvelled at' (106). Elsewhere he argues that 'in this world they which excel other in this influence of understanding . . . ought to be set in a more high place than the residue' (4). From the advantage of their social pre-eminence, these governors who rule by their own merit can set speech to work at its proper function, which consists 'in declaring what is good, what vicious, what is profitable, what improfitable, by them which in the clearness of wit do excel in knowledge, to these that be of a more inferior capacity' (86). Thus the name of his book, *The Governor*, alludes to a governing class which consists both of those who rule and those who teach, and which has a virtual monopoly over speech as well as economic and military power, imposing its will on its receptive inferiors in an uninterrupted stream of prescriptive declarations. Throughout the sixteenth century, an education in the arts of language remained so much a branch of politics that Roger Ascham in his educational treatise *The Scholemaster* saw nothing incongruous about proceeding from teaching his pupils how to write and speak the Latin tongue to teaching them how to run a state.[8]

Central to Elyot's own pedagogic project and to the stability of his 'public weal' is the use of words to achieve the kind of consensus, or verbal agreement, by which the ancient inhabitants of the earth

---

[8] Ascham confesses that some readers will resent his interference in affairs of state: 'some will say, I have stepte to farre, out of my schole, into the common welthe' (*Works*, 222); but he does not apologize for the transition.

selected the original aristocracy. He devotes three chapters to exploring the nature of such agreements: 'Of fraud and deceit' (167), 'Of faith or fidelity' (172), and 'Of promise or covenant' (173). Each chapter heading illustrates his practice of yoking familiar with unfamiliar words in pairs of synonyms, so that he is for ever expanding the vocabulary of his courtly readers while maintaining a tight control over this verbal expansion by means of built-in definitions. These three chapters represent the core of his thinking on the political function of words, and in them he introduces the important concept of 'simplicity' into Tudor discussions of language. 'Truly in every covenant, bargain, or promise', he writes in the first of the three, 'ought to be a simplicity, that is to say, one plain understanding or meaning between the parties' (170). This 'simplicity' is what his constant definitions are meant to impart to every difficult or dangerous word in the text. He explains the concept further in the chapter on 'faith or fidelity':

Wherefore to him that shall either speak or write, the place is diligently to be observed where the proper signification of the word may be best expressed. Considering (as Plato saith) that the name of everything is none other but the virtue or effect of the same thing conceived first in the mind, and then by the voice expressed and finally in letters signified. (172)

For Elyot, as for Plato's Cratylus, the relationship between signifier and signified is by no means arbitrary. A mysterious 'virtue or effect' connects the word with what it expresses, whatever the language, in a way that transcends consensus.[9]

Elyot was well aware that there was nothing simple about conserving verbal 'simplicity'. No matter how strictly policed, words, he admits, are in constant danger of being misunderstood or deliberately rendered ambiguous. As one might expect in his battle to establish an authoritative language, for Elyot the deliberate cultivation of ambiguity is the worst of crimes:

And where any man of a covetous or malicious mind will digress purposely from that simplicity, taking advantage of a sentence or word which might be ambiguous or doubtful or in something either superfluous or lacking in

---

[9] An interesting insight into Elyot's views on the political significance of names can be found in the dedicatory epistle to the *Dictionary* of 1538, addressed to Henry VIII: 'Unto that office of governance is (as it were by the generall consent of all people) one name appropried, in the which although by diversitie of langages, the letters and syllables are oftentymes chaunged, yet the worde spoken hath one signification, which implieth as much as KINGE in englyshe' (sig. A2). For a discussion of Plato's *Cratylus* see Anne Barton, *Ben Jonson, Dramatist* (Cambridge: Cambridge University Press, 1984), 172–3.

the bargain or promise, where he certainly knoweth the truth to be otherwise, this in mine opinion is damnable fraud. (170)

For many writers of both treatises and prose fiction throughout the century, with Roger Ascham and Stephen Gosson prominent among them, the struggle to preserve 'simplicity' or 'one plain understanding or meaning between the parties' in the face of the ceaseless depradations of linguistic fraud was the principal responsibility of the printed text.

Besides being the custodian of linguistic simplicity, the prince of Elyot's imaginary kingdom embodies the conjunction of word and action which is necessary if the verbal covenant is to take effect. His actions are as much a form of instructive language as his speech: 'know that the name of a sovereign or ruler without actual governance is but a shadow, that governance standeth not by words only, but principally by act and example; that by example of governors men do rise or fall in virtue or vice' (165). Elyot explains more fully what he means by 'example' towards the end of the treatise, in the third book. Here he distinguishes between two kinds of experience: the first is the memory of acts we ourselves have performed or witnessed; the second is the knowledge of 'acts committed or done by other men', which 'is called example, and is expressed by history, which of Tully is called the life of memory' (228). Every act of the prince, then, is a text, read by his subjects and woven into the fabric of their selves. As a result, the historical texts that record the exemplary acts of kings and magistrates play a vital role in the process of fashioning members of the public weal. In this educative process, fictional histories make as valid a contribution to the collective memory as factual ones: 'if by reading the sage counsel of Nestor . . . we may apprehend anything whereby our wits may be amended and our personages be more apt to serve our public weal and our prince, what forceth us though Homer wrote leasings?' (231). But if 'leasings' are to help form a society founded on verbal simplicity, the meanings of such lying texts must be agreed on. And the most extended fictional history Elyot includes in *The Governor* is far from eliciting any such agreement.

The story of Titus and Gisippus from the *Decameron* was one of the most popular of Boccaccio's tales, translated into English at least twice before Elyot chose to include it in his treatise.[10] He tells the story as a

---

[10] The tale is told as the eighth story on the Tenth Day: Boccaccio, *Decameron*, trans. G. H. McWilliam (Harmondsworth: Penguin, 1972), 764–94. For earlier English versions

'right goodly example of friendship . . . whereby is fully declared the figure of perfect amity' (136). Amity, as Elyot defines it, is the ideal virtue to set at the heart of the public weal, since it is a condition of perfect mutual understanding: 'Verily it is a blessed and stable connection of sundry wills, making of two persons one in having and suffering' (134). Titus and Gisippus are incapable of deceiving one another, and so apparently incapable of 'fraud'. Their personalities are so interwoven that their very bodies seem to be interchangeable, and one name will suffice for both: 'it seemed none other, when their names were declared, but that they had only changed places, issuing (as I might say) out of the one body, and entering into the other' (136). But their interchangeable names and personalities encourage a verbal and social 'ambiguity or doubtfulness' which quickly disrupts both their friendship and the legal systems of the states they inhabit. Their relationship finds itself rocked when a woman called Sophronia invades their miniature male utopia. The family of Gisippus arranges for him to be betrothed to Sophronia, and on meeting her he falls in love; he then introduces her to Titus, and his friend promptly falls in love with her too. In these circumstances Gisippus has no difficulty in deciding which matters most, his heterosexual betrothal or his homosocial bond. He decides at once to give up the girl, and in doing so re-establishes the 'simplicity or agreement' between the men: 'Nay, God forbid that in the friendship of Gisippus and Titus should happen any suspicion . . . whereby that honourable love between us should be the mountenance of a crumb perished' (140). Without consulting either Sophronia or her family, Gisippus contrives to substitute Titus for himself in the marriage bed. As a result of this action he is banished from the state. Later, when Gisippus is in a legal scrape, Titus returns the favour, substituting himself for Gisippus as chief suspect in a murder trial. Elyot sums up: 'This example in the affects of friendship declares (if I be not deceived) the description of friendship engendered by the similitude of age and personage, augmented by the conformity of manners and studies, and confirmed by the long continuance of company' (149).

But, as Lorna Hutson has recently demonstrated, the story contains a good deal more than the 'description of friendship'.[11] The two men

of the story see *Early English Versions of the Tales of Guiscardo and Ghismonda and Titus and Gisippus from the Decameron*, ed. Herbert G. Wright (London: Early English Text Society, 1937).

[11] Hutson, *The Usurer's Daughter*, ch. 2.

may have fashioned for themselves a perfect medium of communication, an infrangible bond of mutual trust, but they do so at the cost of communication with the societies they inhabit. In order to preserve their own private consensus they break all the other verbal agreements to which they are committed: that is, the inter-familial agreement which is represented by the betrothal vow, and the system of legal agreements which bind the citizens of two states, the states of Athens (where Gisippus betrays Sophronia) and of Rome (where Titus disrupts the trial). Far from providing the cement that stabilizes a public weal, the friends' 'amity' serves only to demonstrate the multiplicity of conflicting interests that craze the social structure, and to show how speech is always slipping from simplicity to fraud and back again: what is simplicity for one social group is fraud for the next. Elyot's novella suggests that amity severs connections as readily as it forges them.

In fact, in his eagerness to divert his readers Elyot has introduced a virus into his treatise that threatens to kill his argument off at birth: the virus of prose fiction. *The Governor* is predicated on the conviction that the stability of a public weal depends on consensus, on 'simplicity'; but fiction seeks to entertain, to relieve the reader's mind from wearisome conformity to precepts, and so eschews both simplicity and stability. Instead it embarks on a quest for the strange, the astonishing, the novel, and constructs itself from misunderstandings and deceits. More specifically, the story of Titus and Gisippus insinuates the recurring topics of Italian prose fiction into Elyot's treatise: plausible strangers who infiltrate aristocratic households and disrupt the organized lives of their inhabitants; educated and sexually dynamic youths who put their skills to work in the service of their own private projects; words (like the names 'Titus' and 'Gisippus' or the term 'friendship') which abruptly shift their significations as their contexts change. And one of the central topics of the tale is secrecy. At the core of the narrative is a 'place secret' to which only Titus and Gisippus have access: the place where Gisippus conceals his friend before smuggling him into the bridal chamber. This secret place metaphorically affirms the possibility that the most sacrosanct verbal agreements can act as camouflage for unsuspected hidden agendas, and that the education of the governing classes in the arts of language can be used to undermine the very political structures it is designed in principle to consolidate.

English writers of fiction—both drama and prose—returned to the story of Titus and Gisippus repeatedly, and used it to question Elyot's confidence in consensual 'simplicity'. The young men's friendship wove itself into texts throughout the reign of Elizabeth, from the lost play of 'Titus and Gisippus' by Richard Edwards to William Painter's *The Palace of Pleasure*, Lyly's *Euphues*, and the plays of Shake-speare. In *Measure for Measure*, the 'bed trick' which the Duke borrows from Gisippus—secretly substituting one woman for another in a lecher's bed, and so conniving at fornication to prevent rape—signals the breakdown of moral categories, and confirms the capacity of language, sex, and legislation 'To make bad good, and good provoke to harm' (IV. i. 14). And the moral dilemmas raised by the story of Titus and Gisippus seem to have made even Elyot think twice about the problems involved in achieving simplicity. Soon after telling it he explains that one of the marks of a true friend is a readiness to make constructive criticisms of one's behaviour. Unfortunately, he goes on, self-serving flatterers have got wise to the fact that their victims no longer trust the 'assentation and praises' which are the stuff of flattery. Instead the sophisticated modern flatterer has recently taken to meting out just the kind of constructive criticism that is the hallmark of friendship. As a result, Elyot complains, 'I am ... not well assured how nowadays a man shall know or discern such admonition from flattery' (151). The complaint casts a cloud over the tale of Titus and Gisippus: might not the unparalleled generosity of the two friends be read as a dangerous instance of mutual flattery? Even in the state of friendship 'ambiguous or doubtful' words cannot be separated from 'simple' ones; the phrases that construct social covenants are also the phrases that mask fraud; Titus and Gisippus are both incomparable examples of amity and devious enemies of the state. Boccaccio's tale lurks at the heart of Elyot's treatise like a spy or a concealed assassin, ready to turn the verbal weapons of the ruling classes against themselves. And for the rest of the century English prose fiction continued to act as a disruptive double agent in the world of the printed text.

## 2.   MONOLOGUES AND DIALOGUES

*The Governor* is a monologic treatise, unfolding its argument through the medium of a single authoritative expository voice. Elyot takes it for granted that there is only one satisfactory way of running a public weal, and that he has the key to it. The voice of dissent is only ever heard obliquely: simplicity is the norm, fraud a temporary aberration.

But sixteenth-century theorists did not always share Elyot's unshakeable confidence in the authority of the printed text. As the century wore on, an increasing number of treatises laid emphasis on the difficulty of achieving consensual simplicity. Some theorists posed as lonely champions of verbal plainness, struggling to preserve the integrity of their pages against the perverse misconstructions of devious readers. Others introduced imaginary antagonists into their texts, whose raucous objections must be suppressed before the argument could be resumed. Many of the most sophisticated texts took the form of dialogues, where a multitude of contesting voices battled to reach an elusive consensus. Elizabethan writers of prose fiction read these treatises with close attention, so that ideas and situations from theoretical texts emerged everywhere in their narratives, subtly altered by their new environment. And in each case it was invariably the most dramatic moment in the treatise, the moment when theory confronts the contingencies of social practice or when an argument trembles on the brink of collapse under the weight of hostile voices, that proved the most fruitful ground for the storyteller's imaginative cultivation.

The form of Elyot's own theoretical texts changed with his changing political fortunes. As his career went on and his hopes of political preferment faded he switched from monologue to dialogue, from confident collaboration with the governing classes to bitter invective against the corrupt counsellors who monopolized the governors' attentions.[12] Soon after the publication of *The Governor* his career as an active politician was abruptly cut short. In 1532 King Henry made him ambassador to the Emperor Charles V, but within a few months Elyot had fallen from grace, Cranmer had replaced him as ambassador, and he found himself back in England, jobless. Two dialogues published in 1533 articulate his frustration over the blighting of his ambitions. In both texts the advocates of simplicity find themselves marginalized like Elyot himself, heroically battling against the triumphant proponents of verbal fraud. The first of these dialogues, *Of the Knowledge which Maketh a Wise Man*, pictures the philosopher Plato in rags, banished from the court of the Syracusan tyrant Dionysius but still struggling to impart his wisdom to the sycophants who have access to the king. In the second dialogue, *Pasquil the Playne*, Pasquil is a miraculous speaking statue in Rome which vents its disillusionment

---

[12] For Elyot's use of dialogue, see Kenneth Jay Wilson, *Incomplete Fictions: The Formation of English Renaissance Dialogue* (Washington, DC: Catholic University of America Press, 1985), 75–107.

with the state of contemporary politics by heckling passers-by.[13] The statue's stony immobility stands for the political impotence of the satirist: both Plato and Pasquil fail to convince their interlocutors. Pasquil shares Elyot's concern with the proper function of words: 'Though I have not so moche lernyng as you', he tells the hypocritical Harpocrates, 'I use alwaye my wordes in theyr propre signification, and to serve to the matter that I reason unto.'[14] He goes on to assure himself (and perhaps Elyot) that however much a wise man may suffer for telling the truth, in time his wisdom will be recognized, 'and than shall repentance cause your simplicitie to be had in renome and perpetual memorie'. But for all his insistence that every word has a proper and immutable significance, Pasquil's use of the word 'simplicitie' differs fundamentally from its use in *The Governor*. There it meant the system of verbal covenants or agreements that guarantees the stability of a public weal. Here it has come to mean a stubborn adherence to a philosophical position that the public weal disowns. In the two years that intervened between *The Governor* and *Pasquil* Elyot seems to have lost much of his confidence in the inviolability of covenants and the authority of the authorial voice.

Monologic treatises too suffered moments of crisis, when the authority of the text was called into question. Antonio de Guevara's *The Dial of Princes*, translated by Thomas North in 1557 and reprinted with additions in 1568, takes an approach to the collaboration between text and reader which is as uncompromisingly authoritarian as the doctrines it adumbrates. In a memorable phrase North describes Guevara's writings as 'a mitridatical electuary, recuering and healing all malignaunt opilations' (third book, sig. *a5*); and the sentence accurately conveys the function of the *Dial*, which is to dose its readers like a literary physician with unpalatable moral tonics.[15] The translator's preface appeals to readers to collaborate with this treatment by 'gyvynge to this present worke gravitie, and to me the interpretor thereof aucthority' (general prologue, sig. *a5*). In this way North

---

[13] For a brief history of Pasquil and the satirical tradition of the pasquinade, see Major, *Sir Thomas Elyot and Renaissance Humanism*, 97–8.

[14] *Four Political Treatises by Sir Thomas Elyot*, introd. Lillian Gottesman (Gainesville, Fla.: Scholars' Facsimiles and Reprints, 1967), 83.

[15] All references to *The Dial of Princes* are taken from the 1568 edition, which includes 'an amplification also of a fourth booke annexed to the same, entituled The Favored Courtier' (title-page). In this edition the first and second books are given a separate series of signatures from the third book and 'The Favored Courtier'. I have therefore given references to books or sections along with signature references.

draws up an agreement with the reader that allows him to proceed with his translation confident that it will not be misconstrued. But of course the agreement serves equally to acknowledge the reader's power to *deny* the text's authority; and this power is comically demonstrated by a character in the text itself.

The chief spokesman for Guevara in the *Dial* is the emperor–philosopher Marcus Aurelius, who delivers an endless stream of precepts on his behalf: precepts on education, on government, on how to endure a state of exile, and the like. But the treatise contains a disruptive element in the shape of the emperor's wife Faustina, who stubbornly refuses to give the emperor the 'aucthority' he demands. In a moment of comic relief which is as welcome as it is unexpected she interrupts one of her husband's interminable disquisitions (ironically enough, on the ideal marriage) with an eloquent attack on his shortcomings as a husband, provoked by his refusal to give her a copy of his study key.[16] She ends by denouncing the whole male sex—Aurelius responds with a misogynistic tirade—and the chapter which began as a dull philosophical disputation ends as a violent domestic tiff. Faustina's rebelliousness is shared by the emperor's children: his son Commodus is a thug, his daughter Lucilla is an inveterate party-goer (which in her father's opinion makes her little better than a whore), and between them Lucilla, Commodus, and Faustina constitute conclusive proof of the abject failure of his domestic policies.[17] Elizabethan writers of prose fiction seem to have been attracted to this chink in the Roman emperor's philosophical armour: William Painter included an anecdote about Faustina in his *Palace of Pleasure*, and John Lyly named the crafty heroine of *Euphues: The Anatomy of Wit* after Lucilla.[18] Like Aurelius himself, Guevara's ponderously didactic text spawned its own recalcitrant literary offspring.

But it was Castiglione's *The Book of the Courtier* (1528; translated by Thomas Hoby in 1561) that finally and brilliantly exploded the myth of the treatise as an unproblematically prescriptive document. Like

[16] *The Dial of Princes*, second book, sig. S4: 'Of the importunate suete of the Empresse *Faustine*, to the Emperour *Marke Aureille*, concerning the key of his closet.'

[17] Aurelius prophetically says of Commodus that 'for that hee hath been evill in my life, I doo ymagyn that hee will bee worse after my death' (second book, sig. P3ᵛ). Lucilla's addiction to parties is mentioned in Ch. 61 of 'The Favored Courtier': 'How at the intercession of many which the Empresse had sent, the Emperour graunted his daughter *Lucilla* licence to sport her selfe at the feaste.'

[18] Painter, *The Palace of Pleasure*, ed. Joseph Jacobs, 3 vols. (London: David Nutt, 1890), ii. 260–3. All references are taken from this edition.

*The Governor*, *The Courtier* represents an effort to reach a verbal consensus; but unlike Guevara or the early Elyot, Castiglione gives no indication that consensus is finally possible. The treatise originated, he explains, in a request from his friend Ariosto that he compose a book describing 'of what sort hee ought to bee that deserveth to be called so perfit a Courtier, that there be no want in him' (15).[19] To fashion this figure Castiglione deliberately rejects conventional methodologies: 'We wil not in these books follow any certaine order or rule of appointed preceptes, the which for the most part is woont to bee observed in teaching of any thing whatsoever it bee' (16). Instead he casts his text in the dialogue form that Elyot favours in his later, satirical, pamphlets. The search for the model Courtier is put into the mouths of a group of courtiers, sometimes garrulous, often idiosyncratic, who repeatedly disrupt any agreement they reach. The Courtier of the title remains fragmentary, incoherent, and ultimately fictional, locked away in a non-existent time and place accessible (like Sidney's 'golden world') only to a hopeful imagination.

The text of *The Courtier* recedes into the past as it is read. Castiglione sets his debate in the court of Urbino ten or twelve years before he sat down to write the treatise, and over twenty years before it was published. His location of the text in a precise historical setting subjects the 'perfit Courtier' to the mutations of time, and time intrudes on the text at every point. *The Dial of Princes* too stresses the insidious effect of time on human affairs; but for Guevara the flux of history has no power to alter meaning:

If tyme could speake, he would certifye us of sundry things wherin we doubt, and declare them as a witnes of sight. Admyt al things perishe, and have an ende: yet one thing is exempted, and never hath end, which is truth, that amongst al things is privileged in such wise, that she triumpheth of time, and not tyme of her. (General prologue, sig. a5ᵛ)

The title North gave to Guevara's treatise, with its allusion to the sundial that marks the passing of the daylight hours, promises its readers that they can model themselves on Marcus Aurelius by means of a strict organization of the hours and minutes of the working day: 'the nature of this dyal of prynces is, to teache us how to occupye our selves every houre, and how to amende our lyfe every moment' (general prologue, sig. aᵛ). For Castiglione, by contrast, time destroys the

---

[19] References to *The Courtier* are taken from the Everyman edition, ed. W. H. D. Rouse (London: J. M. Dent, 1928).

human capacity to organize, eating away at words—he complains in
the preface that the language used by Boccaccio is already outmoded
(11)—and killing the words' users. This built-in obsolescence means
that the act of reading is also an act of mourning. Re-reading his treatise some years after writing it, he tells us how: 'sodeinlie at the first
blush by reason of the title, I tooke no litle grief, which in proceadinge
forward encreased much more, remembringe that the greater part of
them that are brought in to reason, are now dead' (9). Castiglione
obtrudes his own persona on the text very rarely, but when he does
so it is invariably to remind his readers that both text and reader are
slipping backwards into the obscurity of the past. New fashions, new
political configurations, delete his words even as they are read.

The duration of the debate is strictly delimited: four days, corresponding to the four books of the treatise—less than half the time
Boccaccio allows his storytellers in the *Decameron*. Castiglione constantly draws attention to these temporal limits by making disputants
plead the lateness of the hour when they want to avoid confronting
a difficult question, or by making nightfall interrupt the day's debate
(the entire discussion is finally cut short by the dawning of the fifth
day). The narrator intervenes at the beginning of the second book
with a startling evocation of the physical and psychological symptoms
of time's passing. Old men believe that the past was better than the
present, he contends, because they trust the evidence of their decaying
bodies. Their failing senses erode their capacity for enjoyment, so that
they come to resemble passengers on a ship who think that the shore is
moving: 'and yet is it cleane contrarie, for the haven, and likewise the
time and pleasures continue still in their estate, and we with the vessel
of mortalitie fleing away, go one after another through the tempestu-
ous sea, that swalloweth up and devoureth all thinges' (87). Castiglione's version of history is radically unstable. Not only does the body
degenerate, but every aspect of the body's context is swallowed up
by the tempest that 'devoureth all thinges'. The passengers have a distorted view of the shore, and the shore too is rapidly crumbling into
the sea of forgetfulness.

The old men's antagonism to the pleasures of the young is only one
aspect of the diversity of sensory and intellectual perspectives that
separates one disputant from another. From the beginning Castiglione
stresses the differences between disputants more than their agreements. On the first evening the men and women at Urbino consider
and reject a variety of topics for debate before settling on the idea of

constructing the perfect Courtier. Each of these topics illuminates the idiosyncracies that isolate one speaker from the rest, and each rejected topic resurfaces in the course of discussion over the next four days. Gaspar begins by reminding them that 'our mindes, as in other thinges, so also in loving are diverse in judgement' (23), and proposes that each courtier name the particular virtue or vice he or she would prefer to see in a lover. Gaspar's proposition is taken up in the fiercely combative third book, where Julian praises women's virtues and Gaspar responds by listing their vices. Next, Gonzago proposes that the speakers analyse one another's private follies (24), and later in the text this topic too re-emerges, for the follies of certain courtiers repeatedly intrude on the discussion—Gaspar, for instance, poses as a woman-hater, and old Master Morello is obsessed with his own virility. Even after they have settled on the topic of the 'perfit Courtier' the disputants continue to emphasize the difficulty of agreeing on the characteristics he should possess. Count Lewis complains that 'in everie thing it is so hard a matter to know the true perfection, that it is almost unpossible, and that by reason of the varietie of judgements' (31). Differences in age, gender, sexual orientation, and education make final legislation on any issue both arbitrary and controversial.

In fact, only the specific historical conditions under which the debate takes place prevent the 'varietie of judgements' from erupting into open hostility. The Lord of Urbino is sickly and takes no part in the discussion. As a result, the court has been transformed into a temporary matriarchy ruled by the Duchess, an utopia in the aggressively masculine context of Renaissance Italy, in which differences are resolved by debate rather than by armed combat. The Duchess exercises a restraining influence on her male subjects: 'everye man conceived in his minde an high contentation every time we came into the Dutchesse sight. And it appeared that this was a chaine that kept all linked together in love, in such wise that there was never agreement of wil or hartie love greater betweene brethren, then there was betweene us all' (20). Any 'agreement of wil' achieved in the court of Urbino is the product of a time when the aristocracy was, it seems, uniquely qualified to achieve such an agreement, linked by a chain of rational love such as has never obtained before or since. The fourth book tentatively hints at the possibility that Castiglione's idealized Urbino might return at some future date, restored by one of the European child-princes who showed such promise at the time of writing. But the mutations of time make the possibility almost infinitely remote; and in the meantime corruption so dominates the political scene that the 'perfit Courtier' can exist, if at all, only within the confines of Castiglione's text.

But even in the text he never achieves existence. Each time a speaker comes close to painting his portrait it is promptly erased. Count Lewis makes this erasure inevitable when he suggests that the 'varietie of judgements' means that each person in the assembly speaks his or her own private language, and that for every signified there is a baffling multiplicity of signifiers:

> many there are, that delight in a man of much talke, and him they call a pleas-
> ant fellow... And thus doth everie man praise or dispraise according to his
> fancie, alwaies covering a vice with the name of the next vertue to it, and a
> vertue with the name of the next vice: as in calling him that is sawcie, bold:
> him that is sober, dry: him that is seelie, good: him that is unhappie, wittie:
> and likewise in the rest. (31)

The Courtier is constantly being reworked by friends and enemies, his identity remodelled, his names 'covered' with other names. His thoughts and motives are impossible to fathom, and conversely he cannot tell who to trust. As a result, the fear Elyot expressed in *The Governor*, that flattering careerists might learn to disguise self-interest as friendship, is multiplied a thousandfold in Castiglione's Urbino. Bembo gloomily advises that the 'perfit Courtier' should avoid mak-ing friends altogether, since he can never know what his neighbour is thinking: 'because there are in our minds so many dennes and corners, that it is unpossible for the wit of man to know the dissimulations that lye lurking in them' (119). Fraudulent dissimulations infiltrate sexual relationships as well as friendship, as Lord Julian points out in book three: 'men bee now a daies so craftie, that they make infinite false semblants, and sometime weepe, when they have in deede a greater lust to laugh' (237). In fact for Julian words have grown so corrupt that he urges lovers to communicate exclusively in sign language (246). But linguistic duplicity becomes most dangerous when it infects, as it inevitably does, affairs of state. In the fourth book the dis-putants aim to give the 'perfit Courtier' a political role, which for Octavian consists in acting as friend and counsellor to the Prince. He must, says Octavian, 'breake his minde to [the Prince], and alwaies enforme him franckly of the truth of every matter' (261). Unfortu-nately, the simulations of amity described by Bembo are so widespread that most princes have succumbed long since to a state of justifiable paranoia. Most of the ruler's self-professed friends:

speake and worke alwaies to please, and for the most part open the way with lyes, which in the Princes minde engender ignorance, not of outwarde matters onely, but also of his owne selfe. And this may be saide to be the greatest and foulest lye of all other, because the ignorant minde deceiveth himselfe, and inwardly maketh lies of himselfe. (262)

In this courtly wilderness where signs conceal signs, the Prince, like the Courtier, loses all sense of identity. He is what his subjects with a bewildering web of 'lyes and flatterie' have made him (264), and any assault on their verbal construction of him he sees as an assault on his security. The well-meaning counsellor who (like Elyot's Plato) endeavours to show him 'plainly and without anie circumstance the horrible face of true vertue' transforms himself in the Prince's eyes into a 'venemous serpent' (264). Simplicity recasts itself as deviousness—the biblical serpent is the subtlest beast of the field—and to convince this paranoid monarch of his friendship the Courtier must become as deviously subtle in observing 'circumstance' as any flatterer—reversing the tactics of Elyot's flatterers, who appropriated the blunt speech of amity. In the context of all this tactical manœuvring and manipulative self-concealment, only the perfect Courtier could retain much notion of 'true vertue', and only the perfect Prince could recognize his worth.

But instead of overcoming these insuperable obstacles, in the fourth book the perfect Courtier finds himself finally refined out of existence. The book opens with the narrator in sombre mood, meditating once again on the ravages of time: three of the disputants have died before they reached their full potential, a grim omen for the young princes on whom the task of reconstructing Urbino devolves. And in the course of the book it becomes clear that the Courtier himself is subject to time. Julian suggests that the Courtier's political function is better suited to a 'grave person and of authoritie, ripe in years and experience' than to a younger man. At once the disputants launch into a discussion of the qualities appropriate to old age, suddenly adding years to their model youth, ageing him like a sixteenth-century Rip Van Winkle before he has reached maturity. The book ends with Bembo's celebrated rhapsody on the nature of true beauty, but the speech is a swansong, an exquisitely mournful celebration of the shadowy Courtier's transition from old age to death.

It begins as a defence of the proposition that it is appropriate for the Courtier to fall in love, since his political position requires that he be old, and only old men are capable of appreciating what Bembo calls 'true beauty'. In some mysterious way, this 'true beauty' reflects the proportions that give order to the universe. These proportions—the precise relation of part to part which enables a machine to function smoothly—give beauty to 'this great Ingin of the world' (311), and make sailing-ships and buildings the most beautiful, because the most efficiently functional, of human artefacts. The same proportions occur in the most attractive of human bodies; and Bembo argues that in all the creations of God and humanity, 'outwarde beautie' is the 'true signe of the inwarde goodnesse' (309). The desire for true beauty, he claims, has nothing to do with sexual desire. What makes old men uniquely qualified to recognize it is their very blindness and impotence. The loss of their senses liberates them from the confusion that besets the active lover, whose sexual spryness tempts him to blur the distinction between lust and rational love. Old men are 'reasonable lovers' (315) who judge beauty not with their bodily eyes but with 'the eyes of the minde, which then begin to be sharpe and throughly seeing, when the eyes of the bodie lose the floure of their sightlinesse' (318). For them, kissing is the ultimate form of self-expression, since 'the reasonable lover woteth well, that although the mouth be a parcell of the bodie, yet is it an issue for the wordes, that be the interpreters of the soule, and for the inwarde breath, which is also called the soule' (315).

In fact, Bembo's brilliant fantasy implicitly acknowledges the failure of the project of constructing the 'perfit Courtier'. In order to fashion his 'reasonable lover' he has deprived his Courtier of his bodily functions, lifted him out of his political context, and suspended him in an imaginative space that has no connection with the world of devious courtly machinations inhabited by the disputants. Bembo himself warns his colleagues early in the third book that words never act as a trustworthy index to the 'dennes and corners' of the mind, let alone as 'interpreters of the soule'. His sublimely rational old lovers have nothing in common with the cantankerous old men who succumb to the ravages of time at the beginning of book two. They have even less to do with the aged courtier Morello, who interrupts Bembo just as he waxes lyrical about the clarity of an old man's spiritual vision, to insist that old men can and should lead vigorously active sex lives. In fact, true beauty seems to have nothing to do with humanity at all. Once the 'reasonable lover' has reached a state of perfect knowledge, his soul breaks free from the complications of being human: 'for being chaunged into an Angell, she understandeth all thinges that may be understood' (319). At this point the Courtier is effectively dead. For Bembo, Elyot's simplicity becomes available only when the soul leaves the body and the Courtier loses his identity for the last time.

But if the 'perfit Courtier' and the simplicity that enables him to operate remain an elusive fiction, the debate that surrounds him is not. It has been vividly realized in Castiglione's text. The treatise has posited a courtly environment in which differences not only coexist, but make possible the dialogue which enables social interaction. The end of the treatise establishes the conditions under which this culture of debate can come into being. Bembo is brought back to earth by a joke from Lady Emilia, who reminds him that he has not yet left his body, and must return at last to the world where men and women engage in disputations and so ensnare themselves in the nets of misunderstanding. Almost as soon as he falls silent, controversy breaks out once more: Julian and Gaspar take up their quarrel over the merits and demerits of women as if nothing has been said since book three. But Bembo's imaginative visions have not been wholly ineffectual. For a while his words have allowed his hearers to forget time's passing, so that when he falls silent they are amazed to find that the dawn has broken: 'the reasonings . . . with their pleasantnesse had deceived so the Lordes mindes, that they wist not of the going away of the houres' (324). Bembo practises an imaginative deceit, a kind of fraud or flattery, which offers a beguiling but transitory escape route from time, fraud, and flatterers.

The text ends by reminding its readers of the context that gives Bembo's imaginative deceit its beneficent power. The courtiers open windows in the magnificent façade of the palace to see:

already in the East a faire morning like unto the colour of roses, and all starres voyded, saving only the sweete Governesse of heaven, Venus which keepeth the boundes of the night and day, from which appeared to blowe a sweete blast, that filling the aire with a biting colde, began to quicken the tunable notes of the prettie birdes, among the hushing woodes of the hils at hand. (324)

The planet Venus evokes the chain of love with which the Duchess binds the disputants in the imaginary lost world of Urbino. And Castiglione offers his readers the possibility of extending this chain a little, by refusing to close the discussion. If the perfect courtier has never been invented, it is for the readers to go on striving to invent him, by electing a new Duchess and continuing the dispute in the context of their own lives.

Hoby's translation of *The Courtier* was published in 1561, in the third year of Elizabeth's reign. As with the treatises of Elyot and Guevara, English responses to Castiglione's dialogue varied according to the reader's preconceptions about the function of the text. Writers of prescriptive treatises tended to ignore *The Courtier*'s uneasy inconclusiveness and to treat it as a conventional didactic tract. The educationalist Roger Ascham, for instance, seems oblivious to the fact that the book takes the form of a debate. Instead he recommends it in *The Scholemaster* as a beginner's guide to courtly conduct, a wholesome antidote to the poisonous influence of Italian fiction, and a safe substitute for the pernicious practice of sending young men on educational trips to the Continent. 'Advisedlie read, and diligentlie folowed, but one yeare at home in *England*', he claims, the book 'would do a yong jentleman more good, I wisse, then three yeares travell abrode spent in *Italie*' (218). Writers of prose fiction, on the other hand, quickly recognized the dramatic potential of Castiglione's dialogue. In the thirty years that followed the publication of Hoby's translation, writers like Edmund Tilney, John Lyly, and Robert Greene repeatedly exploited the debate culture of Urbino for their own ends, fusing it with other kinds of Italian fiction to produce new, sophisticated prose forms, well suited to expressing the anxieties and unresolved controversies of their times.

The English writers of prose fiction recognized that *The Courtier* had more in common with the fictions Ascham despised than he cared to admit. Castiglione opens his text with a discussion of the language of Boccaccio (11), and his use of the dialogue form owes much to Boccaccio's treatment of *questioni d'amore* in the *Filocolo*. It needed only a closer union of Castiglione's text with aspects of Boccaccio's fictions to make the culture of debate a more unsettling phenomenon than Ascham suspected. Remove the text's central authority—or replace the Duchess with a less restrained, more articulate woman, a Faustina or a Lucilla. Take away the chain of love, or change the nature of that chain, reintroducing the element of sexual attraction which Bembo purged so insistently from the Courtier's relationships. Introduce strangers as participants in the debate, strangers who have the same argumentative brilliance as Castiglione's courtiers but with none of their acceptance of controlling conventions. Transplant the debate from the court to a private household, away from the context where laws are made and policed. Effect just a few of these changes, and Castiglione's elegant threnody to a fictional past may become as insidiously menacing as the subtlest of the Italian erotic fantasies that Ascham attacked with such venom.

## 3. FICTION AS ESPIONAGE

It is ironic that Roger Ascham's *The Scholemaster*, which contains the fiercest of Elizabethan attacks on Italian fiction, should have become a major source of subject-matter for the Italianate English fictions of the following decade; but it is hardly surprising. *The Scholemaster* is the most stylish and imaginative of Elizabethan treatises, and combines the seriousness of a pedagogic handbook with the wit and liveliness of an Italian comedy. Ascham describes its pedagogic function on the title-page: it offers a 'plaine and perfite way of teachyng children, to understand, write, and speake, the Latin tong, but specially purposed for the private bryngyng up of youth in Ientlemen and Noble mens houses, and commodious also for all such, as have forgot the Latin tonge' (171).[20] Bland as it might seem, this description contains the seeds of two narratives that begin to unfold in the course of the treatise and that came to fruition in the following decade. The first is a narrative which was enacted repeatedly on stage throughout the first half of Elizabeth's reign: the story of the perennial struggle to shape the recalcitrant sons of the nobility and gentry into useful servants of the state. The second narrative is hinted at in the statement that the book will prove invaluable for those who have 'forgot the Latin tonge'. Prospective purchasers might infer from this that the book will benefit those who have never known Latin, as well as the genuinely forgetful; in other words, that it will help to provide educational qualifications for upwardly mobile youngsters who wish to gain access to noble households, as well as for the native inhabitants of such households. Both storylines were teasingly developed in the English prose fictions of the 1570s.

But perhaps the most intriguing narrative in the treatise can be described as a kind of spy-story. The book dedicates itself to protecting

---

[20] For an account of Ascham's life and the sources of *The Scholemaster*, see Lawrence V. Ryan, *Roger Ascham* (Stanford, Ca.: Stanford University Press, 1963).

the homes of the aristocracy from infiltration by corrupt Italian customs and linguistic practices: a surreptitious invasion which, Ascham contends, is going on at the time of writing under the very noses of the ruling classes. The ideological structures which keep England secure from Catholic colonization are being stealthily eroded, and *The Scholemaster*'s self-appointed task is to draw attention to this erosion before it becomes irreversible.

Among the factors that contribute to the stealthy demolition of English culture, time is the most obvious. Like the old men in Castiglione's second book, Ascham is always contrasting the state of affairs 'now in our dayes' with the practice of the past (202), elegiacally recalling his last conversation with Lady Jane Grey to prove his point, or praising the pedagogic methods of the Greeks and Romans. Ascham is as conscious as Castiglione of the depredations of time, but he is much more fiercely committed to resisting them. Like *The Courtier* his treatise begins in a mood of nostalgia—begins with a death. He explains that he wrote it at the request of Sir Richard Sackville, who died while it was being written. The book almost died with him. 'Whan he was gone', Ascham muses, 'I cast this booke awaie: I coulde not looke upon it, but with weping eyes, in remembring him, who was the onelie setter on, to do it' (179). Again like *The Courtier*, the book had its origins in a debate, which took place at the house of William Cecil some years before its completion. But despite the time and lives that have passed away since then, and despite Ascham's decision not to reproduce the debate in dialogue form, the text generates an atmosphere of urgency which is absent from the mellower meditations of Elyot and Castiglione. The problems it exposes are immediate and (Ascham thinks) overwhelming ones, and the reader is never allowed to forget the presence of Ascham's ideological opponents.

The book takes as its starting-point an item of gossip that sparked off the debate at Cecil's house: the story of some boys who ran away from Eton 'for feare of beating' (175). The first half devotes itself to a problem of educational psychology suggested by the plight of the Eton truants: how to motivate the reluctant pupil without resorting to the usual Tudor strategy of physical violence. Ascham's solution to the problem is the humane one of appealing to a child's 'will' to learn by making learning pleasurable. But this method has an unexpected and unwelcome side-effect: the schoolmaster who tries to make his lessons entertaining finds himself locked in a ferocious struggle against alternative pleasures that compete with schoolbooks for the child's attention. These rival pleasures reveal themselves gradually but more and more menacingly in the course of Ascham's discussion. In his 'Praeface to the Reader' Ascham compares his text to a work of institutional architecture: 'as it chanceth to busie builders...the worke rose dailie higher and wider, than I thought it would at the beginninge' (178–9). But a little later he betrays an awareness of an alternative, subversive process of education woven into the fabric of his own pedagogic project. At the heart of this subversive education lies the Italian travel which young men undertake as a supplement to their English educational curriculum. Travel in Italy, he contends, erects an alternative schoolhouse which threatens to undermine the foundations of his own school building. This is the schoolhouse of shame, as he warns in a passage heavy with irony: 'a good Scholehouse of wholesome doctrine: and worthy Masters of commendable Scholers, where the Master had rather diffame hym selfe for hys teachyng, than not shame his Scholer for his learning' (229). The passage invests Ascham's title with a dark double meaning: *The Scholemaster* could refer either to the ideal pedagogue or to his corrupt foreign double, who pours his unwholesome doctrines into the schoolboy's mind through all the unguarded entries of his senses.

Ascham confesses that travel in Italy can alter the traveller's identity as radically as any form of conventional schooling, but its effects are very different. Instead of teaching a youth to know himself—that is, to become familiar with what the state expects of him—Italian travel transforms him into a 'mervelous monster', an indefinable hybrid which combines 'at once in one bodie, the belie of a Swyne, the head of an Asse, the brayne of a Foxe, the wombe of a wolfe' (228). This monstrous metamorphosis is brought about, Ascham explains, by unregulated first-hand experience. In this respect his treatise differs fundamentally from Elyot's. Elyot is confident that all the nascent governor needs to acquire political acumen is unlimited access to experience. Ascham, by contrast, sees experience as fraught with dangers, and offers his own carefully regulated text as a safe substitute for the muddled but alluring sensory data garnered from unauthorized sources. On the subject of knowledge gained through travel he warns that 'Learning teacheth more in one yeare than experience in twentie: And learning teacheth safelie. when experience maketh mo miserable then wise' (214). In place of this dangerous hands-on approach he recommends that pupils should be given a good infusion of moral theory, and that they should go on getting it until they reach the ripe old age of 27. This prudent regimen will end by producing an army of upright young men ready to serve the state, fleshly equivalents of Ascham's solid school building, whose mental faculties have been constructed 'according to the square, rule, and line, of wisdom learning and vertue' (216). The juxtaposition of three virtues with three carpenter's tools reflects his conviction of the complementary functions of theory and practice.

As one might expect, Ascham extends his distrust of unregulated experience to embrace a wariness of examples. Elyot takes exemplary histories to be as valid a source of experience as the study of the actions of living men; a store of such examples, both read and witnessed, is the foundation of knowledge. Ascham shares Elyot's belief in the potency of living patterns: 'One example, is more valiable, both to good and ill, than xx. preceptes written in bookes', he acknowledges (218), but this potency has a touch of menace about it. Pupils tend to find bad examples vastly more stimulating than good ones: 'The best examples have never such forse to move to any goodnes, as the bad, vaine, light and fond, have to all ilnes' (220). Indeed, his entire treatise is predicated on the assumption that good is always being overlooked, that the superficially clever pupil he describes as the 'quick wit' will always outshine the less brilliant but more stable forms of wisdom cultivated by the slow. This widespread privileging of brilliance over reliability and of bad over good is, for Ascham, closely related to the current fashion for verbal subtlety and the contempt for consensual simplicity this entails. The 'quick wit' possesses a verbal facility which allows him to shift his position ceaselessly in the service of his own interest: 'sothing, soch as be present: nipping any that is absent ... by quicknes of witte, verie quicke and readie, to like none so well as them selves' (189). Ascham's schoolmaster aims to nurture the opposite qualities of simplicity and reliability, but he is forced to grope for words to describe the accomplishments he prizes in his pupils: 'this ignorance in yougthe, which I spake on, or rather this simplicitie, or most trewlie, this innocencie, is that, which the noble *Persians*, as wise *Xenophon* doth testifie, were so carefull, to breede up their yougth in' (210). The fashionable world has become so seduced by subtlety that at least two of the three words he uses to define the good pupil—ignorance, simplicity, and innocence—were perhaps more familiar to his readers as terms of abuse than as terms of praise.

Ascham's difficulty in finding a suitable vocabulary to describe the qualities of the ideal pupil—difficulties which he resolves by introducing Greek terms for these qualities into his text, including the term 'Euphues' which John Lyly later appropriated for the protagonist of his novel—stems from the infection of the English language by the usage of travellers. On returning from Italy these travellers juggle with the meanings of words and phrases, or substitute their own slippery sign-systems for the agreed linguistic systems which keep social intercourse simple. They communicate with 'signes, tokens, wagers, purposed to be lost, before they were purposed to be made, with bargaines of wearing colours, floures, and herbes, to breede occasion of ofter meeting of him and her, and bolder talking of this and that &c.' (235). The verb 'to breede' insinuates the eventual outcome of these liaisons, and warns of the speed with which these devious linguistic practices will colonize the country, breaking down cultural taboos as they spread.

In fact for Ascham the most dangerous concept to be imported from Italy is the doctrine of freedom of speech. Elyot argued that 'liberty of speech' was essential for preserving good relations between a monarch and his subjects (he discusses the point in his chapter on 'affability', 106–11),[21] but for Ascham unregulated discourse can generate only anarchy. An Italian grows up under disastrously liberal conditions, inhabiting 'some free Citie, as all Cities be there: where a man may freelie discourse against what he will, against whom he lust' (236). Uncensored speech lies at the root of the divisions that form the background to Italian fiction, pitching town against town, fragmenting communities, stirring up 'private contention in many families, open factions in every Citie' (223). *The Scholemaster* is, among other things, an impassioned plea for state control over language. Ascham's concern for a regulated use of words is well known from a celebrated passage in the second part of *The Scholemaster*: 'Ye know not, what hurt ye do to learning, that care not for wordes, but for matter, and so make a devorse betwixt the tong and the hart' (265). This was parodied by Bacon in *The Advancement of Learning*,[22] but it is not, as Bacon seems

---

[21] 'O what damage have ensued to princes and their realms where liberty of speech hath been restrained!' (*The Governor*, 108).

[22] See Francis Bacon, *The Advancement of Learning and the New Atlantis*, ed. Arthur Johnston (Oxford: Clarendon Press, 1986), 26: 'the admiration of ancient authors . . . did bring in an affectionate study of eloquence and copie of speech, which then began to flourish. This grew speedily to an excess; for men began to hunt more after words than matter . . . Then did Car of Cambridge and Ascham with their lectures and writings almost deify Cicero and Demosthenes, and allure all young men that were studious unto that delicate and polished kind of learning.'

to have thought, an uncritical celebration of stylistic ornament. Instead Ascham goes on to suggest that there is a causal relationship between the sloppy use of language and the disintegration of the dominant ideology of the state:

For marke all aiges: looke upon the whole course of both the Greeke and Latin tonge, and ye shall surelie finde, that, whan apte and good wordes began to be neglected, and properties of those two tonges to be confounded, than also began, ill deedes to spring: strange maners to oppresse good orders, newe and fonde opinions to strive with olde and trewe doctrine, first in Philosophie: and after in Religion. (265)

Conscious of this imminent socio-linguistic decay, Ascham seeks to clarify his own usage as painstakingly as Elyot did. 'Headie, and Brainsicke', he explains at one point with pedantic thoroughness, 'be fitte and proper wordes, rising naturallie of the matter, and tearmed aptlie by the condition, of over moch quickenes of witte' (189). By contrast, the quick wits who populate the court change the uses of words whenever it suits them to do so. In a passage which gives urgency to Castiglione's attack on courtly flatterers, Ascham shows how these wits rob words of their proper social functions. If a youth is 'innocent and ignorant of ill, they say, he is rude, and hath no grace, so ungraciouslie do som gracelesse men, misuse the faire and godlie word GRACE' (206–7). Quick wits have nothing but contempt for the quality of 'innocencie' admired by the ancient Persians; but, more importantly, their appropriation of the 'faire and godlie word GRACE', a word which encompasses one of the central tenets of the Protestant faith, initiates the demolition of the verbal hegemony which preserves the English nation as well as the English language. A little later Ascham invokes the word grace in its 'proper' sense, as a protective charm against Catholicism, praying that God will 'preserve us by his Grace, from all maner of terrible dayes' (209). For Ascham a 'faire and godlie word' properly used can resist Armadas; no wonder he advocates the policing of texts. When words can demolish kingdoms, his insistence on the careful imitation of a limited number of prescribed Classical texts takes on the heroic dimensions of a last-ditch defence of the bastions of Protestantism.

At the centre of Ascham's campaign for control of words lies a battle between good and bad books. For every text he prescribes there is a forbidden alternative. He cites Homer and Plato as paradigms of literary respectability, and stylistically pits Italian fictions against the wisdom of the ancient Greeks.[23] When he visited Lady Jane Grey just before her death, he tells us admiringly, he found her reading 'Phaedon Platonis in Greeke, and that with as moch delite, as som jentleman wold read a merie tale in Bocase' (201). Later, Italian texts come into conflict with the divine text itself. Italianate Englishmen 'have in more reverence, the triumphes of Petrarche: than the Genesis of Moses . . . a tale in Bocace, than a story of the Bible' (232). At the same time they 'counte as Fables, the holie misteries of Christian Religion' (232): Italian fictions seem capable of spreading the disease of fiction even into the body of the supreme textual authority, the scriptures.[24]

Ascham's diatribe against Italian books stems in part from a resistance to complexity in narrative. His preferred form of narrative seems to be a simple fable of the kind attributed to Aesop, with its moral carefully attached as a safeguard against misreadings. In an earlier treatise, Toxophilus (1545), he explains that the ancient poets 'oftentymes under the covering of a fable, do hyde and wrappe in goodlie preceptes of philosophie, with the true judgement of thinges' (17). Fiction from Italy, on the other hand, instead of providing a key to the 'preceptes of philosophie', threatens to break down all prescriptive systems with its sheer complexity. Ascham's description of the Italianate Englishman as a monstrous composite beast, a blend of swine, ass, fox, and wolf, signals the traveller's transition from 'simplicitie' to a mental state that eludes definition: his character has grown too subtle to be confined within the structure of a single Aesopian fable. The Italian fictions he brings with him are the textbooks of the disruptive education that challenges Ascham's curriculum at every turn. They inculcate 'not fond and common wayes to vice, but such subtle,

---

[23] He derives the technique, perhaps, from Tyndale, whose Obedience of a Christian Man (1527) complains that the Catholic church's forbidding the laity to read the Bible in the vernacular encourages them to read 'Robin Hood, Bevis of Hampton, Hercules, Hector, and Troilus, with a thousand histories and fables of love and wantonness, and of ribaldry, as filthy as heart can think'. See Stephen Greenblatt, Renaissance Self-fashioning (Chicago, Ill.: University of Chicago Press, 1980), 112–14.

[24] In 1580 Gabriel Harvey was still echoing Ascham's complaint that Italian books had usurped the study of canonical texts in recent years. He tells how, at Cambridge, Cicero, Aristotle, and the rest are regarded as outmoded, while 'Matchiavell' is considered 'a great man: Castilio of no small reputation: Petrarch, and Boccace in every mans mouth: Galateo and Guazzo never so happy: over many acquainted with Unico Aretino: The French and Italian when so highly regarded of Schollers? The Latine and Greeke, when so lightly? . . . all inquisitive after Newes, newe Bookes, newe Fashions, newe Lawes, newe Officers, and some after newe Elementes, and some after newe Heavens, and newe Helles to.' Harvey, Works, i. 69–70.

cunnyng, new, and diverse shiftes, to cary yong willes to vanitie, and yong wittes to mischief, to teach old bawdes new schole poyntes, as the simple head of an English man is not hable to invent' (231).

The allusion to 'new schole poyntes' underlines the problematic aspect of Ascham's attack, which is that Italian fiction uses precisely the same methods to teach its subtle lessons as the ones he recommends for teaching his own pupils. Both schools, the sensual school of experience and Ascham's responsible institution, appeal with equal urgency to the will. Instead of drawing children's minds to learning through kindness, as he recommends, these texts seduce youths with sensuality, so that 'the mynde is sone drawne from troth to false opinion' (230). More importantly, the distinction between 'troth' and 'false opinion' gets lost in the process, so that unsuspecting readers find themselves in the position of the Englishman in Italy, 'baren of discretion to make trewe difference betwixt good and ill, betwixt troth, and vanitie' (227). One of the ways in which Italian fictions effect this confusion is by adopting as their own the moral precepts that Ascham appoints as bodyguards to monitor a traveller's experiences. They make use of 'preceptes of fonde bokes' and parade their fake morality on their title-pages, 'commended by honest titles the soner to corrupt honest maners' (229). Catholic propagandists, in fact, produce books which are unnervingly difficult to distinguish in tone and appearance from *The Scholemaster*. Hence Ascham's careful catalogue, in the second part of his treatise, of the Classical and contemporary texts which are suitable for his pupils' use: a canonical reading-list to which no extraneous text need be added. His own treatise can safely be included on any such list, as its title-page makes plain: it is published '*Cum Gratia & Privilegio Regiae Maiestatis*', with the gracious approval of her majesty's censors.

But Ascham is well aware that his own text offers only a frail bastion against the triumphant inroads of the new fiction. Throughout *The Scholemaster* the vocabulary he uses to describe the decadence of contemporary linguistic and social fashions is that of irresistible excess. When he complains of corruption at court he laments apocalyptically that 'disobedience doth overflowe the bankes of good order, almoste in everie place, almoste in everie degree of man' (209). In the same way, Italian texts overwhelm the carefully controlled system of pedagogic precepts with a flood of corrupt examples: 'for experience, plentie of new mischieves never knowne in England before: for maners, varietie of vanities, and chaunge of filthy lyving' (229). Numerically too Italian fictions breed as fast as the lovers they inflame, and their fertility is the more disastrous because each book has the attractive force of several authorized texts: 'Ten sermons at Paules Crosse do not so moch good for movyng men to trewe doctrine, as one of those bookes do harme' (230); and again, 'ten *Morte Arthures* do not the tenth part so much harme, as one of these bookes, made in *Italie*, and translated in England' (231). Clearly these texts possess in abundance the two stylistic qualities celebrated by Erasmus in his treatise *De Copia*: 'plentie' and 'varietie'. But in place of the metaphor of a river in full spate with which Erasmus opens his account of the persuasive power of eloquence, the metaphor Ascham applies both to his unruly courtiers and to the books they read invokes the appalling energy of a river in flood.[25]

The subversive alternative education Ascham sets in opposition to his own prescribed syllabus is a system operated for the young by the young. Italianate Englishmen have a profound contempt for the prescriptions of their elders, which manifests itself as 'singularity' or self-opinion: they are 'mervelous singular in all their matters: Singular in knowledge, ignorant of nothyng: So singular in wisedome (in their owne opinion) as scarse they counte the best Counsellor the Prince hath, comparable with them' (236). This arrogance is what makes the freedom of speech they exercise so dangerous to the state. Without the restraining influence of schoolmasters or university tutors these young people engage in wide-ranging debates on all current controversies, setting themselves up as 'Common discoursers of all matters' and 'busie searchers of most secret affaires'. In doing so they usurp parliamentary prerogative: freedom of speech in parliament, the right to discuss every political topic without fear of reprisal, was a fiercely defended position throughout the reign of Elizabeth I.[26] By usurping this prerogative Italianate Englishmen undermine the state's authority and increase the likelihood of political unrest. In 1549 Sir Thomas Smith had argued that unmoderated debate among young

[25] Erasmus opens his treatise with the river metaphor: 'The speech of man is a magnificent and impressive thing when it surges along like a golden river, with thoughts and words pouring out in rich abundance.' *Collected Works of Erasmus*, xxiv: *Literary and Educational Writings 2: De Copia/De Ratione Studii*, ed. Craig R. Thompson, *De Copia* trans. Betty I. Knott (Toronto: Toronto University Press, 1978), 295.

[26] See e.g. the arguments for freedom of speech advanced by Paul and Peter Wentworth in Parliament on 9 Nov. 1566, 8 Feb. 1576, and 1 Mar. 1587. *Select Statutes and Constitutional Documents Illustrative of the Reigns of Elizabeth and James I*, ed. G. W. Prothero (Oxford: Clarendon Press, 1913), 118, 120–2, 123–4.

people was directly responsible for the Catholic uprisings in the reign
of Edward VI:

it is ordeyned by the universities that first men should be bachelers, and mais-
ters of arte, ere they should medle with divinitie . . . And now they steppe
over, and fall to divinitie by and by, before they have gotten or purchased
theim anie Judgement throughe the foresaide sciences; which makes theim
to fall to theise dyversities of opinions that we speake of nowe. For all begin-
ners in everie science be verie quicke, and over hastie in givinge theire Judgementes of thinges, (as experience teacheth everie man); and then, whan they
have once uttered and published their Judgementes and opinions, they will se
nothinge that will sounde contrarie to the same, but either they will conster it
to theire owne fantasie, or utterly denie it to be of anie auctoritie . . . in this
science, everie boy that hathe not redde scripture past halfe a yeare shalbe suffered not only to reason and inquire thinges, (for that weare tollerable,) but to
affirme new and straunge interpretations uppon the same never heard of
before. What ende of opinions can theare be while this is suffered?[27]

The passage might easily have served as a source for Ascham's complaints about Italianate Englishmen. More importantly, it suggests
that contemporary politicians would have considered him to have serious grounds for these complaints. Young people in sixteenth-century
England were perceived as being increasingly embroiled in the project
of unsupervised self-education; and by providing textbooks for this
extracurricular activity, writers of fiction could with all seriousness
be accused of inciting them to rebellion.

In retrospect it looks as if Ascham was one of the most sensitive Elizabethan analysts of the new Italian fiction that had taken the English
imagination by storm. He draws attention to precisely those properties
of this fiction—its florid diction, its obsession with male narcissism, its
inventiveness, its parodic demolition of conventional platitudes—
which appealed most strongly to young English writers in the 1570s.
And he supplies these young writers with an intriguing storyline. It is
the story of themselves: of a group of well-educated and headstrong
young men, idle through no fault of their own, with a flashy control
over language and a finger on the pulse of fashion, interested in continental religion and politics, who insinuate themselves by verbal
charm and sexual charisma into the domestic life of an unsuspecting

---

[27] *A Discourse of the Common Weal of this Realm of England*, attrib. Sir Thomas Smith, ed.
Elizabeth Lamond (Cambridge: Cambridge University Press, 1893), 29. For the attribution
to Sir Thomas Smith, see Mary Dewar, 'The Authorship of the "Discourse of the Commonweal" ', *Economic History Review*, 2nd ser. 19 (1966), 388–400.

nation and in doing so destabilize the social and political institutions of that nation at the root. In comparison with these stylish quick wits who like to imitate the Italians, the idealized, old-fashioned English youth Ascham evokes when he speaks of 'the simple head of an English man' sounds irremediably dull. Ascham himself confesses with what sounds like grudging admiration that the qualities of the quick wit and the Italianate Englishman—subtlety, attractiveness, rapid and unexpected changes in the direction of their thought, and a delight in devious double meanings—are the perfect qualifications for authors of poetic fantasies: 'The quickest wittes commonlie may prove the best Poetes, but not the wisest Orators' (189). *The Scholemaster* betrays throughout its length the uneasy sense that Italian fiction has freed the English imagination from traditional conceptions of the art of writing, and that this quiet revolution may be irreversible. A 'mervelous monster' has been loosed on the English literary scene in the shape of the young English inheritors of the tricks of Italian prose fiction. It is a monster which Ascham rightly suspects may be too tricky to be confined in any censorial labyrinth.

## 4. THE POLICING OF FICTION

Ascham's attack on the corrupt alternative education disseminated by foreign erotic narratives forms part of a fierce contemporary debate over the function of fiction. The debate reached its fiercest in the decade and a half that followed the publication of *The Scholemaster* in 1570. This was a period of profound political unrest. In 1569 a Catholic rebellion broke out in the north of England; in the following year a second northern rebellion was suppressed, Queen Elizabeth was excommunicated by the church of Rome and John Felton posted the papal bull of excommunication on the Bishop of London's gate. In 1569 and 1571 the Duke of Norfolk was implicated in Catholic conspiracies, for which he lost his head in 1572. The 'Homily Against Disobedience and Wilful Rebellion', published in 1570 and appointed to be read from every pulpit in the country, ascribed the recent troubles to propaganda spread by Catholic clerical spies who had infiltrated vulnerable English households, 'creeping in laymen's apparel into the houses and whispering in the ears of certain Northern borderers'.[28]

---

[28] *Certain Sermons or Homilies Appointed to be Read in Churches in the Time of Queen Elizabeth of Famous Memory*, ed. John Griffiths (London: SPCK, 1864), 637. In fact, the

And throughout the decade Protestant polemicists contributed to the mood of paranoia by issuing a barrage of tracts which detailed the clandestine activities of Catholic infiltrators at every level of the social hierarchy.[29]

The publishing trade felt the impact of this political turbulence. From 1569 to 1573 the state tightened its control over publishers by issuing a series of proclamations 'agaynst seditious and trayterous Bookes, Billes and Writinges', which encouraged Her Majesty's subjects to hand in any texts they suspected of containing Catholic propaganda to a local government official. The first and second proclamations (issued in March 1569 and July 1570) specifically denounced texts like Felton's bull which libelled the state authorities; but the third proclamation, in November of the same year, spread the net of suspicion more widely. Its stated aim was:

> to geve admonition and warnyng, specially to the simple sort of her good lovyng subjectes, that they be no wyse abused with the wicked practises of ... fugitives and rebelles, by any their adherentes secretly remaynyng or repayring into the Realme, and wandring in corners, movyng good subjectes to be disobedient to the lawes, and scattering false rumors and newes, both by speache, and by bookes and wrytinges ... [30]

Readers of *The Scholemaster* would recognize the scenario: devious Catholic travellers fresh from foreign parts worming their way into the confidence of the 'simple sort' by means of cunningly constructed fictions, 'false rumors and newes'. At the time of the proclamation, the word 'newes' was virtually interchangeable with the recently imported term for short stories translated from French or Italian, 'novels', and both words carried connotations of 'innovation' at a

first English Catholic priests trained at the seminary at Douai (founded in 1568) did not arrive in England until 1574, but the association of Catholicism with domestic espionage was by that time well established. It had been made as early as 1527, when Tyndale wrote: 'in every parish have they spies, and in every great man's house, and in every tavern and ale-house. And through confession know they all secrets, so that no man may open his mouth to rebuke whatsoever they do, but that he shall shortly be made an heretic.' *The Obedience of a Christian Man*, quoted in Greenblatt, *Renaissance Self-fashioning*, 91.

[29] For a convenient summary of the events of the 1570s see Alan G. R. Smith, *The Emergence of a Nation State: The Commonwealth of England 1529–1660* (London: Longman, 1984), pt. 2.

[30] *A Transcript of the Registers of the Company of Stationers of London 1554–1640*, 3 vols. ed. Edward Arber (London: privately printed, 1875–94), i. 453. Another proclamation, aimed at books attacking Lord Burghley, was published in Sept. 1573. Catholic texts were not the only ones to be policed: in June 1573 a proclamation was printed against the Presbyterian *Admonition to the Parliament* (by Thomas Cartwright) of the previous year.

time when this was almost synonymous with 'rebellion'.[31] Under these circumstances the debate over the proper function of fiction, and especially prose fiction, acquired an urgency unheard of in more stable times.

This urgency was intensified by the difficulty of distinguishing the two sides of the debate. On one side stood practitioners of and apologists for fiction of all sorts—verse, plays, and prose fiction, united under the common term 'poetry'. On the other stood the 'poet-haters', as Sidney calls them in *An Apology for Poetry*.[32] In the past commentators have tended to divide the two sides crudely into laughter-loving hedonists and cold-blooded Puritans, but the division is not so easily made. Poets and poet-haters often claimed to subscribe in theory to a similar conception of the function of the printed text. For Ascham and thinkers like him each text played a vital role in defending or sabotaging the verbal simplicity essential for the orderly running of the Elizabethan state. Ideally each text should constitute a carefully organized space designed to teach its readers how to understand and uphold the covenants that formed the basis of the public weal. The poet-haters held that poets tended to bring this textual space into disrepute: first, by inventing stories whose 'morals' could be seen as conflicting with the interests of the state; and secondly, by sacrificing simplicity for subtlety, a kind of intellectual titillation which for Ascham and the composers of the *Homilies* amounted to sedition.[33] Yet in the 1570s an interest in different kinds of intellectual subtlety pervaded even those texts that were most committed to the defence of simplicity. Attacks on fiction were capable of engaging in the same stylistic, structural, and imaginative experiments as fiction itself, while writers of fiction chose to make the dangers of poetic lies and verbal inventiveness the subject of their fictions.

In fact, any attempt to differentiate between theorists, attackers, and practitioners of fiction in the period is to some extent artificial. Both attacks and defences of poetry in the 1570s and 1580s were for the

---

[31] See Sara Warneke, 'A Taste for Newfangledness: The Destructive Potential of Novelty in Early Modern England', *The Sixteenth Century Journal*, 26 (1995), 881–96. See also J. Paul Hunter, '"News and New Things": Contemporaneity and the Early English Novel', *Critical Inquiry*, 14 (1988), 492–513.

[32] *An Apology for Poetry*, 121.

[33] The 'Homily Against Disobedience and Wilful Rebellion' warns of 'the *subtile* suggestions of . . . restless and ambitious persons' and 'The ambitious intent and most *subtile* drifts of the Bishops of Rome' (*Certain Sermons or Homilies*, 626 and 630: my emphases).

most part written by poets: George Gascoigne, Stephen Gosson, Thomas Lodge, Philip Sidney, and George Puttenham all practised the arts
they also discussed in theoretical terms. Stephen Gosson the 'poet-
hater' dedicated his attack on contemporary fiction, *The Schoole of
Abuse*, to the poet Sidney, not because he had not thought hard
enough about the tastes of his dedicatee (as Spenser claimed) but
because he assumed that any responsible artist would share his convictions.[34] Both theorists and practitioners of poetry showed an equal
interest in the conflict between what poetry was traditionally and the-
oretically supposed to achieve and its repeated failures to achieve it.
The commonest contributions to the debate draw attention to the
interplay between poetic theory and practice by being literally
bound up with the fiction they discuss, in the form of dedicatory epistles, addresses to the reader, plot summaries, and other authorial intru-
sions on the text. Theorists and practitioners, attackers and defenders
of poetry agree with Ascham in identifying the terrifying political
consequences courted in the acts of reading and writing fiction; Gosson punningly associates the word with the sword, while Sidney
acknowledges that poetry is capable of doing 'more hurt than any
other army of words' (125). The chief difference between poets and
their antagonists seems to lie in the fact that the first are prepared—
indeed heroically eager—to embrace the danger along with the
delight, while the second, by definition, are not.

Poets and poet-haters shared the same educational background, cultivated the same stylistic idiosyncrasies, were even from time to time
the same people. At the beginning of his career as a professional writer, the young poet Thomas Lodge wittily exposed this paradox in his
pamphlet *The Defence of Poetry* (1579). He published the *Defence* in
response to Stephen Gosson's brilliant piece of anti-theatrical polemic,
*The Schoole of Abuse* (1579), and the fact that Lodge's reply seems to
have been suppressed by the censors as soon as it appeared suggests
how seriously the Elizabethan authorities treated the controversy

---

[34] Spenser wrote to Gabriel Harvey: 'Newe Bookes I heare of none, but only of one, that
writing a certaine Booke, called *The Schoole of Abuse*, and dedicating it to Maister *Sidney*, was
for his labor scorned: if at leaste it be in the goodnesse of that nature to scorne. Suche follie is
it, not to regarde aforehande the inclination and qualitie of him, to whom wee dedicate
oure Bookes.' Quoted by Arthur F. Kinney in his edition of Gosson's criticism, *Markets of
Bawdrie: The Dramatic Criticism of Stephen Gosson* (Salzburg: University of Salzburg, 1974),
43–4. All references to Gosson's criticism are taken from this edition. For a stimulating
account of Gosson's handling of English national identity, see Hadfield, *Literature, Politics
and National Identity*, ch. 4.

over fiction by the end of this decade of debate.[35] In the *Defence* Lodge accuses Gosson of belonging to the same school of sophisticated discourse that Gosson condemns in poetry—much as the King of Navarre accuses Berowne of intellectual hypocrisy in *Love's Labour's Lost*: 'How well he's read, to reason against reading!' (I. i. 94). The *Defence* repeatedly stresses Lodge's conviction that he is tackling an opponent with whom he has everything in common but his argument. At one stage, after summarizing the points in Gosson's argument with which he agrees, he concludes affably: 'in all that I like your judgement, and for the rest to[o] I approve your wit' (84).[36] For Lodge, Gosson is one of Ascham's quick wits who scorns the education that formed him: 'You say that Poets are subtil; if so, you have learned that poynt of them; you can well glose on a trifeling text... Witt hath wrought that in you, that yeares and studie never setled in the heads of our sagest doctors' (65–6). In this way Lodge ranges himself on the side of the authorities and places Gosson in the position of youthful irresponsibility he assigned to the poets in *The Schoole of Abuse*; the *Schoole* itself becomes an example of the offences it undertakes to discipline, Lodge becomes the schoolmaster and Gosson the recalcitrant pupil. Readers who had read both treatises might well find themselves in a state of bewilderment over which is the conservative text and which the radical one. In fact, Lodge suggests that a minor change will place both polemicists on the same side. Gosson need only undergo one of the metamorphoses which delighted the Classical poets, and he will change sides as if he were swapping one set of chess pieces for another: 'I will have you therfore to tast first of the cold river Phricus, in Thracia, which, as Aristotle reporteth, changeth blacke into white' (72). He is merely proposing that Gosson take another step along the path he embarked on when he turned against poetry, and commit a second act of witty apostasy.

Although *The Defence of Poetry* is a less accomplished polemic than *The Schoole of Abuse*, the point it makes is telling. Gosson came from an educational background almost identical to that of two of the most sophisticated contemporary writers of prose fiction, George Pettie and John Lyly. He studied under Dr John Rainoldes (who later turned

[35] Smith notes that 'The book was issued privately in 1579, and was withdrawn immediately' (*Elizabethan Critical Essays*, i. 61). The most likely explanation for such a hasty withdrawal is intervention by the High Commission.

[36] References to Lodge's *Defence of Poetry* are taken from *Elizabethan Critical Essays*, ed. G. Gregory Smith, 2 vols. (Oxford: Oxford University Press, 1904), i. 61–86.

to anti-theatrical polemic himself ) at Corpus Christi College, Oxford, and like Pettie and Lyly seems to have been stimulated by the exuberant brand of rhetoric practised by Rainoldes and others at Oxford in the 1570s.[37] By 1579 Gosson was an experienced playwright.[38] He confesses the paradox of his theatrical connections at the beginning of the *Schoole*: 'I take upon mee to drive you from Playes, when mine owne woorkes are dayly to be seene upon stages' (74). Like the Marprelate tracts of the 1580s, his treatise derives much of its polemical energy from its dramatic representation of the transgressions it condemns. At one point the abuses Gosson exposes become a play mounted for his private entertainment: 'it is a right Comedie, to marke behaviour' at theatres (92), and he went on to choose the structure of a Classical comedy for his last work of dramatic criticism, *Playes Confuted in Five Actions*. The *Schoole* is pervaded by an imaginative energy which a twentieth-century reader might find astonishing in a work that advocates the policing of the imagination. Gosson fills it with metaphors of festive excess: with comically active musicians who like to 'creepe through a ring, or daunce the wilde Morice in a Needles eye' (84); with a Roman emperor who invites a horse to dinner (90); and with sado-masochistic women who cut their bodies to fit their gowns (117). The tract opens with an anecdote about the Emperor Caligula, who after extensive preparations for war at sea 'gave allarme to his souldiers in token of battaile, and charged everie man too gather cockles' (72). The empty action resembles the actions both of Gosson and of the poets; of Gosson, because he modestly doubts his own ability to complete his ambitious project of re-educating the Elizabethan public in their response to fiction; and of the poets, because the theatrical special effects over which they preside

---

[37] John Rainoldes was long held to be one of the principal forerunners, if not the originator, of the ornate rhetorical style known as 'euphuism'. For this view of him, see the introduction to John Rainoldes, *Oratio in laudem artis poeticae*, ed. William Ringler, trans. Walter Allen Jr. (Princeton: Princeton University Press, 1940). Since the publication of Ringler's edition, however, the *Oratio* was found to be a version of a treatise on poetry by a colleague, Henry Dethick, and recent scholarship has inclined toward the view that Rainoldes was only an influential disseminator of certain stylistic traits, designed to 'test the limits of language', which were widespread in Oxford and elsewhere during the 1560s and 1570s. See James W. Binns, 'Henry Dethick in Praise of Poetry: The First Appearance in Print of an Elizabethan Treatise', *Library*, 30 (1975), 199–216. See also Ernst Cassirer, *The Platonic Renaissance in England* (London: Nelson, 1932 and 1953), 173–5, which discusses euphuism as a manifestation of the 'Gorgianic flexibility of language' being explored throughout 16th-cent. Europe.

[38] For details of Gosson's career, see *Markets of Bawdrie*, introduction.

invariably end in bathos: their actors engage in tremendous theatrical business with drums and trumpets, but 'when they have sounded Allarme, off go the peeces to encounter a shadow, or conquere a Paper monster' (78).

The anecdote about Caligula might seem at first to justify Lodge's suspicions that Gosson was being wittily complicit with what he condemns; to signal the text's status as a work of entertainment and to hint at the slightness of the charges he brings. His unwillingness to take seriously his role as public prosecutor seems to be further confirmed by the authorities he uses to back his argument. Unlike the earlier polemicist John Northbrooke, Gosson avoids using biblical authority to support his case against the theatre, because, he tells us, the players 'dare not abide the field, where the word of God dooth bidde them battayle' (99).[39] Instead, he appeals to the 'Antiquityes' (99) which are the traditional province of the poets themselves, comparing himself first with Ovid—albeit the Ovid who wrote *Remedia Amoris* (73)—and later with Ulysses, the wily creation of the archetypal poet, Homer (98).

But as Gosson lists the festive absurdities perpetrated by poets, a sense of menace becomes increasingly evident, peeping out from behind his apparent enjoyment of his subject. Hidden among the comic anecdotes and nonsensical images conjured up by poetry Gosson detects a fundamental threat to order itself. The harmless 'visard that Poets maske in' (77) resembles the Grecian wooden horse, which was welcomed into Troy only to undermine the town's foundations: 'if you looke well too *Epaeus* horse, you shall find in his bowels the destruction of *Troy*' (77). Poets and playwrights are the most insidious of Catholic spies; like the Greeks concealed in the horse's belly, England's enemies have succeeded in penetrating her defences under the cover provided by poetry. For Gosson, the enemies whom Ascham located safely abroad in Italy, or in the monstrous shape of the Italianate Englishman at home, have by imperceptible degrees become naturalized: 'Compare *London* to *Rome*, and *England* to *Italy*, you shall finde the Theaters of the one, the abuses of the other, to be rife among us' (91). At the same time the horrible composite beast which was Ascham's Italianate Englishman seems in Gosson's treatise to have spawned a deviant alternative nature, an ugly

---

[39] John Northbrooke published *Spiritus est Vicarius Christi in Terra: A Treatise wherein Dicing, Dauncing, Vaine Plaies or Enterludes with Other Idle Pastimes . . . are Reproved* in 1577. A second edition appeared in 1579.

parody of the 'golden world' later celebrated by Sidney, which interpenetrates and destabilizes what he conceives to be the 'true' natural order. Poets and their accomplices are the 'Dragons that are hurtful in *Affricke*', the '*Basiliskes* of the world' (90), who wield, like Ascham's Italians, the power to transform their victims into bestial imitations of themselves: they carry the 'Cuppes of *Circes*, that turne reasonable Creatures into brute Beastes' (77). Gosson elaborates on this grotesque alternative nature created by the poets in his response to Lodge's *Defence*, the *Apologie of the Schoole* (1579). The poets substitute an alternative, chaotic hierarchy for the 'true' political and religious hierarchy of the public weal: a poetic power structure that is dominated by the crazy antics of the pagan Pantheon. Led by the irrepressibly potent god Jupiter, these imaginary divinities fight without harming one another, commit acts of petty felony, and most disastrously of all are endlessly reproductive:

Bicause they are gods, they never die; bicause they are married, they dayly multiplie, for none can be so fruitfull as they; thus never dying, and ever encreasing, some of them in time shall be driven to dwell in the ayre, some in the water, some in the earth, some in hell when house rome is scant, for heaven will not hold so great a company. (126)

Gosson concludes that this absurd creation, overladen and groaning with excess gods, finally proves poets to be the 'monsters of nature', irresponsibly prolific outcasts from the social order.

In the *Schoole* the process of anarchic proliferation encouraged by poetry is more insidious. The metaphor Gosson uses is that of an endless chain that finally chokes the nation: 'For as Poetrie and Piping are Cosen germans: so piping, and playing are of great affinity, and all three chayned in linkes of abuse' (85). This chain, a parodic inversion of the Neoplatonic chain of love by which the Duchess united the courtiers of Urbino, means that for Gosson the most seemingly insignificant imaginative acts can end, as they do in his treatise, by spreading civil discord. Virgil's poetic treatment of a gnat and Ovid's of a flea can produce a destructive chain reaction that ends with the demolition of order itself. Poetry stimulates piping and playing, these in their turn promote prostitution and dicing, and these lead inexorably to the destruction of rational discourse as it is taught in the universities and enshrined in state legislation. The absurdities invented by the poets end by making an absurdity of the state. Gosson compares the general abandonment of civic responsibility provoked by the proliferation of poetic fantasies with what would happen if the chief of the poetic gods were to unleash universal madness: 'if [Jupiter] shuld pull his hand from the frame, it were impossible for the world to indure. All would be day, or al night; All spring, or all Autume; all Summer, or all winter; all heate or all colde; all moysture, or al drought' (107). In *The Governor* Elyot maintained that if order were relinquished nothing would remain 'except some man would imagine eftsoons *Chaos*' (2). At the end of the *Schoole* Gosson conjures up 'a huge *Chaos* of foule disorder' brought about by the unrestrained imaginations of the poets (110).

The drama of the poets' offences and their disastrous consequences is enacted on a metaphorical level throughout the treatise by references to food. The *Schoole* can be read as the account of a guest's heroic resistance to the temptations he encounters at an Epicurean banquet. At the beginning Gosson pauses to survey with apparent relish the rich feast of material available to him as a writer: 'And in my opinion the worlde giveth every writer so large a fielde to walke in, that before he set penne to the booke, he shall find him selfe feasted at *Syracusa*, uncertaine where to begin, or when to end' (76). But the feast is an elaborate trap, like the banquet Satan spreads for Christ in *Paradise Regained*.[40] It takes place at Syracuse, the court of the tyrant Dionysius, and it tempts its guests to taste the 'Cuppes of *Circes*' offered by the poets (77) and to indulge in the deadly surfeits offered by the players, which harm their audiences 'more, then if at the Epicures table, they had nigh burst their guts with over feeding' (87). The wise guest approaches the banquet of textual possibilities with infinite circumspection. After describing the Syracusan feast Gosson adds: 'I cannot but commende his wisedome, whiche in banqueting feedes upon that, that doth nourish best' (76). Gosson himself is the host who provides the most nourishing of imaginative repasts; at his meal, musicians and poets behave as they ought. Poetry celebrates heroic military achievements of the past without recourse to fiction (82), while quiet piping accompanies each course, so that 'the sound of the one might draw the hearers from kissing the cupp too often; the sense of the other put them in minde of things past' (82). He goes on to suggest that such moderation need not preclude enjoyment: 'I am neither so fonde a Phisition, nor so bad a Cooke, but I can allowe my patient a cup of wine to meales, although it be hotte;

---

[40] ii. 340 ff.

and pleasaunt sauces to drive downe his meate, if his stomake bee queasie' (88). But Gosson gives his healthier readers less substantial fare. His ideal diet contains no food at all: '*Plutarch* likeneth the recreation that is gotte by conference, too a pleasaunt banquet' (88); and he recommends that when we do experience physical hunger we follow the dietary example of 'our English predecessors' (90): 'they had a kind of sustenaunce in time of neede, of which if they had taken but the quantitie of a beane, or the weight of a pease, they did neyther gape after meate, nor long for the cuppe, a great while after' (91). By degrees, Gosson has drawn his readers from the anticipation of an orgiastic intellectual feast to the meagre diet of a single bean. His apparently exuberant appropriation of the metaphors of abundance loved by poets conceals a reductive rhetoric, a rhetoric devoted to slimming down the disorderly abundance of subjects available to the rhetorician, which is the precise antithesis of the *copia* propounded by Erasmus in his celebrated treatise.[41] Indeed, for Gosson *copia* is the preferred technique of the corrupt poet, who distributes 'copye of abuses' (110) in the same way as Ascham's quick wit disseminated 'varietie of vanities'.

Gosson's solution to the disastrous extremes encouraged by fiction, which mean that human beings are 'ever overlashing, passing our boundes, going beyonde our limites, never keeping our selves within compasse' (100), is that of imposing and enforcing a protective network of inescapable laws. His aim is to achieve the enviable situation where the fallen citizens of England are relieved of the necessity of making any choices for themselves at all. For Gosson, choices are only ever binary—the choice between good and evil—and he has none of Elyot's confidence that a good education will render its recipients capable of choosing wisely. He explains his scepticism about the ordinary citizen's capacity for choice in the course of the terrifying display of formal logic which makes up his third anti-theatrical tract, *Playes Confuted in Five Actions*: 'The minde of it self is simple without mixture or composition, therefore those instructions that are given to the minde must bee simple without mingle mangle of fish and flesh, good and bad[;] where both are profred, the hereditarie corruption of our nature taketh the worst and leaveth the best' (162). For Gosson even more than for Ascham, the cast of mind shared by common citi-

---

[41] For an account of Erasmus' theory of *copia*, see Terence Cave, *The Cornucopian Text: Problems of Writing in the French Renaissance* (Oxford: Clarendon Press, 1979), esp. ch. 1.

zens, those the proclamation referred to as the 'simple sort of . . . good lovyng subjectes', is both fragile and crude. It responds to every choice it is offered, not with an attempt to compromise or to reconcile the two choices as Castiglione's courtiers might have done, but by seizing on the worst and easiest option. Such a crude and vulnerable mental structure needs to be constantly protected by the more knowledgeable minds of the state authorities, who in Gosson's England as in Elyot's would seem to outdo their subjects in intellect as much as they do in power. Gosson ends the *Schoole* with an appeal to these authorities to impose universal censorship, to reduce the cacophony of contemporary poetry and music to silence. Besides their sheer fertility, the threat such artists pose to Gosson's simple state is nothing less than the threat of complexity. The variety they offer engenders confusion: 'where hony and gall are mixed, it will be hard to sever the one from the other' (77), and the alternative nature they create cannot be analysed by conventional means: 'the secretes of nature, [are] searched by witte: the Anatomy of man, set out by experience: But the abuses of plaies cannot be showen, because they passe the degrees of the instrument, reach of the Plummet, sight of the minde' (95). Gosson's solution to the intricate complexities exposed in contemporary culture by recent fiction is to outlaw complexity itself.

In Gosson's linguistic dictatorship, only two modes of discourse are appropriate for the inhabitants of a healthy state. For ordinary citizens, there is silence—the silence of obedience which contemporary texts repeatedly imposed on women—and it is for women that Gosson especially recommends this course of resistance to the seductive eloquence of the poets. He urges his women readers to 'Close up your eyes, stoppe your eares, tye up your tongues; when they speake, aunsweare not; when they hallowe, stoope not' (118). For the ruling classes he recommends a different approach to language, urging them to adopt an authorized form of discourse, an ideal medium for communication to which his own text provides the preface. The last major social malpractice he tackles in the *Schoole* is the abuse of formal logic at the universities, and he interweaves his analysis of the academics' inclination to sophistry with an attack on the art of fencing:

the Arte of Logique was firste sette downe for a rule, by which wee mighte *confirmare nostra, et refutare aliena*, confirme our owne reasons, and confute the allegations of our adversaryes, the end beeing trueth . . . Those dayes are now chaunged, the skil of the Logicians, is exercysed in caveling, the cunning of Fencers applied to quarrelling. (102–3)

This association of logical discourse with swordsmanship is no arbitrary comparison. Gosson goes on to argue that the proper form of discourse for the ruling classes combines speech and action: he urges his shy academic readers to 'Thunder in words, and glister in works' (109), and encapsulates the union of the two concepts in a pun which contracts words and works into a single versatile weapon: 'Let . . . the word and the sword be knit togither' (109). And he ends by transforming his treatise itself into an offensive weapon directed against the poets and their accomplices, exhorting the mayor of the City of London to punish the offenders his text has identified. The text which began with an illustration of futility in the anecdote about Caligula ends by encouraging the violence which Caligula failed to mete out. For Gosson only the authorities can practise the arts as they ought to be practised. He begs the magistrates not to use their powers like the 'evill Poets' who 'break the feete of their verse, and singe out of tune' (114), but instead to break the poets themselves so that they will 'singe out' in a horrific parody of verse. Violent physical punishment is the artistic activity best suited to a fallen world; and he reinforces the point with a metaphor that shockingly anticipates George Herbert's association of music and bodily torture.[42] In dealing with the recalcitrant poet, player, or musician the authorities must play on a specialized instrument of their own, the rack: they must 'play the Musition, streatch every string till he breake, but sette him in order' (114). Any other art form, he implies, threatens a far more drastic and universal breakage.

The metaphor of the rack as a musical instrument suggests that Lodge was right to point out that *The Schoole of Abuse* is locked in a perverse symbiotic relationship with the arts it attacks. The title of the treatise makes self-conscious use of the double meaning that can be read into the title of *The Scholemaster*. Ascham's book identified two sets of schoolmasters operating concurrently in contemporary England: the official pedagogues who base their curriculum on authorized texts, and the secretive Italian schoolmasters who nurture their pupils on erotic fiction. In the same way Gosson's title can be read either as announcing his ambition to 'school' current social abuses—that is, to bring them under the control of the state—or else as a warning of the presence of a school that teaches abuses in

---

[42] Herbert compares Christ's body to a musical instrument in 'Easter': 'His stretched sinews taught all strings, what key | Is best to celebrate this most high day.' *The English Poems of George Herbert*, ed. C. A. Patrides (London: J. M. Dent, 1974), 61.

the heart of London; a perverse reader might even take the title for an invitation to use *The Schoole of Abuse* as a guide to the most fashionable abuses in the capital. Gosson expresses his anxiety that his text might be given this second, unauthorized, reading when he warns himself that 'my Schoole so increaseth, that I cannot touch all, nor stand to amplyfie every poynte' (102). The more thoroughly he examines social abuses, the more inflated and unwieldy his school will become, as if in imitation of the abuses themselves. If he is not careful, the evident pleasure with which he uses metaphor in his polemic will lead him to duplicate rather than to suppress the 'copye' of poetic abuses. He dissociates his pamphlet from this danger by accusing other polemicists of succumbing to it. Less wary opponents of the theatre—he does not say who—have allowed themselves to be tainted with their own subject-matter: 'whilst they fill their Bookes with other mens faultes, they make their volumes no better then an Apothecaries Shop, of pestilent Drugges' (110). Poetry's secret influence is so addictive that even the poet-haters can find themselves unexpectedly hooked on fiction.

*The Schoole of Abuse* represents Gosson's theoretical bid to police the imagination; but like his dedicatee Sidney he did not rest content with theory. In the same year, 1579, Gosson published his own work of prose fiction, a text designed to police itself: *The Ephemerides of Phialo*. The book is a kind of anti-romance that insists on resolving all its tensions and explicating all its uncertainties before they can germinate to produce the dangerous imaginative prolixity that makes the other fictions of the 1570s so unstable. In place of the constant deferrals that propel a conventional narrative, the *Ephemerides* constructs itself around a series of interruptions which obstruct deferral. At one point the protagonist Phialo, a youthful disseminator of good counsel reminiscent of Lyly's Euphues, interrupts himself in the middle of one of his interminable monologues (just as Gosson interrupted himself in the middle of the *Schoole*) and warns himself not to amplify his own analysis of misconduct too far, 'leste I chaunce to passe my limites as farre as *Priamus*, which was registred to be the father of fiftie Children, and but xxvii of them lawfully begotten' (sig. I4$^v$). Priam's sexual excesses are those of the poets themselves, since Troy was the favourite stamping-ground of the poets. Phialo is warning himself not to commit an illegitimate imaginative act—in effect, not to commit poetry.

As with Guevara's *Dial of Princes*, the title of *The Ephemerides of Phialo* proclaims the mission of the text, which is to regiment its readers' use of their time. An ephemeris was a calendar often published along with almanacs, detailing astronomically propitious moments for important engagements—childbirth, marriage, business transactions, and so on.[43] By aligning itself with these precise chronological instruments, Gosson's *Ephemerides* sets itself up in opposition to the anarchically informal treatment of time in contemporary fiction. The book is so closely bound up with Gosson's criticism that it begins with a theoretical refutation of Lodge's *Defence* and ends with an apology for Gosson's polemical writings. In between, the narrative stubbornly refuses to turn into a conventional piece of prose fiction.

The story opens as if it is about to launch into a simpler version of *Euphues*, a variation on the theme of the prodigal son that had proved so popular in Tudor fiction and drama, describing the misdemeanours and eventual repentance of a young man who finds himself torn between the allure of pleasure and the dictates of social convention. A student called Phialo leaves his studies at university in Siena and gravitates towards the fleshpots of Venice. He is followed to Venice by his young friend Philotimo, who rebukes him for abandoning his degree and accuses him of squandering the financial resources left him by his father: 'Hath thy father wasted his treasure on thee in *Sienna*, that thou shouldest mispend thy time in *Venice*?' (sig. A4ᵛ). The scenario was a familiar one to Gosson's contemporaries; the fable of the not-so-penitent prodigal had provided the basis for narratives throughout the sixteenth century, from John Redford's *Wit and Science* (1531–4) to Lyly's *Euphues* (1578). Such readers might expect that Phialo will reject Philotimo's advice as Euphues rejects the advice of Eubulus, or else that Phialo and Philotimo will forge a fickle friendship of the kind Euphues forges with Philautus. Neither of these expectations is fulfilled. Instead Phialo attacks Philotimo in his turn, telling him that he has failed in the first duty of friendship, which is to offer advice in as palatable a form as possible. He then proceeds to instruct him in the right way to do it. The first part of the story effectively ends here; the *Ephemerides* cuts itself short before it can blossom into a full-blown narrative, and instead mutates into an instructive pamphlet, a beginner's guide to courtesy where there is no room for the complex web of ironies that activates the *Euphues* books. What began as a fiction ends by refusing all the plot devices that enable fiction to unfold.

---

[43] For an account of the ephemeris see Keith Thomas, *Religion and the Decline of Magic* (Harmondsworth: Penguin, 1978), 347–8.

Misunderstandings are a staple of plot, and Phialo is committed to eliminating misunderstandings. In the second part of the book he finds another friend, Jeraldi, immersed in reading *The Courtier*, and puzzling no doubt over the problems of social exchange raised by the 'varietie of judgements' and the secret 'dennes and corners' of the mind. Phialo undertakes to resolve all the problems left unresolved by Castiglione's treatise, and he does so by insisting that there is no need for any anxiety over other people's hidden agendas. For Phialo there can be no real doubt about the state of mind or social position of any member of the public weal; relationships between all citizens are as simple as the amity of Elyot's Titus and Gisippus. God has planted such knowledge in the heart of a man:

that seeing the image of himselfe in another, acknowledging presently his owne weakenesse, and deeply considering that wee have all one maker, GOD; one father Adam; one Nurse, the earth; he shoulde love him unfaignedly, embrace him with curtesie, frankely streatch out his hande to succour him, and sette foote by foote unto death to defende him. (sig. E2)

In such a state of unanimity there is no room for the conflicts and deceptions that produce narrative. Castiglione's Bembo, who articulated the most elaborate theory of Neoplatonic love in *The Courtier*, was eventually exposed as a dreamer whose vision bore little relation to social reality; but Gosson never hints that there might be any difficulty in putting Phialo's theories into practice.

In the third and final part of the *Ephemerides*, Phialo defuses sexual desire, the most explosive of topics both in treatise and in fiction. In the process he demonstrates his power over women and so proves himself the philosophical superior of Guevara's Marcus Aurelius, whose theories crumble when challenged by Faustina and Lucilla. By sheer force of eloquence—conveyed perhaps by his magnetic presence, since it certainly does not make itself felt on paper—Phialo succeeds in throttling an incipient romance in the cradle, and persuades a penitent whore to change her name from Polyphile to Theophile. This last book is much the most successful as entertainment, largely because the whore is the first figure in the *Ephemerides* to offer any resistance to Phialo's moral terrorism. Phialo and Jeraldi entice the unfortunate Polyphile to supper with the aim not of taking advantage of her sexual profligacy but of obliterating it. Faced with a full-frontal attack on her profession, Polyphile puts up a vigorous defence, advocating an Epicurean philosophy rather like that of Milton's Comus:

'The beasts of the earth, the fishes of the Sea, the foules of the ayre, the
Sunne, the Moone, the course of the Starres, the foure Elementes, the
whole Worlde was made for our use, and this use is the roote of all our
pleasure' (sig. H4–H4ᵛ). Her description of a genial and fertile nature
resembles the fertile alternative universe inhabited by the poets in
Gosson's polemical writings. Briefly the *Ephemerides* comes alive; but
Polyphile's vigorous version of the proper use of things is sadly short-
lived. Phialo demolishes it at a touch, replacing it with a world of
dualisms ('There are but twoo pathes layde open before us', sig.
R2ᵛ) where the right choice is always the restrictive one, and where
the body which Polyphile celebrates is subjected to the disciplinary
violence advocated at the end of the *Schoole*, 'beaten with the Flayle,
toste with the Fanne, brused with the Stone, parcht with the heate of a
Fiery Oven', until it has been refashioned as God and Phialo would
have it (sig. R5). Phialo ends by consigning his own fiction to silence.
He tells Polyphile that if she follows the correct path 'You shall finde
suche grace . . . as neither eye hath seene, nor eare hath hearde, nor
fleshe hath felte, nor thought conceived, nor *Phialoes* tongue is able
to rehearse' (sig. R5ᵛ). This reference to the book of Isaiah suggests
that the sign that divine grace has resumed its proper ideological
supremacy is a lapse into wordlessness.[44] Sure enough, when Polyphile capitulates, reduced no doubt to exhaustion by Phialo's relentless
moralizing, she loses both her name and her voice. By this point in the
book Phialo has succeeded in destroying all the means by which poets
fabricate their dangerous erotic fictions; and although Gosson tells us
in his prefatory epistle that his friends had pleaded with him to produce a second volume, it is hard to imagine how they could have
expected him to expand a work that repudiates its own genre and
decries all the techniques of verbal expansion.

*The Ephemerides of Phialo* is an attempt to beat the poets at their own
game: a kind of literary mole. Just as contemporary fictions masquer-
ade as responsible publications (as Ascham puts it, they are 'commended by honest titles the soner to corrupt honest maners', 229),
so Gosson's novel masquerades as an erotic fiction in order to lure
irresponsible readers into studying what is in effect a didactic tract.
Both Gosson and Ascham represent erotic fiction as the textual
equivalent of a spy in the world of print. Like the rebels and traitors

[44] Phialo is referring to Isa. 64: 4: 'For since the beginning of the world men have not
heard, nor perceived by the ear, neither hath the eye seen, O God, beside thee, what he
hath prepared for him that waiteth for him.' See also I Cor. 2: 9.

mentioned in the proclamation of November 1570, erotic fiction
creeps into respectable households in order to disseminate its anarchic
propaganda, 'wandring in corners, movyng good subjectes to be dis-
obedient to the lawes, and scattering false rumors and newes'. But
Gosson himself might have predicted that his project of undermining
fiction from within was doomed to failure. Fictional texts, like Catholic agents, feed on those aspects of the mind that are most difficult to
police, sexuality and the imagination, and the element of danger they
contain is precisely what makes them attractive. The Tudor authorities
themselves were well aware of the fascination exerted by texts that
have been banned. In 1599 Francis Bacon accused the Earl of Essex
of seeking to have a book banned in order to augment its popularity,
taking advantage of the fact that 'forbidden things are most sought
after'.[45] Gosson's advocacy of censorship and suppression could only
heighten the allure of poetry, and Elizabethan prose fiction throve
on censorship. Both before and after the publication of *The Ephemerides of Phialo*, Tudor fiction constructed itself from material supplied
by the forbidden underworld: secret agents, erotic encounters,
devious infiltrations, clandestine messages, and leaked documents.
Time and again the writers of fiction confess themselves to be playing
with literary fire, and it is precisely this parading of its own temerity
that continues to give the Elizabethan novel its idiosyncratic power.

[45] Bacon was referring to a book by Dr John Hayward, *The First Part of the Life and Reign
of King Henry IV*, dedicated to the Earl of Essex at a time when Essex's ambitions were under
scrutiny. See Richard Dutton, *Mastering the Revels: The Regulation and Censorship of English
Renaissance Drama* (Basingstoke: Macmillan, 1991), 119–21; see also Annabel Patterson,
*Fables of Power: Aesopian Writing and Political History* (Durham, NC: Duke University
Press, 1991), 114–15.

## 2

# Fictions and their Commentaries before 1570

### I.  THE SECRET MEANINGS OF FABLES

The process of producing narrative fictions seems always to have filled Elizabethan writers with anxiety. Authors and commentators agreed that fictions should fulfil two functions—to entertain and to instruct —but the frequency with which title-pages earnestly promise that the ensuing text will be 'both pleasant and profitable' or just 'very profitable to be known and read' suggests that some commentators remained permanently sceptical about the profit that accrued to the reader from texts which claimed to be pleasant. During the first part of Elizabeth's reign writers of fiction worked to overcome this scepticism by producing plain narrative forms which stressed their own social utility. Among the most popular of these forms was the fable, a narrative which aimed to control its recipients' interpretations by appending a critical commentary to the body of the text in the form of a 'moral': that is, an exposition of authorized readings of the text, designed to establish a notional simplicity of understanding between the author, as custodian of the ideology of the state, and the potentially wayward reader. Elizabethan responses to the complex fiction of the 1570s had their origins in the expectations raised by these apparently primitive literary models.

But the simplicity produced by the interaction between a fable and its commentary was decidedly notional. By the 1560s the various uses of the word 'fable' had come to encapsulate the duplicitous nature of fiction, and often enough the moral commentary only reinforced this duplicity.[1] Depending on the respective ideological

---

[1] For an account of the fortunes of the fable in the 16th cent., see Patterson, *Fables of Power*. See also her chapter 'Censorship and the 1587 "Holinshed's" Chronicles', in Paul Hyland and Neil Sammuells (eds.), *Writing and Censorship in Britain* (London: Routledge, 1992), 23–35.

positions of text and reader, a fable could be either a legitimate rhetorical device or a downright lie; and these two aspects proved difficult to disentangle. Stephen Hawes testifies to the usefulness of fiction in *The Pastyme of Pleasure* (1509): 'For often under a fayre fayned fable | A trouth appereth gretely profitable',[2] while in *The Arte or Crafte of Rhetoryke* (1532) Leonard Cox complains that 'it is the nature of poetes to fayne and lye' (sig. B5ᵛ). These two views of poetic 'feigning' had coexisted for centuries. The antagonism between the two positions was not absolute. Poets could be praised for their pleasurable teachings and damned for their deceitfulness in the same text, as Richard Rainolde demonstrated in *The Foundacion of Rhetorike*. In one place Rainolde expatiates on the endless errors and 'monsterous lies against God' spawned by the fertility of the poetic imagination (sig. G); in another he celebrates the 'godly counsaile' concealed in the most fertile poetic text of all, Ovid's *Metamorphoses* (sig. A3). His definition of a fable epitomizes this moral ambivalence: it is 'a forged tale, containing in it by the colour of a lie, a matter of truthe' (sig. A2ᵛ). Its nature as a 'forgerie' needs to be kept firmly in check by the 'truthe' contained in the moral: 'The morall is called that, out of the whiche some godlie precepte, or admonicion to vertue is given, to frame and instructe our maners . . . the fable was invented for the moralles sake' (sigs. A2ᵛ–A4ᵛ). For Rainolde, the lies of fiction should be not merely regulated but dictated by their preconceived instructive purpose.

But many Elizabethan moral commentaries do not look as if they generated the fable they accompany. Instead they look like a selection of the cleverest or most topical readings of an infinitely pliant text. The fable's dual status as a lie—an act of treason against the verbal simplicity favoured by the state—and as a persuasive instrument of immeasurable value to the ruling classes, was complicated by what commentators saw as its unusual susceptibility to multiple readings. The English fabulists admiringly acknowleged the plurality of interpretations made available by their texts, while at the same time trying to restrict the reader's choice between readings by incorporating a number of safety devices into their narratives. The moral commentary was the most obvious of these devices, but the wittiest commentators showed an alarming tendency to recognize and collude

---

[2] *The Works of Stephen Hawes*, introd. Frank J. Spang (Delmar, NY: Scholars' Facsimiles and Reprints, 1975), sig. C5ᵛ.

with the ambiguities generated by the texts they were supposed to elucidate.[3]

In *The Governor*, Elyot defines a fable as a fictional example invented to supplement the factual examples supplied by history. For Elyot the fable's status as fiction is unimportant, since properly defined it is a tool used by responsible orators and pedagogues employed by the public weal, and so exists in the same relationship to the governor's memory as a 'truthful' history. In fact for Elyot the concept of 'pure' fiction hardly exists at all, since most of the best-known fictions are allegorical or even literal accounts of real historical events. To those who assert that 'the histories of the Greeks and Romans be nothing but lies and feigning of poets', he replies that 'the most Catholic and renowned doctors of Christ's religion' have endorsed their authenticity (230), and goes on to defend as harmless any odd 'leasings' that may have crept into such narratives. George Puttenham develops Elyot's point in *The Arte of English Poesie*. For Puttenham, the principal task of the poet is not to produce fables but to act as a scrupulous recorder of things 'right as they be in deede' (14); he distinguishes them from preachers, philosophers, and historians only by their use of metre and the inventiveness of their style. Like Elyot, Puttenham insists that most of the pagan fables are allegorical histories and that anything improbable or obscene in these histories has nothing to do with the poets:

that *Saturnus* should geld his father *Celius*... and other such matters as are reported by them, it seemeth to be some wittie devise and fiction made for a purpose, or a very notable and impudent lye, which could not be reasonably suspected by the Poets, who were otherwise discreete and grave men, and teachers of wisedome to others. (22)

This implies that whenever poets do engage in producing fables, the 'purpose' of the text is of paramount importance in making it acceptable to the rulers they serve. But the passage also exposes the fact that the distinction between a 'wittie devise and fiction' and an 'impudent lye' is not so easy to make. Perhaps it is because of this difficulty that

---

[3] Rainolde himself provides a fascinating example of the way a fable's commentary could get out of hand. In his example of 'An Oracion by a fable' (*Foundacion of Rhetorike*, sig. A4 ff.), his detailed explication of a political fable delivered by Demosthenes is considerably longer than the narrative it explicates, and includes two further political fables, each of which presumably merits equally careful analysis. For two instances of what seems to be carefully cultivated ambiguity in political fables, see Patterson, 'Censorship and the 158 "Holinshed's" Chronicles'.

Puttenham lends so little space in his treatise to the discussion of fiction; for him, tragedy, comedy, satire, and the rest seem to be almost exclusively preoccupied with the representation of historical 'fact'. He inserts his most extended discussion of fiction into his chapter on history, where he surrounds it with qualifications designed to protect his poets from the charge of spreading lies:

These historical men ... used not the matter so precisely to wish that al they wrote should be accounted true, for that was not needefull nor expedient to the purpose, namely to be used either for example or for pleasure ... which made the learned and wittie men of those times to devise many historicall matters of no veritie at all, *but with purpose to do good and no hurt*, as using them for a maner of discipline and president of commendable life. (32, my emphasis)

It would appear that for Puttenham, fables were produced by serious 'historical men', custodians of authorized learning, for specific pedagogic and political purposes sanctioned by the state. Any deviation from this strictly limited fictive practice threatened to breed the 'monstruous imaginations' that jeopardize his project of raising poetry to the status of a disciplined and well-regulated 'art'.

Puttenham's contemporaries tended to share his suspicion of fiction. One of the few genres that sixteenth-century commentators regularly treated as fiction—that is, as imaginative fabrication, as opposed to allegorical history—was the animal fable. In *The Governor* Elyot remarks: 'I suppose no man thinketh that Aesop wrote gospels, yet who doubteth but that in his fables the fox, the hare, and the wolf, though they never spake, do teach many good wisdoms' (231). But even the animal fable was carefully fenced in with cautions and instructions to prevent its misuse; after all, from Chaucer's *Parlement of Foules* to Skelton's *Speke Parrot* the animal fable had acted—and continued to act—as a versatile vehicle for political satire. In 1570 Thomas North published a translation of a collection of fables called *The Morall Philosophie of Doni*, attributed to the Indian philosopher Bidpai. North's preface warns that these stories about court politics in the world of the beasts must be studied with close attention if they are not to mislead their readers. According to North, animal fables constitute a universal alternative language which can help to overcome the divisions between verbal languages. Such fables enable information to be communicated freely between one culture and another by means of a sign-system composed of 'things'—rather like

the bags full of objects used in conversation by the inhabitants of
Swift's Lagado:

> Of wordes and of examples is a sundrie sort of speache,
> One selfe same thing to mindes of men in sundrie wise they teache,
> Wordes teache but those that understande the language that they heare,
> But things, to men of sundrie speache, examples make appeare.[4]

At the same time, North recognizes that this alternative sign-system is
as vulnerable to unauthorized readings as any other language. The
philosopher Bidpai interlaces his fables with one another in a pattern
reminiscent of the intricate framework of Ovid's *Metamorphoses*: one
tale interpenetrates another, stories unfold within stories, and North
implies that readers who approach such a structure without due care
will quickly find themselves lost in the labyrinths of ideological
error. To prevent the proliferation of unauthorized readings he invests
the work's structure with an almost mystical status, averring that it
reproduces exactly the complex paths taken by the philosopher's
mind in its meditations on political life. He prefaces the book with
repeated injunctions to read the fables in the precise order in which
they are printed: 'the similitudes and comparisons doe (as they saye)
holde hands one with the other, they are so linked togithers, one
still depending of another: which if you sever, desirous to read any
tale or storie by it selfe, not comparing the Antecedent with the
Sequele...you shall be farre from understandinge of the matters'
(5–6). Later North's warnings against misreading the text get more
insistent: 'To reade such a Booke (worthy Reader) thou must call
thy wittes together uniting them and thy understanding with the
due order of the woorke' (16–17). Those who fail to read attentively,
he tells us, are like the blind man 'that wanting his sight, taketh upon
him to go over Mountaynes, Hilles, and Dales, through most
daungerous and perillous wayes' (17). Properly construed, Bidpai's
language of 'things' provides an invaluable guide through the
complexities of court politics. Misread, it spells disaster. North never
specifies the *kind* of disaster a misreading of the political fable will
invoke; but the metaphor of the blind man might have offered his sixteenth-century readers a clue. The 'Homily against Disobedience and
Wilful Rebellion', added to the book of homilies after the Catholic
rising of 1569, made use of a similar metaphor drawn from the

---

[4] *The Morall Philosophie of Doni*, 9; all references are taken from *The Earliest English Version
of the Fables of Bidpai*, ed. J. Jacobs (London: David Nutt, 1888).

scriptures (Matt. 15:14) to describe the clandestine activities of the papist clergy in the households of northern England: 'ignorant mass priests, as blind guides leading the blind, brought those seely blind subjects into the deep ditch of horrible rebellion'.[5] On the basis of the passage from Matthew, blindness had become a familiar metaphor for the condition of opposing the state religion. But North's simile differs from the biblical one in that his blind men choose to wander into 'daungerous and perillous wayes' of their own volition, and are therefore wholly responsible for the consequences. He was clearly eager to ensure that any appropriation of his text by enemies of the English state could never be attributed to negligence or shortsightedness on the part of the translator.

Translators of Ovid's more elusive and erotic fiction were as eager as North to guarantee that their texts participated in the communication of official doctrine. In his translation of the first four books of the *Metamorphoses* (1565), Arthur Golding anticipates the fears of North and Gosson about the delusions that could be spread by fictions not mediated by accredited servants of the state—especially when these fictions describe the exploits of pagan deities who 'with whoordome, theft, or murder blotted bee' (sig. *2).[6] Like North, he enjoins the reader to 'bringe with him a stayed head' (sig. *3v) and to read the fables strictly in sequence. Two years later, when he published his version of all fifteen books, he prefaced his translation with bolder assertions of the work's legitimacy. He repeats Elyot's claim that fables are not fictions at all, but fact expressed in memorable form, and describes the *Metamorphoses* as an encyclopaedia of ancient learning: Ovid's 'darke philosophie of turned shapes' (sig. A2) expresses, not the violent and unpredictable changes that disrupt the world of sexual politics, but a methodical account of ancient history and science just waiting to be decoded by the enlightened scholar. Claims that Ovid was a serious moral philosopher had been widespread since before the time of the medieval *Ovide moralisé*, and surface repeatedly throughout the sixteenth century: William Baldwin's much-reprinted handbook *A Treatise of Morall Phylosophie* (1548) ranks Ovid alongside Plato and Aristotle as one of the deepest thinkers of ancient times, and

---

[5] *Certain Sermons or Homilies*, 637. 'The sixth and last part of the homily against disobedience and wilful rebellion' takes the blindness of ignorance as its theme.

[6] Golding published his first translation of Ovid in 1565 as *The Fyrst Fower Bookes of P. Ovidius Nasos Worke, intitled Metamorphosis*. His complete translation appeared in 1567 as *The .xv. Bookes of P. Ovidius Naso, entytuled Metamorphosis*.

even Francis Bacon embarked on his own idiosyncratic search for
occult knowledge in Ovid's pages, reading them as an allegorical
key to lost scientific insights.[7]

But Bacon's investigation of Ovid's 'darke philosophie' exposes a
problem that became central to later fiction: that of imposing limits
on the possible readings of a text like the *Metamorphoses*, which
could sustain such a plethora of meanings. On the one hand, Ovid's
work concealed philosophical and scientific data so potent that it
could be safely handled only by the most highly qualified scholars.
On the other, its semantic richness invited all readers, no matter
how inexperienced or unlearned, to test their own inventiveness by
investing the text with new significance. The paradox finds itself
disarmingly expressed in a little pamphlet by the young author T.H.
(perhaps Thomas Howell) called *A Fable of Ovid treting of Narcissus*
(1560). T.H. agrees with Golding that the structure of the *Metamorphoses* has been organized with almost architectural precision, so that
any accurate reading of a single fable needs to take strict account of
its context:

> Hys tales doe joyne, in suche a godly wyse,
> That one doth hange upon an others ende . . .
> Thus Ovid bydes hys readers for to knowe
> The thynges above as well as those belowe.

> (sig. B<sup>v</sup>)

But for all this structural precision, any one fable can elicit an astonishing range of morals, as T.H. shows when he lists possible interpretations of the fable of Narcissus. Echo, for instance, can be allegorized
either as a woman who falls in love too easily, or as an unrequited
lover, or as a shameless flatterer; T.H. shows no anxiety about the contradictions involved in accepting all three readings. In fact, despite his
youth and 'umbelnes' (sig. B<sup>v</sup>) he is eager to make his own contribution to this expository free-for-all, and is justifiably proud of the ingenuity with which he does so. He sees Echo as the archetypal
schoolmaster, whose habit of repeating the ends of sentences mimics

---

[7] Bacon's fables were translated by Sir Arthur Gorges in 1619 as *The Wisedome of the
Ancients*. His retelling of the myth of Orpheus illustrates the scientific bias of his version of
the Classical fables: for Bacon, Orpheus' rescue of Euridyce signifies 'The most noble worke
of naturall philosophy', which is 'the restitution and renovation of things corruptible' (57).
Baldwin's *Treatise of Morall Phylosophie* was edited by Edward Arber as *The Sayings of the
Wise; or, Food for Thought. A Book of Moral Wisdome, Gathered from the Ancient Philosophers*
(London: privately printed, 1907).

the schoolmaster's task of reminding his pupils of the 'ends' of their words and actions:

> As who shoulde saye we ought to regarde the cause
> And ende of speche ofte spoke wyth lyttell, pause.

(sig. C2<sup>v</sup>)

T.H.'s innovative moral involves a pun on 'ends' which does not work in the Latin, and his youthful exuberance seems almost to have betrayed him into a narcissistic pride in his own wit which places him in direct competition with the wit of Ovid. For the Elizabethan fabulists, reading fiction was clearly as creative and adventurous an exercise as that of writing it. The text seems capable of yielding any number of incompatible meanings, even the most ridiculous of which may be validated by the premiss that its author is an acknowledged canonical authority. In the *Foundacion of Rhetorike* Richard Rainolde articulates this sense of *legitimate* imaginative fertility when he praises Aesop as both a philosopher and a legislator: 'his fables in effect contain the mightie volumes and bookes of all philosophers in morall preceptes, and the infinite monumentes of lawes stablished' (sig. B<sup>v</sup>). The sentence simultaneously celebrates the semantic richness of Aesop's texts and warns that they must only be read within the monumental framework of what the state considers lawful.

The fable in the sixteenth century, then, could be defined as a text that specialized in transmitting information in coded form. It was therefore inevitable that sixteenth-century authors should take advantage of the genre to probe potentially inflammatory political secrets as well as philosophical ones. In 1553 the publisher William Baldwin wrote a satire called *Beware the Cat*, one of a succession of texts that appropriated the animal fable for the purposes of Protestant polemic. But Mary I came to the throne before Baldwin's fable had got into print, and as a result *Beware the Cat* remained unpublished until 1570, when its ideological stance had been vindicated by the outbreak of government-sponsored anti-Catholic propaganda that followed the northern rebellion of 1569. Clearly Baldwin was well aware of the need for discretion when incorporating political and religious controversies into his publications; he received a salutary reminder of this in 1555, when the first edition of what was later to become *A Mirror for Magistrates* was suppressed by the Marian censors.[8] Fables offered

---

[8] For an account of the complicated publication history of the *Mirror for Magistrates*, see Campbell's edition, introduction, pp. 3–60.

various strategies for concealing the identity and political affiliations of the fabulist, but for the writer who was disaffected with the current administration the safest strategy was always silence.[9]

There is another sense in which the delay in the publication of *Beware the Cat* seems peculiarly appropriate. Baldwin's text is perhaps the subtlest of sixteenth-century animal fables, and it anticipates in a number of ways the experimental fictions of the 1570s.[10] Like them it makes parodic use of devices borrowed from more conventional fictions in order to demonstrate their outdatedness, their irrelevance to the sophisticated world of post-Reformation politics. Like simpler fables it includes a commentary, in the form of a marginal gloss which is peppered with anti-Catholic sentiments and misogyny; and it ends with a sardonic moral. It opens with a debate about whether or not the fables of Aesop should be taken literally, which parodies contemporary claims for the historical authenticity of Classical fables, such as Golding made for the *Metamorphoses*. A little later it divulges the recipe for a magic potion that allows the drinker to understand the language of the beasts; and the inclusion of this recipe (whose principal ingredient is hedgehog) might be read as, among other things, a comic tribute to the fable's traditional function as a repository for ancient scientific and philosophical learning. But in Baldwin's fable the secrets to be gleaned from the conversation of animals are scarcely philosophical ones. Instead they are the kind of embarrassing domestic revelations which respectable households prefer to sweep under the carpet or leave to gather dust in cupboards. In fact *Beware the Cat* converts the function of fiction from the preservation and selective disclosure of timeless truths to the amassing of confidential information about the clandestine activities of seemingly responsible subjects of the state. In the process it converts the fabulist from the role of pedagogue to that of informer, and so makes its own contribution to the important shift in the status of fiction that took place in the 1560s and 1570s.

[9] John N. King discusses the use of fable for Protestant polemic in 'Spenser's *Shepheardes Calender* and Protestant Pastoral Satire', in Barbara Kiefer Lewalski (ed.), *Renaissance Genres: Essays on Theory, History, and Interpretation*, (Cambridge, Mass.: Harvard University Press, 1986), 386.

[10] For an excellent discussion of *Beware the Cat* and the rest of Baldwin's output, see John N. King, *English Reformation Literature: The Tudor Origins of the Protestant Tradition* (Princeton, NJ: Princeton University Press, 1982), 358–406. See also Edward T. Bonahue, ' "I Know the Place and the Persons": The Play of Textual Frames in Baldwin's *Beware the Cat*', *Studies in Philology*, 91 (1994), 283–300; and *Beware the Cat: The First English Novel*, ed. William Ringler, Jr., and Michael Flachmann (San Marino, Ca.: Huntington Library, 1988), introduction. All references to Baldwin's fable are taken from this edition.

Baldwin's fable also anticipates the fiction of the 1570s in its playful experimentation with the role of the narrator. The tale gets told by a number of competing voices, no one voice privileged above another, whose narratives are arranged in the manner of a Chinese box, story secreted within story, so that the process of reading resembles the opening of a succession of chests filled with confidential documents—a structural device used to brilliant effect by both Gascoigne and Lyly. The chief narrator, whose narrative is reported at second hand by an editor called G.B., is a garrulous priest called Streamer, and Streamer in his turn reports the narratives of three further story-tellers: a servant, a man 'which had been in Ireland', and an eloquent cat. These interlocking narratives fulfil a quite different function from the ones which Golding and North ascribed to the tightly organized interwoven fables of Ovid and Bidpai. Where commentators argued that the structures of the *Metamorphoses* and the fables of Bidpai exactly reproduced the intricate workings of the philosopher's mind, it soon becomes clear that the complex structure of *Beware the Cat* merely enacts confusion. No narrator has final control over the narrative as a whole, and each of the stories it contains is incomplete: the servant and the man from Ireland have access to only a fragment of the stories they tell, and Streamer never hears the end of the tale told by the cat. Besides, as the fable unfolds it emerges that the multiple narrators in *Beware the Cat* represent only a tiny fraction of the millions of competing voices that deluge England daily, threatening to reduce it to the condition of a latter-day Babel. When the principal narrator, Streamer, swallows the potion that allows him to understand the language of the beasts, he finds himself suddenly sensitized to the deafening cacophony that surrounds him:

barking of dogs, grunting of hogs, wawling of cats, rumbling of rats, gaggling of geese, humming of bees, rousing of bucks, gaggling of ducks, singing of swans, ringing of pans, crowing of cocks, sewing of socks, cackling of hens, scrabbling of pens, peeping of mice, trulling of dice, curling of frogs, and toads in the bogs . . . with such a sort of commixed noises as would a–deaf anybody to have heard. (32)

The mingling of household tasks with the 'commixed noises' of the beasts suggests that underneath the orderly everyday activities of sixteenth-century London seethes a melting-pot of conflicting discourses, each perhaps accompanied by its own ideology and its own political agenda, over which no government can ever hope to exert complete control. And the antagonism between these rival languages and ideologies could boil over at any moment in spontaneous acts of violence.

One of the miniature stories told in the course of Baldwin's fable provides an unusual illustration of the kind of violence that could flare up between rival subjects of the Tudor state. It is a story told by an English traveller about an unfortunate Irishman, who murders a person who turns out to have been the chief of the cats, and is murdered in his turn by a vengeful 'kitling'. The Englishman tells the story as a humorous anecdote, but its implications are sobering. It details an outbreak of hostilities between representatives of two groups which were themselves fundamentally antagonistic to English government policies, the Irish and the Catholics (punningly contracted to 'cats' in Baldwin's fable).[11] Both of these groups opposed the imposition of Tudor linguistic policies as fiercely as they did the Protestant religion. The Irish successfully resisted attempts to limit the use of the Irish language—Baldwin's Irishman speaks a few words of Gaelic to remind his readers of the fact—just as Catholics resisted the replacement of the Latin mass with Cranmer's English prayer-book.[12] Resistance to the prayer-book had come to a head in England four years before Baldwin wrote *Beware the Cat*, when the so-called 'Prayerbook Rebellion' broke out in Cornwall (where yet another language, Cornish, seems still to have been widely spoken).[13] For readers of Baldwin's text in the 1550s the issues raised by the clash of languages were very real ones, and the uniform imposition of English throughout the territories ruled by the Tudors was a problem which had an immediate bearing on the security and stability of the Tudor public

[11] Baldwin offers a justification for this reading of the word 'cats' in his tragedy of the poet Collingbourne, where the poet explains how he composed a satirical jingle about Richard III's supporters Catesby and Ratcliffe in which he contracted their names to 'Cat' and 'Rat': 'These metafors I use with other more, | As Cat, and Rat, the halfe names of the rest, | To hide the sence which they so wrongly wrest.' *The Mirror for Magistrates*, ed. Lily B. Campbell (Cambridge: Cambridge University Press, 1938), 357: all references are to this edition.

[12] Attacks on the Irish language were given legal expression in the statutes of Kilkenny of 1366 (see *Irish Historical Documents 1172–1922*, ed. T. C. Curtis and R. B. McDowell (London: Methuen, 1943), 52–9). Alan Bliss points out that after the Reformation 'the Irish language became a symbol of the catholic religion': T. W. Moody, F. X. Martin, and F. J. Byrne (eds.), *A New History of Ireland*, 9 vols., (Oxford: Clarendon Press, 1976), iii. 546.

[13] P. Berresford Ellis examines the evidence for the extent to which Cornish was still spoken in the 16th cent. in *The Cornish Language and its Literature* (London: Routledge & Kegan Paul, 1974), ch. 3.

weal.[14] Indeed, neither Baldwin's readers nor his fictional narrators could fail to have been intensely aware of the instability of the state in the reign of Edward VI. Much of the action of the fable takes place on the roof of the Aldgate, where the limbs of dismembered rebels—including, from 1549 to 1551, participants in the Prayer-book Rebellion—were displayed for the edification of the English public.[15] The multiple voices in *Beware the Cat* might be seen, then, as the uneasy forms of expression best suited to a fundamentally fragmented society, and they set Baldwin's text radically at odds with the complacency of conventional fables, with their tacit assumption that their readers shared a common language, a common religion, and a common ideology.

Streamer's principal objective when he swallows his potion is to gain access to the language of the cats. His interest springs from the fact that Baldwin's cats possess the most highly organized and the most cunningly concealed of all the animal cultures. Besides their own language they have their own legal system, their own sexual mores and their own strictly maintained social hierarchy. Streamer first learns of this culture through stories of the chief of cats, Grimalkin, a sort of feline pontiff who wields the same power over other members of her species 'as the Pope hath ere this over all Christendom, in whose cause all his clergy would not only scratch and bite, but kill and burn to powder' (15). Cat culture occupies the spaces left vacant by human society: cats convene under cover of darkness, on the roofs of the city gates, in the holds of ships, in the furtive corners where adultery takes place, and in the private chambers where clandestine masses are celebrated. All this makes it easy to equate the feline underworld with the secret activities of Catholics under a Protestant administration; and for much of the fable the equation works well enough. But Baldwin never quite allows his readers to conflate the terms 'cat' and 'Catholic'. His cats exhibit a number of characteristics which Protestant propagandists attributed to the Catholic clergy: they are sexually promiscuous, inordinately greedy (Grimalkin devours a whole cow) and given to meddling with magic. But they have other characteristics which set them apart from the church of Rome. They

---

[14] For a thoughtful discussion of the Tudor 'manipulation of language as a form of power', see Gillian Brennan, 'Patriotism, Language and Power: English Translations of the Bible, 1520–1580', *History Workshop Journal*, 27 (1989), 18–36.

[15] 'A Priest had been quartered in July 1548; three Norfolk rebels in August 1549; and four Devonshire rebels in January 1550.' *Beware the Cat*, 59.

keep their laws with rigour, abhor hypocrisy, and inform on the misdeeds of adulterers; and they regularly play rather savage practical
jokes on their Catholic owners. In the course of the fable a cat
scratches the face of a Catholic brothel-keeper, fouls the garments of
a superstitious priest, and ends by literally catching its mistress's adulterous lover by the balls. Baldwin's cats are owned by Catholics and
resemble Catholics, but they also disrupt the clandestine plots of
Catholics. They are in fact the double agents of the animal kingdom,
and as such they resist allegorical classification—in much the same
way as the Italianate Englishman resists classification in Ascham's
*Scholemaster*.

Baldwin's fable ends with a moral or 'Exhortation' which explains
the titular injunction to 'Beware the Cat':

seeing [Streamer] hath in his oration proved that cats do understand us and
mark our secret doings, and so declare them among themselves; that through
help of the medicines by him described any man may, as he did, understand
them; I would counsel all men to take heed of wickedness, and eschew secret
sins and privy mischievous counsels, lest, to their shame, all the world at
length do know thereof. (56)

Cats, in other words, are domestic spies who observe and report on
the 'secret doings' of the households they have infiltrated. Like
other informers they act as a partial check on the diversity of hidden
plots and secret agendas which threaten to reduce the Tudor public
weal to political and linguistic incoherence. One might conclude
that this is also the mission that Baldwin assigns to contemporary
fiction: to investigate and expose the 'privy mischievous counsels'
hatched in the bedchambers and closets of the public weal, and so to
take on the role of informer to the state.

But if the injunction to 'Beware the Cat' is intended to control the
enemies of the state by reminding them that their actions are under
constant scrutiny, it offers little evidence that the observers—the cats
themselves—can be policed with equal efficiency. There is something
unnervingly independent about Baldwin's feline informers. They are
more naturalistic than the beasts that populate traditional animal fables:
they rub up against their owners' legs, play with beads, and mew like
any ordinary tabby, and this contributes to the difficulty of assigning
them any simple allegorical function. They are notoriously unreliable
('Cats change their dwellings often' states the marginal gloss, 52) and
willing to sell their services to the highest bidder: the Exhortation

mentions 'the Devil's cat (which cannot be tied up)' (55). And the devastation wrought by one of Baldwin's cats on a man's genitals associates them with current male anxieties about the secret powers of women. Cats can be witches in disguise; they can creep into the beds of sleeping men and suck out their breath; and their culture seems to be at least intermittently matriarchal, since both Grimalkin and the feline narrator Mouse-slayer are female. Baldwin's cats, that is, defy all attempts to constrain them within bounds or categories. They stand for whatever subjects of the Tudor state cannot be controlled or commanded, and in sixteenth-century anti-feminist literature (to which *Beware the Cat* allies itself by means of the misogynist comments in its margins), women were the most uncontrollable subjects of all. The independence of cats—and perhaps by extension of women, of Catholics, of languages other than English within the Tudor demesnes, and of the written word—is reinforced by the unreliable and fragmentary nature of the information we get concerning them. Far from being a serious and systematic philosopher, G.B. (the editor of Streamer's narrative) seems credulous and naïve, and gathers material for his text from the most dubious of sources. He takes everything Streamer says at face value, and shows equal confidence in the tall tales of servants and travellers when recording the story of Grimalkin. His chief informant Streamer never reaches the end of his narrative, since the effects of his magic potion wear off before he learns the outcome of the story of Mouse-slayer. In this way Baldwin explodes the myth of the authority of text or author: neither the editor nor his narrators are fully in command of their subject-matter, and their readers can either give credence to or dismiss the claims of the text as they think fit. By this means Baldwin sets about changing the status of the fable. Where Elyot, Rainolde, North, and Golding define fable as a vehicle for the transmission of the ideology of the state, Baldwin presents it as a textual space in which threats to the stability of the state may be identified and exposed without any guarantee that they can be brought under state control.

It seems appropriate, then, that the title of *Beware the Cat* should take the form of a warning. The warning alerts Baldwin's readers to the presence of secret, unofficial discourses within the linguistic structures of the public weal: discourses which are used by unidentified enemy agents, and which operate alongside the official discourse privileged by the state. The language of cats is both inaccessible and accessible, both secret and a medium for the leaking of secrets.

Under normal circumstances no man can understand the feline tongue, but 'any man' (as the Exhortation points out) can acquire the knowledge which permitted Streamer to decipher it. The language of cats resembles the traditional fable in that it is a code for concealing and revealing information; but the information Baldwin's fable conceals and reveals is exclusive to nobody, and might be precisely the kind of sensitive material that the people to whom it relates wish to keep under wraps. In other words, the warning to 'Beware the Cat' could apply equally to the enemies or to the rulers of the public weal. For Baldwin, fiction is a political no man's land which survives and flourishes in English territory, a subtle infiltrator in the simple world of authorized texts, which masquerades as a respectable citizen but which might be serving anyone or no one. It was this secretive and ambivalent textual territory that English writers chose to explore in the fiction of the 1570s.

## 2.  PAINTER'S DISINTEGRATING PALACES

By the 1560s the animal fable was a relatively domesticated genre: Classical precedent and a long fabular tradition in English had effectively drawn its teeth.[16] Continental prose fiction, on the other hand, was wild. Its early translators handled it as if it were an expensive and highly dangerous exotic beast which needed to be kept at bay with every editorial control at their disposal. The 1560s brought two major shipments: William Painter's *The Palace of Pleasure*, which appeared in two volumes in 1566 and 1567, and Geoffrey Fenton's menagerie of Franco-Italian romantic thrillers, the *Tragicall Discourses* of 1567. If the animal fable could unleash the multiple readings which Baldwin and Rainolde practised on it, this new continental fiction set off a veritable stampede of interpretative dilemmas. Neither Painter nor Fenton knew quite how to deal with their material. They responded to its blend of complexity, variety, and strangeness with a mixture of excitement and suspicion, and tried to bring these conflicting responses under control by means of lengthy prefatory essays and elaborate glosses, which struggle vainly to fit the new fiction into the

---

[16] Though not altogether so. Animal fables continued to act as a voice for the dispossessed and the disaffected for many more centuries, as Annabel Patterson points out in *Fables of Power*. See also her fascinating discussion of censorship and the fable in 'Censorship and the 1587 "Holinshed's" Chronicles'.

procrustean bed of Elizabethan poetic theory. But their unruly imports resisted all attempts to simplify them, and the translators' efforts to give them fabular morals inevitably degenerated into absurdities. These absurdities are worth investigating, because the sophisticated writers of the following decade chose to construct their own narratives out of the contradictions which emerged when English translators encountered Italian domestic fictions.

At the time Painter published the first volume of *The Palace of Pleasure* in 1566, the most popular story-collection in England was William Baldwin's *A Mirror for Magistrates* (first published in 1555 as *A Memorial of suche Princes, as since the Tyme of King Richard the Seconde, have been Unfortunate in the Realme of England*): a series of biographies of princes and nobility gathered out of chronicles and translated into verse. In it Baldwin and his fellow contributors treated the lives of the ruling classes as exemplary political texts of the kind Elyot recommended when he wrote in *The Governor* that 'by example of governors men do rise or fall in virtue or vice' (165). With clockwork regularity the princes in the *Mirror* rise and fall, driving home the message which the allegorical figure of Sorrow 'brayed' to Thomas Sackville in his celebrated Induction:

> come I am, the drery destinie
> And luckelesse lot for to bemone of those,
> Whom fortune in this maze of miserie
> Of wretched chaunce most wofull myrrours chose
> That when thou seest how lightly they did lose
> Theyr pompe, theyr power, and that they thought most sure,
> Thou mayest soone deeme no earthly joye may dure.[17]

The cyclical fortunes of great men impart an illusory stability to the very instability they illustrate. They reassure the ruling classes that reading the *Mirror* will help them to avoid the falls it describes, and remind them that any fall is part of a providential pattern whose shape can be traced throughout history. In addition the tragedies conform on the whole to the concept of 'decorum', the principle that there is an appropriate poetic genre for every political function, an appropriate style for every social class.[18] Tragedy deals with princes

---

[17] *Mirror for Magistrates*, 302.

[18] For an Elizabethan account of decorum, see Puttenham, *The Arte of English Poesie*, ch. 23: 'What it is that generally makes our speach well pleasing and commendable, and of that which the Latines call Decorum.'

and great men, as the original title of the collection insists, and the 'cases of Princes are sithens taken for the highest and greatest matter of all',[19] so that Baldwin's collection would seem to participate in the hierarchy of poetic genres which helped to reinforce the power-structures of sixteenth-century culture. But *A Mirror for Magistrates* also served as a salutary reminder for Elizabethan writers of the danger involved in producing narratives—whether historical or fictional—that come under the scrutiny of a rigorous system of state censorship. The first edition was deemed by the Privy Council to cast aspersion on the Marian regime and was suppressed; the extent to which this affected later readings of the text may be gauged by the addition in 1563 of a tragedy about a minor poet, Collingbourne, who was 'cruelly put to death for makyng of a ryme'—a little satirical jingle in the form of an animal fable, cocking a snook at Richard III and his closest allies. The tragedy was the work of Baldwin himself, who prefaced it with a discussion of the perils of making fiction which must have been close to his heart, as the author of a sophisticated satire in the form of an animal fable which had not yet got into print. The most frequently reprinted collection of stories in the reign of Elizabeth, then, was also perhaps the most widely available testament to the vulnerability of imprudent storytellers.[20]

Painter was intensely aware of this vulnerability. The two volumes or 'tomes' of *The Palace of Pleasure* are packed with passages of anxious self-justification designed to forestall the critiques of the 'blaming tongues and unstayed heades' he imagines to be combing his text for controversial material.[21] His anxiety seems to have increased rather than subsided as time went by, since the second of the two tomes opens with a far more rigorous defence of his editorial policy than the first. The sources of this anxiety seem to have been twofold. In the first place he is eager to explain the pedagogic principles that underlie the *diversity* of the collection—a diversity which means that alongside exemplary instances of good conduct his histories contain 'the uglye

[19] Ibid. 26.

[20] In the prose preface to the tragedy of Collingbourne, Baldwin tells one of his interlocutors: 'where as you say a poet may faine what he list: In deede my thynke it should bee so, and ought to be well taken of the hearers: but it hath not at al times been so allowed'. The drift of the tragedy is aptly summed up in the first line: 'Beware, take heede, take heede, beware, beware'. *Mirror for Magistrates*, 346–7. An excellent recent study of *A Mirror for Magistrates*, including Collingbourne's tragedy, can be found in Hadfield, *Literature, Politics and National Identity*, ch. 3.

[21] *The Palace of Pleasure*, i. 10.

shapes of insolencye and pride, the deforme figures of incontinencie and rape, the cruell aspectes of spoyle, breach of order, treason, ill lucke and overthrow of States and other persons' (i. 5). In the second place, he seeks to gloss over the radical shift in emphasis which the new continental fiction brought with it—a shift from the exalted tragedies of princes and governors to the domestic tragedies that befall the nobility, the gentry, and the commonalty in the bosoms of their families. This was not an innovation—Tudor literature had its share of tales lamenting the fate of commoners and minor gentry[22]—but the sheer abundance of stories recounting the sudden falls suffered by private citizens in or near their homes was what marked out the collections of Painter and Fenton as forerunners of a new development in Elizabethan storytelling. The title of Fenton's *Certaine Tragicall Discourses* boldly advertises this development, and he states it plainly in his second story, where the lovers Livio and Camilla 'albeit were neither princes nor governors of kingdoms, yet . . . encountered in one moment a change and sinister subversion' which gives their story the structure of tragedy.[23] Ascham found the shift in emphasis from prince to subject a 'sinister subversion' in itself; an ominous instance of the social flexibility that had reduced sixteenth-century Italy to a permanent state of war. Painter and Fenton derived much of their material from French versions of the Italian short stories of Matteo Bandello, Bishop of Agen; and Bandello might be described as Ascham's public enemy number one.[24] His stories contain every element that could contribute in Ascham's eyes to the demolition of English cultural values: coded messages exchanged between lovers, secret encounters and undetected adulteries, plots hatched by clever and rebellious children to circumvent the orders of their parents, and murders whose perpetrators sometimes escape unscathed. And all this in the context not only of the traditional locations of political power,

[22] The largest collection of such tales could be found in John Foxe's mammoth work of Protestant martyrology, the *Actes and Monuments* of 1563, which contains the carefully documented histories of martyrs of every social rank. It might be argued that Fenton's Italian tragedies—with the claims for authenticity mounted in the dedicatory epistle—constituted a dangerous foreign counterpart to this mighty collection.

[23] *Bandello: Tragical Tales*, ed. Hugh Harris, introd. Robert Langton Douglas (London: Routledge 1924), 145. All references to *Certaine Tragicall Discourses* are taken from this edition.

[24] For an account of Bandello and his French translators Belleforest and Boaistuau, see René Pruvost, *Matteo Bandello and Elizabethan Fiction* (Paris: H. Champion, 1937). See also Robert J. Clements and Joseph Gibaldi, *Anatomy of the Novella: The European Tale Collection from Boccaccio and Chaucer to Cervantes* (New York: New York University Press, 1977).

the court or the battlefield, but also of the households of Europe, the bedchambers, the gardens, the doors, windows, thresholds, and even the chimneys of private houses. These narratives are full of domestic servants, physicians, confessors, and mistresses who have open access to the secrets of their superiors, and who use these secrets freely for their own ends. They suggest in fact that sophisticated power-games take place under the noses and behind the backs of professional politicians, over which the politicians themselves have little authority.

Above all, Fenton's collection is dominated by fierce and unpredictable women, women who boldly refuse to succumb to the 'female' virtues of obedience, chastity, and silence. Instead they follow their own inscrutable agendas, and are often wild: they take on the properties of beasts at will, drain their male lovers with their sexual energy, experiment with sorcery and murder, and practise cannibalism in the bedchamber. In Fenton's text even paragons of female virtue are capable of aggressive self-assertion, as a lustful abbot finds when his intended victim robs him of his sword: 'Wherewith, she flourished here and there, bestowing her blows with such skill to the disadvantage of her enemy, that who had seen her desperate dealing with the sword would have judged that she had been traded in the only exercise of arms all the days of her life' (282). And Painter's women are no easier to control than Fenton's. The 1566 volume of *The Palace of Pleasure* includes ten stories from Marguerite de Navarre's *Heptameron* and recognizes women as a major component of its audience: the epistle to the reader dedicates the collection to a wide-ranging audience which includes 'the Lady, Gentlewoman or other of the feminine kinde' (i. 12). The 1567 volume of the *Palace* more subtly and strikingly acknowledges the prominence of women in contemporary fiction. It opens with an account 'of divers stout, and adventurous women called Amazones . . . bycause of dyvers Womens lives plentifull variety is offered in the sequele' (ii. 159, 165). Painter might almost have been placing his book under the auspices of an alternative, matriarchal, government, where conventional power structures are reversed, as they are in Christine de Pizan's feminist treatise *The Book of the City of Ladies* (1404–5, translated into English in 1529).[25] The bulk of the narratives in the 1567 volume derives from the stories of Bandello and of his French translator François de Belleforest, and the women in these stories are capable of reverting to their Amazonian heritage at any

[25] By Brian Ansley. It was translated again by Earl Jeffrey Richards (London: Pan, 1983).

time: Fenton describes the chaste swordswoman and her equally combative mother as 'two imps derived of the blood of the ancient Amazons' (282). The women in Italian fiction, in fact, help to emphasize
the contingent nature not only of patriarchy but of all sixteenth-century hegemonies.

Both Painter and Fenton try to subdue these powerful women in
their dedications by giving them a secure niche in the Elizabethan
social structure. The word 'palace' in Painter's title suggests that his
collection combines luxury and ornament with an official function,
sanctioned by the ruling classes. He takes pains to identify his metaphorical palace with the building inhabited by England's queen, and
dedicates his work to the Earl of Warwick, among other reasons
because he is 'daily resiant in a Palace of renowmed fame, guided by
a Queene ... garnished with great learning, passing vertues and rare
qualities of the minde' (i. 6). Fenton takes his efforts to invest his narratives with a respectable social status even further. He dedicates the
*Tragicall Discourses* to a woman, Lady Mary Sidney (the mother of
Sir Philip), and goes on to claim that all the good women in the collection serve only as illustrations of the qualities of his patron:

To whose virtues ... I have chiefly respected to give due renown, by preferring a true portrait of your conversation and life in the virtues, gifts, and orna-
ments, of the noble Angelica, chaste Parolina, constant Julia, and renowned
Carmosina ... For if ever the Queen of Caria was meritorious for her magna-
nimity and bountiful disposition, the Queen of Sheba ... was had in honour
for her wisdom ... or if the constant Lady Blandina ... hath purchased a
crown of eternity in keeping her faith and vow to God and the world ... or,
if any other, either of antiquity or familiar experience, of what degree and
condition soever, have been noted of renown for the gift of nobility in any
sort—your Ladyship may boldly challenge place with the best. (44–7)

Mary Sidney would seem to constitute a richly varied story collection
in herself, encompassing all classes, all periods, and all forms of narrative. By associating his own printed collection with her living one
Fenton makes his text an extension of its dedicatee, and frees his narratives from the stigma of being an unfamiliar literary mode in a foreign country. It is worth noting that the Elizabethan collection that
most openly embraces the novel's subversion of authority, *A Petite Pallace of Pettie his Pleasure*, has no formal dedication.[26]

---

[26] For the suspicions attached to books without dedications see Lorna Hutson, *Thomas
Nashe in Context* (Oxford: Clarendon Press, 1989), 69.

At the same time Painter and Fenton aim to give their translation
literary respectability by associating them with a well-established
genre, that of history. Both editors preface their collections with ponderous effusions in defence of history, which carefully gloss over the
differences between Classical history and the continental novel.[27] To
emphasize the links between the two traditions Fenton peppers his
narratives with Classical allusions, while Painter begins both volumes
of the *Palace* with extracts from the works of Livy and Aulus Gellius.
He seems to have chosen some of these extracts for their resemblance
to Bandello's novels: stories of spies in the bed chamber (Candaules
and Gyges), suicidal women (Panthea and Lucretia), and articulate
whores (Lamia, Flora, and Lais). Some he chose to translate from versions by Bandello himself, as if to suggest that the wayward Italian had
taken up the mantle of his Roman ancestors. And in the 1566 dedication he speaks of all his narratives, both continental and Classical, as if
they were an integral part of the humanist curriculum: they are
'proper and commendable Histories, which I may boldly so terme
because the Authors be commendable and well approved' (i. 4).
Like Chaucer, however, he omits to specify the source of all this commendation and approval.

Painter's view of the function of these 'commendable Histories' is
very close to Elyot's. They are 'probable examples' which alternately
attract their readers to actions which are sanctioned by the state and
deter them from doing wrong:

as all histories be ful of lessons of vertue and vice, as Bookes, sacred and prophane, describe the lives of good and bad for example sake, to yelde meanes
to the posterity, to ensue the one and eschue the other, so have I thought to
intermingle amongest these Novels the severall sortes of either, that ech Sexe
and Kinde may pike out like the Bee, of ech Floure, Honny, to store and furnishe with delightes their well disposed myndes. (ii. 301)

Exemplary narratives should be 'well disposed', highly organized so as
to simplify the reader's task of organizing the mind where they are to
be stowed. The 1567 dedication describes the study of history as part
of a larger body of knowledge, 'the immortall storehouse of all posses-

----

[27] The title-page of Fenton's *Tragicall Discourses* conflates the two traditions, claiming that
the narratives have been 'written out of French and Latin' (39) despite the fact that the Latin
element is confined to a number of references to Classical literature and mythology, inter-
polated from time to time into Belleforest's text, which itself interpolates Classical references
into the narratives of Bandello. See the introduction by Robert Langton Douglas to Fenton,
*Bandello: Tragical Tales*, 18 and 33–5.

sions' which is the liberal arts (ii. 150). Remove one element from this intellectual edifice and the whole structure will collapse: 'To be short every science is so necessary, as the same taken away, reason is deprived and the Life of Man (of due order and government) defrauded' (ii. 150). Painter's histories and novels are as necessary for the orderly operation of the Elizabethan state as an actual palace. In fact the palace metaphor implies that the book itself is as tightly orga-nized as a work of architecture, and that each story has the same math-ematically precise relation to its neighbours as the parts of a building. This sense of structural inviolability extends to the collection itself, where Painter develops the architectural metaphor from the title-page: the story of Horatius stands 'as it were at the gate of this palace' (i. 15), while the stories from Italy occupy the garden.[28] From his the-oretical commentary one gets the impression that Painter saw his collection as the literary equivalent of a House of Memory: one of the unchangeable mental edifices described by Thomas Wilson in his *Arte of Rhetorique*, where every architectural feature serves as a mnemonic.[29]

But alongside his efforts to authorize narratives in prose, Painter has a second agenda which threatens to disrupt the first: he delights in variety. Among his good and bad examples he scatters anecdotes which serve only to 'exhilarate' his readers' minds: 'pleasaunte dis-courses, merie talke, sportinge practises . . . deceitfull devises, and nip-ping tauntes' that have nothing to do with service to the Elizabethan state (i. 5). He signals his craving for variety and the unease he feels about it in the endless apologies which punctuate his texts: apologies for his failure to include religious examples alongside secular ones, apologies for dealing with 'unlawfull love' (i. 5), apologies for describ-

[28] A somewhat duplicitous garden, as it is described in the conclusion of the second tome: 'Every sort and sexe that warfare in the fielde of humayne life, may see here the savourous fruict (to outwarde lyking) that fansied the sensuall taste of Adam's Wyfe. They see also what griefs sutch fading fruicts produce unto posterity: what likewise the lusty growth and spring of vertue's plant, and what delicates it brauncheth to those that carefully keepe the slips thereof, within the Orchard of their mindes' (iii. 431).

[29] Wilson describes the art of memory invented by Simonides, which uses images pro-jected onto the features of rooms and buildings as mnemonics, in *The Arte of Rhetorique* (1560 edn.), sig. a5$^v$. This method is invaluable, he explains, for reminding oneself of things one is very likely to forget, such as the fact that 'My frende (whom I toke ever to be an hon-est man) is accused of thefte, of adoutrie, of ryot, of man slaughter, and of treason'. One can see how this might slip his mind. North seems to conceive of the fables of Bidpai as another mnemonic system, since he says that 'it may in maner be called an artificiall memorie' (*The Morall Philosophie of Doni*, 15). See Frances A. Yates, *The Art of Memory* (Harmondsworth: Peregrine, 1969).

ing 'persons that bee vicious', and for the unrestrained inclusiveness o
his selection. To some readers, he admits, 'it shal not peradventure
seeme fit and convenient to mingle holy with prophane, (according
to the proverbe) to intermedle amongs pleasant histories, ernest epistles, amid amorous Novels, learned Letters' (ii. 279), but he justifie
the mixture with an appeal to the abundance of invention found in
all good texts, whatever their function: 'For amid the divine work
of Philosophers and Oratours, amongs the pleasant paynes of auncient Poets, and the Novell writers of our time, merry verses so wel
as morall matters be mingled, wanton bankets so well as . . . effectual
declamations and persuasions pronounced' (ii. 279). The passage i
not so much a defence as a celebration. Instead of claiming that mixtures have a political or moral duty to perform, Painter simply invoke
the entire store of his readings to illustrate the heterogeneous wealth
of available texts. He sees no reason to restrict or police this wealth
in one novel he transforms the story of the Sibylline books into a
lament for the literature lost at the dissolution of the monasteries, literature which had been preserved for centuries by the 'idle Monkes
Ascham held in such contempt.[30]

Painter regards the 'pleasaunt store' of his own 'readings' as a treasury to be raided at will (ii. 151). And in sorting through this treasury
the texts that strike him as worth translating are the unconventiona
ones—the novel ones. He explains that he chose from the works o
Livy narratives which struck him as 'straung' (i. 4), a term which ha
connotations of both 'innovative' and 'foreign'; the word crops up
repeatedly elsewhere in his collection. The story of the Amazons i
'an Hystory rare and *straunge* to the unlearned' (ii. 159), and the novels
of Bandello are 'so *straunge* and terrible as they be able to affright the
stoutest' (i. 364). The poets who wrote commendatory verses for Fenton's *Tragicall Discourses* were equally struck by their strangeness. Peter
Beverley claims that they have a 'stranger hue' than conventional stories (52), while George Turberville describes them as 'strange and tragical affairs' (51); and Turberville later went on to translate some of
Bandello's strange and tragical affairs for himself.[31] Ascham was quite

---

[30] Ascham, *Works*, 231. Painter sees the books that were destroyed by the Sibyl as 'A
good example for wyse men to beware, howe they despyse or neglecte auncient bookes
and monumentes. Many the like in this Realme have bene defaced, founde in Religious
houses . . . whiche bookes by the ignoraunt, have ben torne and raised, to the great griefe
of those that be learned' (i. 98).

[31] In his *Tragical Tales* of 1576.

right to accuse these translators of smuggling dangerous foreign material into the homes of their English readers, since the books themselves
seem to revel in their strangeness, their foreignness to Elizabethan
culture.

One of the ways in which Painter compensates for the doubtful
moral status of his palace is by falsifying the social status of its inhabitants. In 1566 he describes them as 'renowmed wights' whose 'princely partes and glorious gestes' make them sound as impeccably
aristocratic as the knights of chivalric romance (i. 14). The 1567 dedication gives a still more misleading account of their social class. It
states that history—and, by implication, Painter's histories—'displaieth
the counsels, advises, pollicies, actes, successe, and endes of Kinges,
Princes and great men' (ii. 150). From the description one might
expect the collection to be another *Mirror for Magistrates*, almost exclusively preoccupied with the behaviour of the ruling classes, but in fact
the stories tackle a wide diversity of occupations, from medicine to
prostitution, from robbery to fishing—as Painter acknowledges elsewhere.[32] And he arranges them in an order which sometimes suggests
that he was more interested in setting up witty comparisons than in
propping up the social hierarchy. The story of the Amazons is followed at once by an account of the collapse of male government,
which describes 'the great Alexander: and in what wise from vertue
hee fell to vice' (ii. 165). Later Painter engineers a still more cheeky
juxtaposition when he swings abruptly from a series of philosophical
letters by Plutarch to a set of mock-philosophical precepts on the art
of sex, ascribed to 'three arrant honest Women, which for lewdnesse
wer famous' (ii. 301). The excuse he gives for the transition is that it
will 'variate' the diet of his readers (ii. 259), but Ascham, in *The Scholemaster*, may have seen it as yet further evidence that Painter dealt in
'varietie of vanities, and chaunge of filthy lyving' (229).

Painter's thirst for variety finds its most disturbing manifestation in
the novels derived from the words of Bandello and the '*sondrie kindes*
of cruelties' they unfold (i. 364, my emphasis).[33] At the centre of these

[32] '[T]he contentes of these Novels from degre of highest Emperour, from state of greatest Quene and Lady, to the homelye Cuntry peasant and rudest vilage girle, may conduce
profite for instruction, and pleasure for delight' (ii. 157). It is interesting that this frank statement of the diversity of classes encompassed by his novels implicitly addresses his women
readers.

[33] Painter makes no distinction between the novels he translates from the French of Belleforest and those he translated directly from Bandello's *Novelle*. In the first volume of the
*Palace of Pleasure* he alludes to all seven of his translations from Bandello and Belleforest as

novels is an army of women who repulse all the efforts of a fragil
patriarchy to keep them under control. In story after story thes
women attack and demolish traditional constructions of masculinit
and femininity. Zilia condemns the Lord of Virle to three years c
exercising the 'female' virtues of silence and obedience, while Barbar
forces her suitors to practise the womanly art of spinning. Juliett
assumes a 'manly stomach', and Violenta shows 'greater courag
than is wont to belong to her sex'. The Countess of Salisbury sets her
self up in opposition to the King of England like an Amazon challen
ging a latter-day Alexander:

This worthie Prince (I say) who before that time like an Alexander, was abl
to conquere and gain whole kingdomes, and made all Fraunce to quake fc
feare, at whose approch the gates of every Citie did flie open,... whose hel
met was made of manhods trampe, and mace well steeled with stout
attemptes, was by the weakest staye of dame Nature's frame, a woma
(shaped with no visage sterne or uglie loke) affrighted and appalled. (i. 335)

At the same time women repeatedly violate the social hierarchy b
marrying outside their station. Giletta takes up medicine so as t
arrange a match for herself with Bertrand, who is her social superior
the Duchess of Malfi contracts a secret marriage with her servant, an
the Countess of Salisbury marries the king. The most audacious o
Bandello's female saboteurs is Violenta, a woman who has no socia
status at all. Because of her low birth she agrees to marry her aristo
cratic lover in secret, but he never publicly acknowledges the relation
ship, and eventually marries again. Violenta responds, as her nam
implies, by usurping the male prerogative of violence. With the help
of her maid Giannica she transforms her bedchamber into a spac
where she can operate the barbarous machinery of sixteenth-centur
justice without recourse to official legislation. In this most private o
spaces she dismembers her husband piece by piece, and from it sh
emerges to give herself up to the judicial system which had failed t
act on her behalf. Beside its suggestion that exploited women ca
take the law into their own hands, Violenta's history provides a

'these tragicall Novelles and dolorous Histories of Bandello' (i. 364), and in the dedication t
the second volume he mentions his translations from Boccaccio, Bandello, Ser Giovanni
Fiorentino, and other Italian and French authors, without mentioning Belleforest b
name. Given that my concern is with Elizabethan *perceptions* of Italian texts rathe
than with the Italian texts themselves or with their French adaptations, I have chosen t
follow Painter's practice, referring to his translations of Belleforest's novels as if they wer
Bandello's.

unnerving instance of women banding together to keep secrets from men—even from the men who share their beds. She entices her husband into the house and has sex with him without offering a clue to her murderous intentions. Her partnership with Giannica is the savage counterpart of Giletta's partnership with Julia, when they conspire together to smuggle Giletta into her husband's bed. Bandello's heroines have none of the garrulousness ascribed to women by convention: they are highly efficient secret agents operating on their own behalf. Men have no access to women's agendas, and women know all the secrets of men. This is not to say that Bandello's world is an Amazonian utopia. At the end of most stories the mechanisms of patriarchy are inexorably reinstated. The Lord of Virle forces Zilia to become his mistress by threatening her with death; Violenta and the Countess of Celant are executed; Giletta and the Countess of Salisbury suffer a relapse into connubial obedience. But Bandello offers no guarantees that these mechanisms will not be thrown into confusion again whenever a new generation of Amazons chooses to challenge them.

Of all Bandello's novels in *The Palace of Pleasure*, the story of Romeo and Julietta contains perhaps the highest concentration of elements that might feed Ascham's anti-Italian prejudices. It is perhaps no coincidence that this is also the novel of Bandello's most frequently translated, imitated, and cited in Elizabethan England.[34] The story takes place in an Italian city riven by factions ('as all Cities be there', Ascham might have added, 236). Law and order have broken down: families ignore government injunctions to lay down their arms, children ignore the commands of their parents, love affairs are conducted in secret with the help of clandestine messages and illegal drugs, and illicit lovers are aided and abetted by a devious Catholic church which has access to all the secrets in the state. Those who seem to conform are secretly doing the opposite. Apparent obedience masks a plot, as when Julietta seems to concede to her father's demand that she marry Paris, and apparent crimes hide attempts to restore order, as when Romeo kills Thibault while trying to make peace during a riot, or when Friar Lawrence is caught with a crowbar in the vicinity of the lovers' corpses. Under the pressure of these events communication

---

[34] Arthur Brooke translated it into verse in 1562; Pettie alludes to it twice (*A Petite Pallace of Pettie his Pleasure*, ed. Herbert Hartman (London: Oxford University Press, 1938), 34 and 125); the title of Whetstone's pseudo-Italian story 'Rinaldo and Giletta' in *The Rocke of Regard* (1576) echoes it; and further references to the story abound before Shakespeare converted it to drama in the mid-1590s.

breaks down like other kinds of ideological apparatus. Every time the lovers meet they fall silent, as if to signal their exclusion from official discourse, and in the end it is a failure of communication—a misplaced letter—that leads to their deaths. The 'amity' which held Elyot's public weal together is altogether absent: Julietta tells Romeo that 'all the lawes of Amity are deade and utterly extinguyshed' (iii. 101), and the lovers can only plot to restore it by cunning (she hopes that 'this newe aliaunce shall engender a perpetuall peace and Amity betweene his House and mine', iii. 88). In fact in this novel all the covenants and agreements that go to make up Elyot's 'simplicity' have been broken. The situation is as complex as Ascham could have feared, and official legislation proves powerless to disentangle it.

Painter tried in vain to accommodate a narrative of this complexity within his simple definition of history. At the end of the 1567 dedication he added a list of morals designed to explain the 'pith and substance' of each story and so to allocate them an official function (ii. 154). In the course of this list he explains that 'Iulietta and Rhomeo disclose the hartie affections of two incomparable lovers, what secret sleights of love, what danger either sort incurre which mary without the advise of Parentes'. But the moral is patently at odds with the narrative. The lovers' danger stems not from their disobedience but from the feud which splits the Veronese state, and it is their clandestine affair that finally reconciles the warring factions. At the end of the story a monument is erected which commemorates the lovers' deaths and confirms the culpability of their parents. Romeo and Julietta's disobedience of their parents is cancelled out by their parents' disobedience of the Veronese law.

Arthur Brooke's earlier version of the story, *The Tragicall Historye of Romeus and Juliet* (1562), demonstrates yet more effectively the inadequacy of simple readings of Italian fiction. Among the lessons Brooke draws from the story in his preface is a warning to beware of 'superstitious friers' and an invective against 'auriculer confession (the kay of whoredome, and treason)'.[35] But there is no hint of such a moral in the narrative itself: at the trial of Friar Lawrence the governor of Verona describes him as 'that good barefooted fryre' and commends him

---

[35] In William Shakespeare, *Romeo and Juliet*, ed. G. Blakemore Evans, The New Cambridge Shakespeare (Cambridge: Cambridge University Press, 1984), 213–14. References to Brooke's version are to this edition. The quotation from Shakespeare's *Romeo and Juliet* is taken from the Riverside Shakespeare, like all Shakespeare references in this book.

for his service to the state.[36] Intelligent readers could only have concluded that traditional, crudely moralistic ways of reading were
unequal to the task of dealing with contemporary fiction. And at
least two readers signalled their awareness of this inadequacy. In
1576 George Pettie constructed an entire story collection, *A Petite Pallace of Pettie his Pleasure*, from the awkward relationship between the
novel and the moral readings with which it had been encumbered
by convention; contemporaries would have recognized and enjoyed
his parody of Painter. And in the mid–1590s Shakespeare placed
new demands on the sophisticated readings of his audience by creating
a new Friar Lawrence, an ambiguous figure who inhabits a twilight
zone between the night-time of the lovers and the daylight of Veronese public life.[37] Shakespeare's Friar finds all moral distinctions labyrinthine in their complexity:

> O, mickle is the powerful grace that lies
> In plants, herbs, stones, and their true qualities;
> For nought so vile that on the earth doth live
> But to the earth some special good doth give;
> Nor ought so good but, strain'd from that fair use,
> Revolts from true birth, stumbling on abuse.
> Virtue itself turns vice, being misapplied,
> And vice sometime by action dignified.

> (II. iii. 15–22)

Just as Ascham predicted in *The Scholemaster*, Bandello's novels had
helped to effect a revolution in Elizabethan fiction which left its practitioners 'baren of discretion to make trewe difference betwixt good
and ill, betwixt troth, and vanitie' (227). And Painter with his richly
varied *Palace of Pleasure* was a reluctant agent of this revolution. In retrospect it seems hardly surprising that an advocate of simplicity like
Ascham should have preferred to demolish his palace wholesale, as
Spenser's Guyon pulls down the 'pleasaunt bowres and Pallace
brave' which conceal the enchantress Acrasia, rather than pause to disentangle its constituent parts.[38]

---

[36]  *Romeo and Juliet*, 246.

[37]  Friar Lawrence's twilight existence is suggested by the lines which introduce him
(whether one takes the lines to belong in the previous scene or not): 'The grey-ey'd
morn smiles on the frowning night, | Check'ring the eastern clouds with streaks of light,
| And fleckled darkness like a drunkard reels | From forth day's path and Titan's fiery
wheels' (II. iii. 1–4).

[38]  See *The Faerie Queene*, ed. A.C. Hamilton (London: Longman, 1980), II. xii. 83. All
references to *The Faerie Queene* are taken from this edition. By 1582 Ascham's self-appointed

### 3. FENTON'S MONSTERS

In the course of their careers both Painter and Fenton seem to have involved themselves in shady dealings.[39] In 1561 Painter was appointed clerk of the ordnance of the Tower of London, and so became a small component in the defensive machinery of the English state. But in public life as in his writing he was accused of betraying his trust: during the 1580s he was charged with conspiring to embezzle government funds by transferring gunpowder from Windsor to the Tower of London and then charging it to the accounts as if it were a fresh supply. The accusation may or may not have been well founded; Painter certainly confessed to some sort of misconduct. But there is no doubt at all that Geoffrey Fenton led what can be described as a devious double life. His practice of dedicating books to major public figures—among them William Cecil Lord Burghley, Sir Henry Sidney the Lord Deputy of Ireland, and Queen Elizabeth herself—at last bore fruit in 1587, when he was made principal secretary of the Irish Council. But by that time he had already been employed in Ireland for several years. From 1580 until Elizabeth's death he acted as one of the queen's informers in Ireland, a government spy who was disliked and distrusted by his colleagues. In fact, the careers of Bandello's principal Elizabethan translators echo contemporary responses to the continental fiction they purveyed; Painter and Fenton claimed that their fictions were of immeasurable value to the state, while their critics condemned them as duplicitous, untrustworthy, offensive. Fenton's career suggests something more: that treachery to one person might be loyalty to another, and that duplicity might be given an official function, even rewarded with high office. It might also hold a clue to the reasons why the ambitious young men who imitated the Italian novel persisted in following such dubious for-

---

successor Gosson would certainly have liked to see Painter's construction demolished: 'I may boldely say it, because I have seene it, that the *Palace of Pleasure*, the *Golden Asse*, the *Aethiopian historie* . . . have been throughly ransackt, to furnish the Playe houses in London. How is it possible that our Playemakers headdes, running through *Genus* and *Species* and every difference of lyes, cosenages, baudries, whooredomes, should present us any *schoole-mistres of life, looking glasse of manners, or Image of trueth*?' *Markets of Bawdrie*, 169.

[39] For an account of Painter's career, see Renée Pigeon, 'William Painter', in the *Dictionary of Literary Biography*, 2nd ser. cxxxvi. 259–63. For an account of Fenton's career see the introduction to *The French Bandello: A Selection. The original Texts of Four of Belleforest's Histoires Tragiques Translated by Geoffrey Fenton and William Painter, Anno 1567*, ed. Frank S. Hook (Columbia, Oh.: University of Missouri Press, 1948).

eign models. A writer who knew how to report or even to duplicate the subterfuges of Catholic infiltrators might prove himself invaluable to the counter-espionage activities of the Elizabethan state.[40]

Fenton's later career as writer, informer, and politician suggests one way of reading the story collection with which he chose to launch his career as an author, *Certaine Tragicall Discourses*. After testing the waters of publication with these Italian domestic narratives he turned his attention to translating texts with a more direct bearing on Elizabethan foreign policy. *A Discourse of the Civile Warres and Late Troubles in Fraunce* (1570) deals with events which were of immediate topical interest to the Elizabethan government, the religious wars in France from 1568 to 1569; while *The Historie of Guicciardin, Conteining the Warres of Italie and Other Partes* (1579) documents the contexts of Bandello's fictions by charting the troubles in Italy from 1492 to 1529. In each case Fenton used the art of translation as a means of conveying inside information about England's Catholic enemies into the public domain. *Certaine Tragicall Discourses* might be said to have served a similar purpose: Fenton's prefatory epistles and title-page make little distinction between Bandello's histories and the history of the civil wars in Italy and France, and his commentary treats Italian prose fiction as if it were a record of the hostile movements of an enemy nation, the natural precursor to his more explicitly political translations of the following decade.[41] Through the medium of the 'novel' the collection exposes the workings of Catholic ideology in the households of Italy, France, and Spain, while the narrator poses as a prurient observer whose gaze penetrates the most intimate spaces of his subjects' lives, and who cannot resist interrupting the stories at the most inapposite moments to remind his readers of the Protestant position on the events he records.[42]

But Fenton's text could also be read as presenting a serious challenge to Protestantism. If his later translations examine civil wars in

---

[40] A point that is made by Lorna Hutson in *The Usurer's Daughter*, where she describes a humanist education as the perfect training for 'a textualized intelligence service', (105). *The Usurer's Daughter* also contains the best recent account of Fenton's fiction: see pp. 129–51.

[41] The title-page describes the collection as 'No less profitable than pleasant, and of like necessity to all degrees that take pleasure in antiquities or foreign reports' (39).

[42] His version of the story of the Sieur de Virle, for instance, introduces diatribes against Jeanne La Pucelle and St. Denis which have no equivalent in Belleforest's original. The myth of La Pucelle, he opines, 'seems as true as that which they are ashamed to put in a chronicle of credit touching their Saint Denis; whom they affirm was executed at Paris, and came from thence with his head in his hand, which he buried in the abbey' (460).

foreign states, his *Tragicall Discourses* enacts a civil war within its own confines, a war between the Catholicism of its protagonists and its aggressively Protestant commentary. Like Painter's interpolations in *The Palace of Pleasure*, Fenton's remarks—which elaborate on the comments of the French translator Belleforest—engage with the subjects of Italian fiction with the zeal of a Reformation army; but the heroes and heroines of Bandello's narratives prove as impervious to these attacks as they do to the crude moral values Fenton tries to foist on them.[43] The sheer inventiveness of their misdemeanours and the exuberant flexibility of their rhetoric tie Fenton's ponderous logic in knots, and trick him into contradicting himself on issues where he tries to be most dogmatic. The triumph of Italian inventiveness over English dogma begins with the uneasy relationship between the dedicatory epistle and the body of Fenton's text. In the epistle Fenton erects an elaborate framework within which he proposes to contain and control the stories that follow, but when he turns to the stories themselves this framework rapidly falls apart, and the reader is left with the impression that the ideological position he adheres to has been irreparably damaged and is on the verge of collapse.

The dedication attempts to fit Bandello's texts into a traditional generic mould, and so replaces the term 'novel', which Painter uses throughout his collection, with the more familiar term 'history'; but Fenton's history takes a more rigid form than Painter's. For Fenton, history is a comprehensive collection of representative instances drawn from all possible acts performed by humanity, a universal key to all past and future contingencies. He quotes Cicero as saying that it constitutes 'an image or portrait of all things that have passed since the beginning of the world', and claims that it also predicts all future

---

[43] Fenton acknowledges in his dedicatory epistle that he has translated his narratives from the French: 'I have bestowed some of my vain hours, whilst I was in the other sides the Sea, in forcing certain Tragical Discourses out of their French terms into our English phrase' (44). In his commendatory verses to the volume Sir John Conway represents the process of translation as an act of violence against a devious Frenchman: 'He, labouring with effect, hath, by his learned pain, | Enforced a Frenchman tell his tale in English language plain' (49). George Turberville's commendatory verses refer to the translation from 'French to English phrase' as if it entailed the liberation of the stories of 'Bandel' from an obscurity which has been maliciously contrived, perhaps by Bandello's French adapters, in order to conceal his texts from 'simple common sense': 'The French to English phrase, his mother language he, | The dark to light, the shade to sun, hath brought, as you may see . . . And what, before he took his painful quill to write, | Did lurk unknown, is plainly now to be discerned in sight.' Fenton's readers, then, like Painter's, seem to have associated his narratives with the name of Bandello rather than Belleforest. It is therefore as versions of Bandello's texts that I discuss them.

events 'even until the last and extreme dissolution of the same' (41).[44]
Individuals are merely elements in a repeated pattern, ripples on the
surface of an essential human nature: 'in this world the nature of
man in all ages, although the single persons be changed, remaineth
still one' (43). The historiographer devotes his art to the task of reducing even 'single persons' to conformity, since Fenton claims that he is
capable of removing the differences between generations, making a
young man 'old, not in years... but in experience and wisdom'
(41). In an austere variation on Richard Rainolde's breakdown of
the fable into its component parts, he states his belief that individual
narratives can be converted into the abstract terms of a universal
moral system: 'in every act', he writes, 'there be certain special principles and rules for the direction of such as search out their disposition'
(42), and, while philosophy teaches these rules directly, history figures
forth 'under certain forms and shapes of men and their doings past, all
and every such diversity and change, which philosophy doth teach by
way of precepts'. It complements the Scriptures by acting as every
man's guide to the laws of the properly organized state, teaching its
readers their precise position in the social hierarchy. From it, he tells
us, magistrates learn how their predecessors used their power, private
persons learn how to obey the magistrates, a citizen 'what belongeth
to his proper office', and a woman how to perform her duty in the
miniature commonwealth of marriage.

   One might argue, in fact, that Fenton's version of history is dedicated to annihilating the vagaries of time. In this it falls into line with
North's *Dial of Princes* and Gosson's *Ephemerides of Phialo*, which
announce their project of controlling time in their titles. *Certaine Tragicall Discourses* aims to rescue young men from the vicissitudes of
youth and to fix past and future events like insects in amber, so that
even the most radical of changes, the tragic falls of the *Mirror for Magistrates*, can be shown to have a fixed place among the immutable workings of Providence. Indeed, Fenton seems to consider some sort of fall
to be an invariable element of most men's lives, not merely those of
the aristocracy. Histories are 'the only and true tables whereon are
drawn in perfect colour the virtues and vices of every condition of
man, bothe their flourishing time, whilst they embraced the first,
and miserable fall when they grew in delight with the wickedness of
the last' (42). The characters he approves of are those who resist

----

[44] See Cicero, *De Oratore*, 2. 9. 36.

such changes, the virgins who remain 'assured and constant in vertue' (45), the men who 'became masters of them selves' (46). To be virtuous for Fenton is a matter of preserving oneself from maturity to death in a state of statuesque spiritual immobility.

But the collection itself denies the providential predictability of history. Fenton's selections from among the novels of Bandello are sensational, journalistically preoccupied with exceptions to the rules, with monsters who live beyond the bounds of the acceptable, or paragons whose accomplishments can never be repeated. Fenton replaces the animal fable with a more disturbing genre, the monster story. Pandora is the 'second Medea and execrable monster of our time' (184), the widow of Cabrio is a 'tyrannous monster', the Countess of Celant is a 'devouring monster' (315), and the Albanian captain seems to have been 'bred in the deserts of Africa, the common nurse of monsters' (209). The stories transplant what was constructed as monstrous, strange, or foreign into the heart of the familiar: the murderous exploits of Pandora take place 'not in the Anthropophagans, Scythia or amongst Cannibals or Amazons, ancient murderers of their children, but in the heart and midst of Europe' (157); and in the ninth tale the proem complains that the 'wild nations' of the south and east are more scrupulous in keeping order 'than diverse countries in the heart and bowels of Christendom' (367). Fenton's monsters manifest themselves not in the distant continents that were busily being plundered by European colonists, nor in the safe confines of the London lunatic asylum known as Bedlam, but in the households, the bedchambers, and even the inner organs of the European gentry.

This terrifying and unconfined proximity of the monstrous might call to mind Puttenham's words about the disastrous effects of undisciplined fiction. If the imagination becomes disordered, Puttenham warned—if it begins to represent things to the mind 'otherwise than they be in deede', or to manufacture fictions—'then doth it breede *Chimeres* and monsters in mans imaginations, and not onely in his imaginations, but also in all his ordinarie actions and life which ensues' (15). The Elizabethans associated the word 'monster' with the Latin *monstrare*, to show; in *The Tempest*, Trinculo's first instinct on encountering the monster Caliban is to parade him as a peep-show round the fairgrounds of England (II. ii. 30–7).[45] Monsters were those who were

---

[45] Chris Baldick discusses the history of the word 'monster' in *In Frankenstein's Shadow: Myth, Monstrosity, and Nineteenth-Century Writing* (Oxford: Clarendon Press, 1987), ch. 2.

different, whether by reason of their shocking physical deformities or, less often, by reason of their excellence, and who were displayed to the public as striking instances of God's hand in human affairs. But Puttenham's 'monstruous imaginations or conceits' are less readily located and displayed than conventional wonders; they inhabit the dens and corners of the mind, and have an unnerving habit of breeding further monsters in the minds of their beholders. An Elizabethan reader perusing Fenton's volume, which displays monster after monster in a seemingly endless procession, might well have suspected as Ascham did that these foreign texts might not deter their readers from imitating their protagonists at all, but might instead transform them into monsters in their turn: maybe the 'mervelous monster' which is the Italianate Englishman (228). Most disturbingly of all, perhaps the metamorphosis did not need to take place, and the monstrous was already present in the Elizabethan subject, just waiting to be invoked.

What makes Fenton's protagonists monstrous is their susceptibility to extremes of passion. The most dramatic form this passion takes is rage, whether provoked by jealousy or resentment, and this rage dismantles the illusion of a rational plan behind the collection with an almost physical violence. In the fourth story an exemplary wife is cut to pieces by her jealous Albanian husband, after which:

beholding in her diverse undoubted arguments of death, he began the like war with himself, using the same means and ministers with his own hands, imbrued yet with the blood of his innocent wife; showing (notwithstanding this horrible part and act of despair) diverse and sundry signs of special gladness and pleasure in his face. (209)

The glee with which the husband perpetrates his sado-masochistic atrocities goes well beyond the requirements of instruction or even deterrence, and exposes instead an area of the mind where instruction cannot penetrate and where the disordered imagination reigns supreme. Shakespeare produced his own version of the fourth story in *Othello*, where he took Fenton's exploration of the savage recesses of the mind to their horrific conclusion.[46] What makes *Othello* terrifying

See also Kathryn M. Brammall, 'Monstrous Metamorphosis: Nature, Morality, and the Rhetoric of Monstrosity in Tudor England', *The Sixteenth Century Journal*, 27 (1996), 3–21, for a suggestion that the monstrous was of particular topical interest during the 1560s and 1570s.

[46] For possible links between Fenton's Albanian Captain and *Othello* see Paul N. Siegel, A New Source for *Othello*?', *PMLA* 75 (Sept. 1960), 480.

is the ease with which Iago sows Othello's imagination with monsters through the medium of elaborate fictions: the 'green-eyed monster' jealousy is only one of a plurality of hideous creatures that populate the play as a result of Iago's half-finished narratives. The tragedy is thronged with monsters, from the 'monster in thy thought | Too hideous to be shown' which Othello thinks he has detected in Iago's mind (III. iii. 107–8) to the 'civil monster' which is a cuckolded husband (IV. i. 62–4), from the 'monstrous' lie told by Iago about Cassio talking in his sleep (III. iii. 427) to the 'monstrous act' that brings the play to a close (V. ii. 190). *Othello* might be read as Shakespeare's exploration of the insidious effect on the mind of fictions like Fenton's: their exposure of the ubiquity of the monstrous in the Western imagination, and of the ease with which the monster-stories recounted by travellers—the kind of stories popularized by the medieval travel-writer Sir John Mandeville, and which Othello tells Desdemona in the course of their courtship—might acquire a more sophisticated and insinuating form, and so become the dominant narratives in the history of Europe.

The most pervasive and uncontrollable passion treated by Fenton is the passion of desire. The epistle claims that the *Tragicall Discourses* touches on love only to teach its readers how to reject its anarchic influence. But all Fenton's stories without exception take love as their central topic, and the one certain conclusion they reach is that love always and everywhere resists the rigid moral controls imposed on it by the responsible historian. In fact, the stories have little to do with what the dedication claims to be the primary function of history, the inculcation of 'outward policy' in the children of the ruling classes (41). Instead (as one of the commendatory poems points out) Fenton's subject is the protean metamorphoses of the mind in circumstances when the 'wit' has been rendered most inadequate to its task of organizing the evidence of the senses—when the powers of the intellect have been usurped by sexual obsession, the 'bane that comes by view' (52). The very first story in the book dismisses the illusion that it will have anything to do with 'outward policy' when it proclaims that it describes not the 'sumptuous buildings of princes'—the palaces which Painter used to suggest his collection's alluring blend of pleasurable excitement and political orthodoxy—but instead:

the marvellous effects of love; which . . . seems more strange than the curious construction and frame of any palace for necessity or pleasure, theatre, or place of solace, builded by art or industry of man, or other stately court (what square, quadrant, or triangle form soever it contains), or other mystical work, yielding cause of wonder to the university of the earth. (59)

Painter reproduces the same passage in his own version of the narrative without commenting on its displacement of his palace metaphor.[47] Set at the 'gate' of Fenton's collection it announces the tension between the architectural rigidity of his theory of history and the strangeness, the 'marvellous effects' and wonderful causes, which the novels disclose in the impenetrable microcosm of the mind.

Fenton may have chosen to open his collection with the story of Anselmo and Angelica because it describes an ideal love-affair to measure against the disastrous ones that dominate the collection. The story tells of a time when Anselmo's family, the Salimbeni, was locked in a struggle to the death with the family of the Montanins, one of those aristocratic feuds which filled Bandello's Italy and which helped to substantiate Ascham's claim in *The Scholemaster* that Italian cities existed in a permanent state of civil war (226). In time the Montanin family finds itself reduced to a single household, and the head of the household, Charles Montanin, is imprisoned for debt and condemned to be executed under the terms of a 'tyrannous statute' (70). Meanwhile, Anselmo has fallen in love with Charles's sister Angelica, whose name denotes the perfect Neoplatonic association between her 'right Angelike beautie'—as Bembo calls the outward manifestation of inward excellence in *The Courtier* (319)—and her virtue. Anselmo resolves to 'expose immediately the fruits and effects of semblable virtue' (81) by delivering Charles from his debt. In gratitude Charles offers Anselmo his sister in recompense, and the ensuing marriage unites both the lovers and their families, producing a hermaphroditic union which makes 'of two bodies, erst and long disjoined, an equal will and entire mind' (113).

Bandello knew both Castiglione and Bembo personally, and like Bembo's speech at the end of *The Courtier* this novel defines love as a semi-divine power which draws its possessor from an appreciation of transient physical beauty to a knowledge of transcendent spiritual truths. The story is a happier version of the tale of Romeo and Julietta, where the lovers' virtue reunites a divided society without recourse to a tragic denouement. But for Fenton the heroism of Anselmo and Angelica is complicated by its context. Their actions, like those of

[47] *The Palace of Pleasure*, iii. 288.

Titus and Gisippus, are designed to circumvent a law, and so set them
in direct opposition to the laws of the state—even if the state is a corrupt one, an unjust commonwealth in an Italy which is the 'only
storehouse for partialities and civil factions' (62). Moreover, the virtue
Anselmo manifests in uniting the warring families is repeatedly stated
to be unique: Anselmo himself calls it 'a thing exceeding the common
course and order of nature' (79), and in this way marks it as benevo-
lently monstrous. And, like all Fenton's versions of Bandello's novels,
the story portrays the choice between good and evil as a difficult,
perhaps an insoluble, conundrum. In a central episode the heroine
Angelica finds herself confronted like Shakespeare's Isabella with a
choice between two courses of action both of which are equally
repugnant to her: she must either agree to surrender her body to
Anselmo in return for her brother's release or else hold herself guilty
of ingratitude; so that in her perplexity she longs to be the protagonist
of a simpler story, such as the Classical tale of Virginia (99). For all its
depiction of ideal characters who act as a foil for the confused or corrupted minds in the other novels, the first discourse retains its identity
as one of Ascham's excessively subtle Italian narratives, refusing to
indicate a plain path for its reader to follow, and concentrating instead
on the strange, the excessive, the monstrous.

But the aspect of the first story which most seriously challenges
Fenton's moral strategy is this: that the love which prompts Anselmo
to reconcile the warring families is virtually indistinguishable from the
passion which propels other characters in the collection to acts of
horrific violence and despair. As love always does in the *Tragicall Discourses*, Anselmo's passion subjects him to the most appalling extremes
of physical distress, in this case the anguish reserved by Elizabethan law
for the worst offenders, 'the torment of the wheel' (65). The story
ends by dissociating love from the unflattering picture of it painted
in the dedicatory epistle, arguing that the emotion has been unfairly
depicted in the past 'in colours of rage, folly, and frenzy', and that in
a noble heart like Anselmo's it obeys the 'laws of so necessary and
ancient institution of nature' (115). Yet Anselmo's reaction to love
goes as far beyond institutional 'laws' by reason of its honourable
intensity as Pandora's later 'frenzy' does by reason of its savagery.
And the passions experienced by less exemplary lovers in Fenton's collection resist rules equally vigorously and are just as extreme. The
proem to the first tale announces that Anselmo's love produces
more remarkable effects than the most startling achievements of

human architecture, and elsewhere in the collection love continues to vanquish architectural restrictions. The third story describes Pandora's departure from convention as an exodus from the 'palace of reason' (185), and in the sixth story, where a lustful abbot finds himself attracted to a goldsmith's daughter, his fantasies again subject him to incomparable agonies and shatter both spatial and legal limitations as easily as Ascham's Italian fictions do: 'the whole cloister or circuit of his abbey could scarcely comprehend the sundry imaginations of his brain' (274). The abbot's passion and Anselmo's have everything in common, and Fenton's readers must ask themselves a puzzling question: how is it that two kinds of love which have identical symptoms can produce such contradictory results?

Elyot differentiated rational love from irrational desire by giving rational love another name, 'amity'.[48] It might be argued that the amity that brings the first story to its happy conclusion is only *initiated* by Anselmo's tormented passion for Angelica, and that the two kinds of love, while forming an alliance in this one instance, differ fundamentally. After all, the story concludes that only when desire takes root 'in the noble heart' does it become the 'fountain . . . of all civil and good order' (115). By good fortune Anselmo's passion finds an outlet in amity, but under other circumstances, in a less 'noble' heart like the abbot's, it might just as easily erupt in acts of murder, rape, or suicide. The trouble is that Fenton fails to draw a clear distinction between love's rational and irrational aspects. While the first story contends that it is unjust to portray love as a 'frenzy', the ninth, which relates the murderous adventures of the Lady of Cabrio, insists that 'love is an undoubted rage and fury' (369). In the second tale the lovers Livio and Camilla suffer death by coitus, and the Argument struggles in vain to moralize this embarrassing incident. To do so it must argue that the love they experience has nothing in common with Anselmo's regulated passion for Angelica. Accordingly the Argument agrees with the first story that ideal love is a 'necessary means to reform the rudeness of our own nature' (119), but goes on to warn that when it is undertaken 'without advice or judgement'—a moralistic view of love cannot accept that it is ever involuntary—desire inflames the most unruly aspect of the mind, the imagination, and so prompts the lover to 'throw himself headlong into the gulf of a

[48] See *The Governor*, book. 2, ch. 11: 'The true definition of amity and between what persons it happeneth'.

foolish and cunning phantasy'. But even within this one story Fenton
betrays an inconsistent attitude to desire. The narrative that follows
the Argument pays no attention to the existence of 'reforming' love,
and declares instead that, far from having a legitimate origin in the
divine or natural order, love is only ever a symptom of the plague of
individualism, a narcissistic inflation of the self: it is a 'humour of
infection derived of the corrupt parts in ourselves' (121), and later a
'rage or humour of frantic folly, derived of ourselves' (156). A later
Argument reverses the definition of love advanced in the first story
and the Argument to the second; in the twelfth it is simply a 'passion
of most dangerous and perverse corruption' (471) which only leads to
right action rarely and by chance. For Fenton, love alters its significance according to the evidence offered in each separate tragical
story and in each separate incident in each story. The characters
draw contradictory conclusions about it from the evidence of their
own experiences, and commentators too can infer no universal truths
about it from their histories, no coherent view of the function of
desire in a well-run public weal, despite the fact that its symptoms
remain consistent.

If the dedication stressed the importance of extracting universal
'principles and rules' from Bandello's novels, Fenton's stories themselves concentrate less on the universality of such laws than on the
question of how laws of all kinds are endlessly reinterpreted as circumstances change. The Ferrarese who rapes Julia in the eighth story
claims he is doing so for the most impeccable of motives, and explains
that he has earned the right to possess her body by following the traditions of romance: 'if long service with sincere loyalty may seem meritorious, you alone can judge my diligence and I accuse your cruelty'
(359). Julia replies by objecting to his appropriation of judicial terms
for his own ends: 'Neither deserve I of right the imputation of cruelty,
and much less of unseemly rigour as you term it' (360). A little later
she insists that he has used the word 'meritorious' in a corrupt sense:
'Neither can I answer you with other terms but commit you to the
*merit* of your folly' (360, my emphasis). The Ferrarese has enlisted
the legal language of reward and punishment in support of his criminal
actions, and other protagonists of Fenton's discourses are equally skilful at manipulating the jargon of universal 'principles and rules' to suit
their current requirements. In the third story when Parthenope urges
Pandora to commit adultery with him he uses the vocabulary that
Anselmo used to describe Angelica: 'measuring your heavenly shape,

with the outward show of singular courtesy that seems to occupy all your parts, I cannot resolve of any cruelty to consist in you' (165)— the statement again parodies Bembo's Neoplatonic effusions. When Parthenope deserts her, Pandora in her turn sees the revenge she exacts as an enactment of the universal principle of justice: she claims that 'his just chastisement should import a terror to all traitors that hereafter should seek to seduce any lady by sugared words' (183). Each subject defines Fenton's 'principles and rules' differently, and this multiplicity of conflicting definitions frustrates all Fenton's efforts to endow Bandello's text with a simple moral structure. The Argument to the twelfth story succinctly expresses the confusion to which these constant frustrations give rise. The Argument ascribes the anarchy that threatens to demolish Fenton's architectonic view of history to the insidious operation of desire, and proceeds to offer yet another definition of that passion, couched once again in the contradictory terms we have come to expect:

I may boldly avouch that which we call affection to be a passion resembling in some respect the condition of true amity, and not much unlike, for the most part, the general evil which the Grecians call *philauty*, and we term by the title of love, or vain flattery of ourselves, chiefly when we see any so friendly to his desires, that, to satisfy the inordinate thirst or glut of his greedy appetite, he forgets both honour and honesty. (471)

The passage is remarkable for the timidity with which it 'boldly avouches' an opinion of love; it succeeds only in confirming its elusiveness. Words prove inadequate and contingent glosses on its metamorphic effects: it is 'that which we *call* affection', and its 'title of love' is a misleading euphemism for self-flattery. It can be defined only by what it resembles, and it resembles both 'the condition of true amity', the friendship that binds Elyot's public weal, and the Greek *philautia*, the narcissism Ascham detects in quick wits and Italianate Englishmen, and which in Ascham's treatise threatens to overwhelm all society's attempts to impose its regulations. Love is whatever people want it to be, and Fenton's constant redefinitions betray his uneasy sense that it may be held to represent every private transaction that cannot be policed.

Later in Fenton's argument we are told that love disseminates fictions throughout the state. It obscures the 'true' nature of things —the essential rules privileged in the dedication—under a fictive veil that reveals only 'what images of virtue, courtesy, or bountiful disposition soever our lovers do imagine in them whom they serve, dimming the eyes of the world with a mist of dissembled substance' (472). The chief instrument of these deceptions is the lover's jargon, which yields up its sensuous derivation under scrutiny: 'their meaning is sufficiently manifest in the sugared orations and discourses of eloquent style, which those amorous orators seem to prefer, when their minds (occupied wholly in the contemplation of their mistresses) do commit the praise of the perfection in their ladies to the filed forge of their fine tongue' (472). Fenton's *Tragicall Discourses*, dominated as they are by the elusive condition of desire, by the 'filed forge' of the lovers' stylistic mannerisms, and by the narcissism which isolates loving individuals from the rigid social structures which ought to contain them, doom themselves to an inevitable and perpetual subversion of their own 'principles'.

The stories of Pandora and the Lady of Cabrio provide two of the most striking instances of this subversion. In both cases clever and independent women take over the spaces of domestic architecture and seize the reins of power with disconcerting ease; moreover, neither woman suffers the horrific punishments to which she would have been condemned by the Elizabethan legal system. The Lady of Cabrio transforms her house and grounds into a network of booby-traps designed to destroy its male inhabitants, and incites one of her husband's servants to murder him: 'truly', Fenton comments, 'the domestical servant, in credit or trust with his master, and evil-given or affected towards his lord, is more to be feared than a whole army of enemies standing in battle array in the field' (375). After his death the Lady usurps her husband's power and establishes a Machiavellian state in his household, where she draws up devious domestic 'policies' and where her son accuses her of abusing the 'majesty royal'. The extent to which her policies succeed implies that there might be hundreds of such barbarous miniature kingdoms in the 'heart and bowels of Christendom', and that any family might be harbouring its own serial killer in its most carefully guarded inner chambers.

Pandora offers equally disturbing evidence of this possibility. Like the Lady of Cabrio she runs riot through her husband's household, sleeping with pages, corrupting servants, and converting her bed-chamber into an operating theatre where she can abort the foetus of an unwanted child. In addition, she is the incarnation of Ascham's neuroses: all his prejudices against Italy could be confirmed by reading her story. From the first the narrative ascribes her conduct to her

nationality: she begins as an 'Italian imp' (159) and ends by being 'Ita-
lianated with all subtleties' (185), melting effortlessly into the background among her sophisticated Italian contemporaries. When her
lover deserts her, leaving her pregnant, Pandora threatens to transform
herself into one of Ascham's Italian enchantresses: ' "Ah!" saith she,
"why was not I traded in the magical sciences of the Colchian
Medea or the Italian Circe...?" ' (176). But instead of subjecting
others to a Circean metamorphosis she undergoes one herself, her
anger converting her into a composite beast more dreadful by far
than the Italianate Englishman: her conduct exceeds 'the brutal cruelty
of the wolf, tigress, or lioness' (183), and she later becomes a 'bitchfox', an 'execrable monster', and a 'bitch of Hyrcania' (184). The
excesses to which her sense of justice leads her play havoc with Fenton's efforts to control his narrative. His account of the final stage of
her transformation is an uneasy fusion of pietistic disapproval and fascinated voyeurism:

Truly, I know that virtuous ladies (sprinkled with the dew of pity) will not
only tremble at the remembrance of the inordinate cruelty of this cursed
mother, but also open the conduits of their compassions, weeping on the
behalf of the torment wherein unnaturally she plunged the innocent imp
which nature had formed of the substance of herself; who, converted from
the shape of a woman into the disposition of a devil, raging without measure,
that she could not be delivered, howled out at last with a horrible cry full of
impiety and blasphemy in this sort: 'seeing (saith she) that both God and the
devil deny me their assistance, I will (in spite of their powers) rid me of thee,
O cursed and execrable creature!'

Wherewith, possessed wholly with the spirit of fury, having her eyes sunk
into her head, her stomach panting, and her face all full of black blood, by the
vehemency of the conflict which she had endured, began to leap with all her
force from the top of the coffer down to the ground...

Certainly, good ladies, my heart, abhorring no less the remembrance of this
bitchfox, than my spirit troubled with trembling fear at the continuance of her
cruelty, gives such impediment to my pen that it is scarce able to describe unto
you the last act of her rage: wherein this limb of the infernal lake, not worthy
any longer to bear the name of a woman, proceeding to the end of her enter-
prise, takes up her son with her bloody and murdering hands, whom, without
all compassion and contrary to the order of a Christian, she beats with all her
force against the walls, painting the posts and pavements in the chamber with
the blood and brains of the innocent creature newborn. (182–4)

Despite his assertions that his penmanship has been inhibited by his
outrage, Fenton amplifies the bloody details of the abortion with

ornate fluency over several pages, while punctuating his account with
increasingly feeble gestures towards an ever more distant 'norm' of
female behaviour. He sanctimoniously reminds his audience that Pandora is acting 'without measure' and 'contrary to the order of a Christian', and appeals to his trembling and tear-stained women readers as if
to reassure himself of the uniqueness, the monstrosity, of Pandora's
violence. But not all his readers need have concurred with his shrill
condemnation of her actions. For one thing, Pandora's rage has its justification, as he himself admits in the proem to the ensuing discourse.[49] She has been abandoned in pregnancy, and her violence
(like Violenta's in *The Palace of Pleasure*) expresses the anger of a
woman who has no access to the machinery of justice. And the end
of the story suggests that Pandora may not be so monstrous—that it
may not be so easy to make a pedagogic example or demonstration
of her. We never learn whether she was punished for her illegal abortion, and she finally disappears without trace into the 'company of
other ladies':

Whereof, going to bed, she caused certain baines to be provided; wherein
washing herself, the next day (being hallowed and a feast of great solemnity)
she was carried in a rich couch to visit the company of other ladies, amongst
whom she was not worthy to keep place, being the shameful butcher of her
own blood and wicked enemy to the life of man. (185)

In Fenton's misogynistic fantasies, the female 'enemy to the life of
man' lurks in the heart and bowels of polite society, scrupulously
observing the external formalities, and even participating in the education of the young—the murderous Lady of Cabrio ends her career as
a respectable governess. Bandello's Amazons cannot easily be told
apart from the traditional categories of wives, mistresses, and virgins:
they are equally at home in palaces and in schoolrooms, and the patriarchal legal system cannot quite control them.

   Fenton does not fail to supply instructions on the prevention of
female rebellions like Pandora's. In the story of Luchino and Jani-
quette he warns the mothers and tutors of young girls to keep them
under control by means of savage corporal punishment: 'For as the
philosopher termeth them to be a kind of cattle more apt to decline
than any other reasonable creature; so (saith he), if they get once the
bit between their teeth, and crop of the herb of riotous will, it is

---

[49] '[A] certain jealousy sprung of an unjust mislike (as she thought) is ready to cover the
fault of Pandora', (187).

harder to reclaim them... than the wild haggard or rammish falcon by any cunning or devise of their keeper' (408). He ends his collection with two stories that demonstrate the way wild women could be tamed by violence; both the story of Zilia and the story of Genivera end with their heroines being terrorized into submission. But several of Fenton's stories militate against the neatness of this closure. By avoiding punishment Pandora and the Lady of Cabrio escape from the moral framework of Fenton's text, and so provide graphic illustrations of the difficulty of containing the threats to order posed by sophisticated Italian operators. Even the simplest examples of female good conduct show the same tendency to excess, the same capacity to evade moral containment, as Pandora does. The virtuous woman in the sixth story takes up the Amazonian art of swordfighting, and Julia in the eighth is commended for her chastity but condemned for the act of suicide by which she preserves it. At the beginning of the third tale Fenton announces his intention to 'treat upon tragical affairs, proceeding of unnatural lust, with lascivious disposition, the only master pock and chief fountain from whence distilleth all poisoned humours of infection, overflowing at length the channel of his quiet course with unruly waves of inordinate cruelty' (158). Pandora and her sisters are the unleashers of this deluge, sweeping away the scheme proposed by Fenton for his *Tragicall Discourses* and bringing the threat of chaos to his creation. It is perhaps no accident that Ascham, who advocated the policing of texts like Fenton's, should have reserved the most violent of the anecdotes in *The Scholemaster* for his account of the education of a woman, Lady Jane Grey. Lady Jane's devotion to study—which is expressed in terms of her contempt for Italian fictions[50]—derives from a pedagogic programme which is as aggressive as Fenton could have wished: whenever she puts a foot wrong in the presence of her parents, she tells Elizabeth's approving tutor,

I am so sharplie taunted, so cruellie threatened, yea presentlie some tymes, with pinches, nippes, and bobbes, and other waies, which I will not name, for the honor I beare them, so without measure misordered, that I thinke my selfe in hell, till tyme cum, that I must go to *M. Elmer*, who teacheth me so jentlie, so pleasantlie, with soch faire allurementes to learning, that I thinke all the tyme nothing, whiles I am with him. (201–2)

[50] Ascham finds her 'readinge *Phaedon Platonis* in Greeke, and that with as moch delite, as som jentleman wold read a merie tale in *Bocase*' (201).

The passage offers a horrifying instance of the lengths to which some Tudor parents would go—to the extent of infringing the 'measure' and 'order' which they presumably meant to inculcate in their offspring—in order to suppress the 'natural' wildness of women. It is perhaps not the least of Ascham's objections to Italian fiction that it offers glimpses, here or there, of women who will not submit to such treatment, and who are willing and able to turn the tables of domestic violence on their self-appointed masters.

Fenton's collection, then, replaces the apparent simplicity of the animal fable or exemplary history with the savagery, the subtlety, and the moral ambiguity of the monster-story. Opening the *Tragicall Discourses*, Elizabethan readers found themselves investigating not the moral and philosophical secrets enshrined in the traditional fable but the monstrous secrets that lurk behind the ornate façades of aristocratic buildings throughout Europe: the capacity for aggressive self-assertion that conceals itself beneath the obsequious mask of the wife, the mistress, or the household servant; the ferocious sexual drives which periodically overwhelm the human mind and body, which resist the imposition of rules and restraints of any kind, and which can commandeer at will the limitless resources of the intellect. Far from elucidating the universal principles that govern every aspect of a Christian society, as printed texts were supposed to do, these stories shed a baleful light on the areas of sexual and domestic conflict where 'measure' and 'order' hold no sway—the areas which philosophers, pedagogues, politicians, and official historiographers would rather leave unexplored, shrouded in the secrecy of silence. Fenton's monsters are yet more cunning and more bafflingly camouflaged than Baldwin's cats, and resist with still fiercer tenacity the efforts of their author to contain them within the bounds of conventional structures of narrative and interpretation. Like a descendant of the mythical king Minos of Crete, Fenton endeavours to enclose his hideous progeny within the strict architectural limits of a pedagogic system, but in the process he finds that his narratives themselves have become an elaborate trap which allures its youthful readers into seeking out the very dangers it is designed to eliminate. In the conclusion to the thirteenth tale, Fenton expresses the pious hope that his cornucopia of repellent examples will contribute to the education of its youthful readers, 'lest, in remaining still in the labyrinth of sensuality, they serve not hereafter as a fable and stage play to the posterity of the multitude' (560). The 'labyrinth of sensuality' suggests a vastly more complex architectural edifice than that of a palace—an edifice that both contains and draws attention to the mistakes that the palace would like to hide. And the youthful writers of the following decade chose to linger in and to extend the labyrinth Fenton had unwittingly constructed, and to adopt the labyrinth as the presiding metaphor for their own outrageous fictions.

# 3
# George Gascoigne and the Fiction of Failure

George Gascoigne specialized in the fiction of failure. His narratives in prose and verse record the mournful resilience of youths whose aspirations fade and superannuated lovers whose hopes are dashed, and he aligns his own career with those of his protagonists, both in his poems and in the playfully elusive epistles he places at the beginning of his works. His characters devise elaborate plots for their own advancement, only to find their strategies overthrown by unexpected developments, their plots demolished by devious counter-plots, their complex efforts at subterfuge slipping out of control by reason of their sheer complexity. Their willingness to improvise, to seize every opportunity to get what they want, is signalled by the term Gascoigne uses to describe the narratives that contain them: 'adventures', with all its Elizabethan connotations of hazard, chance, the absence of a coherent design. His prose fiction *The Adventures of Master F.J.* (1573) consists of a series of risks or hazards rashly undertaken.[1] Master F.J. twice 'adventures' to enter his mistress's chamber (37, 75), the narrator 'adventures his pen' on F.J.'s behalf (39), and the text itself finds its way into the public domain as a result of another 'adventure'—the risk taken by the narrator when he divulges the story of F.J.'s clandestine love-affair to an unreliable friend (40). *A Hundreth Sundrie Flowres*

[1]  All references to *The Adventures of Master F.J.* are taken from *An Anthology of Elizabethan Prose Fiction*, ed. Paul Salzman (Oxford: Oxford University Press, 1987). I have chosen to cite from this edition because it is the one most widely available to students and scholars at the time of writing. The standard edition of the *Adventures* is to be found in *A Hundreth Sundrie Flowres*, ed. C. T. Prouty (Columbia: University of Missouri Press, 1942), which should be consulted to clarify the relationship between the various explanatory epistles I discuss in this chapter. See also Prouty, *George Gascoigne*, 191, for a bibliographical description of the *Flowres*.

the volume in which the *Adventures* first appeared, is another perilous game of chance, as the printer confesses in an explanatory letter. Despite his anxiety that the censors will not like it, the printer 'adventures' to present the volume 'unto all indifferent eyes' in the hope that its sheer diversity will protect it from censorship.[2] None of these risks pays off: F.J.'s mistress loses interest, the narrator's friend betrays his trust by releasing F.J.'s story to the press, and the collection itself was withdrawn from circulation by order of the High Commission. But Gascoigne's obsession with abortive projects might leave his readers with the sneaking suspicion that he not only anticipated this act of censorship but actively courted it, for reasons that may become apparent.

At the same time, Gascoigne's interest in failure defines itself against the fiction of a carefully structured career, a well-planned life. In his preliminary epistles he seems to present his personal history as a fable or parable, an exemplary course of instruction born from a collaboration between a benevolent Providence and the generosity of his patrons, as well as from his own struggles for self-advancement.[3] His prefaces divide his literary productions into different categories, each of which corresponds to a different stage in his moral development. He began his career, he tells us, by writing as a 'deformed youth', a purveyor of adolescent sexual fantasies; went on to refashion himself as a 'reformed man' by assuming the serious role of a satirist; and ends as a 'grave Philosopher', who passes his time in the blameless pursuit of translating the works of Augustine and Pope Innocent III.[4] His autobiographical sketches in verse and prose can thus be read as versions or fragments of an orderly narrative, a reworking of the parable of the Prodigal Son, in which his youthful 'adventures'—his bigamous marriage, his accumulating debts, his futile efforts to forge a career as

---

[2] The epistle from the printer in *A Hundreth Sundrie Flowres* is reproduced in *The Complete Works of George Gascoigne*, ed. John W. Cunliffe, 2 vols. (Cambridge: Cambridge University Press, 1907), vol. i: *The Posies*, 475–6. All subsequent references to Gascoigne's works, except *Master F.J.*, are to the Cunliffe edition.

[3] The fullest expression of this partnership can be found in the celebrated poem 'Gascoignes woodmanship', in which God and the Lord Grey of Wilton combine to put Gascoigne's talents to a suitable use. *Gascoigne, Complete Works*, i. 348–52. See Jonathan V. Crewe, *Trials of Authorship* (Berkeley, Ca.: University of California Press, 1990), ch. 5.

[4] Gascoigne's translation of St Augustine's *De Contemptu Mundi* was included in his pamphlet *The Droomme of Doomes Day* (1576); his treatise *A Delicate Diet, for Daintiemouthde Droonkardes* (1576) was partly based on Pope Innocent's sermons. *Complete Works*, ii. 209–49 and 451–71.

courtier, lawyer, soldier, and writer—serve as a training-ground for a discreet maturity spent usefully in the service of the state.[5]

Gascoigne refers again and again to this imaginary progression from prodigality to reformation. In *The Adventures of Master F.J.* the narrator suggests that this is the pattern all English writers ought to follow in the course of their careers, and expresses his disappointment that:

amongst so many toward wits no-one hath been hitherto encouraged to fol-low the trace of that famous and worthy knight Sir Geoffrey Chaucer, and after many pretty devices spent in youth for the obtaining a worthless victory might consume and consummate his age in describing the right pathway to perfect felicity, with the due preservation of the same. (5)

In the dedication to his satire *The Steele Glas* (1576) he adds the ex-amples of Plato and Aristotle to the list of distinguished authors who began their careers by living 'very ryotously' (ii. 136); and in his tem-perance tract *A Delicate Diet, for Daintiemouthde Droonkardes* (1576) he aligns himself with St Augustine by stressing his recent retreat from the 'thryftlesse workes' of his adolescence (ii. 453). In this version of Gascoigne's biography, the latter end of his career redeems the begin-ning. His youthful pride in intellectual athleticism, his gift for extem-porization, his love of risks, his adventurousness, justify themselves retrospectively by being harnessed at last in the service of the ruling classes; the 'lost time which I misbestowed in wryting so wantonlie' (ii. 453) is finally recovered by being absorbed into the orderly sched-ule of the public weal. The dedication to *The Droomme of Doomes Day* (1576) bears eloquent witness to this absorption. It is filled with the sense of time wasted, and of the insistence with which this wasted time demands atonement. In it he confesses that he has been 'giltie of much time mispent' and acknowledges that 'both the tyme, and my duetie doe challenge in me the fruites of repentaunce' (ii. 211); and he brings home the urgency of this repentance by specifying the pre-cise time-scale within which he has accomplished the translation. A friend has urged him 'almost twelve moneths past' to write something more morally uplifting than love-lyrics (ii. 211), and the dedication was completed on the 'second daye of Maye. 1576' (ii. 214). The manuscript in which he found *The Droomme of Doomes Day* testifies to his eagerness to redeem his past by his present actions. It has lain unread in his library for fifteen years, throughout the period of his rio-

---

[5] For an account of Gascoigne's career see Prouty, *George Gascoigne*. For reworkings of the Prodigal Son parable by writers of the period see Helgerson, *The Elizabethan Prodigals*.

tousness, and yet it remains directly relevant to the needs of the present moment—it is 'very meete to be redde as the present tyme requireth' (ii. 214). The title he gave it, with its allusion to the appointment with God at the day of doom which must finally be kept by the whole of creation, proclaims his new awareness that he is working within a temporal framework controlled by Providence. The tone of this dedication could not be more different from the informal, extemporary tone of the epistles in his first miscellany, *A Hundreth Sundrie Flowres* (1573), and it is tempting to accept Gascoigne's account of his reformation without a second thought.

Of course, he took considerable pains to encourage this acceptance. His presentation of himself as a penitent prodigal invites his aristocratic readers to participate in the narrative of his career by giving it a happy ending—that is, by putting his gifts to work on their own behalf. He makes this invitation explicit in the three epistles that introduce his second miscellany, *The Posies* (1575). *The Posies* is an extensively revised and expanded version of *A Hundreth Sundrie Flowres*, which had fallen victim to state censorship two years earlier.[6] The first of its epistles is an impudent address to the censors themselves, 'the reverende Divines' of the High Commission (i. 3), and in it Gascoigne freely admits the justice of their decision to suppress the earlier volume. Like all humanity, he confesses, readers are *magis proni ad malum quam ad bonum*, more inclined to evil than to good, so that if any text seems to jeopardize the moral 'reformation' of its readers there is every reason to ban it as a potentially seditious document. The question then arises as to whether or not *The Posies* may reasonably be regarded as a 'Whetstone of Vanities', and whether its author deserves to be branded a 'corrupte Merchaunte for the sale of deceyptfull wares' (i. 4). Gascoigne never denies the power of his texts to corrupt or deceive their readers; in the second of the three epistles he goes so far as to confess that they might have the poisonous properties of hemlock (i. 13). Their status, as he declares in the second epistle, is that of a 'two edged swoorde' (i. 14), a duplicitous ideological weapon which is capable of being wielded in a variety of antagonistic causes.[7] *The Posies*, Gascoigne explains, is made up in equal parts of 'deceyptfull wares' and 'morall discourses' (i. 13), good grain and chaff. All

---

[6] See my Introduction.

[7] The metaphor anticipates Sidney's comparison of poetry to an equally duplicitous weapon: 'With a sword, thou mayest kill thy father, and with a sword thou mayest defend thy prince and country' (*An Apology for Poetry*, 126). See below, s. 4 of this chapter.

three of his preliminary epistles stress the same thing: that it is up to the reader to employ these two-edged texts and their wayward author in such a way as to render them of service to the state. Gascoigne has consented to the publication of *The Posies*, he tells the censors, 'To the ende that thereby the vertuous might bee incouraged to employ my penne in some exercise which might tende both to my preferment and to the profite of my Countrey' (i. 5). *The Posies*, then, represents a transitional phase in Gascoigne's development, a crossroads in his literary career. The mixture of moral and deceitful texts it contains is arranged in such a way as to enable readers to judge for themselves both the rhetorical charisma of its clever author and the alternative routes his 'giftes' might take. Read one way, the collection could lead to these gifts being deployed to the benefit of the nation. Read in another, the craftiness they celebrate could lead to the corruption of an entire generation. It is the responsibility of the reverend divines, the epistle suggests, to ensure that both Gascoigne and the 'yonger sort' who admire his work end up as reformed prodigals rather than as unreformed—perhaps even Catholic—saboteurs. The question of whether *The Posies* should be censored as the *Flowres* was is therefore of only marginal importance: what is essential is that the talents of its author should not be ignored.

Before he gains steady employment, however, Gascoigne's career has no coherent structure: his lack of control over the anarchic variety of his experiences betrays itself repeatedly in the two collections of his works. Despite the lip-service they pay to the parable of the Prodigal Son, neither the *Flowres* nor *The Posies* has a convincing plan—at least not one which is accessible to its readers. In *A Hundreth Sundrie Flowres* the absence of a visible design is everywhere apparent. The first part of the collection is straightforward enough: it contains two plays, *The Supposes* and *Jocasta*, the first an adaptation of a comedy by Ariosto, the second adapted from a tragedy by Lodovico Dolce. But the second part is decidedly problematic. It opens and closes with two stories about abortive love-affairs—the tales of Master F.J. and Dan Bartholmew of Bath—and both stories are left 'unperfect', bereft of the expected moral summary (80). In addition, the unplanned nature of the collection is positively paraded in the trio of explanatory letters which introduces the first and second parts of the volume. The first part opens with a letter headed 'The Printer to the Reader', explaining the convoluted paths by which the manuscript of the collection reached the press. The printer claims that he received it from a gentleman, who was given it by a friend, who collected its contents from a number of other gentlemen and who insisted that he did not want it printed. To confirm this explanation the printer draws attention to the letter which introduces the second part, headed 'H.W. To the Reader'.[8] Here the mysterious H.W. confesses his own 'rashness' in having smuggled the collection into print against the express instructions of its editor. This confession is followed by a letter from the editor himself, G.T., who says that he is sending H.W. the manuscript on the sole condition that he retain it for his own private use. In other words, the gentlemen who wrote the letters which introduce the second part want the reader to believe that the publication of the collection was a spontaneous and slightly treacherous act, for which its editor could not be held responsible. The printer, on the other hand, thinks that this whole elaborate story is a hoax, contrived with 'clerkly cunning' to deflect the attacks of critics and censors:

Now I feare very muche (all these words notwithstanding) that these two gentlemen were of one assent compact to have it imprinted: And yet, finding by experience that nothing is so wel handled now adayes, but that some malicious minds may either take occasion to mislike it themselves, or else finde meanes to make it odious unto others: They have therefore (each of them) politiquely prevented the daunger of misreport, and suffered me the poore Printer to runne away with the palme of so perillous a victorie. (i. 476).

In these three letters *A Hundreth Sundrie Flowres* introduces its readers to a 'perillous' literary environment where malicious minds 'misreport' the texts of their rivals, where apparently rash or random acts conceal 'politique' agendas which can damage those who are not privy to them, and where the plot that underlies the production of a text can only ever be guessed at. The *Flowres* presents itself as a publication which is not straightforwardly 'pleasaunt and profitable', either to the public or to the state, despite the protestations on its title-page. It springs from the private agendas of anonymous gentlemen, and it fails to make these agendas plain. The very real 'daunger' involved in such literary subterfuge emerged when *A Hundreth Sundrie Flowres* was withdrawn from circulation.

What persuaded the printer to publish the collection, he tells us, was the exuberant variety of its contents. The verses it contains need not be read 'in such order as they are sorted', but may be perused at

---

[8] 'H.W. to the Reader' and the epistle that follows it, 'The letter of G.T. to his very friend H.W. concerning this work', are reprinted in *An Anthology of Elizabethan Prose Fiction*, 3–4.

will: 'you may take any one flowre by it selfe, and if that smell not so pleasantly as you wold wish, I doubt not yet but you may find some other which may supplie the defects thereof' (i. 476). Nothing could be further from North's injunctions to read *The Morall Philosophie of Doni* in the exact sequence in which it is presented, or his insistence on the need for readers to give 'aucthoritie' to his translation of *The Dial of Princes*. There is no authorized reading of *A Hundreth Sundrie Flowres*, no notion of an author's claim to ownership or control of a text. Some of the poems announce the identity of the author in their titles: 'Gascoignes good morow', 'Gascoygnes good nyghte' 'Gascoignes recantation'. Others claim to have been composed by 'sundry gentlemen' identified only by their mottoes or 'posies', thus giving the impression that the collection is the product of a secret coterie of clever and sexually prolific youths, not bound by a systematic code of learning and manners as North's texts claim to be.[9] The second version of the collection, *The Posies*, modifies the emphasis on anarchic inventiveness which characterized the first. For one thing it lays full responsibility for the composition and publication of its contents on a single writer, announcing itself as *The Posies of George Gascoigne Esquire*, so both dispersing the mystery of the volume's authorship and locating itself within the social hierarchy. For another it classifies the texts it contains under separate headings, entitled respectively 'Flowers', 'Hearbes', and 'Weedes', and by this means claims to offer its readers a guide to the rationale informing its layout: the flowers are pleasant, the herbs are profitable, and the weeds are a waste of time. But the apparently orderly disposition of *The Posies* is something of a red herring. Flowers, herbs, and weeds are not as easy to distinguish as they might at first appear. 'I have not ment', Gascoigne explains, 'that onely the Floures are to be smelled unto, nor that onely the Weedes are to be rejected' (i. 13). All three types of vegetation can flourish equally well in a formal garden or in an untended wilderness, and Gascoigne leaves his readers to decide for themselves which of these two spaces his collection represents.

The concept of the formal garden occurs repeatedly in contemporary texts as a metaphor for delightful usefulness; but the metaphor of the wilderness crops up with equal frequency throughout Gascoigne's

---

[9] H.W. describes the original manuscript of the collection as 'a written book, wherein he had collected diverse discourses and verses invented upon sundry occasions by sundry gentlemen (in mine opinion) right commendable for the capacity' (*An Anthology of Elizabethan Prose Fiction*, 3).

areer, and he invariably associates it with joblessness.[10] In *The Tale of Iemetes the Heremyte* (1576) he confesses that he has had a tendency to wander wyldlye' in his youth, and hints that his wanderings will only nd when Elizabeth chooses to 'sett me on worke' (ii. 476). In *The Princely Pleasures at Kenelworth Castle* (1575) he assumes the persona f Sylvanus, god of the woods, and so marks himself out as an inhabit-ant of the wastes of unemployment. Dressed in the dishevelled gar-ments of a satyr, he runs breathlessly alongside Elizabeth's horse ointing out unusual botanical specimens that have seeded themselves 1 the castle grounds: shrubs and trees that conceal the forms of out-f-favour courtiers, consigned by the queen's displeasure to a lifetime 1 the wilderness, and waiting for a word from Elizabeth to restore hem to their 'prystinate estate' (ii. 131).[11] At the time Gascoigne 00 was an exile from civility, a man without a stable role. He had wasted his talents, he confesses in *The Posies*, by writing about the wildernesses' of erotic desire, and 'he that wandereth much in those wildernesses, shall seldome continue long in one minde' (i. 17). *The Posies* presents itself not as a solid architectural structure like Painter's *The Palace of Pleasure*, but as a ruin whose outlines have been lost beneath encroaching weeds: 'And if hereafter you see me recover mine estate', he tells the younger members of his audience, 'or reedifie he decayed walls of my youth, then beginne you sooner to builde ome foundation which may beautifie your Pallace' (i. 14). Gas-coigne's second miscellany, like his first, would seem to be a text with-out a clearly defined position or 'estate' in the public weal, and one which is therefore capable of bringing unspecified danger to unwary wanderers. And once again the High Commission took this danger eriously enough to suppress the whole collection.

At the same time, the reluctance to 'continue long in one minde' is precisely what Gascoigne considers his greatest asset in the job market. The quality which he offers to interested patrons is his 'quick capa-ity', meaning, in part, the capacity to think on his feet and to speak persuasively at the drop of a hat. Of course as Ascham points out, an

[10] North refers to *The Dial of Princes* as a garden: 'In publishinge this my worke, I have bserved the maner of them that plant a new gardein, wherein they set Roses which give pleasaunt Savour to the nose, they make faire grene plattes to delight the eyes, they graft uitful trees to be gathered with the handes, but in the end as a man I may have erred' (gen-ral prologue, sig. ★5ᵛ).
[11] Gascoigne's breathlessness was implied by Robert Laneham in his account of the enter-ainments: 'Here her majestie stayed her horse to favour Sylvanus, fearing least he should be riven out of breath by following her horse so fast.' Quoted in Prouty, *George Gascoigne*, 89.

aptitude for improvisation can be a liability as well as an asset: 'com
monlie', *The Scholemaster* explains, 'men, very quicke of witte, be also
verie light of conditions: and thereby, verie readie of disposition, to b
caried over quicklie, by any light cumpanie, to any riot and unthrif
tines when they be yonge: and therfore seldome, either honest o
life, or riche in living, when they be olde' (189). And Gascoigne ha
an unnerving tendency to ally himself with Ascham's quick wits. I
*The Posies*, for instance, he echoes the passage just quoted when h
confesses that 'witte and I did (in youth) make such a fray, that
feare his cosen wisedome will never become freendes with me i
my age' (i. 16). In fact, in most of his references to his own accom
plishments Gascoigne seems as ready to stress his own capacity for cor
ruption as he is to proclaim his usefulness. In *Dan Bartholmew of Bath*
he associates 'quicke capacitye' with the ability to manufactur
unauthorized fictions, 'To tell a tale without authoritye', which is
sign of 'small discretion' (i. 96). *The Adventures of Master F.J.* point
out that the English poet's 'quickness of invention' has seldom beer
properly used (5), and *The Posies* warns its youthful readers that acro
batic mental tricks should not be tried at home: 'If you see me sinke ir
distresses (notwithstanding that you judge me quick of capacitie) ther
... eschue betymes the whirlepoole of misgovernment' (i. 14). Mos
disturbingly of all, in his play *The Glasse of Governement* (1575) Gas
coigne uses the term 'capacity' to describe the mental qualities o
two brothers who fail to achieve the moral reformation that redeeme
the biblical Prodigal, and who fall victim to horrible fates as a result
Their tutor Gnomaticus complains that they share the disastrous inde
pendence of mind that afflicted the ancient philosophers, 'whos
opinionate judgementes did eclipse the rest of their comendabl
capacitie: wherupon also hath sprong the damnable opinion o
*Atheysts*. For the mind of man is so heavenlie a thing and of sucl
rare excellencie, that it alwaies worketh and can not be idle' (ii. 69)
Quick capacity, then, is always working even when it is unemployed
and the result of such unsupervised activity might be religious as wel
as political dissent, the spread of atheism as well as of misgovernment
In other words, the reformation of George Gascoigne should be a
matter of vital importance to the Elizabethan censors, since withou
it there could be no knowing what his working mind—and the work
ing minds of his fascinated readers—might get up to.

Like Ascham's quickness of wit, Gascoigne's quick capacity sets itsel
up against its opposite, 'simplicity', and its antagonism to simplicity i

what makes it dangerous, uncontrollable, wild. Throughout his work he wavers between two uses of the word simplicity, one with positive, the other with negative connotations. The first is Elyot's in *The Governor*, where simplicity is an agreed meaning or system of meanings, a set of known definitions within which the subjects of a state agree to operate. This is the definition Gascoigne alludes to in *The Posies*, when he tells his younger readers that he is concerned as a 'reformed man' to 'protect' his youthful productions by reducing them to 'simplicitie' (i. 13). The other definition of the word militates against this project; it identifies simplicity with stupidity, an inability to manipulate words and situations to one's own advantage, an incompetence in the art of rhetorical improvisation. This second definition pits the interests of the private subject against the interests of the state, since the subject who dismisses simplicity as stupidity is also likely to dismiss the 'simple' system of meanings by which the state defines what is legal and what is illegal, what is profitable and what is corrupt. The two meanings of the word are constantly coming into conflict in Gascoigne's texts, as he oscillates between mocking the dullness of his enemies and arguing the case for his own moral reclamation. Inevitably the conflict even enters the works of his so-called 'reformation': when in *The Steele Glas* he names the parents of Satire as 'Playne dealyng' and 'Simplycitie', he is forced to explain in the marginal gloss that he means 'Not ignorant symplicity but a thought free from deceite' (ii. 144).

As one might expect, the most striking instance of the conflict between these two kinds of simplicity occurs in the preliminary epistles of *The Posies*. The letter to the 'reverende Divines' explains why Gascoigne felt the need to 'protect' *The Posies* against the slurs of hostile readers. The first version of the collection, he claims, was taken by the censors as an exercise in wilful obscurantism, a tissue of 'clowdes and figurative speeches' which might conceal (or be read as concealing) coded references to scandalous goings-on among the ruling classes (i. 3). The epistles in *The Posies*, then, are ostensibly designed to elucidate the 'darke places' that had brought down the wrath of the censors on the *Flowres* (i. 9); they are designed, in fact, to make Gascoigne's poems consensually simple. 'I will explane', he tells his readers, 'that which being before mistically covered, and commonly misconstrued, might be no lesse perillous in seducing you, than greevous evidence for to prove mee guiltie of condemnation' (i. 10). At the same time, all three letters display an almost unseemly eagerness to exonerate Gascoigne himself from the charge of stupidity. The second epistle casts itself as a response to the clever young men who may 'wonder at my simplicitie' in publishing his censored texts a second time (i. 9), while in the first epistle, his elucidation of the 'darkest' and most 'dangerous' text in the collection, *The Adventures of Master F.J.*, ties itself in knots in its efforts both to acknowledge and to deny the subtle allusiveness of the narrative. Some readers, he explains, have interpreted Gascoigne's prose fiction as a *roman à clef* written 'to the scandalizing of some worthie personages, whom they woulde seeme therby to know' (i. 7). His response is scathing: while he mocks the 'simplicitie' of such accusers, his main objection to their accusations seems to stem from their assumption that he would be stupid enough to allow his less sophisticated readers to decode any scandalous references he might have made. 'Alas, alas', he laments ironically, 'if I had bene so foolishe as to have passed in recitall a thing so done in deede, yet all the world might thinke me verie simple if I woulde call John, John, or Mary, Mary' (i. 7). The remark is hardly a refutation of his accusers' charges, although a more vigorous refutation follows: 'I doe here protest...that there is no living creature touched or to be noted therby.' Admirers of Gascoigne's 'quick capacity' might conclude that, however many worthy personages might be libelled in his fiction, he is too skilful an operator to allow any particular dignitary to be 'noted' in the text. The passage resembles a witty pastiche of the translators' apologies that precede the works of Ovid, Aesop, and Bidpai, where the 'dark philosophy' concealed within the texts of the fabulists is represented as both dangerously potent and deserving of respectful study. Gascoigne even seems to ally his collection with these collections of fables by changing the title of *The Adventures of Master F.J.* to *The Pleasant Fable of Ferdinando Jeronimi*, with all the promise of moral probity this entails. The difference is that Ovid's *Metamorphoses* was an authorized text with an established place in the humanist curriculum. Gascoigne's text, by contrast, remains a loose cannon, not only unauthorized but subject to censorship, and all the perilous talents it displays are presumably waiting to be exploited by the first comer to recognize their potential.

## 2.   SETTING THE SINGULAR TO WORK

Despite their opposition to simplicity, Gascoigne's quick capacities are not as clever as they like to think; and the source of their many excursions into folly is what Ascham calls their singularity, their narcissistic arrogance. As *The Scholemaster* puts it, they are 'verie quicke and readie, to like none so well as them selves' (189), and their conviction of their own brilliance is such that it bereaves them of loyalties and allies and leaves them politically isolated. But arrogance is not the exclusive province of those who delight in parading their mental gifts. As Gascoigne's satire *The Steele Glas* points out in its detailed survey of contemporary vices, every section of Elizabethan society has its own brand of 'singularity'—its prejudices, its self-serving agendas, its capacity for building elaborate castles in the air and for pulling the wool over its own and other people's eyes—which can be summed up in their fondness for the crystal mirror of flattery, that 'shewes the thing, much better than it is' (ii. 148), as against the honest, old-fashioned mirror made of steel, which reflects things as they are. Consensual simplicity exists, if at all, in a constant struggle with the singular, and Gascoigne's texts take as their theme the clash between the desires that motivate the private subject and the laws by which the state attempts to regulate the lives of its unruly citizens.

His comedy *The Supposes* (1566) is one of his wittiest explorations of this struggle. It derives its title from the wide variety of prejudices or 'supposes' which govern the expectations of its audience and of its cast of fictional characters. The audience, as the prologue points out, is liable to approach the comedy with a range of different 'supposes' about what it will contain, each of which corresponds to their own private predilections or desires. Those who delight in intellectual games will expect the play to be full of logical conundrums, 'the sophisticall handling of subtill Suppositions' (i. 188); those who are more interested in sex will expect it to be full of innuendo. What these various expectations have in common is their acknowledgement of the divorce between different people's understandings of the same verbal signs, and the rich diversity of imaginary scenarios or narratives to which these disagreements can give rise; this is what the play explores. *The Supposes* consists of a web of misunderstandings which temporarily reduces the social hierarchy to chaos. '[T]his our Suppose', the prologue explains, 'is nothing else but a mystaking or imagination of one thing for an other. For you shall see the master supposed for the servant, the servant for the master: the freeman for a slave, and the bondslave for a freeman: the stranger for a well knowen friend, and the familiar for a stranger' (i. 188). The catalyst for these misunderstandings is a secret agreement between a clever

young man and his equally clever servant that they should swap identities in order to give the young man access to the woman he loves.
This reversal of roles is rendered necessary by the fact that the master,
Erostrato, is a Sicilian stranger whose birth and financial expectations
are unknown in the town of Ferrara, and who therefore has little hope
of gaining access to the woman as a legitimate suitor. At the same time
his status as a stranger is what makes the role reversal possible. Like an
accomplished spy, he can assume any role he likes in a foreign town
where nobody knows who he is; in playing the part of a servant he
manages to worm his way into the household of his lover, causing
minor outbreaks of hostility between the inhabitants of Ferrara and
those of Sicily and Siena, and bringing into question the very identity
of the Ferrarese state. As one character remarks to Erostrato's father at
the height of the play's confusions, 'the worlde is large and long, there
maye be moe *Philoganos* and moe *Erostratos* than one, yea and moe *Fer-
raras*, moe *Sicilias*, and moe *Cathaneas*: peradventure this is not that
*Ferrara* whiche you sent your sonne unto' (i. 223). If the play had
not been a comedy, the outcome could have been disastrous for
the young man's lover, dangerous for Ferrara, and fatal for Erostrato
himself.

But for all his skill at role-playing, Erostrato has little control over
the chain of 'supposes' he sets in motion. His disguise initiates a series
of frantic improvisations, which culminates in the arrival of his father
at precisely the moment when his presence can do most damage. As
Erostrato's servant complains to Fortune:

> If at any time before thou haddest conducted him, this enterprise had bene
> cut off without care in the beginning: and if never so little longer thou
> hadst lingred his jorney, this happie day might then have fully finished our
> drifts and devises. But alas, thou hast brought him even in the very worst
> time, to plunge us al in the pit of perdition (i. 232).

The state authorities in the play seem to have as little skill in unravel-
ling the mistakes brought about by Erostrato's machinations as the
young man does himself. In his perplexity over the apparent disap-
pearance of his son, Erostrato's father exclaims, 'oh eternall God, is
there no judge? no officer? no higher powers whom I may complaine
unto for the redresse of these wrongs?' (i. 228). But the answer he
gives himself is not encouraging: both advocates and judges have 'insa-
tiable jawes' and will take no interest in cases that bring them no
profit. The play's denouement is finally brought about, not by the

extemporizing skills of servant or master, nor by the intervention of the law, but by the forces that have control over time itself. These forces lie outside the reach either of the private subject or of the state; as one of the characters observes while the comic ending unfolds, 'I think that not so much as a leafe falleth from the tree, without the ordinance of god' (i. 241). In comparison with Providence, even the subtlety of an author can look like stupidity, as the prologue suggests when it catches itself giving away the plot of the play: 'But what? I suppose that even already you suppose me very fonde, that have so simply disclosed to you the subtilties of these our Supposes: where otherwise in deede I suppose you shoulde have hearde almoste the last of our Supposes, before you coulde have supposed anye of them arighte' (i. 188). This is the one expectation that the play fulfils: that its 'subtilties' will sort themselves out in the end; but the diversity of the supposes that emerge along the way can only be reduced to consensual simplicity by divine intervention, the 'ordinance of god'.

The Supposes comfortingly places the potentially treacherous operations of Erostrato's 'quick capacity' within a providential framework; but the 'mystakings or imaginations' in Gascoigne's later texts are not so easy to disentangle. His second collection punningly associates itself with Ariosto's comedy by taking the title The Posies of George Gascoigne Esquire. In doing so it brands its author as a master of disguises, a cunning dissembler who can adopt whatever 'pose' he likes and who can play at will on the 'supposes'—the expectations, fantasies, and assumptions—of his simple readers. This is the portrait of the artist he presents in the third of the preliminary epistles. Here he alludes to the metamorphic powers of St Paul, who could:

transforme himself into all professions, therby to winne all kinde of men to God: saying that with the Jewes he became a Jew: with them that were under the law, he seemed also under the lawe: with the feeble, he shewed himselfe feeble. And to conclude, he became all things to all men, to the ende that hee might thereby winne some to salvation. (i. 15)[12]

Gascoigne possesses the same metamorphic powers, the same capacity to melt into any background as the Apostle; but the ends to which he employs these powers are very different from St Paul's. He freely admits that his skills in versification have been employed for the most part in the service of sexual intrigue. In addition, they have not been used for the benefit of a single master, but have adapted

---

[12] See I Cor. 9: 20–2.

themselves to the needs of successive employers: most of his eroti
verses have been written for other men. The 'posies' or mottoe
with which he signs his 'poesies' are a private code designed to concea
his identity from an inquisitive public: 'For when I did compile an
thing at the request of other men, if I had subscribed the same wit
mine owne usuall mot or devise, it might have bewrayed the sam
to have beene of my doing' (i. 17). He seems, in fact, to have live
his life as a literary mercenary, an arch domestic secret agent who pan
ders to the pornographic whims of his readers instead of to their mora
well-being; and the title of *The Posies*, with its layers of alternativ
meanings, illustrates the difficulty of confining either Gascoigne'
texts or Gascoigne himself to a single responsible function.

The protagonists of Gascoigne's narratives seem as incapable as he i
of finding safe employment for their talents. Each of them fails to sub
scribe to the comic consensus which was brought about by Provi
dence at the end of *The Supposes*. In both *The Adventures of Maste
F.J.* and the narrative poem *Dan Bartholmew of Bathe*, the male prota
gonist begins by supposing himself in control of his own sexual intri
gues, the mastermind of his own adventures. But he quickly learn
that his mistress is a more adept manipulator of 'supposes' than him
self, and ends by being discarded by her in favour of a less self
satisfied—or less exhausted—lover. Neither F.J. nor Bartholmev
shows any sign of being elevated by his misfortunes to the status of
responsible citizen, as Erostrato was; they are still seeking their privat
sexual fortunes at the end of their adventures as energetically as the
were at the beginning. The same tenacity in clinging to shattered illu
sions is shown by the indigent mercenary 'Miser' in the satirical poen
'*Dulce Bellum Inexpertis*', who continues to dream that his fortune wil
be made by war in the teeth of ever-accumulating evidence that i
will not. The Green Knight, another of Gascoigne's abortive Romeos
is equally unable to disengage himself from his fantasies: the poem tha
announces the knight's abandonment of his sexual adventures, 'The
greene Knights farewell to Fansie', ends with a postscript that recant
his recantation: 'Fancie hath not yet his last farewell' (i. 382). None o
these narratives ends with a satisfactory sense of closure; none of thei
protagonists succeeds in transforming himself into a penitent prodigal
F.J. and the Green Knight fail to supply their stories with a moral; an
the story of Dan Bartholmew peters out with the narrator feebly con
fessing that 'my borrell braine is all to bloont | To give a gesse wha
ende this man shall have' (i. 136). In the same way, the collection a

whole fails to achieve a moral ending. The last section of *The Posies* comprises the group of texts entitled 'Weedes', so called because their contents are 'neither pleasant nor yet profitable' (i. 13). Like Erostrato in *The Supposes*, Gascoigne is incapable of bringing either his collection or his career to a comic conclusion without assistance from a higher authority. But unlike *The Supposes*, *The Posies* shows little evidence that such an authority has intervened, as yet, in its author's history.

Fortunately, Gascoigne did not have to wait long after the publication of *The Posies* before he began to win recognition at court. In August 1576 he was sent as an observer to the Low Countries by the Elizabethan government, and described what he saw in a brilliant piece of journalism, *The Spoyle of Antwerpe*. It seems appropriate that 1576 should have been the year when he found royal favour, since he had anticipated such a development at the beginning of the year when he presented the queen with a magnificent New Year's gift: a manuscript written out and illustrated by Gascoigne himself, containing a transcription in English, Latin, French, and Italian of an entertainment he had written for Elizabeth's visit to the house of Sir Henry Lee in the summer of 1575. The title of the manuscript is *The Tale of Hemetes the Heremyte*, and it is effectively an extended happy ending. The narrative weaves together the stories of Gandina, Contarenus, Loricus, and Hemetes, and it is told by one of Gascoigne's many unreliable narrators, the hermit Hemetes who is one of the protagonists. Each of the characters in the story falls in love, and each in turn encounters an impediment to their love's consummation. Gandina and Contarenus find their courtship cut short by a king, Gandina's father, who disapproves of the match. Loricus is unable to fathom the feelings of the woman he loves, except by the 'straunge essay' of pretending to love someone else (ii. 481). Most awkwardly of all, Hemetes falls in love with a woman who never stays in the same shape for more than five minutes at a time. All four lovers respond to their dilemmas by taking to the road; and all four, after experiencing the 'varyablenes of... adventures' in foreign parts (ii. 479), eventually make their way to the place where all dilemmas are resolved, 'a place, wheare men were moste stronge, and women most fayre, the country most fertyll the people most welthy, the government most just, and the princes most wourthy' (ii. 482)—England, of course, and more specifically Woodstock, where Elizabeth is waiting to restore them to prosperity.

This solution of Gascoigne's to the problem of his career is more satisfactory—and more sophisticated—than a simple reformation. If he had chosen once again to stress his moral apostasy, his withdrawal from the sexual adventurousness that had shaped his early literary productions, he would merely have rendered the works of his youth redundant. Instead he suggests that the queen herself occupies the erotic territory he had been exploring for so long, and that she alone can control its complexity, its wildness. The situations encountered by the four lovers are not straightforward moral choices of the kind he tackled in his treatises. Instead they raise a number of tricky political questions, the questions of whether or not a subject should obey an unjust monarch (Gandina's father), of what 'straunge' tactics should be deployed to 'fynde surely owte' the thoughts of a subject who conceals her allegiance 'most closely' (Loricus' secretive lover, ii. 481), and of how to respond to the complex signals given out by a subject who is 'wonderfull of condicion' (Hemetes' metamorphic lady, ii. 482). Unlike Gascoigne's earlier narrators—G.T. in *The Adventures of Master F.J.*, the Reporter in *Don Bartholmew of Bathe*, the Author in the Green Knight sequence—Hemetes the hermit is neither baffled by the complexities of the stories he relates nor willing to gloss over them; he presents his narrative in all its intricacy as a puzzle to be solved by its audience, and particularly by Elizabeth. The difference between Hemetes and these other narrators lies in his openness: he is ready, as none of the others were, to remove all the mystery from his own situation. He tells Elizabeth his life history, conducts her into his most private space—the 'symple hermytage' he occupies (ii. 484)—demonstrates his commitment to an orderly schedule determined by God (he retires to say his 'orysons' at the end of the narrative), and expresses his devotion to the service of the queen. Hemetes is 'symple', but the world he inhabits is not.

The same is true of Gascoigne in the dedication. Much of the epistle is devoted to a commentary on the self-portrait he drew as a frontispiece to the manuscript, which shows him as a soldier kneeling in full armour with a pen behind his ear, a book in one hand, a lance in the other. The portrait provides an answer to the various readings of Gascoigne's character that had been practised by his enemies in the course of his career; an answer which he presumed 'thus rudely to draw in sequens, before the skyllfull eyes of your lerned majestye' after he had reflected on the condition in which he found himself 'my youth myspent, my substaunce ympayred, my credytt accrased

ny tallent hydden, my follyes laughed att, my rewyne unpyttyed, and
ny trewthe unemployed' (ii. 476). Gascoigne's problems, he opines,
ave sprung from what lies concealed beneath the show represented
y the portrait: from the disjunction, that is, between 'seeming' and
being' which he identifies in *The Steele Glas* as endemic in Eliza-
ethan culture.[13] The outward appearance of a man, he explains, is
othing but an elaborate shell, a camouflage that covers up his inward
orruption: 'I coumpt the thoughtes of man to be fowle, how fayr
oever his pretences are/ nott unlike the filthynes of his fleshe and
ntrayles, which are clenly covered with a fyne fyllme of comely sky-
ne' (ii. 475). The heroic figure drawn at the beginning of the manu-
cript is a cover in more senses than one: by opening the manuscript
lizabeth is looking inside Gascoigne's shell, and will find there not
ust the evidence of past wildness—'pryvy thoughts' filled with 'con-
ynuall regreats' (ii. 475)—but also 'tallent hydden' and 'some suffy-
yency to serve' his monarch (ii. 476). Once again his text stands at
crossroads, depicting him 'In dowbtfull doompes, which waye
vere best to take', like the wanderers in Hemetes' narrative, and the
equest he places at the core of the epistle is that the queen 'will
ouchsafe *gracyowsly to looke ynto* your loyall subject' in order to assess
is potential (ii. 477, my emphasis). The request does not imply that
Gascoigne's former life of 'straunge adventure' should be swept
way, but that 'yt deserveth deeply to be considered' in all its 'won-
lerfull varyetie' (ii. 474), and that once it has been examined it will
lemonstrate his fitness for the 'straunge adventure' of the court.

The extent to which his sophisticated erotic follies found a haven in
he court is suggested by one of his last texts, a loose imitation of Pet-
arch's *De Remediis Utriusque Fortunae* called *The Grief of Joye*, which he
ublished in 1577 and 'adventured' (once again) to dedicate to Eliza-
eth (ii. 514). The text takes as its theme the proposition that 'There is
griefe, in everie kind of joye' (ii. 519); its dominant metaphor is that

---

[13] Gascoigne, *Complete Works*, ii. 147–8:

> That age is deade, and vanisht long ago,
> Which thought that steele, both trusty was and true,
> And needed not, a foyle of contraries,
> But shewde al things, even as they were in deede.
> In steade whereof, our curious yeares can finde
> The christal glas, which glimseth brave and bright,
> And shewes the thing, much better than it is,
> Beguylde with foyles, of sundry subtil sights,
> So that they seeme, and covet not to be.

of the 'maze' Gascoigne finds himself in as he contemplates the goo
things and the bad, the 'jollitie' and 'anoye' that have accrued to hir
as a result of his youthful experiences (ii. 518–19). The setting fo
these labyrinthine contemplations is the court. The second of th
four songs in *The Grief of Joye* is effectively an extended love-poem
to all the women in the court, which cheekily returns to the cloud
allusiveness that had got him into trouble with the censors. In plac
of the explanatory marginal gloss which elucidated *The Steele Gla*
and *The Droomme of Doomes Day*, the margin is littered with tantalizin
initials, and one mysterious woman whose initials are withheld i
identified as the subject of all his erotic literary effusions, his 'Frendl
foe' who addresses him as 'Bartholmew' (ii. 530). In Elizabeth's court
the contradictions, the puzzles, the coded exchanges, the adventure
of Gascoigne's unreformed days are as vigorously active as ever; bu
the skills he manifested in recording them have at last acquired at
official function: to express the *legitimate* subtleties of contemporar
sexual politics as they unfold under the watchful eye of the queen.

The *Grief of Joye*, like *Hemetes the Heremyte*, supplies the ending tha
was absent from Gascoigne's unreformed narratives. It does not, how
ever, supply a moral, nor any other kind of closure; the poem stop
abruptly in the middle of a disquisition on horsemanship, with th
explanation that the author will not finish the text unless he has th
queen's approval. Gascoigne ended his career, then, not so mucl
reformed as trusted, not so much tamed as on a leash: operating a
the queen's sharp-eyed poetic informer on the machinations o
the aristocracy. But he left a dangerous legacy to his successors in th
form of Master F.J., the man who never found a stable place in th
public weal, the duplicitous secret agent at the heart of English pros
fiction, who infiltrates the domestic arrangements of the ruling classe
without bothering to ask their permission. *The Adventures of Master F.J*
offers no guarantee that such a man will necessarily reach the saf
haven of official employment as Gascoigne did. And the consequence
of this failure to employ such a shifty double agent, the narrative seem
to warn, could be little less than disastrous for the Elizabethan state.

## 3.  CREEPING INTO HOUSES

*The Adventures of Master F.J.* as it appears in *A Hundreth Sundrie Flowre*
reads like an extended exercise in courting censorship. In *The Posie*

Gascoigne associates the first version of the story with the 'ydle Bookes or wanton Pamphlettes' which were banned by the High Commission (i. 4); and in doing so he seems to imply that the unruly texts of his wilderness years could have the same contaminating influence over their readers as the 'seditious and trayterous Bookes, Billes and Writinges' issued by the Catholic church and denounced in the government proclamations of the early 1570s. And the *Adventures* seems to insist on this association with an almost suicidal perversity. The narrative unfolds in a region of England which the government might have characterized as a seed-bed of sedition: the 'north parts of this realm' where rebellion broke out in 1569, and where devious Catholic dissidents poured 'false rumours and news' into the ears of unsuspecting English subjects.[14] Like the other texts of Gascoigne's wilderness years the *Adventures* sets itself up in opposition to reformation, whether of 'manners' or of religion. It is peppered with allusions to treason, infiltration, espionage, duplicity, and clandestine Catholic practices, and transforms the conventions of Petrarchan poetry into an elaborate code designed to enable clever youngsters of both sexes to hatch secret plots against their elders. In the words of the 'Homily Against Disobedience and Wilful Rebellion', *The Adventures of Master F.J.* describes one of Gascoigne's quick capacities 'creeping... into the houses and whispering in the ears of certain Northern borderers', and in doing so it delivers a veiled warning and an ultimatum to the Elizabethan ruling classes.

The text describes the burgeoning and withering of an affair between a sophisticated young man, F.J., who is a guest in the northern household where the action takes place, and a woman called Elinor. It begins as an extended critical commentary on F.J.'s love poetry, written by an admiring friend of the poet's who signs himself G.T.; but it quickly develops into a full-blown narrative whose length and complexity seem to take G.T. by surprise, as if he had never expected a domestic subject to yield so much material: 'I do dwell over-long in the discourses of this F.J., especially having taken in hand only to copy out his verses' (14). Little by little, as the story unfolds, embarrassing snippets of information fall into the reader's hands as if by accident. A close reading of one of Elinor's letters engenders the suspicion that she has a private secretary, and it soon emerges that he is only the latest in a line of lovers with whom she has long been secretly

---

[14] See Ch. 1, s. 4.

embroiled. Some way into the commentary the narrator happens to mention that Elinor is married; and a few pages later he casually hints that F.J.'s love-life is as changeful as that of his mistress. *The Adventures of Master F.J.* has the dangerous unpredictability of a succession of ambushes, and neither the protagonist nor the narrator seems to know quite what to make of what G.T. calls 'this thriftless history' (80).

The adulterous affair takes place in the house of Elinor's father (another piece of information which is dropped as it were in passing) under the nose of her husband, in violation of the laws of hospitality. Central to the text, then, is the concept of the 'friendly enemy': the trusted wife, guest, servant, or daughter, who occupies the domestic space governed by the male head of a household, and who exploits the intimacy afforded by cohabitation to pursue his or her own private agenda in defiance of the patriarch's authority and without his knowledge. The lovers deploy all their rhetorical resources to cover their tracks, while at the same time the convoluted nature of their strategies means that their coded exchanges are constantly slipping out of their control, constantly betraying them into mutual misunderstandings or accidental self-exposure. Time and again texts 'bewray' their authors —by giving away too much about their illicit lusts, by being intercepted by unwelcome third parties, or by generating confusion through their cunningly contrived obscurity. As the affair unfolds the texts passed between the lovers grow more and more impenetrable: 'I understand not . . . the intent of your letters', Elinor tells F.J. (8), and her letters produce in him 'a confusion to my dull understanding' (10). If at first these protestations seem disingenuous, by the time Elinor consents to sleep with F.J. she has him well and truly baffled, 'as one that could neither conjecture the meaning of her mystical words, nor assuredly trust to the knot of her sliding affections' (28-9). The lovers describe one another's language as 'strange', with all the connotations of 'foreign' that the word brings with it; and this is hardly surprising, since both seem well versed in the French and Italian customs which are the stock-in-trade of adulterers. Like *Beware the Cat*, *The Adventures of Master F.J.* explores a situation where friends are always recasting themselves as enemies and where the familiar is always being reconstituted as the exotic, and like Baldwin's fable it might best be described as a spy-story in a domestic setting.

Words are the ultimate 'friendly enemy' in G.T.'s narrative. They are two-edged swords of the kind Gascoigne warns his readers to flourishe wisely' in *The Posies* (i. 14): like swords they can inflict damage when they need to, and like swords they can be used either in attack or in defence. The association of words with weapons was a popular one with Elizabethan authors. In *Hemetes the Heremyte* Gascoigne uses it to express his ambition to serve the queen as effectively on paper as in action, depicting himself equipped 'with penn to fighte, and sworde to wryte a letter' (ii. 473), while in *The Schoole of Abuse* Gosson punningly connects the word with the sword to reinforce his conviction that printed texts should work at all times in collaboration with the system of state censorship (109). But in *The Adventures of Master F.J.*, as in *The Posies*, the anagrammatic association of words with the sword demonstrates above all the potential treachery involved in the cunning deployment of rhetoric. At the moment when the adulterous affair is consummated, Gascoigne introduces a sword into the narrative, a duplicitous weapon that summarizes the difficulty of sorting friends from foes in the intricate verbal environment the lovers have constructed. Meeting with Elinor in a gallery at midnight, F.J. terrifies her by bringing his sword along with him, and she at once reads his weapon as a sign that he plans to assault her. F.J. hastens to reassure her that he has brought his sword 'for their defence and not to offend her in any wise' (30); but only a slight syllabic alteration can change defence into offence, as he soon discovers to his cost. Next morning the sword is stolen from his chamber by a witness of their midnight meeting, and thus becomes the potential cause of 'offence' against the lovers, a silent testimonial to their treachery. Later in the narrative, when the lovers lose the last traces of their trust in one another, their friendship breaks down into just the kind of hostility Elinor had anticipated. The 'fair words' with which F.J. tries to heal the rift convert themselves in the space of a paragraph into a savage, phallic sword-thrust: 'he drew upon his new-professed enemy and bare her up with such a violence against the bolster that, before she could prepare the ward, he thrust her through both hands and etc.' (61). At this point the rules of the game of verbal fencing give way to the lawlessness of physical conquest, and the 'rapier' (another name Gascoigne gives to F.J.'s sword, 34) fulfils its potential as an accomplice to rape. In the context of the *Adventures*, words, phrases, tokens of friendship, and the actions they accompany, can reverse themselves at a moment's notice, just as the two elements in the phrase 'friendly enemy' can acquire a different weighting under different circumstances, or a sword can be drawn in sport or in anger.

The fact that *The Adventures of Master F.J.* is available in print is the effect of another act of friendly enmity, this time committed by the gentleman H.W. against his 'familiar friend' G.T. (3). In his letter to the reader at the beginning of the second part of *A Hundreth Sundrie Flowres*, H.W. explains that G.T. lent him the manuscript on condition that the 'original copy' be returned when he had finished with it, a request with which he has happily complied. But in eliciting this promise G.T. has forgotten that, with the advent of the printing press, the original copy has lost its uniqueness, and that the return of a manuscript is no guarantee that it will not continue to circulate beyond the confines of the privileged circle to which its author chooses to show it. In the age of print the Petrarchan love-poem has ceased to be an intimate textual container for the sexual indiscretions of the ruling classes, shown to a select audience as a token of friendship.[15] Instead it is in danger as never before of escaping from its confinement and entering the public domain.

This danger is brilliantly evoked in the middle of the narrative. Soon after the affair's consummation, G.T. transcribes one of F.J.'s poems called 'Beauty shut up thy shop' (38), in which the triumphant lover claims that his mistress has cornered the market in the best of Beauty's wares and that she has left nothing to her rivals but cosmetics. But G.T.'s commentary on these verses suggests that their celebration of Elinor's singularity has become common property since its composition, in more ways than one. First of all, he explains, Elinor has made sure that this and other poems by F.J. have 'come to view of the world, although altogether without his consent' (39). Secondly, it is by no means certain that the poem is about Elinor, since it addresses a woman called Helen, and G.T. thinks he knows who she is. And thirdly, G.T. points out that a single love-poem can be adapted to a diversity of contexts: 'marry peradventure if there were any acquaintance between F.J. and that Helen afterwards, the which I dare not confess, he might adapt it to her name, and so make it serve both their turns, as elder lovers have done before and still do and will do world without end Amen' (39). In this way the claims to exclusivity and authenticity mounted by Petrarchan love poetry are exposed as an elaborate sham. Instead G.T. implies that any modern love-poem

---

[15]  For a discussion of the guarded 'publication' of love poetry 'between intimates in private rooms', and of H.W.'s violation of this intimacy, see Patricia Fumerton, ' "Secret" Arts: Elizabethan Miniatures and Sonnets', in Stephen Greenblatt (ed.), *Representing the English Renaissance* (Berkeley, Ca: University of California Press, 1988), 93–133.

makes 'common' the spaces which the aristocracy and the gentry have hitherto regarded as their private preserve. He explains this process in another revealing passage a few pages later. One of the greatest pleasures experienced by an illicit male lover, he explains, springs from the 'secret intercommoning of joys' in verse (41). At the same time the act of making his happiness 'common'—to however limited an audience—inaugurates a process that eventually wipes out all his proprietorial pleasure in the affair. 'I have always been of this opinion,' he explains:

that as to be fortunate in love is one of the most inward contentations to man's mind of all earthly joys, even so if he do but once bewray the same to any living creature immediately either dread of discovering doth bruise his breast with an intolerable burden, or else he leeseth the principal virtue which gave effect to his gladness, not unlike to a 'pothecary's pot which being filled with sweet ointments or perfumes doth retain in itself some scent of the same, and being poured out doth return to the former state, hard, harsh, and of small savour, so the mind being fraught with delights, as long as it can keep them secretly enclosed, may continually feed upon the pleasant record thereof . . . but having once disclosed them to any other, straightway we lose the hidden treasure of the same, and are oppressed with sundry doubtful opinions and dreadful conceits. (41)

The whole of *The Adventures of Master F.J.* is just such a spilled jar, pouring out the 'hidden treasure' of aristocratic intrigue to satisfy the curious noses of its readership, and so depriving it of the value it derives from being kept private, from enclosure. This process is enacted in the shift of emphasis from verse to prose; as the narrative unfolds the proportion of prose to verse increases with alarming rapidity, like a pool of ointment spreading after it has escaped from its metrical container. And as the private enclosure of verse breaks down, so the exclusivity of aristocratic ownership comes under threat. Elinor's sister, Dame Frances, describes her as a 'commodious common' which has been grazed by a variety of gentlemen, and announces her own intention to conduct an experiment to see if F.J.'s 'enclosure thereof might be defensible against her said secretary' (26). All F.J.'s efforts at enclosure fail, and it is a secretary, the humble wielder of the pens and pencils that make and break property deals, who helps to engineer its failure.

At the same time the reader is constantly being reminded of H.W.'s act of treason in letting the story spread still further by releasing it to the press. G.T. interjects occasional asides to the specific reader he imagines to be scanning his manuscript—'I think you have not read... Ariosto', he tells H.W. as he prepares to narrate the fable of Suspicion (47), and at the moment when he describes the sexual act between the adulterers he breaks off to remark, 'Were it not that I know to whom I write, I would the more beware what I write' (30). These asides implicate the rest of his readers in F.J.'s criminal act of trespassing on the domestic property of his host. But G.T., H.W., and the general reader are not the only eavesdroppers on F.J.'s purportedly clandestine affair. Nearly all his communications are overseen or overheard, and the reader is kept guessing as to who may or may not have access to his letters, poems, and conversations. At the beginning of the narrative, F.J.'s first letter to Elinor turns out to have been read by Elinor's current lover, an ugly and untalented secretary. At the end, a story is told in which a housemaid spies on a pair of adulterers through a keyhole. In the meantime the house inhabited by F.J. and Elinor seems to be riddled with chinks and crannies through which observers—both masters and servants— can study the secret activities of its inmates. Under these circumstances the paranoia of the illicit lover who commits his thoughts to the 'blabbing leaves of bewraying paper' (11) proves justified, and, more seriously, the anxiety of the censors about the text's capacity to disseminate 'false rumours and news' turns out to be well founded.

The sharpest observer in the book is Elinor's sister Frances, who sees through the coded messages exchanged by the lovers with unnerving ease. When she tells F.J. about her suspicions, he is quick to protest that she must have misunderstood a conversation she has overheard by chance: 'Fair lady... you either mistook me or overheard me then', he insists, and assures her that 'I cannot love, and I dare not hate' (18). But later it emerges that F.J.'s protestation that he 'cannot love' was itself overheard by his mistress as she stood in the 'portal of her chamber' (26), and was taken by her as evidence that he has been lying to her from the start. Meanwhile Dame Frances continues to spy on F.J., watching him as he returns across a 'large base court' from his assignation with Elinor (31). She does so, G.T. explains, because she is 'no less desirous to see an *issue* of these enterprises than F.J. was willing to cover them in secrecy' (31, my emphasis). Texts, speeches, and buildings are full of 'issues', exits and entrances through which secrets and rash words are always escaping; and the more elaborate the security systems adopted by intriguers to protect themselves from prying eyes, the more vulnerable they make themselves to equally ingenious strategies of penetration and discovery.

Even when the penetration of a security system by outsiders seems impossible, the tightest of such systems has already been breached by the paranoid fantasies of the people it is designed to protect. G.T. makes this point in the fable of Suspicion, which he tells about half-way through his narrative, at the moment when F.J. succumbs to para-noid fantasies about Elinor and her former lover.[16] In Ariosto's fable, Suspicion inhabits the most elaborately defended of all households, a labyrinthine seaside rock with only one 'issue'; yet the miserable householder passes his days in abject terror that this fortress will be found and invaded by his former wife, the woman who lived with him in a previous existence and who became so frustrated with his irrational fears that she stabbed him to death with a knife. As a precau-tion against another such misfortune, Suspicion surrounds himself with the protective paraphernalia of a head of state—bulwarks, guards, and innumerable suits of armour—and stuffs his bed with porcupine's quills to keep himself awake. He emerges only after dark when the rest of the world is asleep, at which time 'with stealing steps he stalketh about the earth, infecting, tormenting, and vexing all kinds of people with some part of his afflictions, but especially such as either do sit in the chair of greatest dignity and estimation, or else such as have achieved some dear and rare emprise' (50). The passage is one of sev-eral in the course of the *Adventures* that draw a parallel between the situation of the householder or lover who fears betrayal by his 'friendly enemy' and that of the frightened monarch who suspects his closest advisers. The fable of Suspicion could also be read as Gas-coigne's impudent comment on the paranoia of the Elizabethan advo-cates of state censorship. Such 'grave judgementes', as he calls them in *The Posies* (i. 3), aim to fortify the world of the printed text against infiltration by corrupt foreign influences; but in doing so they could be said to 'infect' the texts they scrutinize with the very corruptions they condemn. Suspicion's irrational terror of his former wife pene-trates his defences more efficiently than any spy could have done; and the fable of Suspicion itself resembles a foreign infiltrator at the heart of Gascoigne's history. The fable is the only text in *The Adven-tures of Master F.J.* that has no audience within the narrative: G.T. tells

---

[16] The fable comes from Ariosto's *Orlando Furioso*, canto 2. See Prouty, *George Gascoigne*, 210 n.

it for the benefit of his friend H.W., and F.J. never reads it.[17] This translation from the Italian might almost have crept into G.T.'s history as a cheeky response to the anxieties voiced by Ascham about the insidious effects of translations from the Italian. It implies that such suspicions are self-fulfilling, and that readers like Ascham will always engender what they dread.

The presence of Suspicion at the centre of the *Adventures* might well have been inferred from the history that precedes it. Suspicion resembles the 'ugly hellish monster' secreted at the heart of a Cretan labyrinth (46), and as it advances *The Adventures of Master F.J.* becomes increasingly labyrinthine. F.J. draws attention to the tortuous development of his affair in his second letter to Elinor, where he compares their correspondence to an 'endless labyrinth' which baffles all his efforts to chart its involutions (10). The twisting of a maze is mimicked in the disjunction between the different acts of reading that take place in the course of the history. The reader gains access to F.J.'s letters and poems in a different order from the one in which Elinor reads them: G.T. presents us with F.J.'s texts in the supposed order of their composition, but the difficulty of smuggling these jottings to Elinor means that she frequently does not receive them until several pages after their first appearance, and indeed one poem never reaches her at all (24). Readers who want to remind themselves of the verses to which Elinor responds are continually forced to disrupt the linear progress of the narrative by turning back to the place where these verses are printed out in full. The effect, of course, is to challenge the insistence by authoritarian writers like North, Fenton, and Golding that there is only one 'correct' order in which to read a text, that a narrative has an architectural rigidity which a reader must not presume to violate, and that one of the functions of a responsible book is to regulate the leisure time of the reader by imitating the disciplined schedule of a well-organized day. G.T. stresses the informality of his narrative both by insisting on the selective nature of the act of reading (with reference to a particularly seedy sonnet he recommends that 'he that liketh it not turn over the leaf to another', 43) and by the emphasis he lays on the role of 'opportunity' or 'occasion'

---

[17] Earlier in the narrative we are told that one of F.J.'s poems, 'A cloud of care hath covered all my coast', was never given to Elinor because 'F.J. himself had so slender liking thereof' (23–4), and we never hear whether he presented her with the famous lyric 'And if I did what then?' (79); but in both cases we can presume that F.J. read through his poems at least once after he had written them.

in bringing the protagonist's plots to fruition. F.J. and Elinor both agree that they met by 'hap', although they are less certain as to whether it was 'good hap' or 'mishap' that brought them together (6, 10). Soon after their meeting Elinor 'took occasion' to dance with F.J. (7); F.J. next bewailed his 'lack of opportunity' to converse with her (11), and then 'took occasion' to do so by entering her room to heal her of a nosebleed (13); later he 'found opportunity' to lose a sonnet sequence 'near to his desired mistress' (14), and later still when Elinor's secretary left her it was 'an opportunity of good advantage' to her hopeful new lover (15). In other words, their affair consists of a series of rapidly improvised responses to unexpected contingencies, and as such it constitutes by far the most exuberant of Gascoigne's celebrations of the extemporary skills fostered by a 'quick capacity'.

By disrupting the linearity of conventional narrative time *The Adventures of Master F.J.* suggests that time itself is a flexible commodity, one that can be put to different uses by different subjects. Being denizens of the night, the clandestine lovers take advantage of the temporal as well as the physical spaces that have been left vacant by the other occupants of the household, and signal their increasing disdain for their public duties by taking to their beds during daylight hours and by wearing their night-clothes at the dinner-table. The 'occasions' for their meetings occur in the intervals between one household activity and the next, so that when F.J. chooses to dine with Elinor in her chamber he must send 'a *supersedias* ... into the great chamber unto the lord of the house' to excuse his absence (28). The sense given by the narrative that its subjects operate according to different time-scales is wittily expressed by Elinor's confidante Dame Pergo, who tells a story in which two lovers find themselves embarrassingly incapable of synchronizing their desire for one another. The story describes how a knight fell in love with Pergo in her youth and loved her for seven years without getting anything in return; and how after the knight's desire had at last changed to hatred Pergo found that she loved him after all, and loved him unrequited for a further seven years before losing interest in her turn. She ends by asking F.J. to judge which of the two lovers suffered most from this failure to reach an agreement. Without an answer to this question, she tells him, there can be no reconciliation between them, and no possibility that their relationship can end in marriage. Predictably, F.J. gives judgement in favour of the knight, telling Pergo that the chief fault was hers for failing to seize the 'occasion' for marriage

when it presented itself (58); but his partisan response is hardly calculated to reconcile the lovers' differences and restore them to the status
of productive members of the public weal. Pergo's tale unfolds the
potentially disastrous consequences of the 'varietie of judgements'
which Castiglione explored in *The Courtier* where men and women,
the old and the young, cannot reconcile their assessments of contemporary trends, and where the possibility of reaching a consensus on
any issue is always receding into an imaginary past. In the *Adventures*
this diversity of opinions has degenerated into open warfare between
men and women, between public duty and private desire, between
one subject's deployment of their time and another's; and the narrative
gives little indication that these disputes can end in a peaceful settle-
ment. At the end of the text F.J. composes a poem in which he complains that Elinor is passing her time in dalliance with her newly
favoured secretary while F.J. kicks his heels in frustrated unemployment. But he predicts that a time will come when their roles will be
reversed and when she will find herself unemployed in her turn: that
'tides of turning time' will put an end to her erotic fishing for new
lovers, and that 'Then will I laugh and clap my hands, | As they do
now at me' (79). Like Pergo, F.J. sees history as a succession of sudden
reversals in which competing private interests gain the ascendancy by
turns, and where the possibility of compromise is subordinated to the
desire to get the upper hand. This ruthlessly competitive environment
is what prompts G.T. to describe the *Adventures* as a 'thriftless history',
a narrative whose resistance to the temporal, rhetorical, and legislative
conventions by which a state organizes itself renders it useless to the
public weal—disorderly, and therefore politically as well as poetically
disruptive.

## 4.   LOOKING FOR AN ISSUE

The artful disorder of *The Adventures of Master F.J.* conceals a bipartite
structure of surprising neatness. The story of the monster Suspicion is
told at the highest point in F.J.'s fortunes, after he has composed a
sequence of triumphal verses in which he celebrates his acquisition
of Elinor and the illusion of control that this victory brings with it.
Some pages beforehand, Dame Frances has supplied him with information to suggest that Elinor is in fact controlled by nobody but herself—'she seemed to accuse Dame Elinor for the most unconstant

woman living' (26)—and it is just when F.J. thinks himself finally to have mastered his mistress that this information begins to sap his confidence. G.T. announces the fact in terms that recall the ancient metaphor of the wheel of Fortune: 'And here I will surcease to rehearse any more of his verses until I have expressed how that his joys, being now exalted to the highest degree, began to bend towards declination' (43). Abruptly an organizing power seems to exert itself over the text, a power which is inscrutable to its protagonist, and which is associated with traditional representations of divine intervention in human affairs as exemplified in the fall of great men.[18] At this point the neatness of the narrative's structure begins to make itself apparent. After the fable has been told, the events of the first half begin all over again, but this time in reverse, and with Elinor, not F.J., acting as the devious master of ceremonies. In the first half F.J. had worked to establish the rules of their game of adultery: he showered Elinor with secret letters, entered her chamber under the pretence of curing her nosebleed, developed his courtship in a parlour game, overcame a temporary access of jealousy on her part, and finally consummated the affair on the bare boards of a gallery. But after he has celebrated this consummation in verse the sequence of events starts to run backwards. F.J. succumbs to suspicion as Elinor did earlier; he then presides over a second parlour game as Elinor presided over the first—but F.J. finds that the rules have changed, and that where Elinor was elected 'queen' of the assembly on the first occasion, on the second F.J. is merely elected 'governor', with a duty to answer questions, not to ask them. Soon afterwards Elinor enters his chamber to cure him of his jealousy as he cured her of her nosebleed—but what begins as a reversed courtship, with the woman wooing the man, ends as a rape, with F.J. violently struggling to regain possession of Elinor's body and mind. His struggle fails, and the episode is succeeded by the call of a cuckoo mocking his cuckoldry as he had earlier mocked the husband's. Finally the narrative peters out in a series of ironic reworkings of F.J.'s adventures in prose and verse. There is no conclusion, no moral, no 'issue' from the labyrinth in which the lovers have involved themselves: the history of Master F.J. remains 'unperfect' (80), its ending marked

---

[18] See *The Mirror for Magistrates*, ed. Campbell:

Loe here (quoth Sorowe) Prynces of renowne,
That whilome sat on top of Fortunes wheele
Nowe layed ful lowe, like wretches whurled downe,
Even with one frowne, that stayed but with a smyle. (316)

only by a few bitter verses which acknowledge that its protagonist remains as baffled by his adventures as he was at the beginning.

But readers of the *Adventures* might be less inclined than G.T. to abandon hope that there might be a way out of the perplexities charted by the narrative. Throughout its length the history seems to insist that there could be another outcome to the tangled web of events it describes; an emergence, that is, from the darkness of secrecy and confusion into the light of official employment. The possibility of this alternative 'issue' is hinted at in the many allusions to darkness and light that accompany the twists in F.J.'s fortunes. The courtship of F.J. and Elinor resembles the bewildering interplay of torches and shadows in the rooms and corridors of an Elizabethan mansion, where the sudden flaring of a light serves only to dazzle the unwary passer-by. In F.J.'s first letter to Elinor he tells her that meeting her in the North Country is like coming across fire in the middle of an icy waste; and he quickly moves from this imagined collision between heat and cold to a startling encounter between darkness and light. Elinor is a 'blazing star' with the power 'to dim my dazzled eyes', he announces in his first poem (8), and in his second he compares himself to a moth that is suicidally attracted to the flame of a candle (11–12). Soon afterwards Elinor bursts into flame in her turn ('The flames began to break out on every side', 12), while F.J. continues to explore the dazzling interplay of darkness and light in successive verses—from the poem 'In prime of lusty years' (21–2) where he describes his own sexual incandescence and the searing brightness of Elinor's eyes, to the mournful stanzas where he compares her jealousy to a sudden onset of gloom, 'A cloud of care hath covered all my coast' (23–4). All of F.J.'s encounters with Elinor take place in semi-darkness, either in the torchlit evening or by moonlight, or 'in the grey morning' half-way between night and day (10, 78), and all of these encounters leave him blinded. As he expresses it in his second poem:

> I must confess these dazzled eyes of mine
> Did wink for fear when I first viewed thy face.
> But bold desire did open them again
> And bade me look, till I had looked too long

> (12)

Elinor, on the other hand, never quite loses control of her senses. As G.T. puts it, she remains 'one that could discern the sun before her chamber windows were wide open' (10); for all her protests about

he 'darkness' of F.J.'s erotic language (9), she seems completely at
ome in the confusing domestic twilight she inhabits. F.J.'s poem 'A
Moonshine Banquet' (32–3) sums up his perception of their respective
ositions. In it, Elinor plays the part of a kind of alternative moon-
goddess, a producer of potent reflected rays who borrows her light
oth from the moon—who 'shamed to shine where she her beams
lisplays'—and from the sun—who becomes jealous of her blazing
eauty and maliciously invests her eyes with his own scorching heat.
Her ability to scorch gives rise to the rumour that she loves to torture
nen, and it needs all F.J.'s 'deep foresight' to 'espy' that this is malicious slander, a calumny devised by the sun in revenge for her rivalry
of his powers ('But I with deep foresight did soon espy | How Phoe-
us meant, | By false intent, | To slander so her name with cruelty').
Nevertheless, readers who have examined F.J.'s earlier accounts of his
own torments and bedazzlement might conclude that his 'foresight' is
tself a form of blindness, a clever conceit which enables him to dismiss
rom his mind Elinor's association in his own verses with 'shame',
deceit', 'error', and 'treason'. For all its evocations of different sources
of light, the poem 'A Moonshine Banquet' exposes the fact that F.J.
nd Elinor consummated their affair in total darkness, so that F.J.'s
efforts to represent himself as a clever spy who employs his piercing
vision in the service of his secret 'queen' only add to the evidence
of his myopia in the world of domestic politics.

  Elinor's chief rival in her capacity as the queen of erotic fire and
lomestic twilight is Dame Frances, F.J.'s kinswoman who is also the
laughter of the lord of the household. In contrast to Elinor, Frances
occupies the sunlit space of the park adjoining the mansion. It is
nere that she meets F.J. when he is out looking in vain 'for the coming
of his mistress into her appointed walk' (24), and here that she explains
s Elinor never does the significance of the baffling hints she has
lropped in the confusion of the house's interior. It is from the park
hat she returns, after taking 'the fresh air of the morning' (31), to
teal F.J.'s sword from his bedchamber and so demonstrate her awareness of his clandestine activities. And it is in the park that she walks
with Elinor's confidante, Dame Pergo, to hear the calling of the
cuckoo and to let her know that she has 'espied' the fact that Elinor
s 'cuckolding' F.J. (63). If Elinor is the undisputed mistress of the
nansion, who knows 'all privy ways of that house very perfectly'
nd who can convey herself into any of its chambers 'unseen and un-
erceived' (59), Frances is the mistress of the open air, the discoverer

of secrets who none the less refrains from exposing them, the un-
masker of acts of treason who devises ingenious counter-plots to
defray their potentially calamitous results. As the champion of light
and air she offers an alternative course of action to F.J., an issue
from the verbal obscurity into which his sexual secrets have plunged
him. When she first meets him in the park she attempts to reach an
agreement with him which is the precise antithesis of the ambivalent
contract he is in the process of forging with Elinor: an agreement
founded on kinship and on 'friendly meaning', where mutual confidence may be taken on trust 'without adventure' and where plainness
takes the place of obfuscation (25). She attempts, in fact, to restore
consensual simplicity to F.J.'s discourse, and F.J. signals his recognition
of this attempt by swearing 'by this sun' that he will honour his obligations to her. At the same time G.T. is eager to insist that Frances'
respect for simplicity has nothing to do with naïvety, the dull 'simplicity' which Elinor mocks in her last letter to her discarded lover (76)
She is a more accomplished spy than either F.J. or Elinor; she possesses
a 'singular capacity' (27) which enables her to participate in the lovers'
word-games and even to conduct an 'experiment' upon them (20, 26)
and she is the informer who finally furnishes F.J. with ocular proof that
Elinor has renewed her relations with her secretary. The darkest point
in F.J.'s adventures follows his descent into the gloom which surrounds Suspicion, who lives in a hole 'so dark and obscure as scarcely
either sun or air could enter into it' (47). To escape from this obscurity
F.J. has only to fulfil the terms of the contract he drew up with Frances
in the grounds of the mansion, where she designated herself his
'Hope' and gave him the title of her 'Trust' (26), and so pitted her
own 'friendly meaning' against the double meanings engendered by
his relationship with his 'friendly enemy' Elinor. But Frances's hopes
of restoring F.J. to simplicity are dashed almost as soon as she has
voiced them, when F.J. accidentally informs her of his conviction
that the term 'trust' itself is subject to suspicion and that 'in *Trust* is
treason' (27).

The rival contracts drawn up with F.J. by Elinor and Frances are
only the most prominent strands in a matted web of rival contracts
woven and unwoven in the course of the narrative. Each of these contracts exists in constant competition with the rest, and all of them are
eventually broken. Private agreements threaten to supplant public
obligations: Elinor's marriage vow clashes with her clandestine agreement with F.J., and their secret contract assumes the status of a public

ommitment when challenged by the still more secret pact she has
made with her secretary. Similarly F.J.'s public obligation to his host
s threatened by his private covenant with Elinor, which then threa-
ens to destroy his more formal agreement with Dame Frances. In
ddition to these major contracts, the inhabitants of the household
ome together in the evenings to play parlour games which involve
urther temporary agreements, additional rearrangements of the shift-
ng system of duties and promises that governs the structure of Gas-
oigne's labyrinth. In each case, the honouring of one contract
necessitates the breach of another, and faithfulness to one friend provokes the enmity of many. Rivalry between competing agreements
rupts before the narrative has even begun, when H.W. breaks his
promise to the narrator G.T., in order, as he claims, to fulfil his duty
o the public: 'as one that thought it better to please a number by
ommon commodity than to feed the humour of any private person
by needless singularity' (3). He then informs his readers that they
oo are involved in the competition between contracts, since only
heir approval of the text can preserve his alliance with the friends
he has betrayed: 'if it fall out, contrary to expectation, that the readers'
udgements agree not with mine opinion in their commendations, I
may then—unless their courtesy supply my want of discretion—
with loss of some labour accompt also the loss of my familiar friends'
3–4). In this way he plunges his audience into an environment which
ecalls the court of Urbino in the sheer 'varietie of judgements' it can
ccommodate, and in the dizzying diversity of contractual obligations
which these judgements can entail. Unlike the court of Urbino, however, the household in the *Adventures* contains no moderating figure
by whom the diversity of opinions can finally be arbitrated. In the
nd, it is for the reader alone to decide whether there is any possibility
of restoring the complex tangle of duties and promises to some kind of
onsensus.

G.T. is constantly reminding his readers of their status as arbitrators
by deferring to their critical judgement each time he hazards an opinion of F.J.'s verses. 'These verses are more in number than do stand
with contentation of some judgements' (23), he confesses after copy-
ng out one of F.J.'s lyrics; 'This ballad, or howsoever I shall term it,
percase you will not like' (33); and, later, 'It will please none but
earned ears . . . So I leave it to your judgement' (52). Meanwhile,
he process of arbitration moves from the periphery to the centre of
he narrative. In the second half of the *Adventures* two 'notable

histories' are told (73), one by Dame Pergo, one by Dame Frances
and in each case F.J. is forced to take on the role of moderator or
judge of the dilemma posed by each story—the role taken by the
High Commission with regard to Gascoigne's text. By acting as moderator F.J. is made to reconsider the code of values by which he judges
texts—whether spoken or written—and to articulate for the first time
the process by which he reaches his verdict. As he does so, the reader
too are encouraged to scrutinize their position as arbitrators.
Throughout the narrative the grounds on which the reading public
makes its critical judgements are as uncertain as G.T.'s reactions to
F.J.'s verses. On the one hand G.T. expects his reader H.W. to concur
with his view that 'good letters' ought to include 'wholesome lessons
tending to the reformation of manners' (4). In saying so he aligns himself with conservative moralists like Golding and North, whose views
he parrots in a hackneyed sentence: 'For who doubteth but that poets
in their most feigned fables and imaginations have metaphorically set
forth unto us the right rewards of virtues and the due punishments for
vices?' (4). On the other hand, G.T. and H.W. expect their readers to
take pleasure in the sophisticated inventiveness of the poems they present them with: H.W. considers the gentlemen who have contributed
poems to G.T.'s volume 'right commendable for their capacity' (3)
and G.T. asseverates that 'I found none of them so barren but that
in my judgement, had in it *aliquid salis*' (6). The two editors, then
expect reactions to the volume to be divided between admiration
for its wayward inventiveness and awareness of its serious moral function. H.W. combines the two reactions in his description of the 'commodity' he has reaped from reading the text, which was 'to sit and
smile at the fond devices of such as have enchained themselves in
the golden fetters of fantasy, and having bewrayed themselves to the
whole world do yet conjecture that they walk unseen in a net' (3).
The sentence implies that sophisticated readers are capable of remaining serenely detached from the 'trifling fantasies, humoral passions and
strange affects' they enjoy, so that not only will they derive amuse-
ment from the text, but their recognition of its moral failings will
prove that their 'capacities' are quicker than the poets'. Such readers
that is, can take their place as useful members of the public weal not
just in spite of but *because of* their appreciation for Italianate subtlety.

Nevertheless the sophisticated readers addressed by H.W. remain
morally suspect, since they are willing to collude with his treachery
in order to obtain the imaginative commodities they covet. The diffi-

ulty of reconciling delight in wit with moral probity is implicit in
G.T.'s use of the term *aliquid salis* to convey the quality of F.J.'s
poems. The phrase conjures up a radically different critical perspective
from the moralistic one defended by Golding and North; a new per-
pective which Gascoigne articulates in his pioneering treatise on pro-
ody, 'Certayne notes of Instruction concerning the making of verse
or ryme in English'.[19] The readers and would-be poets Gascoigne
addresses in this treatise are fashionable devotees of the 'crystal glasse':
narcissistic poseurs who take a positive delight in the disparity
between the representation of a thing and the thing itself. For such
reader–poets, poetry has lost its function as a vehicle for religious
and philosophical knowledge; instead it has become at once a form
of self-advertisement and a form of camouflage, a flamboyant demonstration of their rhetorical skills and a means of deflecting attention
from their private agenda. To fulfil these functions a poem needs to
contain *aliquid salis*, that is, 'some good and fine devise, shewing the
quicke capacitie of a writer' (i. 465). These devices are disconcertingly
similar to those used by adulterers to conceal their clandestine activ-
ties. The poet is to avoid hackneyed comparisons such as allusions
to crystal eyes and cherry lips, 'For these things,' Gascoigne explains,
are *trita et obvia*'. Instead, he goes on:

would either finde some supernaturall cause wherby my penne might walke
in the superlative degree, or els I would undertake to aunswere for any imper-
ection that shee hath, and thereupon rayse the prayse of hir commendacion.
Likewise if I should disclose my pretence in love, I would eyther make a
straunge discourse of some intollerable passion, or finde occasion to pleade
by the example of some historie, or discover my disquiet in shadowes *per Alle-
oriam*, or use the covertest meane that I could to avoyde the uncomely cus-
omes of common writers. (i. 466)

In avoiding the trite and obvious Gascoigne's fashionable poet stands
in imminent danger of avoiding the honest and safe. He values the
straunge' above the familiar and loves to show off both his respons-
veness to contingent 'occasions' and his mastery of the art of using
shadowes' to cover his tracks. Such skills lift him above the run of
common writers', but at the same time they risk placing him beyond
the pale of ideological as well as stylistic convention. Gascoigne's pro-
osal that the male poet should use his lover's 'imperfections' as the
asis for flattery draws attention to this danger, and it is one that F.J.

[19] Appended to *The Posies* of 1575: i. 465–73.

and Elinor are forever running into. Their affair, which is based in par on their admiration for one another's evasive linguistic manœuvres, i fundamentally hostile to the plain language that permits the formula tion of legal agreements. When F.J. first suspects that Elinor's letter have been penned by her secretary his response is not to denounc her indirectness but to embrace it: 'these your letters', he tells her 'frame in me an admiration of such divine esprit' (10), and the sen tence seems to encapsulate his erotic attraction to deviousness an infidelity as well as to clever writing. He grounds, in fact, his 'prays of hir commendacion' on her 'imperfection'. From this point or even the plainest declarations of mutual attraction between the lover couch themselves in the 'straunge discourse' they have adopted a their private code, so that their very misunderstandings are an integr part of the understanding they have reached with one another. Whe Elinor resolves to resort to 'flat plain dealing' and to declare her attrac tion to F.J. in unequivocal terms, the best she can do is to tell him: ' swear unto you here by my father's soul, that my mother's younges daughter doth love your father's eldest son above any creature living (28); the contorted sentence articulates her desire in terms that reca the familial obligations that are being violated by her adultery. It i only when they succeed in speaking plainly that the lovers lose thei peculiar private understanding. In the first half it is when F.J announces plainly that he cannot love that Elinor falls out with him and it is when Frances tells F.J. the plain facts about Elinor's promiscu ity that F.J. falls out with his mistress. On the one occasion in the sec ond half when F.J. gives Elinor access to 'the certainty of his thoughts and 'plainly expressed with whom, of whom, by whom, and to whom she bent her better liking' (61), their friendly agreement is abruptl terminated. Their relationship, then, relies not on simplicity but or its antithesis, fraud. For Elyot, fraud was 'an evil deceit, craftily ima gined and devised, which under a colour of truth and simplicity enda mageth him that nothing mistrusteth' (*Governor*, 169); an act o sabotage, a virus that threatens to unknit the network of agreement that binds together the fabric of the public weal; and Gascoigne's read ers might implicate themselves in this process if they allowed thei admiration for the subtleties of wit to blind them to its consequences

One way in which Gascoigne's readers can retain their standing a good citizens is by acting as spies, informers, cunning sifters of th secrets of the narrative's protagonists. By this means they can restor some kind of simplicity to Gascoigne's text, and justify G.T.'s com

lent at the end, where he tells H.W. (and by implication the eaves-
ropping public) that 'you will easily understand my meaning'. G.T.
leans that his readers will easily recognize and forgive the 'petty trea-
on' he has committed in 'using sundry names for one person, as "the
)ame", "the Lady", "Mistress" and etc., "the lord of the castle", "the
laster of the house", and "the host"' (80); he implies that this loose
sage of honorifics is no more than a minor breach of decorum. But
)etty treason' had much more serious implications than G.T. seems to
iggest. The phrase was a legal term for a crime that was only a step
elow high treason: the murder of a subject by one of his or her
ibordinates or dependents; so that Gascoigne's narrator would seem
> be accusing himself, however mockingly, of conspiring with F.J. to
estroy the reputation and perhaps even the feudal status of an English
oble family. And this is not the only 'meaning' Gascoigne's narrator
xpects H.W. to 'understand'. An alert reader will have detected
everal acts of treachery in the course of the *Adventures*: an inclination
> celebrate subtlety at the expense of simplicity, for instance—that is,
> undermine the grounds on which meaning may be easily under-
:ood; a willingness, too, to divulge the tricks of the adulterer's trade
nd to publicize the sexual secrets of noble households; and a tendency
> transgress the narrative conventions favoured by the moralists, such
s a straightforward style, an orderly disposition of the text, an
xplanatory gloss on the less accessible passages, and a plain moral con-
lusion. And alongside all these petty treasons such a reader might
ave detected a betrayal which is not so petty: F.J. and Elinor's sly
itroduction of Catholic customs and values into a Protestant English
ousehold. The lovers' subtlety has what Ascham might have regarded
s a distinctly Catholic flavour. Both of them look towards the Catho-
c countries of Europe for activities with which to fill their leisure
me: F.J. translates sonnets and stanzas from the Italian, cultivates
ie 'French manner of dancing' and sings *alla napolitana* (21), while
linor writes (through her secretary) in a Roman hand (8), kisses in
panish (11), favours fashions from Piedmont (34), and cultivates
:alian habits (16). Both lovers communicate with one another
irough cyphered speech and 'mystical words', whose obscurity
latches the perceived impenetrability of Catholic doctrines and litur-
ical practices. F.J. woos Elinor under the guise of curing her nose-
leed by a prayer or charm of the kind that Catholic priests were
ipposed to dispense; and both lovers fashion images or idols of
leir secret bedfellows: F.J. dances 'with the image of St. Frances in

his hand, and St. Elinor in his heart' (19) and constructs an 'idol' o
Elinor 'in his inward conceit' (37), while Elinor uses the secretary a
her 'holiest idol' (26). Elinor shares with Catholic priests a fondnes
for fine linen and sprinkled water, and when she transfers her atten
tions from F.J. to the secretary, the narrator describes the change a
an act of sexual apostasy, a parodic 'reformation of her religion' (62)

Most dangerously of all, like Catholics the lovers owe allegiance t
an authority quite different from the governor of the domestic com
monwealth in which they find themselves. After frequent militar
skirmishes and ambassadorial approaches F.J. gains employment as Eli
nor's servant and later as her governor, and Elinor sets up her 'court' a
the household's queen who rules according to the peculiarly Italia
principles of 'politic government' (37, 68). Under these condition
the multiple titles G.T. gives to his characters might be seen as th
consequence not of his 'homely manner of writing' (80) but of th
rival political systems that have been set up in Elinor's home. As 'Mis
tress', Elinor rivals her father's title of 'master of the house'; as 'th
Lady' she holds sway over F.J. in competition with 'the lord of the cas
tle'; and the different titles G.T. gives her father invoke the differen
obligations F.J. violates by wooing his married daughter. Like Bald
win's *Beware the Cat*, Gascoigne's *Adventures* depicts an English societ
which is radically at odds with itself, riven with rival factions and com
peting languages; but in the *Adventures* the alternative political system
devised by the genteel invaders of an aristocratic household is vastl
more seductive than the furtive community exposed by Baldwin'
feline informers. For all their misadventures, F.J. and Elinor ar
witty, fashionable, beautiful, eloquent, and succeed at least for a tim
in establishing a little earthly 'heaven' of their own, 'their affairs bein
no less politicly governed than happily achieved' (37). And at the en
of the tale they get away with it. F.J. goes on to court new mistresse
(including, perhaps, the woman called Helen) and Elinor is lef
entwined with her secretary. Even the revised ending in the secon
version of the tale, *The Pleasant Fable of Ferdinando Jeronimi*, fails to sup
ply the moral conclusion the censors might have demanded. Of th
three conspirators, it is the innocent Dame Frances who dies as a resul
of F.J.'s actions, and the inference the narrator draws is a disturbin
one: 'thus we see that where wicked lust doeth beare the name o
love, it doth not onelye infecte the lyght minded, but it maye als
become confusion to others which are vowed to constancie' (i
453). Not only have the criminals not been brought to justice, bu

ieir secret activities threaten to wipe out the honest citizens. For this
:ason it seems inevitable that the High Commission should have
ecided to censor both versions of Gascoigne's thriftless history. In
oth, the clandestine Catholics who crept into northern houses in
*Certain Sermons or Homilies* are left free to continue the processes of
ifiltration and indoctrination; so that both versions might be seen
; militating not only against 'reformation of manners' but against
.eformation itself.

As one might expect, Frances is the chief of Protestant counter-
spionage in the text, the Walsingham of the household.[20] She re-
ognizes F.J.'s dual allegiance almost at once, so that when she meets
im under a 'tree of reformation' in the park she is not fooled by his
uritanical appearance for a moment: 'I little thought,' she tells him,
>y your evensong yesternight to have found you presently at such a
1orrow mass, but I perceive you serve your saint with double devo-
on' (24). She recognizes, in fact, that his Catholic idolatry of Elinor
onceals itself beneath the mask of apostasy, and that his appearance
yesternight' at the reformed service of evensong bears no relation to
1e tenets of his duplicitous faith, his devotion to his saint. When F.J.
ffers his services to Frances as a means of deflecting attention from his
ctual mistress, she responds with a biblical quip to remind him of the
ilemma that faced all Elizabethan Catholics: 'I have heard say oft
mes . . . that it is hard to serve two masters at one time' (25). Never-
1eless like a good spy-master she chooses not to expose his sexual and
eligious treason but to exploit her knowledge to recruit him to her
ause. Her appropriation of his sword might be read as an attempt
0 win him back to Protestantism: the homily on Bible-reading
escribes the scriptures as 'sharper than any two edged sword', and
ne sword was widely used by English Reformation poets as an
mblem of a monarch's powers over his doctrinal enemies, so that
·J.'s weapon might conceivably be taken as a metaphor for his
ιith.[21] Unfortunately on this occasion Elinor proves more adept at
eeping the sword than Frances; she steals it back from Frances's
hamber, using techniques acquired either through long practice or

---

[20] I am not proposing a deliberate allusion to Walsingham in Gascoigne's use of the name
Frances', but the coincidence is interesting.

[21] The reference to the two-edged sword is biblical: see Heb. 4: 12 and Rev. 1: 16, 19: 15.
or a discussion of the sword as a token of divine justice see King, *English Reformation Liter-
*ture*, 188–206. See also 'A fruitful exhortation to the reading and knowledge of Holy Scrip-
1re', *Certain Sermons or Homilies*, 3.

native cunning, 'according to old custom or wily policy' (36)—and s
might be said to demonstrate the tenacity of the 'old custom' of Eng
lish Catholicism.[22]

Frances's most elaborate strategy for returning F.J. to the ideologic
fold is the story she tells towards the end of the narrative. In it sh
describes how a husband discovers through the offices of a househol
spy—a maid 'of subtle spirit' (69)—that his best friend is sleeping wit
his wife. Instead of confronting his friend with this discovery, the hus
band chooses to signal his awareness of his wife's duplicity in secret b
paying her cash each time they make love. When at last his wife ask
the reason for these payments he tells her that they are intended t
represent the new contractual understanding that has been establishe
between them by her breach of marital trust: intended, that is, 't
make thee understand thine own whoredom' (71). Chastened, th
wife devises a strategy of her own to break off with her lover, whic
is to make him swear that he will grant her a request before she tel
him what it is. The lover agrees, and she makes him promise to sto
courting her; and by this indirect means directness and simplicity ar
restored between all parties: 'thus being become of one assent, [th
lover] remaineth the dearest friend and most welcome guest tha
may be, both to the lady and her husband, and the man and wife s
kind, to each other, as if there never had been such a breach betwee
them' (72–3).

The most striking aspect of the story is the determination of all par
ties to avoid at all costs the exposure of their domestic secrets. Th
husband sacks the maid who has apprised him of his wife's adultery
and threatens to kill her if she mentions it again; his coded allusion
to his wife's infidelity take place in the privacy of their bedchamber
and when his wife seeks to discover the 'secret cause' of her husband
odd behaviour she enters his private study and locks the door behin
her (70). Unlike the fortified dwelling of Suspicion, where husban
and wife have no access to one another's secrets, this household pre
serves the security of its inmates by the exchange of secret informatio
within a strictly limited domestic circle, and the alliances it protect
prove the stronger for this system of private communication. By tell
ing the story, Frances presents F.J. with an issue from the labyrinth c

---

[22] The phrase 'old custom' was frequently used by Protestants to describe Catholicism.
lost play called *Old Custom* was performed in about 1547, which personified the Roma
clergy as 'Old Blind Custom', and an allegory called *New Custom* was produced in abou
1570. See King, *English Reformation Literature*, 274.

is affair, just as the wife presents her lover with an 'issue' from his treachery: F.J. need only forswear his contract with Elinor and his talents will be restored to useful employment in the service of his legitimate allies. Unfortunately, however, there is more than one way of reading Frances's story. If F.J. were to see *himself* as the husband and the *secretary* as the lover, then the little fable could be read as an exhortation to Elinor to return to her affair with F.J.. Such a reading would be supported, ironically enough, by Frances's own contention, in a conversation with Dame Pergo, that lovers can be cuckolded as well as husbands; and this would seem to be the way F.J. reads the story, since after it has been told he at once returns to hoping that his mistress will come back 'lovingly to embrace his service in wonted manner' (74). Either way, the 'issue' proffered by Frances turns out to be a dead end; F.J. never renounces Elinor, never marries Frances, and the *Adventures* ends, like Johnson's *Rasselas*, with a conclusion in which nothing is concluded.

*The Adventures of Master F.J.*, then, is a bold and brilliant bid for employment which refuses to take no for an answer. It corroborates Ascham's alarmist forebodings that the infiltration of Protestant English culture by corrupt Catholic practices is proceeding apace under the noses of the aristocracy, and it confirms his fears that Italianate fictions of all kinds might act as a vehicle for this process. Above all, it demonstrates its author's aptitude for the detection as well as the perpetration of the secret abuses it describes. Despite the anonymity in which its authorship is shrouded, Gascoigne offers his readers— aristocracy, gentry, and censors alike—abundant evidence that he is the hidden amanuensis who sets it before an admiring public. As the title-page of *The Posies of George Gascoigne Esquire* announces so flamboyantly, it is Gascoigne who creates both F.J. and his verses, Gascoigne who devises the cunning strategies by which he enters Elinor's service, and Gascoigne who exposes them; and it is Gascoigne who cheekily uses Frances as a ventriloquist's dummy to teach the Elizabethan authorities how to deal with unemployed 'quick capacities' like F.J. and himself. Set a thief to catch a thief, as Frances's fable tells the English governing classes (the husband sets his wife to catch her lover): employ the busy brains of your educated subjects in the secret service of the state, or before you know it they will be secretly employed by someone else; either in the service of their own private objectives, or more disturbingly in the service of a rival political faction which appreciates and rewards their abilities as the Elizabethan

state has failed to do. Quick capacities are two-edged swords whic
can be used to defend a state and its religion or to destroy then
double agents able to evade detection by their 'politic governmen
of their own enterprises, while exposing the plots of less competei
agents, and willing, if they are sufficiently disaffected, to sell their skil
to rival masters. Given legitimate employment, quick capacities wi
strengthen the fabric of the public weal with their powers of observa
tion and information-gathering. Unemployed, they will prov
'friendly enemies' capable of weakening the linguistic ligatures tha
bind the public weal together.

Gascoigne's impudence and daring in launching this challenge ar
astonishing. After all, he possessed all the hallmarks of a 'friendl
enemy' of the Elizabethan state. His father was a Catholic, many c
his patrons and allies were members of the Catholic aristocracy, an
in 1572 he himself was accused both of atheism—often used as a syno
nym for heresy—and of acting as a spy for foreign powers.[23] It is eas
to conclude from the hostile reception of both versions of the *Adven*
*tures* that his daring was ill-judged and that his impudent bid fo
employment failed. But it would be rash to reach this conclusio:
too hastily. Imitations of Gascoigne's adventurous productions, sucl
as George Whetstone's moralistic revision of *The Posies*, *The Rocke* (
*Regard* (1576)—which signals its ideological reliability by taking a cas
tle as its presiding metaphor—and John Grange's exuberant romanc
*The Golden Aphroditis* (1577)—which celebrates rhetorical sophistica
tion with unsophisticated enthusiasm—suggest that his contempor
aries did not consider his dazzling display of verbal craftsmanship t
have damaged his prospects of advancement. Indeed, they had goo
reasons for thinking it had improved them. Gascoigne ended hi
career not only as a privileged commentator on the secret lives o
the women at Elizabeth's court, but as an agent in the service of Si
Francis Walsingham, entrusted with carrying sensitive documents t
London from the French court and the Low Countries. The offenc
he gave the censors, then, does not seem to have disqualified him fron
taking an active part in the defence of the realm. C. T. Prouty attrib
uted Gascoigne's eventual success in finding employment to the evid
ence supplied in his moral treatises that he was a reformed characte

---

[23] See Prouty, *George Gascoigne*, 61: the accusation reads: 'Item he is a notorious Ruffian
and especiallie noted to be both a spie; an Atheist and a godlesse personne'. For atheism a
heresy, see Nicholl, *The Reckoning* 43–4. For Gascoigne as one of the literary 'intelligencer
in Walsingham's service, see ibid. 171–3.

and a model citizen.[24] But it is equally tempting to speculate that Elizabeth and Walsingham employed him because they suspected that he was not. By setting him to work as he asked them to, the English authorities might be said to have silently recognized the rather unpleasant principle that 'petty treason' to a private subject could be loyalty to the state; and to have acknowledged the legitimacy of Gascoigne's brilliant display, in a domestic setting, of the duplicitous skills required by a public servant in Elizabethan England.

[24] Prouty, *George Gascoigne*, 93: 'His strenuous literary efforts or his friends, Bedford, Grey, and Gilbert had proved to the world that the "ydle poett" was no more; that a reformed character had supplanted the riotous youth.'

## 4

# George Pettie, Gender, and the Generation Gap

### I.  CORRUPTING THE CANON

Reading *A Petite Pallace of Pettie his Pleasure* (1576) is a little like enter
ing a library where the books have come alive and taken to flappin
from shelf to shelf, exchanging pages and passages with other book
to the horror of the monkish librarian. Fables from Ovid's *Meta
morphoses* jostle with histories from Livy, Tacitus, and Plutarch, an
each of these canonical texts seems to have been invaded by th
erotic novels of Bandello.[1] The narrator makes quixotic leaps fron
Protestant seriousness to Catholic frivolity, from misogyny t
pseudo-feminism, from the moral platitudes of a Golding or a Fento
to passages in which he simperingly propositions his female reader
By this means he ensures that his Elizabethan audience will find i
his stories not a steel mirror of exemplary virtues and vices but a cryst
one that presents a confused and constantly shifting reflection of the
own divided culture. His narratives, like his prose style, construc
themselves from a series of oppositions—rival values, competin
obligations, antagonistic authorities—all of which are expressed i
terms of two central conflicts: war between the genders, and wa
between the generations. Of all the fictions discussed so far, Pettie
most fully bear out Gosson's fear that his contemporaries are 'eve
overlashing, passing our boundes, going beyond our limites'; but th
commercial success of the collection, suggested by the many edition
it had gone through by 1614 (six at least), testifies to the interes

---

[1]  For the fullest account of Pettie's sources, see the notes to Herbert Hartman's edition c
*A Petite Pallace of Pettie his Pleasure* (London: Oxford University Press, 1938), 273–309. A
references are to this edition.

oused in the Elizabethan public by its disquieting dissolution of
onventional boundaries.[2]

Pettie's text has its roots in earlier English fictions. The women
who populate his novels are literary cousins of Painter's Amazons,
politically active and unfailingly eloquent, whose power over the fan-
sies of men confounds all bids by the state authorities to control
men's reason. They are related too to Baldwin's cats, secret agents in
the miniature commonwealth of the household, who speak a different
language and subscribe to a different set of values from the ones
favoured by the men who seek to master them. And they bear more
than a passing resemblance to the heroines of an even earlier story-
collection, an anonymous volume called *The Deceyte of Women*
(.1520).[3] Here too the continental novel has invaded the territory
of canonical texts: biblical histories and Classical myths are interleaved
with witty erotic anecdotes translated for the most part from *Les Cent
Nouvelles nouvelles*, a pornographic French story-collection of the
fifteenth century, and the familiar misdeeds of Jezebel and Delilah
pale into insignificance beside the sophisticated con-tricks of more
modern wives and mistresses. Like Gascoigne's Elinor, these women
have complete control over the nooks and crannies of domestic architecture, and an inexhaustible capacity for finding new uses for familiar
household fittings. One wife tricks her husband into climbing into a
clothes-chest for a wager; she then pretends that the lid of the chest
has stuck, and spends the rest of the day having sex with her lover.
A second wife conceals one of her young men in the attic while she
sleeps with another—so violently that the bed collapses under the
strain. When her husband unexpectedly returns while the two men
are still in the house, she manages to persuade him that she has been
sick, that the violence of her feverish tossing and turning has broken
the bed, and that her lovers are doctors who have come to alleviate
her suffering. A third wife slips out of her husband's bed to sleep
with her lover in the adjoining room on the pretext of letting in the
dog. In comparison with the energy and ingenuity of these women,
the men in the collection look stupid, maimed, or impotent. One
wife takes advantage of her husband's lack of an eye to allow her
lover to escape undetected; the lover of another pretends to have
lost his manhood in a bid to get access to his mistress; and the wife

---

[2] Hartman lists the known editions in his text, pp. xviii–xxi.

[3] Discussed in Margaret M. Schlauch, *Antecedents of the English Novel 1400–1600* (Warsaw:
WN, and London: Oxford University Press, 1963), 100–8.

who pretends to be letting in the dog is so disappointed by her lover
performance that she directs a volley of abuse at him under the guis
of shouting at her pet. The power of women to rob men of thei
potency is summarized in the penultimate story, a lively retelling c
the myth of Hercules and Iole:

She caused him for to lay away the lyons skinne and caused him to be clothe
with soft clothes of sylke, she caused hym for to were a croune of rosemar
upon his head, and golden rynges upon his fyngers . . . she caused hym for t
gyve hym selfe to womens busynes and ydlenes, in so muche that he wer
and satt among the women and tolde ryddels and fortunes as the chyldre
did, and sate and spon yarne at the dystaffe as the women dyd. Now behold
how the worthy Hercules is brought to femynyne workes through the decey
of Yole to his utter confusyon, the which was wont to be so manly in all hi
feates. Now beholde, what myschyefe, what marvayles and what folyshne
that the false and subtil women can brynge to passe, yea that semeth unpos
syble for to be, that can they doo and bryng to passe. (sigs. K$^v$–K2)

Women are the undisputed rulers of the arts of 'ydlenes' or leisure
controllers of the imagination, mistresses of 'marvayles' and practi
tioners of the 'unpossible'; and they are capable of dissolving th
boundaries between masculinity and femininity at a touch, and so c
drawing the strongest of men into their territory. Indeed, the text'
retelling of the story of Adam and Eve states explicitly that this i
their goal.

They are also capable of demolishing moral categories at will, an
this power is demonstrated by the competing sets of values that con
front one another throughout the collection. The volume is ostensibl
designed to warn men against debilitating female influences; its title
page announces that it is intended for 'the instruction and ensampl
of all men, yonge and olde', and the stories taken from canonica
sources relentlessly hammer home the message that women ar
never to be trusted. But the collection's parade of examples of femal
ingenuity lends a note of desperation to these warnings. At the end o
the story of Judith and Holofernes the anonymous editor exclaim
despairingly, 'who is it that can take hede of the deceyte of women
except he doo utterly abstayne their company, for they be so fals
and so full of deceyte that al the hede that a man can take is to lytle
(sig. C4$^v$). And the conclusion of the collection confesses that such
abstinence is impractical, 'for without women may none be ful
made, further, there as is no women is none made' (sig. K4). In fact
like Stephen Gosson's *Schoole of Abuse* the text seems to have been

nfected by the female values it deplores, and the continental novels it ontains are full of symptoms of this infection. The women in these necdotes are never caught out, and the editor seems as eager as ley are to avoid getting them into trouble. The story of the wife who locks her husband in a trunk ends with a prayer whose mock-iety parodies the narrator's sanctimonious utterances elsewhere in le volume: the husband, he says, shall never discover her adultery wythout a myschaunce fall that this booke come to his hand for to ead, the whiche God forbyd. Amen.' (sig. D2). Later he addresses vomen readers directly, in the tale of the woman who pretends to e ill: 'ye prety trulles that love to cary stones: learne this prety con-eyt against ye be sicke' (sig. D4ᵛ); this kind of 'instruction' makes onsense of the collection's claims to protect 'all men, yonge and lde' against the machinations of the opposite sex. One story tells of learned man who has read so many misogynistic tracts that he des-airs of ever preventing his wife from cuckolding him. When he nds that she has indeed been unfaithful he can only lament the lim-ations of a formal education: 'I have redde of muche deceyte, lyschefe and subtil wayes that women have to begyle their husbandes vythal, but thys subtyl meanes I never saw nor red afore this tyme. .nd therfore he fel in gret melancholy and dyed in short tyme after, or because that he had studied so longe in vayne' (sig. K). It would eem that the devious alternative education which Ascham ascribed o the translated fictions of the 1560s was already well established by le time of Henry VIII, and that fictional women and the authors vho compiled their histories were its devious co-founders.

In *A Petite Pallace of Pettie his Pleasure*, as in the earlier story-collec-ion, women again take most of the blame for disrupting the humanist ducational curriculum. The first of the preliminary epistles, written y a young man called R.B. and addressed 'To the gentle Gentle-vomen Readers', mimics the act of petty treason committed by Gas-oigne's H.W. when he sent *A Hundreth Sundrie Flowres* to the printer vithout permission. Once again the author of the stories—an *alter ego* f George Pettie's called G.P.—never meant them to be published, as e tells us in his 'Letter . . . to R.B.' (5). And once again the young man o whom the author entrusted his manuscript was forced, by his own onfussion, to 'transgresse the boundes of faithfull friendship' in order o get it into print (3). At the same time, R.B.'s epistle to the 'Gen-lewomen Readers' rewrites the terms of this betrayal. In *A Hundreth* *Sundrie Flowres* H.W. justified his treachery with a mocking allusion

to his duty to the state.[4] R.B., on the other hand, ascribes his pett
treason to his all-consuming libido. He informs his women reader
that 'the great desire I have to procure your delight' supplied him
with the motive for his action, and that 'to speak my fancye withou
feayninge, I care not to displease twentie men, to please one woman
for the freindship amongst men, is to be counted but colde kindnesse
in respect of the fervent affection beetweene men and women' (3)
Already, then, the competition for women's attention has driven
wedge between two male friends—R.B. and G.P.—and this is onl
the first of many instances throughout the collection of the displace
ment of male agreements by rival contracts between men and women

In addition, R.B.'s confession implies that the *Petite Pallace* cater
not for the standard school curriculum but for the alternative syllabu
followed by wayward pupils at the school of idleness. He contrast
Pettie's collection with 'former Pallaces of Pleasure', since the latte
'containe Histories, translated out of grave authors and learned writers
and this containeth discourses, devised by a greene youthfull capacitie
and reported in a manner *ex tempore*' (4). The *Petite Pallace* lays no
claim to the authority or the pedagogic usefulness that Painter and
Fenton claimed for their collections, and it never proposes to supple
ment the productions of learned writers, as G.T. did in *A Hundret.
Sundrie Flowres*. By characterizing the text as the spontaneous effusio
of a 'greene youthfull capacitie', principally designed for the entertain
ment of women, R.B. signals the radical challenge it poses to the pre
ceptual rigour of conventional schoolbooks, and places it squarely a
the centre of the struggle for control of young minds and bodie
which was the topic of Ascham's *Scholemaster*.

Fenton claimed to hold the key to immutable truths, and as a resul
his collection was riven with involuntary contradictions. *A Petite Pal
lace of Pettie his Pleasure* claims only to put across a medley of disparat
points of view, and proclaims its concern with singularity and subjec
tivity by alluding to Pettie's private tastes in its title.[5] As if in deferenc
to Elizabethan storytelling convention, each history opens with a pre
ceptual 'sentence' to be confirmed or modified by the ensuing action

----

[4] H.W. tells his readers that he chose to print the manuscript 'as one that thought bette
to please a number by common commodity than to feed the humour of any private perso
by needless singularity' (*An Anthology of Elizabethan Prose Fiction*, 3).

[5] The title advertises George Pettie's responsibility for the text; but the persona Petti
adopts in the collection is that of the dissolute improviser and pseudo-moralist G.P..
have therefore chosen to refer to G.P., for the most part, rather than to Pettie, in the ensuin
discussion.

ut these sentences are presented not as axioms but as opinions, and
re invariably qualified with the phrase 'I think'. And the judgement
f the narrator, G.P., is almost always at odds with the views of the
ducational establishment. The third story ('Germanicus and Agrip-
ina') tells us that G.P. is 'rather setled into this sentence . . . that our
wne desires not the destines dryve us to all our doynges' (56). In
iis he differs from the 'opinion' of professional astronomers, and he
·els free to reverse his position in the sixth story ('Admetus and
lcest'), where he pronounces that marriages are 'guided by destinie'
nd hastily adds 'I think' (126). The opening of 'Amphiaraus and Eri-
hile' dissents from received opinion in the shape of the 'auncient
hilosophers' (85) when it unfolds G.P.'s private views on riches,
/hile 'Icilius and Virginia' dilates on the fluctuating condition of
·arned opinions about love ('It is a doubt often debated but not
et decided', 103) and offers the most tentative of speculations
bout love's origin ('if an opinion grounded upon reason without
ny proper experience on mine owne part may take place'). Fenton
rgued that human actions were governed by 'certain principles and
les'; G.P. suggests that, if this is the case, we have not yet discovered
1em.

The first narrative in the collection, the story of the life and death of
'amma, would seem to present the perfect opportunity for a didactic
isquisition on the principles and rules of wifely good conduct. Plu-
1rch tells the tale succinctly in his *Mulierum Virtutes*: Camma is a
riestess of Diana, married to Sinatus, and courted by one Sinorix;
inorix murders Sinatus to facilitate his suit, and in revenge Camma
rst agrees to marry him and then kills her second husband and herself
/ith a poisoned mixture of milk and honey.[6] Guevara retells the story
1 *The Dial of Princes* (second book, sig. Q) as a rather grotesque illus-
·ation of the joys of marriage. He urges wives and husbands to imitate
1e conjugal solidarity of Camma and Sinatus: 'in such sorte they
ught to agree and love together, that all those of the commonwealth
1ould rejoice at their behaviours' (second book, sig. P6). At the same
me his version contains a sombre warning about the fragility of the
1atrimonial state. Wives in particular, he points out, are subject to
1e same intensive scrutiny as citizens under an authoritarian political
egime, so that 'it is not sufficient for ladies to be pure good: but also

<hr />

[6] See *Plutarch's Moralia*, ed. E.H. Warmington, Loeb Classical Library, 15 vols. (London:
/illiam Heinemann, and Cambridge, Mass.: Harvard University Press, 1968), vol. iii, trans.
rank Cole Babbitt, 550–5.

to geve no occasion for men to judge that (if they durste) they woul
be evill' (second book, sig. Q$^v$). Castiglione's *The Courtier* characteris
tically complicates this kind of prescriptiveness in its version of th
narrative (208–9). The story forms part of a debate on the positio
of women in the public weal, and the various responses to it fror
different members of the audience confirm its status as a contributio
to an unfinished dialogue rather than an authoritative example. Julia
invokes Camma as support for his encomium of women in boo
three: 'When have you ever seene or red that a husband hath shewe
such a token of love towarde his wife, as did Camma towarde her hus
band?' (208). But his conviction that she offers incontestable evidenc
of women's superiority to men is quickly quashed when he submits 1
to the arbitration of his listeners. The women in the audience ar
deeply affected by Julian's narrative, but Phrisio assumes that he ha
told the story precisely in order to 'make these Ladies weepe' (20ς
and so to ingratiate himself with the objects of his desire, and th
misogynist Gaspar takes the narrative as proof that 'women in ever
thing cleave alwaies to the extremitie' (211). Before Pettie got hol
of the story it had already established its credentials as the focus fo
controversy about the different sorts of influence a narrative ca
exert on its recipients.

G.P.'s version includes elements from both Guevara's and Casti
glione's, both of which he seems to have known. Castiglione set
his narrative in the context of a discussion, so that the debate mus
affect his readers' responses to the story. G.P., on the other hand
sets his debates in the context of a narrative, so that the diversity c
responses elicited by the separate incidents in the story becomes on
of its central themes. G.P.'s Camma, like Shakespeare's Lucrece, i
obsessed with the problem of how her words and actions will b
construed after the event by a potentially hostile public. At on
point, under pressure from Sinorix, she asks herself a question whicl
seems to spring from Guevara's insistence that a wife cannot afford t
give even the slightest grounds for a misreading of her conduct. Sh
asks herself whether there is any more substance behind the wor
'chastity' than the impulse to avoid defamation, which can b
achieved as easily by keeping your sexual adventures secret as by pre
serving your virtue. For a moment the inner, private Camma is at odd
with her outward, public stance; and it is at this point that she ana
chronistically invokes examples from Bandello's novels to suppor
her new definition of sexual morality. Painter read Bandello's tale

of the Duchess of Savoy and the Countess of Salisbury, both of whom resist the advances of political figures, as examples of un-blemished female chastity;[7] but Camma is temporarily tempted to reinterpret them as illustrations of the dangers that arise from failing to capitulate to corrupt authorities. Under the influence of this alter-native reading, the mutual forbearance of Guevara's married cou-ples—expressed in a neat chiasmus, 'she by her pacience ought to suffer the imperfections of him, and he like wise by his wisedome ought to dissemble the importunities of her' (second book, sig. P6)— turns into a labyrinth of social deceptions which stretches to their limits the implications of the word 'dissemble': 'theyr husbandes never heare of it, and though they do heare of it, yet wil thei not har-ken unto it, and though they do in a manner se it, yet will they not beleeve it, and though they doo beeleeve it, yet will they love them the better to have them leave it the sooner' (28). Under the aegis of this new morality, the sexual misdemeanours of wives are protected from reprisal by their husbands' eagerness to preserve at all costs the illusion of conjugal harmony. Of course, Camma quickly restores Bandello's tales to what Painter considered their proper function; but in the meantime the diversity of uses to which a narrative can be put has been established, and her fear that her own account of her rejection of Sinorix will be misread means that Camma is unable to return to the simplicity of her former relationship with her husband. Just as she decides to tell Sinatus about Sinorix, it strikes her that if she does so her husband may suspect that she encouraged her suitor's advances, or that she mistrusted her own ability to resist them unaided. She resolves to stay silent; and the result of this decision, G.P. suggests, is that her husband in his ignorance is unable to protect himself against his murderer. By eliminating the simple understanding that existed between Sinatus and his wife—by destroy-ing their ability to talk to one another—the invasion of Camma's mind by Italianate secretiveness and subtlety seems to be directly responsible for her husband's death.

But G.P.'s conclusion, like all his conclusions, is designed to undermine the reader's confidence that any history can elicit a simple

---

[7]   Painter tells the story of the Duchess of Savoy 'to the singuler praise and commendation of chaste and honest Ladies' (i. 285), and the story of the Countess as another example, sui-ably annexed to the first, of a woman 'whose life tried like gould in the fornace, glittereth at his daye like a bright starry planet, shining in the firmament with most splendent brightnesse bove all the rest, to the eternal prayse of feminine kinde' (i. 334).

reading. After listing the tragic consequences of Camma's virtue—'the husband slaine, the ruffian fled, the lover poysoned, the wife dead, the freinds comfortles, the children parentlesse'—the narrator asks, 'And can the preservation of one simple womans chastitie, countervaile all these confusions?' (37). An intricate network of relationships has been destroyed to save a woman's reputation, and G.P. implies that it was Camma's mismanagement of her negotiations with her lover that made their deaths inevitable: if she had been more willing to countenance a secret arrangement with Sinorix, all this misery could have been avoided. He closes with a phrase that echoes Lord Gaspar's dismissal of the sentimental stories of Lord Julian: 'it is naturally incident to women to enter into extremities' (37). For G.P., Camma is a victim of her own moral extremism, which goes hand in hand with political naïvety; her failure to exercise her private judgement astutely may be a moral triumph, but it is a disaster for the public weal. Like Castiglione, G.P. takes pains to emphasize the high political standing of Camma's lover: Sinorix is a judge and 'the chiefe ruler of the citie' (12–13), and his infatuation with a married woman has serious implications for the running of the state. In his eagerness to justify his courtship he is prepared to argue that the laws of nature should be privileged above the laws of the public weal (17), and he later yields his office as judge to the woman he wishes to seduce. At first Camma exercises the powers he gives her with discretion: 'seeynge you have constituted mee Judge in this case . . . this sentence definitive I give, I condemne you hencefoorth to perpetuall scilence in this sute' (19). But she quickly loses confidence in her capacity to adjudicate between the competing obligations imposed on her as a woman: her duty to Sinorix as her social superior compared with her duty to punish his crimes; her obligation to protect her children compared with her obligation to avenge her husband. For the narrator G.P., Camma's reasoning is as faulty as the reasoning of the infatuated magistrate; and G.P.'s decision to leave it to the readers' judgement 'whether be more worthy reprehension, hee or she' (38) invites them into Camma's world, where there is no place for moral absolutism, where political power resides in the hands of private subjects as well as with public figures, and where decisions about the priority of obligations have lost all the clarity they may have had in the times of Penelope and Lucretia, the exemplary women with whom he ranks his heroine. The frequent dichotomies G.P. constructs in his prose style contribute to the sense that both his protagonists and is readers are constantly being presented with bifurcating paths, with o signposts to indicate which is the most judicious—and least peri- ous—path to follow.[8]

In this way *A Petite Pallace of Pettie his Pleasure* recklessly demolishes the simpler structures of the 'former Pallaces' which inspired it. In his translation of Stefano Guazzo's courtesy book *The Civile Conversation* (1581), Pettie comments that his earlier story-collection had 'already yonne [him] sutch fame, as he which fyred the Temple of Dianae' (1. 7)[9], and two of the stories in the *Petite Pallace* betray his conscious- ness of this literary iconoclasm by taking the demolition of buildings as a central metaphor. G.P. describes the marriage of Camma and Sinatus in architectural terms, as a 'faithfull buildinge' which the adulterer Sinorix conspires to 'raze and beat down' (12). Later, in the course of wooing Camma, Sinorix constructs his own fragile fictional edifice on a misconstruction of Camma's words: he takes one of her courte- ous rejections as a 'firme foundacion' for his continuing suit, but by mistaking the nature of the ground wheron the foundation was layd, his building, as if it had been set in sandes, soone came to ruine' (20–1). Germanicus raises a similar imaginative palace when he courts Agrippina; he tells her that Cupid has promised him sexual fulfilment 'so frankely that if the perfourmance follow, a house with beames of beaten golde, and pillers of precious stones will not coun- ervaile the price of it' (58). But he goes on to confuse the promise made by Cupid with an invitation to political ambition, and his even- ual assassination shows that 'boystrous windes do most of all shake the highest towers' (77). The palace Painter used as a metaphor for his col- ection was a seat of government as well as a space devoted to private pleasure; but for G.P. the quest for private fulfilment inexorably undermines the structures of legitimate government, whether of a household or of a state; and the baroque fantasies generated by sexual desire invariably bring about the collapse of temples, houses, palaces, and agreed moral systems.

But sexual fantasies form only one ingredient in the stew of passions, fears, hopes, and ambitions that is forever engulfing the rival claims of reason and order in the lives of G.P.'s protagonists.

---

[8] For an analysis of Pettie's prose style, see J. Swart, 'Lyly and Pettie', *English Studies*, 23 (1941), 9–18. See also Janel M. Mueller, *The Native Tongue and the Word: Developments in English Prose Style 1380–1580* (Chicago, Ill.: University of Chicago Press, 1984).
[9] References to Pettie's translation of Guazzo are taken from *The Civile Conversation of M. Steeven Guazzo*, ed. Charles Whibley, 2 vols. (London: Constable, 1925).

The fullest account of the human susceptibility to what he calls the 'motions of the minde' occurs at the beginning of the second story in the collection, the tale of Tereus and Progne (40–2). The story opens with a sentence which avers that the human constitution responds to novel circumstances with an almost satanic adaptability, 'as the *Cameleon* chaungeth him selfe into the colour and hew of every thing he doth viewe, so man is made apt to bee transfourmed into any misfortune, and to receive any evill that raigneth upon the face of the earth'. The sentence recalls the pliancy of the Italianate Englishman in Ascham's *Scholemaster*, whose 'busie head' and 'talkativ' tonge' are trained in the art of improvisation by the dangerous school of Catholic Europe (236); or the working minds of Gascoigne's quick capacities, who can adapt themselves with Pauline promptness to any situation. For G.P. it seems that humanity is a race of malevolent shape-shifters, more ready to absorb the lessons of 'evill' than the precepts of official instructors. This resistance to structured learning is aggravated by the competition between generations which G.P. goes on to describe at length. In a passage which anticipates Jaques meditation on the seven ages of man, he explains how the fear of real or imagined threats to their security pits one generation against another in a cycle of perpetual conflict. At birth the baby weeps in anticipation of the pain that will be inflicted on it by its elders. Children 'feare the maister' who struggles to implant their minds with 'lowringe lore', and young adults dismiss the 'toyes' that amuse the child, only to replace them with playthings of their own which set them violently at odds with their parents, 'fantasticall follies' and 'prodigall pride'. When an adult falls in love, the child's fear of the schoolmaster becomes the 'pensife feare of parentes displeasure' which later commutes itself into the fear of harm coming to their own children. Old people labour under the illusion that the world has changed for the worse, betrayed into contempt for the younger generation by their own decrepitude, as they were in *The Courtier*. Finally, hostility between the generations is replaced by the still more urgent 'feare of approaching death' (42). As one might expect from this passage, Pettie's collection is filled with studies of the pain one generation inflicts on another. The father of Admetus laments the parent's acute sensitivity to the pain of a child, comparing it to that of a spider who 'feeleth if her web bee prickt but with the point of a pin' (138). Virginia complains of the intense physical agony inflicted on her by friends and relatives who would not let her marry the man she loved; and 'Tereus and Progne' contains the most savage of all these clashes between generations. Philomela's father is brought to death's door by his parting from his daughter ('if her return bee not with speede, you shall heare of my speedy returne to the earth from whence I came', 47), and later the incipient violence of the parent–child relationship bursts bloodily into the open, when Progne dismembers her young son Itis in a passage almost as laden with sadistic details as Fenton's account of Pandora's home abortion. In Pettie's collection, the rivalry between the allure of pleasure and the syllabus prescribed by the older generation is always lapsing into savagery, and the reconciliation of youth with age seems impossibly remote.

G.P. never rejects outright the humanist conviction that fiction can indoctrinate its readers by example. Instead, he demonstrates that examples affect the understanding in more complex and duplicitous ways than conservative theorists like Fenton could concede. In his translation of the *Civile Conversation* Pettie echoes Ascham when he insists that texts should form the basis of a formal education: if the children of the gentry resist textual instruction, he warns, 'experience must then be your guide, which wyll be but a blynde one; it must be your Scholemaister, but you shall finde it a dangerous one' (i. 8). The *Petite Pallace*, on the other hand, charts with relish the careers of those who have chosen experience as their demonic schoolmaster. Germanicus complains when he fails to reach an understanding with his lover, 'alas how true do I trie that saying, that every commodity hath a discommodity annexed unto it' (59). His experience has confirmed a 'sentence' or precept, but instead of offering an issue for Germanicus' predicament the sentence merely confirms the problematic nature of experience, governed as it is by moral as well as syntactical oppositions. This kind of instruction undermines traditional pedagogic methods even as it purports to acknowledge them. To reinforce his case for learning in the *Civile Conversation*, Pettie asserts that there is a mode of discourse which is capable of communicating the simple 'truth', and like Ascham he identifies this 'truthful' discourse with the Latin tongue, which is the linguistic currency of the humanist curriculum, and whose antiquity exempts it from the fluctuations of time. In the course of defending the validity of English borrowings from the Latin he asks: 'What woord can be more plain then this word *plaine*, and yet what can come more neere the Latine? what is more manifest, then *manifest*? and yet in a maner Latine; what more commune then *rare*, or lesse rare then *commune*, and yet both of them comming of the Latine?' (i. 11). But the world of experience recorded in the *Petite Pallace* has nothing to do with this Latinate simplicity. In his fictions G.P. stresses only the capacity of language for inhibiting consensus, and his characters' stylistic playfulness merely enables them to worry one another's rhetoric to pieces. Progne, for instance, exposes the lies of Tereus with a devastating use of assonance: 'truth which hee pretendeth nothing els but trifling: love lust, woordes wyles, deeds deceit, vowes vanities, faythfull promises faythlesse practises, ernest othes, errant artes to deceive, sorrows subtelties, sighes slightes, groanes guiles, cries crafts, teares treason' (52). From time to time G.P. makes what looks like an unequivocal moral pronouncement, as when the narrator exclaims with evangelical enthusiasm a little earlier in the same story, 'See the just judgement of god, who will suffer no evill done secretly, but it shalbee manifested openly' (51). But the proposition that all evils in this life are subject to providential arbitration quickly becomes debatable when the narrator launches into the ugly details of the murder of Progne's son, little Itis (53–5). Like *The Adventures of Master F.J.* the *Petite Pallace* contains no moderator, no touchstone of good judgement, and in this it differs fundamentally from the *Civile Conversation*, whose authoritative status is guaranteed by the eulogy of Queen Elizabeth which Pettie inserts into Guazzo's text. In the *Conversation* Elizabeth represents the supreme linguistic as well as the supreme political authority. She has a scholar's command of all the European languages, and protects herself from malicious gossip by her manifestation of consensual 'truth' through action: 'you wil say that spight it selfe can not deface her doings any way, and that in spight of spight shee will triumph over all yll tongues' (i. 201). In the *Petite Pallace*, by contrast, the role of arbitrator is constantly being transferred from magistrates to private subjects. Sinorix appoints Camma as his judge, Appius forfeits his judicial rights to Virginia and her father, Progne and Horatius pass peremptory sentence on the husband and sister who offend them, and G.P. asks his readers to pass judgement on his text. Elizabeth's absence from the collection sets it free to investigate the competing claims of rival obligations and agreements in the Renaissance public weal. And G.P. chooses to focus his investigation on an institution which had become an ideological battlefield for religious rivalries: the miniature commonwealth of marriage.

## 2.   MYTHS OF MARRIED LIFE

Since the reign of Edward VI, marriage had been seen as a peculiarly Protestant institution, the backbone of the reformers' literary efforts to tame the anarchy of sexual desire as it had been celebrated for centuries in poetry and romance.[10] But G.P.'s stories play havoc with the notion that marriage contracts can exert any kind of control over their contractors. Instead they represent wedlock as an explosive combination of competing interests, in which private agreements and public duties, the law of the state and the law of desire, Catholic values and Protestant convictions struggle for supremacy. A glance at his sources confirms that each novel in the collection is as painstakingly constructed as one of his sentences, and that he has reworked each story into a witty analysis of the sometimes violent clashes between different authorities which claim dominion over wedlock. The story of Virginia becomes a study of the forces that combine to destroy her hopes of marriage, the forces of paternal as well as political tyranny. The story of Horatius becomes the story of the married sister he murders, allowing G.P. to explore the conflict between the demands of the state of marriage and the demands of the state itself. Scilla's infatuation with Minos becomes a disquisition on the political consequences of a woman's efforts to assert her right to choose a husband over her parents' right to choose one for her; and the myth of Pygmalion transforms itself into a commentary on the futility of constructing conjugal ideals. All of Pettie's married couples experience the same disruptions and embarrassments as Guevara's Marcus Aurelius does in his marriage to Faustina, and nearly all of them end by throwing the public weal into confusion.

The overall structure of the collection reinforces G.P.'s vision of marriage as an unstable mixture of opposites, a reproduction in miniature of the instability of the Elizabethan state. It opens with a description of marriage as the perfectly balanced relationship, a harmonious union reproduced stylistically in G.P.'s use of rhythm, rhyme, alliteration, and assonance: 'in this stately state of Matrimonie, there is nothing fearefull, nothing fayned, all things are done faithfully

---

[10]  See John N. King's discussion of responses to the courtly love tradition in the reign of Edward VI, in *English Reformation Literature*, ch. 5. See also Valerie Wayne's discussion of marriage in *The Flower of Friendship: A Renaissance Dialogue Contesting Marriage* (Ithaca, NY: Cornell University Press, 1992), introduction. All references to *The Flower of Friendshippe* are taken from this edition.

without doubting, truely without doublyng, willingly without constraint, joyfully without complaint' (11). The last story ends with the
opposite view, when the studious Alexius abandons his marriage
because he holds it responsible for confounding order instead of preserving it: 'I se hereby my wit dulled, my understanding blinded, my
memory weakned, my sences sotted' (269). Between these two
extreme opinions the collection demonstrates just how precarious
the 'stately state of Matrimonie' really is—and the word 'stately'
extends the implications of this instability well beyond the confines
of the domestic. As the stories unfold they offer accumulating
evidence of the inaccuracy of the harmonious initial sentence, from
the 'doubting' that provokes jealousy in 'Cephalus and Procris' to
the 'doublyng' which accompanies adultery in 'Minos and Pasiphae',
from the 'constraint' which facilitates Philomela's rape to the 'complaint' uttered by Pygmalion when his lover deserts him. The collection is arranged thematically in pairs of novels: sometimes obviously
so, as with the linked stories of Pygmalion and Alexius which describe
the breakdown of two forms of 'ideal' love, or those of Procris and
Pasiphae, which deal with jealousy; sometimes less obviously, as with
the tales of Camma and of Progne, which concern vengeful wives,
or Germanicus and Amphiaraus, which explore the antagonistic sets
of values that tear partnerships apart. 'Icilius' and 'Admetus' both
revolve around intractable parents and the self-sacrifice of young
lovers, and 'Scilla' and 'Curiatius' contain political betrayals motivated
by desire. Each of these thematic pairs of stories reproduces the uneasy
partnership between spouses that exacerbates the ideological confusions it is intended to resolve.

A comparison between the central story in the collection and the
final story serves to illustrate the orderly diversity of G.P.'s treatments
of matrimony. The twelfth and last novel, 'Alexius', which finishes
with the hero discarding his earthly union in favour of a union with
God, is carefully balanced by the sixth novel, which ends the first
half of the collection with the picture of an ideal relationship explicitly
anchored in this life rather than the next. 'Admetus and Alcest'
describes the only marriage in the book which ends more happily
than it began: it is a redemptive reworking of Painter's 'Romeo and
Julietta', complete with warring families and a secret marriage at a her-
mitage, whose lovers succeed in breaking free from the political and
parental repression which opposes their union, and whose happy ending implicitly condones filial resistance to the authority of parents and

the state. Where 'Alexius' recommends that a man needs constantly to adapt the motions of his mind to changing circumstances (249), 'Admetus and Alcest' celebrates the lovers' constancy in the face of a hostile fortune. Alexius begins by obeying his father, Admetus begins by ignoring his; Alexius comes to see the pleasure of marital intercourse as 'the very pathway to perdition' (269) and sets out on a pilgrimage to escape it, while the lovers forgo both pleasure and power for matrimony's sake, and exchange 'pleasant pallaices' for 'pilgrims peltes' to obtain it (137). Alexius sums up the debates between lovers which fill the book by debating with himself over the relative merits of the official curriculum and the sensual curriculum taught by women. The lovers' story, on the other hand, ends with a debate in which both sides argue the same case, striving to outdo each other in the art of persuasion so as to demonstrate the strength of their commitment to one another. When Apollo rashly promises Admetus a second term of life if he can find someone willing to die in his place, the god provokes a fierce controversy between the lovers over who shall die first. Like the debates that end contemporary stories of male friendship (Titus and Gisippus, Damon and Pithias), this apparent altercation only reaffirms the stability of the lovers' bond, the fact that they possess 'one will in two minds, one hart in two bodies, and two bodies in one flesh' (146). The argument ends, like the quarrel between Pyrocles and Musidorus in the *Old Arcadia*, with the triumph of love over debate itself.[11] Alcest pretends to succumb to her partner's persuasions, only to go off and kill herself while he isn't looking. Love's independence of other laws, even the law of possibility, is then confirmed by Proserpina, the merciful spouse of the god of the dead, who agrees out of pity to let Alcest return to life. Where Alexius rejects marriage because it interferes with his spiritual development, 'Admetus and Alcest' affirms the potency of a private agreement between a man and a woman to overcome the shortcomings of official legislation. The sixth and twelfth stories, in fact, articulate contradictory positions in a dialogue that runs throughout the collection, a dialogue between the private and the public that is never convincingly resolved.

[11] In the *Old Arcadia* Musidorus demonstrates with a fine display of logic the irrationality of Pyrocles' infatuation with Philoclea; but at the end of the debate, having won it comfortably, his love for Pyrocles prompts him to jettison his arguments and urge his friend to 'command me to do what service I can towards the attaining of your desires'. *The Old Arcadia*, ed. Katherine Duncan-Jones (Oxford: Oxford University Press, 1985), 23.

But despite its sentimental ingredients, the ideal marriage of Admetus and Alcest is hardly an unqualified endorsement of romantic love.
For one thing, it is accomplished at considerable cost to the lovers'
respective nations. Admetus' adoption of the garb of a Catholic pil-
grim might be taken to signal his subscription to a different set of
laws than the laws of his country, and the consequences of his pilgrimage are drastic: his father dies of grief when he hears of it.[12] The story
that follows this one, 'Scilla and Minos', tells how a similar act of filial
defiance made possible the invasion of a kingdom by a foreign power.
The happy issue of Admetus' clandestine marriage—its instrumental-
ity in reconciling two warring states—needs to be weighed against the
devastation his country might have suffered as a result of his neglect of
his princely duties. As in so many of G.P.'s stories, the search for the
ideal condition, the perfect partner, the supreme relationship, brings
more dangers with it than benefits. And in the end, both the dangers
of Admetus' joyful union and the reconciliation it effects are nothing
more than an elaborate illusion, a literary hoax, a myth. The restoration of Alcest to life is the one supernatural event in the collection
which is given no rational explanation; G.P. merely lets it stand as a
testament to the powers ascribed by the poets to romantic love. And
he comically consigns the lovers' relationship to the chocolate-box of
fantasy by contrasting it with his own more mundane marital experiences. At the end of the story he drifts off into a daydream about what
it would be like to be married to Alcest, the ideal wife; but in the middle of his dream he is rudely awakened by the protests of his 'actual'
spouse, whom he imagines wishing with equal fervour that he could
be imprisoned inside his fantasies: 'Methinks I hear my wife wish me
such a wife as I have spoken of; verily, good wife, you wish your
wealth great wealth, and God make me worthy of your wife, and
your wish.'[13] As in *The Courtier*, the ideal (whether sexual or moral)
remains trapped forever inside the pages of books along with other

[12]   The metaphor of the pilgrimage of love was an old one by Pettie's time, but the metaphor could be ideologically charged. Fenton had used it to express his hostility to Catholicism in the story of the Milanese lovers Cornelio and Plaudina. Cornelio seeks out his
mistress 'with no less devotion than the papists in France perform their idolatrous pilgrimage
to their idol Saint Tronyon . . . or our superstitious Catholics of England of late days to the
Holy Rood of Chester or image of our Lady at Walsingham' (Fenton, *Bandello: Tragical
Tales*, ed. Hugh Harris, 247).

[13]   I quote here from I. Gollancz's bowdlerized edition of *A Petite Palace of Pettie his Pleasure*, 2 vols. (London: Chatto & Windus, 1908), i. 196–7. Hartman's edition renders the passage as follows: 'Meethinkes I heare my wish, wishe mee sutch a wife as I have spoken of,
verily (good wish) you with your wealth great wealth, and God make mee woorthy of you

fictions; and whenever such fantasies escape from their confinement they wreak havoc with whoever entertains them.

Nevertheless, in G.P.'s collection private fantasies are always escaping into the public sphere and interfering with affairs of state. This is especially the case with the novels he adapts from Ovid's *Metamorphoses*. Each of these novels takes as its subject a particular form of self-deception: the fictions spawned by adolescent infatuation (Scilla), the delusions of jealousy (Procris), the absurd expectations generated by the myth of the perfect lover (Pygmalion). In each case the imagination shows an alarming propensity for creating what it expects to find, as if in anticipation of Puttenham's warning about imaginative monsters in *The Arte of English Poesie*.[14] Not only is the human mind infinitely capable of adapting like a chameleon to evil influences, but it is equally capable of moulding its surroundings into conformity with its own secret fears and desires. And the stories that record the transformative power of fantasy might be said to stand in danger of working a similar monstrous transformation on their inexperienced readers.

Perhaps the most consistent study of self-deception in the book is the ninth novel, 'Cephalus and Procris'. Several of G.P.'s discourses revolve around an associative field of metaphors or concepts which drive home the political implications of the courtships they recount: 'Scilla and Minos' articulates desire in military terms, while 'Germanicus and Agrippina' concentrates on the competing systems of values encapsulated in the word 'worth', and 'Cephalus and Procris' is narrated throughout in terms of the most sensitive of senses, that of sight. Sight is the instrument both of surveillance and of espionage, the means by which public figures control their subjects and private subjects defend their interests. It is also the sense that accumulates images with which to stock the secret spaces of the imagination,[15] and the eye is the organ whose perceptions can be most easily distorted by the '*Chimeres* and monsters' of the mind. Vision first attracts Procris to Cephalus, after she has 'speciallye vewed' him among the young men of Venice (186), and later it is vision that the older generation use to keep the lovers apart. When they discover the object of the girl's desire, her parents have Cephalus sent abroad and she finds herself 'warely watcht' to make sure she does not follow him (190).

wish and your wishe' (146). In this case, Gollancz's version seems to me for once to make more sense.

[14] Quoted at the head of my Introduction.

[15] See Ch. 5, s. 1, esp. n. 5.

Meanwhile, Procris continues to deploy her visual sense in the service of desire. When she watches the banished Cephalus set out to sea, love permits her to defy the laws of perspective ('shee bent her eyes with such force to beehold it, that shee saw the ship farther by a mile then any els could possibly ken it', 190). During his absence she is tormented by imaginative visions of disaster ('Mee thinkes I see the hoysinge waves lyke a huge army to assaile the sides of thy Ship', 190); so that by the time of Cephalus' return her sensitivity to real or imagined visions has grown so intense that she fears it might prove fatal if she sees him again too suddenly:

shee feared least his sodayne sight would bring her sutche excessive delight that her sences shoulde not bee able to support it, and therfore got her into the highest place of the house, and beheld him comming a far of, and so by litle and litle, was partaker of his presence, and yet at the meetinge, she was more free of her teares then of her tounge, for her greetinge was only weepinge, word shee could say none. (192)

Eventually the parents accede to the children's demands and the lovers are married. But the concentration on sight which at first expressed the lovers' sensuous delight in one another quickly undergoes an ugly metamorphosis, and the married couple soon begin to use vision to accumulate evidence of one another's infidelity. Shortly after the wedding Cephalus 'beegan plainly to see and rightly to judge' that Procris is over-promiscuous in distributing her 'retchles regardes and light lookes' to other men (194). To find out whether he has grounds for his jealousy he decides to spy on her: he visits her disguised as a stranger, concealing his name under the impenetrable alias of Sulaphec, and claims to have met her husband in foreign parts and to have heard him say that 'her very sight was so lothsome unto mee, that I could not by any meanes indure it' (197). Procris' reply reveals that her dependence on sight has not yet blurred her judgement: 'what use I reasons to retell [refell?] that which one without eyes may see is but some coyned devise to cosen mee?' (198). But the supposed Sulaphec finally succeeds in corrupting her through the 'ritch sight' of gold (201).

By this stage the sense of sight has acquired a diversity of functions which rob it of any value as an instrument of impartial scrutiny. Its testimony can be used to support whatever prejudice the viewer cares to conceive, and its uses can be reversed as easily as Cephalus reverses his name. Soon after Cephalus' successful venture into the field of espionage Procris too 'beegan to have a very carefull and curious eye' to her husband's doings (202), and succumbs to jealousy exactly as he did, 'sodaynly by reason of one looke which hee cast upon one of his neighbours' (205). To soothe her suspicions Cephalus narrates the myth of Hercules and Deianira, warning her to 'See' the effect of Nessus' shirt and to 'foresee' that she does not fall into the same trap (206). But exemplary texts in the *Petite Pallace* have no power to alter the predispositions of their readers, and besides, the lying tales Cephalus told when in disguise have robbed the art of narrative of any instructive 'credit' it may once have possessed. Procris chooses instead to rely on her own powers of observation to furnish proof of her suspicions, and soon finds them confirmed when she overhears Cephalus addressing a passing breeze as if it were his mistress. Her reaction is predictably visual: she resolves to 'goe see' her husband's lover and to vent her rage in 'scratching her incontynent *eyes* out of her whoorish head' (208, my emphasis). Her hasty execution of this resolve, together with Cephalus' failure to watch where he throws his spear, is what kills her. G.P. concludes that, far from discouraging secret transactions, 'wary watching' is a mere incitement to the contrivance of cunning plots, whether against spouses, against parents or, implicitly, against the state. Subtle means of discovering subtlety merely propagate greater subtlety; suspicion generates what it suspects, as it did in *The Adventures of Master F.J.*. Instead G.P. suggests that wives reform their unfaithful husbands by offering them ocular proof that they themselves are honouring the marriage contract, so that 'when they shall *see* you love them faithfully' (209, my emphasis), they shall be shamed into doing likewise. The simplicity of agreements can only be preserved by practising simplicity; but in the world of the *Petite Pallace* the terms of any agreement contain the seeds of their own undoing, and both marital and legal simplicity labour to protect themselves against insurmountable odds.

In the narrative that follows 'Cephalus and Procris', the consequences of an ill-considered marriage contract find their most striking metaphorical expression. 'Minos and Pasiphae' is the story of the events that preceded the construction of the labyrinth, the architectural trap in which King Minos sought to hide the monstrous evidence of his wife's refusal to be bound by the terms of their nuptial agreement. In G.P.'s version of the myth, the minotaur which is the product of Pasiphae's adultery also acts as a metaphor for the unhappy marriage that produced it. Cephalus' jealousy sprang from what he

took to be his intellectual inequality with his wife; as he lost his respec
for Procris' 'wit', so he lost his trust in her ability to honour the term
and conditions of wedlock (193–4). Minos, on the other hand, waxe
jealous because of the *social* inequality of his union. G.P. taps the roo
of his anxiety at the beginning of the story, in a passage that make
Minos' marriage sound as volatile and ungainly as the body of th
minotaur:

how can there be one harte in two bodies, when the one wisheth one thing
the other willeth another? When the one is disposed one way, the othe
inclined another way, according to the secret instinct of their proper an
peculier natures? . . . So that for one of meane parentage, to bee marrye
with one of princely race, I think as good a match, as beetweene Lions an
Lambes. (210–11)

In other words, by marrying the low-born Pasiphae Minos has intro
duced an enemy into his household and a saboteur into his govern
ment, artificially fusing two antagonistic sets of 'secret instincts', s
that all his political supporters are hostile to his wife and all his wife'
allies are antagonistic to her husband. Accordingly, the first part of th
narrative is taken up with the account of a clandestine plot devised b
Pasiphae against her husband's interests. It tells how she conceives
grudge against one of Minos' favourites, a young man called Verecun
dus: how she seduces him into writing her a love-letter, shows the let
ter to her husband, and succeeds in having Verecundus banished from
the kingdom. But the plot has an unexpected side-effect that backfire
on its deviser: for the letter suddenly apprises Minos of the endles
possibilities for concealed relationships encoded in the fraudulent us
of words. From the moment Minos reads the incriminating text hi
speech is filled with wordplay: elaborate puns which signal his dawn
ing awareness of the multiplicity of secret affairs his wife may be con
ducting. The word 'proper' acquires a double meaning for him
signifying both the delight he takes in his wife's 'proper' appearanc
and the difficulty of defending his exclusive rights to her as his conju
gal 'property': 'the pleasure which her proper person procured him
was drowned with the doubt, lest she would not remaine prope
unto him' (222). The word 'like' is fraught with still more doubl
meanings: 'my chaunce was to chuse one, who if (as the sayinge is
like, like best of their likes, is like to like better of any other then o
my selfe' (223). As Minos succumbs to paranoia about the world o
potential for fraud in words, Pasiphae finds herself effectively trappe

in the dual identity contrived for her by her husband: 'Who wil honour mee for queen, which am suspected for a queane and harlot?' (223). The terms of her covenant with Minos—who agreed to make her his queen in exchange for the exclusive rights to her loyalty (213–14)—have been rendered irremediably ambiguous by her husband's jealousy, and Pasiphae responds to this ambiguity by throwing herself into the illicit sexual activities which are implicit in her binary title.

Predictably, all Minos' efforts to prevent her adultery come to nothing. His strict surveillance of his wife merely obscures the details of her love-life by making her more expert in the arts of concealment, and G.P. articulates the confusions to which her secrecy gives rise by presenting his readers with two alternative versions of her affair with the bull. The first version is the one reported by Ovid, in which she falls in love with a beast, slaughters the cows who compete with her for his affections, and eventually satisfies her desire for him by secreting herself inside a wooden heifer. The second version is an allegorical reading of Ovid's fable, a pastiche of the ingenious contemporary explications of the transcendent 'truths' concealed behind poetic fictions. According to this version, the bull is a man called Taurus who is Minos' private secretary, and the bull's horns belong to the cuckolded king (225). Whichever version is the right one, both of them testify to the power of the paranoid imagination to construct what it fears: 'suspicion and slaunder maketh many to bee that which they never ment to bee' (226).

The offspring of Pasiphae's elusive union, the minotaur, is an awkward fusion of the incompatible elements that fail to achieve reconciliation under the auspices of marriage. The labyrinth which contains it is the web of protective verbal evasions by which a married couple—or the state—protects the myth of its stability; and G.P. reproduces its twists in the 'doubting' and 'doublyng' of his style. But the reader is never offered a direct glimpse of the labyrinth's legendary occupant. It is kept at one remove, like the 'wilde Ægyption with one eye in his forehead' which the wife of Fulvius Torquatus yearns to see in an anecdote narrated at the end of 'Minos and Pasiphae' (227). G.P. tells the tale of Torquatus' wife as a mocking example of female self-restraint. But her self-discipline ends in tragedy: she dies as a result of the intensity of her craving to see the monster, and the anecdote merely serves to confirm the irresistible appeal of the monstrous, the strange, the marvellous, to those who have been forbidden access to it. As with Fenton's *Tragicall Discourses*, the strangest monsters in

Pettie's collection are the ones generated by the unbounded imaginations of its protagonists, and these unruly demons cannot be enclosed in any labyrinth.

### 3. DIVORCING THE STATE

If the stories Pettie derives from Ovid examine the chameleon changes effected by the private imagination, his stories from Roman history explore what happens when the laws of marriage collide with the laws of the state. Each narrative transforms what its sources present as a political incident into a study of the devastation wrought by the intrusion of politics on the private lives of a married couple. Camma's moment of self-doubt arises when she contemplates the official status of her would-be lover; Horatia's death (in 'Curiatius and Horatia') is brought about by the clash between her private commitment to her husband and her public duty to her country; and the tragic ends of Germanicus and Agrippina stem from their inability to choose between the different personal and political connotations of a single word: 'worth'.

Tacitus scatters his account of the couple throughout his *Annales*.[16] While he shows a superficial interest in their dominant characteristics—Germanicus is modest, Agrippina faithful—he always subordinates their private relationship to its political context. G.P. owes only the bare bones of his story to Tacitus. He organizes his narrative around a series of dialogues between the pair, in the course of which the initial understanding they reach is steadily eroded by their divided loyalty to two incompatible legal systems, the law of the state and the law of desire. Every change he makes to his source intensifies this central conflict and foregrounds the different values to which men and women subscribe. Where in Tacitus Agrippina is as politically active as her husband, in the *Petite Pallace* she lives in perpetual terror of Germanicus' overreaching political ambitions. Where Tacitus reports that Agrippina died some time after her husband and suggests that she was murdered by her political rivals, G.P. has her die of grief immediately after her husband's assassination. But G.P.'s most important change is to create a discrepancy between the couple's financial circumstances,

---

[16] See *Tacitus in Five Volumes*, Loeb Classical Library (Cambridge, Mass.: Harvard University Press, 1931), vols. iii and iv, trans. John Jackson.

so that Germanicus spends the entire novel struggling to make what he perceives as his inferior social status equal to Agrippina's. The idea that marriage should be founded on some kind of equivalence between husband and wife was a familiar one: Edmund Tilney's prose fiction *The Flower of Friendshippe* (1568) declares that 'equalitie is principally to be considered in this matrimoniall amitie' (108), but distinguishes equality of birth and fortune from the more necessary equality of understanding that subsists between two compatible personalities. But Tilney's notion of 'equalitie' has nothing to do with the equal distribution of power. One of the interlocutors in his treatise, Pedro de Lujan, tells the company that 'In this long, and troublesome journey of matrimonie, the wise man maye not be contented onely with his spouse's virginitie, but by little and little must gently procure that he may also steale away hir private will, and appetite' (112). Germanicus never succeeds in distinguishing equality of fortune from emotional and intellectual equality, and he seems obsessed with demonstrating to himself and his male peers that he is capable of dominating his wife as well as of equalling her. The elaborate arguments with which he tries and fails to convince himself that he is more than her equal forge an unbroken rhetorical chain which draws the couple inexorably from their first meeting to their premature deaths.

Germanicus' courtship of Agrippina is dominated by his endless reassessments of her value as compared with his own. His first soliloquy considers the question of whether value-systems are to be regarded as social constructs or as universal essences; he never resolves this dilemma. He begins by worrying that Agrippina will marry someone who is 'more woorthy of her then my selfe' by the standards of the social hierarchy (59), but goes on to comfort himself that no man can be 'woorthy' of such a woman in absolute terms. At length he decides to transfer his allegiance once and for all from the scale of economic and hierarchical values privileged by the state to the absolute moral standards represented by Agrippina: 'For shee is the goddesse whom I wil honour with devotion, shee is the prince whom I will obey with duty, shee is the country in whose cause and quarrell I will spend life, living and all that I have' (60). Germanicus has found a means of 'countervayling' Agrippina's worth by founding a private nation to rival Rome, a secret country run by love's laws instead of the laws of the state. So long as he remains faithful to this new constitution there is no reason why the lovers need not remain joined in a stable union. Unfortunately Germanicus' pride makes him incapable of remaining satisfied with the terms of their private agreement. Even as he pledges emotional allegiance to his wife he feels impelled to point out that she is hardly his superior by birth, since he is 'nere kinsman to themperour' (60); and by the end of the same soliloquy he remains as doubtful of their equality as he was at the beginning, and as frantically eager to prove it to the public: 'by how mutch more a man hazardeth him selfe for his misteris sake, by so mutch the more hee manifesteth the constancy of his love, and meriteth meede at her handes the more woorthily' (61). Germanicus has already decided that no man can finally 'merit' Agrippina, so his obsession with matching her condemns him to a life of perpetual hazard.

Agrippina's soliloquies follow a similar course to those of her husband. She begins by flirting with the idea that virginity is a 'worthier' condition than wedlock, but quickly decides that Germanicus is 'worthy of a far more worthy wife then her selfe' (70), and informs her sceptical parents that 'differences or inequalities beetween the married' arise not from unequal fortunes but from the disagreements produced by forced marriages (74). From this point on she gives her unwavering commitment to the public weal of desire, the miniature state which is governed by Cupid: 'love if wee obey his lore . . . raigneth over us like a lovinge Lorde' (75). Once she has pledged her allegiance to this state she never revokes it, and she is still articulating her loyalty on her deathbed. Germanicus, on the other hand, soon tires of his perceived inferiority. He frets because he is unable to support his wife 'according as his princely minde desired' (76), so that when the Emperor offers to adopt him as his heir he accepts at once, not for his own sake (he is 'altogether unworthy' of the succession, 77) but for Agrippina's (she is 'woorthy of all the honour in the world'). The last dialogue between the couple exposes the rift that has opened between their different understandings of value. Agrippina reaffirms her independence of the public weal, declaring that she would regard Germanicus as her own private emperor even if he were the poorest man in the city (81). The ambitions she expresses are exclusively personal ones: 'though you surmount mee in all other thynges, yet wil I not fayle, if it bee possible, to exceede you in good wil' (81). Germanicus ignores her insistence that their bond is founded not on capital but on mutual 'good wil', and insists on continuing his perilous political ascent because 'the best state which ever I shalbe able to bryng you to wilbe to base for your worthinesse' (81). The loving rivalry between the couple—a familiar convention in con-

emporary love-stories—degenerates into a series of professions of
mbition which spiral competitively higher and higher, urged on by
 succession of metaphors of height and depth. Their dialogue can
nly be terminated by the intrusion of a man who acknowledges
either public nor private constructions of 'worth', Germanicus' mur-
erer Tiberius, who 'passed not to pervert both humaine and devine
wes' in his determination to seize the Imperial throne.

   Agrippina's death completes her divorce from the priorities of gov-
rnments and politicians. For her, 'both humaine and devine lawes'
re comprehended in Germanicus, so that her lament for his death
xpresses the death of all her aspirations: 'My life my love, my hope
ıy husband, my joy my *Germanicus* is miserably murthered' (82).
Ier suicide by starvation transports her physically into the alternative,
ınmaterial world she has occupied imaginatively since her betrothal:
;.P. describes her body's literal liquidation as it distils into tears, dis-
ɔlved by feeding on the insubstantial provender of sorrow. But as
lways, having moved his readers with a tragic story G.P. cannot
llow it to acquire the authoritative status of a pedagogic example.
ıstead he proposes that all methods of assessing value fluctuate in
esponse to altered circumstances and changing fashions:

ıere hath bene never any one husband so good, but there may bee others
ɔund as good: yea and though they bee not perfectly so good, yet in respect
f chaung which most women delight in, they are commonly counted better:
; you your selves if you were once married perchaunce would saye, or at
east thinke. (83–4)

'he sentence testifies to the pleasure G.P. takes in deconstructing
ıoral essences and prescriptive platitudes. In a series of rhetorical shifts
. moves from a bland initial proposition, that no husband has a mono-
ɔly on excellence, through a cynical recognition that a wife's judge-
ıent can be affected by her taste for sexual variety (her second
usband may not be 'perfectly so good' but will be 'counted better'),
ɔ an implicit acknowledgement that a husband might never under-
:and the system of values favoured by his wife (the last clause suggests
ıat the unmarried women in G.P.'s audience will never again 'saye'
ɟhat they 'thinke' once they have got husbands). In Pettie's collection
either women nor the men who court them have access to any
greed system of essential values such as the ones invoked by contem-
orary commentators. Instead of principles and rules, G.P.'s conclu-
.ons dispense practical advice on marital contingencies: 'Germanicus

and Agrippina' ends with the pragmatic recommendation that husband ought not to 'seeke and provide better for [his wife] then hee would do for himselfe'. In fact, as soon as the notion of moral absolutes enters into any 'covenant or bargain' in the book, it destroys its adherents' capacity to compromise, to improvise, to adapt; and for G.P. the loss of these skills is invariably fatal.

This is certainly the case in the eighth novel, 'Curiatius and Horatia'. Horatia shares Agrippina's uncompromising loyalty to the private state of matrimony, and it is her obstinate allegiance to this state that propels her into conflict with Rome. Painter's version of the story of Horatius held him up as a 'victorious paterne of valiant chivalrie' (i. 16); G.P.'s, by contrast, fixes on the one moment in the story which makes nonsense of Painter's assessment. This moment occurs after Horatius has achieved heroic status by killing the three Curiatii in single combat. As he returns home he overhears his sister Horatia mourning her dead husband, one of the Curiatii, and promptly kills her for her lack of patriotism. The sister's grief completes her aliena tion from the Roman state, and G.P. has alienation in mind from the opening sentence of his story.

He begins with an account of love's estrangement from the rules that govern the world in general. The strangest natural phenomena, he tells us, such as water that runs uphill or air that 'descendeth into the pores of the earth' (166), have agreed scientific explanations: they do so to 'avoyde vacantnesse'. Only desire has no explanation, since it exists 'farre without the compasse of reason and bounds of nat ure' (167). The story of Horatia charts her progress from modest con formity to the kind of defiant articulacy which her brother takes to life 'without the compasse of reason'. At first she shows an exaggerated respect for the 'bounds' of propriety which frustrates all Curiatius's attempts to court her, to such an extent that he begins to think her no more than a flirt who is expert in all the tricks of mock-prudish ness: 'what shew of shamefastnesse will they make, what visors of vyr ginitie will they put on, what colours of continencie wil they set foorth' (170). Indeed, Curiatius is so certain that her modesty is 'put on' that he himself dons a 'visor' or mask to court her. But Horatia's resistance to Curiatius stems only from an exalted respect for the insti tution of marriage. For a wife, she explains, her husband is a self-suffi cient private estate, an extensive property beyond whose bounds she may not stray: 'Hee is the only play which pleaseth her, hee is the only game which gladdeth her, hee is the field shee delighteth to walke in, hee is the forrest shee forceth to hunt in' (176). It is this definition of the limits and obligations imposed on wives that makes Horatia's behaviour at her husband's death so offensively incomprehensible to her relatives. The public victory of the state represents her personal defeat: 'my triumph, my victory, my prosperytie, my blisse, my peace, my pleasure, is perished' (182), and her conception of herself as the sole surviving citizen of her own private nation lends irony to the words spoken by Horatius as he kills her, which G.P. reproduces almost verbatim from Painter: 'so come it to every *Romaine* that shall lament the death of an enemy to the *Romaines*' (183). When desire propelled Horatia beyond the 'compass of reason and the bounds of nature' she began to define herself by her husband: at that point all her other bonds were severed and she ceased to be a Roman, or even a sister.

At that point, too, she began to manifest a marked affinity with the feline protagonists of Baldwin's *Beware the Cat*, who subscribe to a legal system quite separate from that of their owners, and with Gascoigne's Elinor, who sets up her own private state within her husband's household. Unlike her politic predecessors, Horatia has her dilemma as the servant of two masters savagely resolved by a representative of the state authorities—her brother; but her death might be taken as evidence of the threat posed to the identity of European public weals by the alternative affiliations and loyalties that spring up like weeds within their borders. It would take, one might suspect, only a slight adjustment to harness such loyalties in the interests either of a powerful foreign administration, or of a domestic rebellion, or both.

The other story G.P. adapts from Roman history takes this potential for major political conflict ignited by a seemingly insignificant domestic dispute to an explosively rebellious conclusion. 'Icilius and Virginia' features yet another clash between private and public obligations; but this time the encounter sparks off a revolution.

Once again, the various sources available to Pettie highlight the originality of his treatment. Livy's history emphasizes the part played by Virginia's death in reforming the constitution of the Roman republic.[17] William Painter's, by contrast, warns of the collapse of legal simplicity that attends the abuse of political power. Painter tells the story as the fifth novel in *The Palace of Pleasure*: the Decemviri, officials

[17] See *Livy*, ed. G. P. Goold, trans. B. O. Foster *et al.*, Loeb Classical Library, 14 vols. (Cambridge, Mass.: Harvard University Press, and London: William Heinemann, 1984), vol. ii, trans. B. O. Foster, 143 ff.

appointed to introduce Athenian law into Rome, take advantage of their legislative powers to seize control of the state, stirring up resentment among the citizens in the process.[18] Popular outrage comes to a head when one of the Decemviri conceives a 'libidinous desire, to ravishe a yong virgine' (i. 35) and perverts the law to satisfy his lust. The girl's father Virginius kills his daughter to assert his right to dispose of her, then uses the gesture as an emotive device to raise the Roman people in rebellion. The revolt that follows topples the Decemviri from power and restores the tribunes to supremacy in Rome. Painter closes the novel with the moral that the private misdeeds of public officials initiate political chain reactions: 'upon the filthie affection of one noble man, issued paricide, murder, rebellion, hatred, depriving of magistrates, and great mischiefes succedinge one in an others necke; wherupon the noble and victorious citie, was lyke to be a praye to forren nations' (i. 44–5). Unlike Livy's, his reading of the episode avoids condoning revolution by focusing on the magisterial misgovernment that sparks it off, and his concentration on Appius allows him to skirt altogether the issue of whether Virginius was right to take his daughter's life. Pettie's version, on the other hand, marginalizes Appius in order to place the triangular relationship between father, daughter, and the daughter's lover squarely at the centre of the narrative.

Pettie could have known at least one more Elizabethan version of this story. This was an interlude published in 1575 as a *New Tragical Comedie of Apius and Virginia*, written by an anonymous playwright who signs himself R.B. (not, as far as is known, the R.B. of Pettie' *Pallace*), and based on the Physician's story in *The Canterbury Tales*.[19] Unlike Livy's and Painter's versions, the play focuses on Virginia's relations with her parents, and depicts the family unit as the ideal educational environment. By promising to obey her father and rejecting Classical examples of unruly children, R.B.'s Virginia establishes her identity as the model Elizabethan subject, the antithesis of the disruptive woman or the errant prodigal child. Where the prodigal brother in Gascoigne's *Glasse of Government* end up by being exiled and executed for crimes against foreign states, R.B.'s Virginia emerges triumphant from her father's efforts to test her integrity by espionage. When Virginius eavesdrops on a conversation between his wife and daughter

---

[18] For Painter's version of the story, see *The Palace of Pleasure*, i. 35–45.

[19] *Tudor Interludes*, ed. Peter Happé (Harmondsworth: Penguin, 1975), 152–70. References in the text are to this edition.

he hears, not the incriminating evidence of a secret plot for which so many contemporary fictions used the same device, but conclusive proof of their familial solidarity: 'A, Gods, why doo ye not compel eche Dame the lyke to showe?' (278). The family then celebrates their measured lives in the measures of song: 'Then friendly and kindly, let measure be mixed | With reason, in season, where friendship is fixed' (280). In contrast to the citizens of this perfect miniature state, the Vice's companions, a male and female servant, gleefully disobey their drab superiors, eliciting the Vice Haphazard's remark that 'As pecockes sit perking by chaunce in the plomtree | So maides would be masters, by the guise of this countrey' (288). The country's misrule stems from Apius, who first sets himself up as an abolute monarch, then announces (like Pettie's Sinorix) that he has surrendered his role as a magistrate, inappropriately enough, to Virginia, the paragon of filial obedience: 'I rule no more, but ruled am; I do not judge but am judged' (288). Perhaps the most striking change R.B. makes to his sources is in Virginia's death scene, which he reworks with some ingenuity in such a way as to preserve the audience's sympathy for her father. On hearing of Apius' plot to ravish his daughter, Virginius plans at first to commit suicide; it is only when Virginia asks him to kill her instead that he agrees to do so, on condition that he can kill himself afterwards. Like Isaac in the mystery cycles, Virginia succumbs to a touch of nerves just before her death and asks to have her eyes bound (309), but otherwise father and daughter are in complete agreement about the necessity that she be sacrificed.[20] These revisions of the death scene both add to the story's pathos and enable the audience to subscribe more readily to R.B.'s moral, which recommends Virginia's family (somewhat unfortunately, one would have thought) as a model 'Of bringing up of tender youth' (317).

R.B. presents the parent–child relationship as a microcosm of the just society; G.P. instead sees Appius' behaviour as an extension of the discord which is always being sown between parent and child by their conflicting interests. He begins his inversion of the story's traditional readings in his initial sentence, where he considers the story of Virginia as an example not of virginal chastity but of romantic love, and concludes with Cicero that love between men and women is founded above all on 'similitude of manners' (103). His version, in

<hr>

[20] Isaac succumbs to an access of nerves in a version of the episode from Brome, Suffolk, reproduced in *English Mystery Plays*, ed. Peter Happé (Harmondsworth: Penguin, 1975), 52–70.

fact, continues to investigate the simplicity that consolidates alliances but 'Icilius and Virginia' impudently suggests that such simplicity can only ever be established between members of the same generation. The first half of the discourse devotes itself to the wooing of Virginia by Icilius, the fiancé who figures as her father's chief supporter in Painter's version, and it is not until the second half that Appius emerges as the principal threat to the lovers' union. Icilius is encouraged in his courtship by a 'special freend' of his own age (109), who provides another example of the 'similitude of manners' that bind one mind to another in perfect mutual understanding. Like Elyot's Gisippus (whose example he invokes) this friend stumbles on Icilius while he is lamenting his own economic dependency, which he considers an insurmountable obstacle to his suit. The friend enjoins him by the 'inviolable bond of freindship' to tell him the cause of his private grief (112); when he hears it, he can see no reason why Icilius' parents should not remove the impediment with ease: 'her position is not so greate, but your parentes are able to make yours equal unto it' (113). For Icilius and his generation in the story, friendship is a matter of agreement rather than an economic arrangement; but Virginia is less sure of her parents' perception of the grounds of friendship, as she explains to Icilius in a letter: 'though I coulde finde in my heart to like you above all other, yet I know not whether my freinds will yeeld their consent therto' (115).

Unfortunately Virginia's fears are justified. Her parents favour alliances which are sealed by financial securities as against verbal promises; and G.P. depicts the collision between these parental and filial versions of the bond of friendship as an act of violence that foreshadows and provokes the violence Virginius visits on his daughter. The lovers are forced to part so that Icilius can accumulate capital in the wars, and their parting is a dismemberment as savage as that of Progne's child, Little Itis: 'of all greifes it is most gripyng when freindes are forced to parte eche from other, when one hart is placed in two places, when one member is torne as it were from another when ownes selfe is separated from him selfe, or at least his seconde selfe' (117–18). The 'covetous cruelty' of Virginia's parents, then, threatens the very identities of friendship, of marriage, even of selfhood, and weakens the defensive structures of any network of alliances. This violation of the terms by which bonds are contracted differs only in degree from the sexual violation Appius attempts under the cloak of his judicial authority; and Virginius implicitly acknowledges the fact when he tells the Decemvir that he too is guilty of the fraudulent redefinition of verbal bonds: 'doest thou thinke under the pretence of bondage, to make her bound to thy beastlinesse?' (122). Virginia, on the other hand, holds her father responsible for the danger she stands in: 'partly by your meanes I am fallen into this extremity' (123); like Appius he has 'set down his owne will for a law' (122), and his daughter points out that his insistence on economic guarantees from prospective allies has weakened him irrecoverably. Without the aid of trusted supporters such as the absent Icilius he can give her no protection against her assailant: 'your power is to weake to wreak the wrong which is offred me, and your force is to feeble to fence me from the fury of my foes' (123). The sole amends he can make is to forge a new and dreadful bond with his daughter based, like 'true friendship', on a kind of moral equality: she asks him to 'countervayle the lucklesse and lothsome life which you have given mee' with an 'honourable death'. R.B.'s family unit preserved inviolate the 'measure' by which they invested trust in one another; G.P.'s Roman family loses touch with the moral and legal grounds by which assurance is measured, and is forced to adopt the most extreme of measures to recover their mutual confidence. And the processes by which they sever the bonds of friendship are the same processes as those by which unscrupulous politicians like Appius dismantle a nation's legal system. As in all his discourses, Pettie's narrator shifts the arena of ideological debate from the seat of government to the private household, from the court of law to the domestic dispute; and the shift compels his readers to reassess the part played by the most minor of private controversies in making or breaking the security of the state.

The conflicts between parents and children that break out in 'Icilius and Virginia' and 'Scilla and Minos' produce two of G.P.'s most wittily duplicitous conclusions. In the first, he progresses from the statutory commendation of Virginia's 'noble minde' and her father's 'stout courage' to a pragmatic proposal for avoiding the drastic solution to which they are eventually reduced (124). Old men like Appius, he warns his female readers, are given to 'more then outragious lusts', and the opinions of the old are no more to be taken as moral absolutes than the rash inclinations of the young. Time blurs the ageing subject's judgement, so that 'sutch an one shall measure your deedes by his owne desire, and your life present by his owne life past, when hee shall thinke you to bee naught, bicause hee him selfe hath bene naught

(125). The young, then, have as firm a hold on the concept of duty a
their elders, and need to make their voices heard if mismatches are no
to keep occurring: 'humbly request them you may chuse where yo1
like . . . Dutifully tell them that sutch presinesse of parentes brough
*Pyramus* and *Thisbe* to a wofull end, *Romeo* and *Julietta* to untimel}
death, and drave *Virginius* miserably to murther his owne daughte:
*Virginia*' (125). The insertion of Bandello's example of Romeo anc
Julietta into a list of canonical exempla ranks the contemporar}
novel alongside Ovid's fables and Livy's histories, and implies tha
the new generation of prose fictions can speak for the sophisticated
rhetorically accomplished youth of Pettie's generation with as mucl
authority as the texts privileged by the humanist curriculum. 'Scill;
and Minos' goes still further, offering the different generation
among its readers two alternative moral conclusions. The firs
addresses the readers' parents, and warns of the dreadful fate that awaii
recalcitrant children who oppose their fathers' wishes. The second i
concealed parenthetically inside the first, and addresses itself tc
younger readers after their parents have left the room: 'But (Sover-
aigne) now your father is gone, I will give you more sound advice: ]
will admonishe you all . . . not to binde your selves to the froward fans
of your politique parents' (164–5). Fathers and daughters, children anc
parents are locked in a struggle for sovereignty which demands al
their rhetorical cunning and political deviousness if either side is tc
avoid surrendering to the terms dictated by the other. Perhaps the
aspect of the *Petite Pallace* which contributed most to its author's reputation as the iconoclast who burned the literary temple of Diana wa:
the posture it adopts of blatant partisanship in the struggle. G.P
repeatedly sides with the children against the parents, the school o
abuse against the school of good conduct, the secret kingdom o
love against the public weal within which it operates; and he repeatedly insists that the divergent understandings of different generation:
need to be taken into account in the negotiation of any social contract

### 4.   IDOLS AND PILGRIMAGES

One thing in G.P.'s collection is certain: that the crude moral summaries which close conventional sixteenth-century narratives have
nothing to offer the sophisticated understandings of the youthfu
readers they claim to instruct; and the last two stories in the *Petite Pallac*

furnish conclusive proof of this premiss. 'Pigmalion's friende, and his Image' begins with a sentence that casts doubt on the very possibility of reaching a consensus: 'to resolve certenly upon incertenty, is the way never to be in any certenty:... to determine of those things which are not in our powers to perfourme, is nothing els but to bee deceived of our expectation' (228). The sentence might serve as an admonitory motto for moralists like Guevara or Fenton: to present a reader with moral instructions without recognizing the reader's capacity to ignore those instructions is self-evidently futile.[21]

The uncertain bearing of this sentence on the story that follows it helps to make G.P.'s point. In his improvised variation on Ovid's fable of Pygmalion, the protagonist begins by falling in love with a married woman, and enjoys a comfortable platonic relationship with her for a number of years before the inevitable blot appears on the horizon of their happiness. Indeed, Pygmalion idolizes the woman to such a degree that sexual intercourse would have damaged his mental image of her beyond repair. Instead he restricts the physical aspect of the relationship to the pleasures of masturbation: 'Yea, hee received more pleasure of her by imagination, than of any other woman by the acte of generation' (231). But his female friend eventually tires of the purity of his devotion and deserts him for another, more active, lover; and this desertion provokes Pygmalion into a misogynistic tirade which takes up almost six pages of Hartman's edition, in which he accuses the whole female sex of representing 'wo unto men, as their name importeth' (241). As his pun implies, Pygmalion considers women to be the undisputed mistresses of fraud and double meanings, and his attack urges the impossibility of men forging any amicable contract with them, since the verbal resources by which such deals are made have no place in female rhetoric: 'then farewel reason, thou resteth not in womans head: then farewel wyt, thou wieldest not womens doinges: then farewel fayth, thou art no womans pheare' (233). Moreover, women have a limitless capacity for seducing men into complicity with their fraudulence. They can persuade the wisest of men to 'naughtinesse' by enveloping him in 'counterfeit courtesye' (239), and once they have done so they transfer their attentions to another male victim as soon as the inclination takes them. The

---

[21] More's persona in *Utopia* would have agreed. 'And to be plain with you', he tells Hythloday, 'truly I cannot allow that such communication shal be used, or such counsel given, as you be sure shall never be regarded or received' (46–7). This is a problem explored more fully by Lyly in *Euphues and his England*; see Ch. 6, s. 2 below.

sentence that inaugurates the story, then, could be given at least two readings. On the one hand it could be taken as a warning to men that any agreement they reach with women will constitute a 'resolution upon incertenty', and that they should shun all such agreements as Pygmalion and *The Deceyte of Women* recommend. On the other hand, Pygmalion's diatribe itself resolves upon 'incertenty', first in that it builds its case on the weight of a single experience, and secondly in that Pygmalion proves quite incapable of sticking to his resolution. The misogynistic argument he constructs is an 'image', an elaborate castle in the air which has no bearing on the practical necessity that men form partnerships with women, as was his Platonic 'image' of his married lover, and the inadequacy of both positions is exposed when Pygmalion creates a third and still more fantastic image, the marble statue of an ideal woman with which he falls in love.

Pygmalion's story becomes in G.P.'s hands both a satire on Neoplatonic philosophy of the kind propounded by Castiglione's Bembo and a mocking commentary on men's propensity for cleaving to untenable convictions and for worshipping images they have fashioned for themselves. These propensities, G.P. implies, find their most absurd manifestation in the Catholic worship of idols. Pygmalion's erotic attraction to his statue resembles the misguided beliefs of those who 'love images right well, and verely perswade themselves that images have power to pray for them, and help them to heaven' (244). Such fantasies, he says, are assisted by the current trend for building water-powered automata, like the articulated sculptures in Renaissance gardens which reproduce all the motions of submissive women, 'when images have beene made to bow their heads, to holde out their handes, to weepe, to speake etc.' (245). For G.P. as for other Elizabethan Protestants, Catholicism resembles an elaborate machine for the simulation of miraculous wish-fulfilment—a global version of the mechanical paradise encountered by Nashe's unfortunate traveller Jack Wilton in Rome.[22] Friendship too can resemble such eye-deceiving simulacra; it can either be based on the solid qualities G.P. compares to different artefacts made of stone—jewels, pillars, 'a picture made in marble' or the legendary 'stoane of *Scilicia*' (246)—or else it can be a cunning imitation of stony reliability: 'it is most easy to deceive under the name of a freind'. In fact, Pygmalion's

---

[22] See Thomas Nashe, *The Unfortunate Traveller and Other Works*, ed. J. B. Steane (Harmondsworth: Penguin, 1972), 327–30. All references are taken from this edition.

rift into idolatry throws a new light on G.P.'s witty meditations on lliances and bonds. He founds his arguments on shaky premisses nd faulty reasoning, and such reasoning encourages the formation f bonds which are neither lasting nor reliable. Under these conditions measure of uncertainty in the form of scepticism becomes desirable ather than threatening; to 'resolve certenly' on suppositions and ncertain alliances is a mark of gullibility, not trust. For this reason he story ends with instructions not on the best means of identifying our true friends but on the surest techniques for getting rid of your alse ones.

The last novel completes G.P.'s demolition of fixed moral and deological categories. Its opening sentence articulates not a truism ut a dilemma, the unresolved question of 'what life in this life it ee best to enter into' (248). Instead of answering it G.P. advises hat whatever career his young male readers may choose they should void addicting themselves exclusively to any single way of life. All uman experience is subject to change, and ambitious youths should e infinitely capable of adapting themselves to new contingencies. Alexius', whose title breaks the sequence of titular alliances and mis-lliances that dominate the collection, comically illustrates what is kely to happen to young men who fail to cultivate such politic flex-bility.

The story's protagonist cultivates instead the rhetorical excesses and bsurdities that encourage ideological extremism. In two long peeches, each of which vehemently rejects the premisses of the ther, Alexius argues with equal vigour the case for two antagonistic orms of schooling: the humanist educational programme, which levotes itself exclusively to literary study, and the erotic curriculum aught by women, which takes the body as its principal text. In each ase Alexius is convinced that he has discovered the sole 'pathway to ʾaradise' (260), the exclusive route to personal fulfilment. The first peech is a response to his father's complaint that Alexius is bringing o 'commodity' to the public weal by his excessive dedication to ooks. In it the boy contends that learning was responsible for the oundation of civilization itself, since without it neither cities, laws, or religions would exist; he supports his apology with examples of minent kings and generals who have recognized the need to sponsor earning. The second speech is an extravagant reply to Pygmalion's nisogynistic tirade. Alexius utters it in a flurry of excitement after e has slept with a woman for the first time, and it resembles the

opening novel of Painter's second volume in that it sketches the blue
print for an alternative, Amazonian, form of government, a new stat
in which political power devolves on the superior administrative skil
of women. In it he openly acknowledges the link between the privat
domestic economy and the public political sphere which is implic
throughout the collection—and throughout English prose fiction c
the sixteenth century. He cites the anti-feminist jibe that women ar
'alwayes desirous of soveraintie' as proof that they possess a 'noble an
haughty minde' (266), just as women's proverbial infidelity demon
strates their aptitude for politics, 'seeinge in privy stealthes they ca
practise so politikely that their husbands, though never so wary, sha
never be ware of it'. In fact, in his excitement at losing his virginit
Alexius is prepared to advocate the completion of the proce:
recorded in *The Deceyte of Women* and see men replaced by wome
at the helm of the public weal.

Alexius' conflicting encomiums of learning and women expose th
radical disjunctions in his mind between the component parts of h:
experience: between marriage and sexual abstinence, between th
intellect and the senses, between learning and action. But educate
Elizabethan readers of the two arguments might quickly have decide
that they focus on different aspects of a single well-balanced mal
career. Both speeches exploit the same vocabulary: in the first, learn
ing is the youth's 'chief pleasure', while in the second, sexual pleasur
usurps the diction of the schoolroom, as Alexius learns the eroti
equivalents of the parts of speech, numbers, articles, and the best les
son of all, the 'conjunction of cases, and joyninge of genders togethe1
(260). The boy's artificial divorce between the study and the marriag
bed arises, like Pygmalion's misogyny, from his faulty logic, as G.F
points out: 'his general reasons are altogether sophisticall and full c
fallacies' (268). But, more specifically, G.P. seems to hint that h
derives his fallacious reasoning from an immersion in the ideolog
of the Catholic church. Some of Pettie's readers would have know:
that the story of Alexius was based on the life of a Catholic saint, nar
rated in a popular medieval story-collection, the *Gesta Romanorum.*[2]
Alexius shares with his Catholic prototype a susceptibility to the wor
ship of graven images—his praise of women could be read as a1
extended exercise in idolatry, and he cites the example of the Virgi1

---

[23] See *Gesta Romanorum*, trans. Charles Swan (Toronto: General Publishing, and Londo1
Constable, 1959), 32–8. In this version the tale is highly allegorized: the saint's wife, fc
instance, is interpreted as 'the vanity of the world' (38).

Mary as proof that women have no need for the company of men. Soon after completing his second speech he tires of marriage and adopts the religious life as his new obsession, replacing his earthly bride with a male 'beloved', Christ, as if in imitation of a professed monk or celibate friar. To pursue his new vocation he embarks on a lifelong 'pilgrimage' which presumably confirms his father's fears that he will fail to yield any commodity to his country (270). At the end of his career Alexius, like Admetus, is no more a model citizen for his Protestant readers than he was at the beginning.

G.P.'s conclusion finally undermines any pretensions the text might have had to impart a moral 'lesson'. It does so by the daring expedient of juxtaposing seemingly serious religious precepts with the sexual blandishments of a lecherous priest. G.P. begins by exhorting his male readers to 'forsake wife and wealth, and take up the crosse of Christ and follow him as *Alexius* did' (270); he then advises his female audience to keep their desire for their husbands within reasonable limits for fear of being distracted from the love of God. But both of these recommendations are given an unexpected twist in the last sentence of the collection, in which G.P. executes his most abrupt transition from solemnity to frivolity:

But I could preache better to you in a more pleasant matter, I wil leave this text to maister parson, who while he is unmaried I warrant you wil disswade you so earnestly from sutch idolatrous doting on your husbands, that hee will not sticke to tell you beesides Scripture that you ought too have no respect of persons, but to love an other man or him selfe as well as your husbandes. (271)

Suddenly the anti-matrimonial counsel G.P. has been dispensing transforms itself into the ideal scriptural 'text' for a clerical seducer. The parson who has failed to marry might well be suspected of Catholic leanings, and his exploitation of his clerical position as a cover for his lechery is typical of Elizabethan representations of Catholic confessors.[24] The priest's opposition to idolatry is nothing but sexual opportunism; and this casts a dubious light on the authorial intentions behind the last two novels, with their mockery of the idolizing tendencies of Pygmalion and Alexius. Indeed, the whole collection is full of such sexual blandishments and innuendoes, purportedly directed at the female audience to which the stories were originally told 'in a manner *ex tempore*' (4); from 'Amphiaraus and Eriphile', where G.P.

---

[24] Such as Arthur Brooke's; see above, Ch. 2, s. 2.

claims that 'the girles of our parish think that welch *Sir Richard* hir
selfe can not make a better preache then I can' (102), to 'Admetu
and Alcest', where he offers to give a practical demonstration to h
female auditors of the 'manner' in which the lovers kissed (137
Like the infiltration of Classical narratives by the Italianate nove
these lascivious posturings introduce a seedily seditious undercurren
into what might be taken by the unwary or the obtuse for conven
tional exemplary texts; so that the entire collection can be given a
diverse readings as one of G.P.'s duplicitous conclusions. On th
one hand it is a flashy display of its author's skills in the arts of rhetori
and exegesis, designed to demonstrate his immense potential as a ser
vant of the state; on the other it is a surreptitious invitation to youthfu
disobedience and irresponsibility, which warns of the uses to whic
the author's talents could be put by the ideological enemies of the Eli
zabethan public weal. Like Gascoigne's two miscellanies it is a warn
ing as well as an advertisement, an elaborate piece of blackmail whic
stridently demands that its author be given more useful employmen
as well as humbly requesting it.

The second of the preliminary letters in the collection, 'The Lette
of G.P. to R.B. Concerning this Woorke' (5–7), foreshadows the du
function of the text as a corrupting influence as well as an instructiv
one. In his letter, G.P. expresses the somewhat belated misgiving tha
the collection will have an adverse effect on its inexperience
reader—that R.B. is in greater need of a sexual bridle than a spur—
and announces the narrator's intention to set out on pilgrimage lik
Alexius to expiate the sins of his storytelling youth. But we are onl
introduced to G.P.'s misgivings after we have learned in the first epis
tle that they were fully justified—after R.B. has expressed his greate
commitment to women than to men and has released Pettie's duplici
tous collection to the press. And G.P.'s resolution to go on pilgrimag
with Alexius would seem to furnish pretty inadequate proof of hi
reformation. Rather it suggests that he remains wedded to wandering
perhaps on the Continent, perhaps even in Italy; that he will continue
in fact, to be seduced by foreign manners and ideologies, and that h
will return from his travels in the monstrous shape of an Italianat
Englishman, more rhetorically fraudulent and more sexually profligat
than ever.

The deadly effect the collection might have on its young male read
ers is enacted in the fate of its protagonists. When he falls is love, Alex
ius, like most of the characters in the collection, finds that he ha

wandered into an elaborate verbal maze from which there is finally no escape. Intellectually sophisticated but resistant to guidance, Alexius succumbs to the 'confused *Chaos* of conceits' which G.P. mentions in the novel's prefatory paragraph and quickly finds himself 'lost as it were in a *Labyrinth*, not findinge any way out' (248). Progne strays into a similar architectural trap when she marries Tereus, since he is descended 'of the seede of *Theseus*, who left *Ariadne* in the desertes, to bee devoured, through whose helpe hee subdued the Monster *Minotaur*, and escaped out of the intricate *Labirinth*' (52). Later Agrippina finds that 'the more diligently shee laboured to get out of the *Labyrinth* of love the more doubtfully was shee intricated therein' (75); and Pygmalion implies that all relations between the sexes involve them in the same impasse:

this hatefull love by nature wee follow, it bereaveth us of reason, pollicie hath no place in it, pleasure doubleth our dolour, patience purchaseth no ease, labour is lost, payne prevayleth not, counsayle conduceth not, time tieth and intangleth us, no, nothyng is able to leade us out of this intricate Labyrinth. (237)

Pettie's astute analysis of the various logical and rhetorical snares that inveigle the young into a verbal maze without an exit proves his mastery of the strategies essential for a public servant in the intricate world of Elizabethan politics. But his collection is another such verbal labyrinth capable of ensnaring both its reader and its talented author, and, like Gascoigne's *Posies*, it daringly courts the intervention of the state authorities to provide it with an issue.

Recent work on *A Petite Pallace of Pettie his Pleasure* has rightly pointed out that it is addressed to women in order to make a point to men.[25] But the point is not simply that of demonstrating the author's mastery over his female audience. Pettie's representation of women as the architects of devious domestic policies and the proponents of moral absolutism allows him to explore some of the complex linguistic issues involved in the forging of agreements and the drawing up of contracts in mid-Elizabethan England. On the one hand, his female subjects compose, and elicit from their lovers, the most elaborate forms of fraud; on the other they are the foremost champions of simplicity, and illustrate the dangers that attend the attempt to impose an agreed ideological language on the state. Like foreign powers,

---

[25] See Lucas, *Writing for Women*, ch. 3. See also Hutson, *The Usurer's Daughter*, 112–14.

women compete with Elizabethan officialdom for control of the skills of quick capacities; and their sometimes violent resistance to mastery lends urgency to the task of restoring the educated youth of England to the work of religious and political reformation.

# 5
# The Dissolution of *Euphues*

## I. DOUBLE READINGS

If Pettie's *Pallace* resembles a rebellious library in which every volume
has infiltrated its neighbour, Lyly's two *Euphues* books look like a pair
of insufferably self-important volumes which aspire to form an entire
private library on their own. Between them, they contain representative samples of almost every kind of text known to the Elizabethan
reader: from Italian novella to Roman New Comedy, from childcare
manual to marriage guidance pamphlet, from theological disputation
to alchemical tract, from animal fable to tourist brochure; and the
numerous imitations they spawned within a few years of what Lyly
calls their birth testify to their astonishing capacity for generating
further texts.[1] But in addition to the incipient future fictions they contain, the *Euphues* books also carry the seed of their own redundancy.
In the epistle to the 'Gentlemen Readers' in *Euphues: The Anatomy of
Wit* (1578), Lyly muses that 'We commonly see the booke that at
Christmas lyeth bound on the Stacioners stall, at Easter to be broken
in the Haberdasshers shop', and for a few months each new edition of
the *Anatomy* changed the seasons mentioned in this sentence to com-
ply with its new date of publication.[2] 'Christmas' became 'Midsomer'
and then 'Easter', 'Easter' was altered to 'Christmasse', and in this way
Lyly forced his text literally to keep up with the times. This discreet
acknowledgement of the volume's transience is not just a response

[1] Among many others, the *Euphues* books spawned Barnaby Riche's *The Straunge
and Wonderful Adventures of Don Simonides* (1581 and 1584), in which the protagonist
meets Euphues face to face; Robert Greene's *Euphues his Censure to Philautus* (1587); Thomas
Lodge's *Rosalynde. Euphues Golden Legacie* (1590), which announces that it was 'found after
his death in his Cell at Silexedra', and the same author's *Euphues Shadow* (1592).
[2] R. W. Bond notes these changes to the seasons in his edition of *The Complete Works of
John Lyly*, 3 vols. (Oxford: Clarendon Press, 1902), i. 182. All my references to Lyly's works
are taken from this edition.

to commercial pressure; it also reflects one of his most consisten
observations, that fashions, desires, and intellectual trends exist in
constant state of flux; and Lyly's peculiarity is that he seems to tak
an almost unseemly pleasure in the fact. The epistle goes on to te
us that its author is 'content' that his work should vanish in thre
months 'when as the greatest wonder lasteth but nyne days' (i. 182
Of all Elizabethan writers of fiction Lyly is perhaps the most consciou
of the temporal limits of his text, and the most sceptical of the effor
of contemporary moralists to police their readers' time.

Perhaps Lyly stressed the inevitability of his books' eventual out
moding in order to emphasize the highly topical nature of their con
tents. The *Euphues* books struck at the very heart of the current debat
about the function of fiction. No other work of the period contair
such a wealth of allusion to texts and metaphors germane to the con
troversy; and no other author (always excepting Sidney) possessed th
stylistic mastery which would permit such allusiveness.[3] Once th
debate, the texts, and the metaphors from which they constructe
themselves were no longer current, Lyly's fictions could fulfil thei
ambition to fall into fashionable obsolescence. By the time Rober
Greene put Euphues to sleep on the title-page of his *Menapho*
(1589),[4] Lyly had been long engaged in producing yet more transier
and topical fictions, the comedies he wrote for Elizabeth I.

Lyly proclaimed his preoccupation with exuberant inventivenes
and moral ambiguity when he launched his first volume under th
aegis of 'wit'. According to Elizabethan anatomists, the wit was th
area of the brain into which the evidence of the senses was first pro
jected before being sorted by the understanding and stored on th
orderly shelves of the memory; a gallimaufry or stew of undigeste
images and raw ideas, the most fertile and the most undiscipline

---

[3]  An account of Lyly's style can be found in Morris Croll's introduction to his edition c
the two *Euphues* books, *Euphues: The Anatomy of Wit; Euphues and his England*, ed. M. W
Croll and H. Clemons (London: Routledge, 1916). This was superseded by Jonas A. Barisl
'The Prose Style of John Lyly', *ELH* 23 (1956), 14–35. A more recent discussion is that c
Janel Mueller in *The Native Tongue and the Word*. Another useful account can be found i
Leah Scragg, *The Metamorphosis of Gallathea: A Study in Creative Adaptation* (Washington
DC: University Press of America, 1982), ch. 1.

[4]  Greene's *Menaphon* is subtitled 'Camillas Alarum to slumbering Euphues, in his Mel
ancholie Cell, at Silexedra', but the comments Greene makes in the narrative suggest tha
she did not succeed in waking him. Melicertus thinks that Samela has 'learnd with Lucill
in *Athens* to anatomize wit', and informs her that euphuism is out of date. See *The Li
and Complete Works in Prose and Verse of Robert Greene*, ed. Alexander B. Grosart, 15 vol
(London: Hazell, Watson & Viney, 1881–6), vi. 3 and 82.

region of the mind.[5] To live on your wits was to rely on your gifts of imaginative improvisation, rather than on your reason, the organizing principle that was so carefully nurtured by humanist pedagogues and logicians. The dangers involved in such self-reliance were the subject of John Redford's interlude *Wit and Science* (1531–4), whose hero rejects conventional forms of schooling to pursue a course of study based on unsupervised experiment, and is killed as a result by the dreadful giant Tediousness, then miraculously resurrected by a passing virtue, and finally dressed up by the monster Idleness in the fool's cap and bells belonging to Ignorance, her son.[6] Only the most strenuous efforts on the part of Reason can restore Redford's Wit to the pedagogic programme which ensures that he will win the lady Science (or Learning) for his bride, and even after that the recalcitrant youngster does not lose his taste for imaginative and sexual experiments. Two more versions of the adventures of Wit were performed and published in the reign of Elizabeth, and in each version his adversaries—Fancy, Folly, Wantonness, and the rest—grew more devious and more alluring.[7] By the time Ascham came to analyse the difference between the hard wit and the quick one, the faculty of linguistic and intellectual inventiveness had taken on a vigorous life of its own, and Lyly seems to assume prior knowledge of his character's history when he summarizes the contents of *The Anatomy of Wit* on the title-page: 'wherin are contained the delights that Wyt followeth in his youth by the pleasauntnesse of Love, and the happynesse he reapeth in age, by the perfectnesse of Wisedome' (i. 177).

[5] This description of the wit (or more properly 'wits') as a physical area of the brain is, of course, only one of the many Renaissance definitions of this faculty. More often it is alluded to as a mental action. For an Elizabethan anatomist's view of the operation of the wits, see . Thomas Vicary, *The Anatomie of the Bodie of a Man* (first published in 1548, and reissued by the surgeons of St Bartholomew's in 1577), ed. F. J. Furnivall and Percy Furnivall (London: N. Trübner and Co., 1888), 31. See also Robert Burton, *The Anatomy of Melancholy*, introd. Holbrook Jackson, 3 vols. (London: J. M. Dent and Sons, 1932), vol.1, 165: 'The agent is that which is called the wit of man, acumen or subtlety, sharpness of invention, when he doth invent of himself without a teacher, or learns anew, which abstracts those intelligible species from the phantasy, and transfers them to the passive understanding, "because there is nothing in the understanding which was not first in the sense".' For a full account of the various meanings of the term 'wit' in the Renaissance, see William G. Crane, *Wit and Rhetoric in the Renaissance: The Formal Basis of Elizabethan Prose Style* (New York: Columbia University Press, 1937; reprinted Gloucester, Mass.: Peter Smith, 1964).

[6] See Happé, *Tudor Interludes*, 181–219.

[7] *A New and Pleasant Enterlude intituled The Mariage of Witte and Science*, (c.1569), and *The Marriage of Wit and Wisdom* by Francis Merbury (published before 1579). For the text of the latter, see *English Moral Interludes*, ed. Glynne Wickham (London: J. M. Dent, 1976), 163–94.

Sidney ascribes two functions to wit in the *Apology for Poetry*. The 'erected wit' is the quality that brings the human creative powers closest to the divine; the quality that makes poetry possible (101). Yet wit is also the faculty which most 'abuseth Poetry' (125), and which is most in need of a disciplinary 'Daedalus' to check its exuberant ambition (132). Wit's duplicity emerges again in Spenser's account of the House of Alma, his allegorical topography of the mind and body. Here the eccentric figure of Phantastes, the personification of the faculty that engenders fictions, possesses a 'working wit | That never idle was, ne once could rest a whit' (II. ix. 49), and this constant 'working' brings Phantastes close to lunacy: he has 'sharpe staring eyes, | That mad or foolish seemd' (II. ix. 52). The perilous nature of his creativity is signalled by the resemblance between the monstrous murals that decorate his chamber and the forces of Maleger which besiege the House he occupies. But when Spenser moves on to describe the room belonging to the antithesis of Fantasy, Reason, the elegant wall-paintings in his orderly chamber depict 'All artes, all science, all Philosophy, | And all that in the world was aye thought *wittily*' (II. ix. 53, my emphasis). Wit would seem to resemble Erasmus' Folly in the pluarality of its actions; it both generates the arts and sciences and spawns the rebellious fantasies that threaten to destroy them.

In its capacity for surprising disclosures wit participates in the nature of Alcibiades' Sileni, the grotesque statues described by Plato which can be opened up to reveal the images of gods.[8] The Sileni supplied the opening motif for Rabelais's *Gargantua*,[9] and Erasmus' Folly adopts them as her emblem:

all human affairs, like the Sileni of Alcibiades, have two very dissimilar aspects; so that what at first sight (as they say) seems death when looked into further becomes life, and vice versa. This is true also of what seems beautiful and ugly; rich and poor; disgraceful and glorious; learned and ignorant ... in short, you will suddenly find everything the opposite if you open the Silenus.[10]

Folly's account occurs while she is arguing that a fool gains more wisdom from the experience of innumerable mistakes than the wise man

---

[8] For Erasmus' discussion of the *Sileni Alcibiadis*, see *Erasmus on his Times*, ed. Margaret Mann Phillips (Cambridge: Cambridge University Press, 1967), 77–97.

[9] 'Silenes of old were little boxes, like those we now may see in the shops of Apothecaries, painted on the outside with wanton toyish figures ... but within those capricious caskets were carefully preserved and kept many rich jewels, and fine drugs.' François Rabelais, *The Lives, Heroic Deeds, and Sayings of Gargantua and his Son Pantagruel*, trans. Sir Thomas Urquhart and Peter Le Motteux (London: Chatto & Windus, 1921), bk. 1, p. xvii.

[10] *The Essential Erasmus*, trans. John P. Dolan (New York: Mentor, 1964), 118.

derives from all his theoretical studies; a thesis that Lyly maintains with increasing relish as his work progresses. *The Anatomy of Wit* imitates the more unsettling version of the Sileni which Erasmus discusses in the *Adagia*: the inverted kind, which looks attractive on the outside but when opened discloses something repellent, like the fair human skin which envelops the disgusting inner organs in Gascoigne's dedication to *Hemetes the Heremyte*.[11] Both Lyly and Erasmus associate this kind of Silenus with the ugly wearers of exotic clothing; but Lyly penetrates beneath the clothing to dissect the body itself, exposing not some godlike humanist intellect but the warring elements and conflicting impulses that motivate Marlowe's Tamburlaine. As Lyly's fashionable fictions proliferate, they demonstrate more and more his delight in the disjunction between container and contained, word and matter, public façades and secret agendas. By the time he wrote *Campaspe*, his version of the Sileni had become radically different from that of Erasmus. The Prologue at Court begins by reminding the audience that '*Jupiter* placed *Silenus* Asse among the starres', but goes on to say, '*Alcebiades* covered his pictures beeing Owles and Apes, with a courtaine embroidered with Lions and Eagles' (ii. 316). Lyly's Alcibiades does not hide the figure of a god inside an ugly statue; instead the surface of his text conceals under a courtly veil the confusing mixture of wisdom (the owls of Athene) and apish folly which underlies all human artefacts and endeavours. But this version of the Sileni occurs at the end of a long process during which Lyly was formulating his literary theory and practice; a process that began with the epistle dedicatory of *The Anatomy of Wit*.

The dedication offers an exuberantly sophisticated key to the problems involved in reading the ensuing text. It begins by describing a series of imaginary paintings, examples of the 'muet Poesie' which every Elizabethan apologist used as an analogy for verbal fictions.[12] Both Painter and Fenton used painting to illustrate history's status as

---

[11] See above, Ch. 3, s. 2.

[12] For Puttenham's poem on the topic of *ut pictura poesis*, see *The Arte of English Poesie*, 174:

> If Poesie be, as some have said,
> A speaking picture to the eye:
> Then is a picture not denaid,
> To be a muet Poesie.

For a discussion of the topic, see Lucy Gent, *Picture and Poetry 1560–1620* (Leamington Spa: James Hall, 1981), which contains many interesting insights into Lyly's allusions to the visual arts.

an index to transcendent truths: Painter describes history as the 'picture of verity' (ii. 150), while for Fenton histories are 'the only and true tables whereon are drawn in perfect colour the virtues and vices of every condition of man' (*Tragicall Discourses*, 42). These linguistic paintings possess the power to reduce the intricacies of right and wrong to simple diagrams and vivid colours, the necessary first step in the pedagogic process of attracting readers to virtue and repelling them from vice. But Lyly's paintings are a more unruly form of art. The first portrait in the book offers not a simple pattern of virtue or vice but a problem of interpretation: 'Paratius drawing the counterfaite of Helen . . . made the attier of hir head loose, who being demaunded why he dyd so, he aunswered, she was loose' (i. 179). George Whetstone's miscellany *The Rocke of Regard* began by repelling its readers with the portrait of the diseased Cressida, a blunt warning against misreading the collection as an incitement to lechery.[13] Lyly's volume, by contrast, begins with a depiction of Helen's proverbial beauty, in which the clue to her 'loose' behaviour is so tastefully and wittily concealed that it emerges only when the spectator 'demaunds' an explanation from the artist, who responds with a pun (and at this point the word 'counterfaite' may also assume a double meaning). A picture of Vulcan comes next, followed by one of Venus; and the functions of these two paintings are still more complex. The pictures are described as 'curiously' and 'cunningly' executed—not words which Fenton could apply to his simple coloured charts; and, being set side by side, the ugliness of Vulcan is presumably intensified and the beauty of Venus exalted. But those who remember that Venus was Vulcan's wife and that she committed adultery with Mars will find additional significance in the disparity between their appearances. For these viewers the physical blemishes of the portraits—the fact that Vulcan has been painted with a club foot and that Venus sports a mole—offer a sardonic comment on their blemished marriage. The dedication's list of obliquely revealing paintings ends with an anecdote in which the artist Apelles refuses to let the authority of Alexander interfere with the accuracy of his art. When Alexander tries to conceal a disfiguring scar with his finger, Apelles paints him caught in the act of concealment, 'with his finger cleaving to his face'. Lyly concludes from these pictorial examples that 'in all perfect workes aswell the

[13]  See *The Rocke of Regard*, ed. J. P. Collier (n.p.: Collier's Reprints, 1870), 35, where the reader is approached by Cressida 'whom you may suppose, in tattered wedes, halfe hunger-starved, miserably arrayde, with scabs, leprosie, and mayngie, to complaine as followeth . . .'.

fault as the face is to be showen' (i. 179), and on this premiss he founds
his case for exploring the 'vanities' as well as the 'vertues' of his slippery protagonist, Euphues.

Lyly's pictures with their attendant anecdotes and the conclusion he
draws from them can be read in two very different ways. On the one
hand they can be taken as a variation on the traditional authorial
apology for mixing good and bad examples in a work of fiction;
such a reading would assume that, like Painter and Fenton, Lyly
intends his readers to respond by rejecting the 'fault' manifested by
each portrait and cleaving instead to the unblemished ideal. But it
soon becomes clear that Lyly sees this disengagement of the fault
from the face as an impossibility. According to his sources, the ideal
rulers Cyrus and Alexander both possessed rather comic physical and
behavioural blemishes (Cyrus had a hooked nose and Alexander was a
drunk), and their status as kings, the most potent form of exemplum,
implicitly spreads their 'mixed' condition throughout the societies
they ruled. Both the external proportions of the painterly nude and
the internal workings of the mind exhibit the same structural complexity: 'as every Paynter that shadoweth a man in all parts, giveth
every peece his just proporcion, so he that disciphereth the qualities
of the mynde, ought aswell to shew every humor in his kinde, as
the other doth every part in his colour' (i. 180). And the deeper the
artist or anatomist probes in his investigation of mind and body,
the more contrasts he must needs expose: 'The Surgion that maketh
the Anatomy sheweth aswel the muscles of the heele, as the vaines
of the hart' (i. 180). Beauty and blemish are inextricably interwoven
in the composition of the human frame, and this brings us to the second reading of Lyly's text: the closer, more 'anatomical', reading to
which the book's title seems to enjoin us. According to this reading,
Lyly's anecdote of Parrhasius explaining his portrait of Helen proclaims
not only the artist's integrity in exposing vice but also the capacity of
the vicious to take pleasure in ingenious disguises and to make themselves attractive (Helen's 'loose' head-dress is wittily seductive as well
as morally significant). The story of Apelles painting Alexander could
be read as signalling the artist's simultaneous complicity with and
independence of the strategies by which the ruling authorities conceal
their flaws beneath a propagandistic gloss (Alexander's finger). The
spectator's need to ask the artist to explain his painting, to know the
story of Venus and Vulcan in order to interpret their portraits, and
to be aware that there is a scar beneath Alexander's finger, suggests

too that an 'anatomical' reading is an élitist one, the territory of an exclusive company of clever insiders who have access to the confidential information that enables them to understand the subtleties of a text. Lyly's 'counterfaites', in other words, are of a very different kind from Sidney's speaking pictures.[14] Instead of giving form and vitality to abstract ideals like Sidney's poet, they share the historian's condition of being 'captived to the truth of a foolish world', and they share the world's deviousness. Lyly tells us that if the 'sight' of Euphues seems 'to foolish to be regarded of the learned' his readers 'ought not to impute it to the iniquitie of the author, but to the necessitie of the history' (i. 180). History, whether feigned or factual, of necessity imitates the mixture of disparate elements inherent in its subject, like the portraits of the fictional Helen and the historical Alexander, and Lyly's history demands the same intensive scrutiny as Parrhasius' painting. Read in this way the epistle might be interpreted as Lyly's declaration of his affiliation to, and mastery of, a new form of fiction, concerned not with pedagogic simplicity, nor with Fentonian 'principles and rules', but with a witty imitation of the puzzling complexity of contemporary public and private life.

   The second half of the epistle elicits the same alternative acts of reading as the first. The traditionalist can continue to accept at face value Lyly's protestations that he recognizes his moral responsibility as an author. Lyly assures such a reader that he has chosen to include 'mo speaches which for gravitie wil mislyke the foolish, then unsemely termes which for vanitie may offend the wise' (i. 180), and goes on to apologize for the plainness of his style (which will 'nothing delight the dayntie eare of the curious sifter', i. 180) and to promise that the moral substance of the narrative will more than make up for its stylistic defects ('Where the matter it selfe bringeth credit, the man with his glose winneth smal commendation', i. 181). A proponent of simplicity will gladly concur with his pronouncement that 'a naked tale doth most truely set foorth the naked truth' (i. 181), and will accept his closing definition of the *Anatomy* as nothing but a 'simple Pamphlet'.

   But again an 'anatomical' scrutiny of the epistle exposes a quite different set of meanings. Lyly's apology for his folly in handling the subject of wit involves a display of rhetorical virtuosity that proves him to be supremely witty. 'It may be', he confesses, 'that fine wits

---

[14] See *An Apology for Poetry*, 107.

wil descant upon him, that having no wit goeth about to make an Anatomy of wit' (i. 180). The word 'descant' suggests the fine wits' eagerness to show off their skill by performing elaborate variations on other people's melodies (like Gascoigne's Elinor who played a sexual 'descant... upon F.J.'s plainsong', 62; or Euphues himself, who mocks the friend whose lover he has stolen for failing to learn 'the first noat of Deskant', i. 236); Lyly's seeming confession of the validity of their criticisms only confirms his appreciation of their performance ('their jesting in my mynd is tollerable', i. 180). He proceeds to demonstrate the aptness of the fine wits' jesting by placing himself in the midst of a gallery of rash self-promoters—a butcher who undertakes to give anatomical demonstrations, a horse-doctor who sets up as a physician and so makes himself an 'Asse'—'All which thinges', he says, 'make most against me, in that a foole hath intruded himselfe to discourse of wit' (i. 180). But he immediately places the fine wits alongside him in the gallery of self-made asses when he identifies their peculiar brand of folly: 'Though the stile nothing delight the dayntie eare of the curious sifter, yet will the matter recreate the minde of the courteous Reader' (i. 180). Like the butcher, the horseleech, and Lyly himself the fine wits have exaggerated social aspirations: they are 'curious', not cunning critics; their folly consists in a reliance on the 'eare' rather than the 'minde'; and Lyly describes their objections to the plainness of his style in a parison which no reasonable 'sifter' could construe as anything but stylistically 'dayntie'. By the end of the epistle the fine wits have been reduced to the status of the average English reader: 'It is a world to see how English men desire to heare finer speach then the language will allow, to eate finer bread then is made of Wheat, to weare finer cloth then is wrought of Woll' (i. 181). Every modern Englishman is a 'fine wit' and a 'curious sifter', and hence the irrational slave of his 'humors', the inhabitant of a fantastic world beyond the capabilities of speech to express. Such a reader is impossible to please: 'I cannot feede their humors', he tells us (i. 181). On the other hand he had earlier promised to 'shew every humor in his kinde' (i. 180); so that by anatomizing the 'fine wits' who derided his text Lyly has turned them into its subject, a comic spectacle which 'it is a world to see'. For the wit who has read the epistle carefully, Lyly has achieved an effect reminiscent of that of Erasmus in *The Praise of Folly*, since his readers are never quite sure where wit ends and folly begins, or whether they themselves are the readers who scrutinize or the subject under scrutiny.

At the same time, like the narrative voice in *The Praise of Folly*, he shows himself to participate in the fine wits' folly (after all, he shares their Englishness and hence presumably their appetite for impossibly fine speech). His claims for the 'excellencie' of his subject-matter and the poverty of his style grow increasingly effusive and increasingly suspect. 'The right Coral needeth no colouring. Where the matter it selfe bringeth credit, the man with his glose winneth smal commendation' (i. 181), he simpers, and in doing so convicts his own text of being preoccupied with fakery, encrusted as it is with rhetorical 'colours'. His own 'glose' is accumulating even as he claims to reject it. 'It is ... a greater show of a pregnant wit, then perfect wisedome, in a thing of sufficient excellencie, to use superfluous eloquence' (i. 181), he declares, and his own 'superfluous eloquence' promptly aligns him with the 'pregnant wit', the master of exuberant verbal excess. Lyly immediately confirms his alignment with wit by illustrating his point with an example which removes all hope that his text is in a moral sense 'a thing of sufficient excellencie': 'Venus according to the judgement of Mars, was then most amyable, when she sate close by Vulcanus'. This is brilliantly witty. Lyly's readers have been placed in the position of Mars judging his lover Venus; their aesthetic judgement of his text has been conflated with Mars's covert act of visual adultery; and Lyly has incidentally implicated himself in the adulterous act, since earlier in the epistle he was responsible for setting the portrait of Venus alongside that of her husband for the delectation of Mars and other connoisseurs of the erotic. It would seem that an admiration for stylistic ornament entails a predilection for sexual and social transgression, as in the case of Gascoigne's Master F.J.. One might be reminded of Puttenham's definition of figurative language as an abuse of speech, a crime against the simplicity favoured by the state.[15]

Lyly's text seems to be implicitly accusing itself of inciting its readers to sensuality. It goes on to accuse itself of duplicity. He assures us that 'a naked tale doth most truely set foorth the naked truth ... that paynting is meter for ragged walls then fine Marble, that veritie then shineth most bright when she is in least bravery'(i. 181)—all of which things, as he said earlier in the epistle, 'make most against' himself, since his text has been conspicuous for its use of verbal 'paynting' and other stylistic mannerisms, and since in the next epistle we shall hear that, far from being 'naked', it is clothed in the very latest fashions. Lyly's sub-

---

[15] *The Arte of English Poesie*, 228–9. See my Introduction.

ject would seem to be the careful cultivation of falsehood, the concealment of crumbling moral edifices under a fine linguistic veil, the
obscuring of 'veritie' by rhetorical 'bravery'; all the abuses, in fact,
that Guevara, Ascham, and later Gosson associated with contemporary
fiction.

As the petitions he wrote to Elizabeth show, Lyly was one of the
most accomplished letter-writers of his time.[16] The *Anatomy*'s opening epistle is a brilliant exercise in tricky prose, a cornucopia of alternative readings. Even more ingeniously than Gascoigne or Pettie, he
interweaves what seem to be traditional apologetics—excuses for
presenting a morally mixed text, assurances of his own 'gravitie',
expressions of preference for matter over style, disingenuous self-
deprecation— into what on closer, more 'anatomical', reading proves
to be an exposition of his text's sophistication, its sensuality, and its
participation in and bettering of the politician's shiftiness. Lyly's concealment of the 'witty' reading has proved only too successful for the
modern reader, who until recently has been naïvely prepared to
believe him when he calls the *Anatomy* 'simple', and has failed to see
that the epistle transforms the entire narrative into one of the devious
fictions it ostensibly repudiates.

2. HEADY MIXTURES

The observation in the epistle that 'paynting is meter for ragged walls
then fine Marble' forms the opening link in one of the many chains of
analogies that bind Lyly's text together from start to finish. The dedication resembles an outwardly opulent and authoritative building
which on closer inspection proves alarmingly unstable, like the palace
of Pride in the first book of *The Faerie Queene*, whose 'wals were high,
but nothing strong, nor thick', and whose 'hinder parts... | Were
ruinous and old, but painted cunningly' (I. iv. 4–5). The narrative
that follows is full of collapsing edifices, from the town of Troy
invoked by Eubulus (i. 188) to the towns that are undermined by rabbits, moles, and frogs in Euphues' misogynistic tract the 'cooling
Carde' (i. 249); from the towns of Sodom and Gomorrah which
Euphues compares with Athens (i. 274) to the building erected by the
Empress in Euphues' final letter, which is being stealthily dismantled

---

[16] For the best of Lyly's letters see *Complete Works*, i. 26–7, 28–9, 64–5, 68–9, and 70–1.

by her courtiers ('The Empress is no more to be suspected of erring then the Carpenter that buildeth the house bee accused bicause theeves have broken it', i. 321). Potentially splendid structures of all kinds are continually being erected and then destroyed, usually in a secretive or insidious manner: by the wiles of Greeks, by the invisible tunnelling of small animals, or by the midnight depredations of robbers. The narrative as a whole resembles one of these disintegrating buildings. From the traditional Elizabethan reader's perspective it looks like a morally impregnable structure such as Whetstone's miscellany *The Rocke of Regard*, which used a fortress as one of its presiding metaphors;[17] while the more penetrating reading demanded by the epistle dedicatory reveals it to be always on the brink of collapse, unbalanced by its own sophistication.

The proponent of simplicity need go no further than the style to find evidence of the narrative's moral integrity, composed as it is from the superficially uniform building-blocks of euphuism—the figures of parison, paronomasia, alliteration, and so on, which lend the most irrational statements an apparently architectural reliability.[1] Fixed, the traditionalist might think, in these stylistic containers, are gems drawn from the fund of human wisdom: allusions to Classical literature, natural history, animal fable, and Ovidian mythology together with an abundance of familiar proverbs. And the overall structure of the *Anatomy* reproduces the euphuistic dichotomy on a monumental scale, balancing the Italianate narrative of the love-affair between Euphues and Lucilla in the first half of the volume with a collection of instructive documents written by the reformed Euphues in the second. The book seems to provide a built-in safe-guard against Euphues' initial abuses of wit, by afterwards making him repent of his follies and turn to instructing the reader in the proper uses of the intellect. The overall impression the *Anatomy* gives is that of being unequivocally safe; no 'ragged walls', only 'fine Marble'. It therefore comes as a shock to enter the narrative by way of the epistle and find that, like Lyly's description of Naples, the 'very walles and windowes' of the story show it 'rather to bee the Tabernacle of *Venus*, then the Temple of *Vesta*' (i. 185). Wherever the architecture of the book is not in a state of collapse it is being misused. For Eubulus the streets of Naples are nothing more than the squalid setting

---

[17] Whetstone explains that he has 'guarded' his collection with its title (p. i), and named one of its sections 'The Castle of Delight'.

[18] See n. 3 above.

or a perpetual orgy, with 'dronken sottes wallowinge in every house,
in every chamber, yea, in every channell' (i. 188), while Philautus
compares the treacherous Euphues to a sluttish swallow, 'which in
the Summer creepeth under the eves of every house, and in the Winter leaveth nothing but durte behinde hir' (i. 234). Even the treatises
that make up the second half of the book are thronged with disreput-
ble buildings. The penitent Euphues urges his friend Philautus to 'Fly
the places, the parlours, the portalles, wherein thou hast bene conver-
saunt with thy Lady' (i. 256), and advises him to 'come from the court
to *Athens*' (i. 309), from the seat of government to the seat of learning;
and the last four epistles are all devoted to similar exhortations to flight
from the urban centres of corruption, from the letter to the exiled
Botonio which urges him to 'Choose that place for thy palaice
which is most quiet' (i. 314), to the letter to Livia which congratulates
her on her decision to quit Naples. But flight is no guarantee of moral
purgation; elsewhere Euphues complains that Athens itself is full of
'subtile practises in chambers', that the Athenian 'temple of *Vesta*
where virgins should live' has become infected with Neapolitan corruptions (it is 'lyke the stewes, fraight with strompets', i. 274). From
this perspective, far from creating authoritative palaces or storehouses
full of the collective wisdom of mankind, the *Anatomy* seems to focus
on the inevitable infiltration both of social institutions and of the
mind's most secret recesses by the anarchy of the senses. Its stylistic
containers do not resemble building-blocks so much as fleeting
instances of humanity's persistent and often futile efforts to impose
some verbal shape on the protean matter of sexual and intellectual
experience.

The story's demolition of the stylistic structures which reinforce
transcendent values and ideals begins in its first two sentences. The
narrative opens with a sentence that reproduces stylistically the balance between disparate elements from which both a perfect youth
and a perfect society might be constructed; a parison in which each
element exists in harmony with its companion elements: 'There
dwelt in *Athens* a young gentleman of great patrimonie, and of so
comely a personage, that it was doubted whether he were more
bound to Nature for the liniaments of his person, or to fortune for
the encrease of his possessions' (i. 184). Like genial fairy godmothers,
Nature and Fortune have each contributed their gifts to the story's
protagonist, making him a miniature model of what Eubulus calls
'sober government'. But as soon as the perfect parison of the book's

first sentence has been established an additional element disrupts it
equilibrium: 'Nature impatient of comparisons, and as it were disdain
ing a companion, or copartner in hir working, added to this comli
nesse of his body suche a sharpe capacitie of minde, that not onel'
shee proved Fortune counterfaite, but was halfe of that opinion tha
she hir selfe was onely currant' (i. 184). Nature's superfluous gift c
a 'sharpe capacitie of minde' undermines the physical and economi
prosperity into which the boy has been born, and from this momen
on his acerbic intelligence continues to demolish familial and socia
structures until it brings about the death of Lucilla's father, the chie
representative in the book of political as well as parental authority
The syntactical dichotomies or 'euphuisms' associated with Euphue
invariably stress, not the co-operative harmony between one part c
a sentence and the next, but the domination or supplanting of on‹
thing by another. Like his patron Nature, he is impatient of compar
isons and disdainful of co-partners, and this is reflected in the phrase
that describe him, whose components strain against each other as i
they are about to fly to pieces: he is 'of more wit then wealth, anc
yet of more wealth then wisdome' (i. 184). Another destructiv‹
euphuism encourages him to distance himself from his contempor
aries: 'Seeing himselfe inferiour to none in pleasant conceiptes, h‹
thought himselfe superiour to al in honest conditions'; and this i‹
turn encourages him to abandon political and economic co-partner
by 'leavinge his countrey' and 'loathing his olde acquaintance' (i
185). Later, his lover Lucilla is described in a still more powerful anc
ominous series of destructive euphuisms. Her beauty 'stains' th‹
beauty of other women, her 'modest bashfulnesse caused the othe
to looke wanne for envie', and finally it is hinted that she disseminate
duplicity like a malevolent star: 'as the Sunne dimmeth the Moone
that she cannot bee discerned, so this galant gyrle more faire then for‹
tunate, and yet more fortunate then faithfull, eclipsed the beautie o
them all, and *chaunged their coulours*' (i. 199, my emphasis). Wher‹
beauty has such reductive powers, which it employs exclusively tc
subdue competitors and to stir up antagonism, it comes as no surprise
to hear in the following sentence—before Euphues has even me
Lucilla—that under her influence the youth will soon have 'broke
the bondes of marriage, and forbidden the banes of Matrimonie' (i
199). Ascham described Italianate Englishmen as 'mervelous singule:
in all their matters' and went on to trace the disastrous political con‹
sequences of this singularity. Lyly dramatizes the political and persona

consequences of such solipsistic narcissism, both in the succession of treacherous actions that characterizes Euphues' relationship with Lucilla and in the stylistic details of his text, in the conflict between the 'harmonious' forms of euphuistic dichotomy and the 'destructive' forms which rupture agreements throughout *The Anatomy of Wit*.

In the first part of the *Anatomy* Euphues' wit derives its powers both of creativity and of destruction from its association with excess. From the moment when Nature gives him an inordinately sharp capacity of mind, Euphues discards the safety of temperate words and actions and shapes his career from extremes, 'using jesting without meane, and abusing mirth without measure' (i. 184). His delight in excess is both what attracts the wise old citizen Eubulus to him and what alerts him to the dangers the boy is courting. The old man notes his 'myrthe wythout measure, yet not wythout witte', and warns him of the probable effects of his untutored brilliance: 'by how much the more I love the highe climbinge of thy capacitie, by so much the more I feare thy fall' (i. 189). The sentence recalls the metaphor of the wheel of fortune which gave shape to so many traditional narratives of the rises and falls of princes, and in doing so it serves as a reminder that for Elizabethan readers the tension between temperance and excess was a matter of concern not merely for the well-being of a private subject but for the health of a nation. Elyot saw the avoidance of extremes and the temperate reconciliation of diverse ingredients as prerequisites for any stable social structure. The qualities which govern his ideal governor exist in a state of equilibrium which is precariously maintained by the dominant virtue of temperance, 'the moderatrice as well of all motions of the mind... as of all acts proceeding of man' (122). Virtue itself is 'an election annexed unto our nature, and consisteth in a mean which is determined by reason, and that mean is the very midst of two things vicious, the one in surplusage, the other in lack' (130); the preservation of this delicate balance is the overriding preoccupation of *The Governor*. For Eubulus as for Elyot, the conservation of temperance is a task beset with dangers. He tells Euphues that 'Thou art here amiddest the pykes betweene *Scilla* and *Caribdis*, readye if thou shunne *Syrtes*, to sincke into *Semphlagades*' (i. 189), and he considers Euphues' 'election', or choice of action, not merely to determine the fate of an individual, but to constitute a major political decision: 'for hee well knewe that so rare a wytte woulde in tyme eyther breede an intollerable trouble, or bringe an incomperable Treasure to the common weale' (i. 186). In *The Faerie Queene* the undisciplined and intemperate body quickly grows monstrous (II. ix. I), and Spenser depicts it as besieged by the monsters of Maleger's army, who in their turn resemble the 'raskall routs' of Irish freedom–fighters (II ix. 15), so that again personal prodigality has a direct bearing on insurrection. In the first half of the *Anatomy* Lyly is careful to underplay the political ramifications of Euphues' behaviour, but they nevertheless invade his text at every juncture. It is easy to overlook the fact that Lucilla's father is 'one of the chiefe governours of the citie' (i. 199) and that Lucilla is 'heire to his whole revenews'; that Philautus is 'towne borne childe' whose father had 'great countenaunce' while he lived, while Euphues 'crepte into credite' with Lucilla through his friendship with Philautus like the secret agent of a hostile power, and finally that Euphues' status as a foreign national is emphasized whenever he is mentioned, from the opening of Eubulus' speech when the old man sends his 'hoarie haires' as 'ambassadors' between them (i. 187), to Philautus' eventual recognition that Euphues shares his countrymen's skill in destroying cities: 'Couldest thou not remember *Philautus* that *Greece* is never without some wily *Ulisses*, never void of some *Synon*, never to seeke of some deceitfull shifter?' (i. 232). It is also easy to overlook the frequency with which Euphues and Lucilla are said to be breaking the laws of Naples.[19] The Greek Euphues' infiltration of Naples closely resembles the Italianate Englishman's infiltration of the homes of the English aristocracy in *The Scholemaster*. And wit's corruption of the Neapolitan state is as difficult to extirpate as it is to prevent; in the final letter, the reformed Euphues paints a vivid picture of the Empress at Naples as she struggles vainly to legislate against the 'excesses' of her unruly courtiers (i. 319). Just as in Ascham's celebrated treatise, what is at stake in the *Anatomy* is not merely the reformation of a prodigal but the security of a kingdom.

In fact the Elizabethan traditionalist might easily have convinced himself that Lyly was an uncritical disciple of Elizabeth's former tutor, if only on the evidence of the sheer abundance of references to *The Scholemaster* with which the *Anatomy* is loaded. The name of Euphues himself recalls the first of the seven qualities Ascham ascribes

[19] Philautus is said to have won Lucilla 'by right of love, and shoulde have worne hir by right of lawe, had not *Euphues* by straunge destenie broken the bondes of marriage, and forbidden the banes of Matrimonie' (i. 199). Philautus later complains that both Euphues and Lucilla have 'committed perjurie' (i. 233), and Euphues replies with a reference to Euripides 'who thinkes it lawfull for the desire of a kingdome to transgresse the bounds of honestie and for the love of a Lady to violate and breake the bands of amitie' (i. 235). He concludes that 'any impietie may lawfully be committed in love, which is lawlesse' (i. 236).

to the ideal pupil, the condition of being 'apte by goodnesse of witte, and appliable by readines of will, to learning' (194). In *The Scholemaster* as in the *Anatomy*, the quality of 'Euphues' is as apt to be corrupted as it is to be educated. One of the qualifications for the ideal pupil is that he should be physically attractive, but Ascham complains that most able-bodied aristocratic youths are never submitted to the discipline of schooling: 'commonlie, the fairest bodies, ar bestowed on the foulest purposes'. Lyly's Euphues confirms the worst of Ascham's fears for the fate of witty and well-made young men. He is one of those quick wits whose very sharpness makes them peculiarly susceptible to temptation; *The Scholemaster* compares them to 'over sharpe tooles, whose edges be verie soone turned' (189), and Lyly uses the same analogy for his protagonist's predicament: 'the teenest rasor soonest tourneth his edge' (i. 184–5). Euphues takes the 'bridle' of his career into his own hands and 'rashly ranne unto destruction', and in doing so he imitates Ascham's young Englishmen, who disdain the 'bitte' and 'bridle' of God's grace and 'go, and ryde, and runne, and flie' to the corruptions of Italy (228). Lyly's narrator blames the boy's rashness on irresponsible parents who 'are more desirous to have [their children] mainteine the name, then the nature of a gentleman'. These recall the parents in *The Scholemaster* who take more trouble to seek expert advice about horses than about their children (193), and the reformed Euphues later repeats this complaint in a pedagogic treatise of his own, *Euphues his Ephoebus*: 'sooner will they bestow an hundreth crownes to have a horse broken, then a childe well taught' (i. 267). Inevitably the old man Eubulus adopts Ascham's arguments when he urges Euphues to return to his studies, and, when his urgings fail, the narrator's explanation for their failure again echoes *The Scholemaster* analogy for analogy. Clever adolescents, he points out, prefer the 'blossome before the fruite' (i. 195), just as Ascham's quick wits 'shewe forth, faire blossoms and broad leaves in spring time, but bring out small and not long lasting fruite in harvest time' (189). Like Ascham he notes with astonishment the rapidity with which a 'fyne wytte' assimilates information; and finally he comments on their willingness to modify the meanings of words to suit their own convenience: 'if one bee harde in conceiving, they pronounce him a dowlte, if given to study, they proclayme him a duns... if full of wordes, a sotte, if without speach, a Cypher, if one argue with them boldly, then is he impudent, if coldely an innocent' (i. 195). The passage reproduces Ascham's comments on the linguistic abuses cultivated by cunning

youths, which lead inexorably to the misuse of 'the faire and godli
word GRACE' (206–7), a term that is subjected to equally cavalie
treatment in *The Anatomy of Wit*.[20] With supreme impudence, Lyl
would seem to have fused Ascham's treatise with the abuses it attack
by pillaging it from stem to stern for material with which to construc
his Anglo–Italian fiction. His text does not merely invade the canon o
prescribed texts, as Pettie's collection did by transforming Classica
fables and histories into sophisticated novellas; instead Lyly import
Italian fiction into the very heart of the humanist pedagogic project
by transforming Ascham's impassioned plea for the retention of th
Classical canon into the basis for an erotic romance. It is hard to
think of a better way of bearing out *The Scholemaster*'s warning
about the insidious corruption of contemporary England by seductive
Italian subtlety.

Where the *Anatomy* differs radically from *The Scholemaster* is in th
delighted admiration with which the narrator seems to contemplat
the moral and linguistic outrages perpetrated by wit. The circumspec
tion with which Lyly communicates this delight is part of what make
*The Anatomy of Wit* such an extraordinarily *double* text—a text suscept
ible of so many rival readings. At the beginning of the narrative Lyl
repeats almost verbatim what he said in the epistle about the inter
mingling of good and evil in every aspect of experience: 'As therefore
the sweetest Rose hath his prickel...so the sharpest witte hath hi
wanton will, and the holiest head his wicked way' (i. 184). Variation
on this motif recur throughout the *Anatomy*, until it acquires the
authoritative resonance of a philosophical dictum. Lyly may have
derived the notion of the pervasiveness of contraries from anothe
student of rhetorical duplicity, Castiglione. The fourth book of *Th
Courtier* contains a panegyric on temperance to which Elyot, Ascham
and Eubulus would all readily have subscribed, that culminates in it
restoration of the golden age 'which is written to have beene whe
Saturnus raigned in the olde time' (273). But Castiglione had earlie
taken a less favourable view both of the 'olde time' and of humanity'
capacity for achieving moderation. In the second book he propose

---

[20] In the first half of the *Anatomy* Euphues persistently misuses the word grace i
Ascham's terms, as in his response to Eubulus, when he uses the word to mean a private predilection: 'so many men so many mindes, that may seeme in your eye odious, which in a
others eye may be *gratious*' (i. 190, my emphasis). The word does not resume its prope
meaning until Euphues' dispute with Atheos in the second half: 'There is no heart s
hard...that by grace is not made as supple as oyle' (i. 305).

that 'since ill is contrarie to good, and good to ill, it is (in a manner) necessarie by contrarietie and a certaine counterpeise the one shoulde underproppe and strengthen the other, and where the one wanteth or encreaseth, the other to want or encrease also: because no contrarie is without his other contrarie' (89). Under these conditions, any increase in good over a particular period elicits a corresponding growth in the incidence of wickedness; and, conversely, an excess of wickedness presupposes a corresponding abundance of goodness. Hence Castiglione explains that when old men complain that the present is more vicious than the past, they are inadvertently acknowledging its relative merit, 'for no ill is so evil, as that which ariseth out of the corrupt seed of goodnesse' (90). From this perspective Elyot's plea for temperance is also a plea for cultural mediocrity. According to Castiglione, extremes of behaviour signal humanity's increasingly fine achievements, and human intellectual growth is inextricably bound up with moral decline:

And therefore where nature nowe bringeth forth much better wittes than she did tho, even as they that be given to goodnesse doe much better than did those of their time, so also they that bee given to ill doe much worse . . . And that the wittes of those times were generally much inferiour to these now adayes, a man may judge by all that hath proceeded from them, as letters, painting, statues, buildings and all other things. (90)

The modern wit with its extremes of conduct is a measure, in fact, of the rich artistic achievements of the present as compared with the drab heritage of the past.

Lyly repeats Castiglione's contention that 'no contrarie is without his other contrarie' in a complicated passage which occurs after Euphues has given the most impressive evidence of his verbal skills in the book, when he confutes the accusations of the aged Eubulus. For neyther is ther any thing, but that hath his contraries' (i. 196), the narrator opines at this point, and with characteristic evasiveness he uses the phrase in such a way that both the moralist and the proponent of wit can read it as supporting their respective positions. The sentence occurs after a disquisition on 'fine wytte' which is prompted by the young man's rhetorical display: 'a quicke understanding, is able to atteine to more in a moment or a very little space, then a dull and blockish heade in a month' (i. 196). Here the word 'blockish' recalls the quick wit's insulting names for the hard wit in *The Scholemaster*, and it is by no means certain that the narrator does not share the fine wit's contempt for pedestrian intellects. The wit-loving reader might assume that he does, and that when the narrator tells us there is nothing without its contraries he is merely stressing the enormous gulf that separates the fine from the 'blockish' mind. The moralist, on the other hand, might assume that the phrase 'neyther is ther any thing, but that hath his contraries' refers to the ensuing sentence, which explains that nothing can preserve its identity without an opposite to define itself by: 'the finest edge is made with the blunt whetstone, and the fairest Jewell fashioned with the harde hammer' (i. 196). Lyly compounds the confusion between these two possible readings by intimating immediately afterwards that his *Anatomy* maintains a profoundly ambivalent attitude to wit:

I go not about (gentlemen) to inveigh against wit, for then I wer witlesse, but frankely to confesse mine owne lyttle wit, I have ever thought so supersticiously of wit, that I feare I have comitted Idolatry agaynst wisedome, and if Nature had dealte so beneficially with mee to have given me any wit, I shoulde have bene readyer in the defence of it to have made an Apologie, then any way to tourne to Apostacie. (i. 196)

This astonishing sentence tells us that the narrator delights in wit to a dangerous extent—it has made him commit 'Idolatry agaynst wisedome', tarred him in fact with the same brush of Catholic superstition that Ascham applied to his Italianate Englishmen—but fails altogether to inform us whether he is engaged in attacking wit or defending it. The end of the authorial interpolation does not resolve this dilemma; it merely lists, again with echoes of *The Scholemaster*, the dangerous 'humors' to which the undisciplined wit is subject: 'they be secure of perills, obstinate in their owne opinions, impatient of labour, apte to conceive wrong, credulous to beleeve the worst' (i. 196). The entire passage might elicit a third reading which moderates between the witty and the moralistic reader: that quick wits are self-evidently wedded to immorality, but that the energy with which they articulate their resistance to moral convention is precisely what makes them attractive.

The attractiveness of energetic immorality lies at the core of the doctrine of contraries presented at the beginning of the narrative. 'As ... the sweetest Rose hath his prickel,' the narrator opines, 'the finest velvet his brack, the fairest flowre his bran, so the sharpest witte hath his wanton will, and the holiest heade his wicked waye' (i. 184). He goes on to suggest that this fusion of wit with will, of holi

ness with wickedness, is widely held to be more attractive than un-
adulterated excellence: 'And true it is that some men write and most
men beleeve, that in all perfecte shapes, a blemmish bringeth rather a
liking every way to the eyes, then a loathing any waye to the minde'
(i. 184). This comment is hardly controversial unless we notice that
the narrator seems to be equating *moral* mixtures (the holy head
with its wicked way) with *aesthetic* ones (the perfect shape with its
blemish). The allure of physical beauty has seduced most men into laying greater emphasis on aesthetic than on moral considerations, and
this is confirmed by the fact that the blemish brings pleasure 'to the
eyes' instead of revulsion 'to the minde'. But the narrator quickly
goes on to suggest that the mind like the body has its contraries: 'in
the disposition of the minde, either vertue is overshadowed with
some vice, or vice overcast with some vertue' (i. 184); although he
does not say so openly, the reader may conclude that 'most men'
will find this mixture of qualities in the mind more attractive than
moral and intellectual simplicity. Lyly carefully insists that these opinions are not his own—they merely represent what 'some men
write'; but the fact that 'most men' are inclined to believe what is
written would seem to invest his own text with the same iconoclastic
persuasiveness as those of his fellow writers, and to make it equally
vulnerable to the charge of moral irresponsibility. Contemporary culture, Lyly seems to imply, has learned to equate subtlety with corruption, and to celebrate it none the less, and the *Anatomy* repeatedly
testifies to the validity of this dangerous equation. The narrator
comes close to confessing as much when he tells us, first that 'none
[was] more wittie then *Euphues*, yet at the first none more wicked',
and then that 'witte is the better if it bee the deerer bought' (i. 185).
At the outset of their careers the best intellects, it seems, may be identified by their resistance to every form of discipline or control. It is a
test of the resourcefulness of Euphues' mind that he succumbs so
rapidly to the temptations of Naples: 'the finest cloathe is soonest
eaten wyth Moathes' we are told and, as even Eubulus acknowledges,
'the most delicate wyt is ... moste subjecte to yelde unto vanitie' (i.
189). The *Anatomy* never ceases to entrap its readers in this constant
tension between moral probity and intellectual brilliance; between
'good', in the sense of technically accomplished, art, and the good
art which attempts to guide its recipients along the more pedestrian
paths of good conduct. It would seem that fiction that aspires to wit
must always resemble the subtle Italianate fiction condemned by

Ascham, and must inevitably succumb to the 'overlashing' excesse
condemned by Gosson, no matter how wittily it concurs with thei
strictures on subtlety and excess. Lyly's is the art of the fallen worlc
the practical, contingent art which makes nonsense of the absolutis
pronouncements of a Fenton or a North, or of the idealistic enthu
siasm of Sidney's apologist. It is also an art like Gascoigne's, whic
proclaims its author's willingness to participate in the still more bewil
dering discourse of sixteenth-century politics, and which indicates th
dangers that might enmesh the Elizabethan government if its witt
author remains, like Euphues, a stranger to the court.

## 3 . EUPHUES THE SECRET AGENT

Euphues' arrival in the dangerous and delightful field of Italianat
fiction coincides with his entry into the city of Naples. As soon a
he gets there he finds himself practically deafened with verbal echoe
of earlier Elizabethan fictions. Naples is described as 'a place of mor
pleasure then profite, and yet of more profite then pietie' (i. 185), an
the description parodies the title-pages of those story-collections c
the 1560s which advertised themselves as 'No less profitable than plea
sant' (Fenton's *Tragicall Discourses*) or 'very requisite for delighte an
profit' (Painter's *Palace of Pleasure*, ii. 147). Euphues' response t
Naples is that of the unruly reader who is always implicitly presen
in the dedications to these collections, and who has less interest i
the moral instructions to be derived from the ensuing text than i
the vicarious erotic thrills it can afford him. Bandello's French trans
lator Belleforest prefaced his translation of the *Histoires tragiques* wit
an embarrassed acknowledgement of the ease with which suc
readers might be seduced into thinking his stories pornographic: 'E
quoy que de prime face il semble que ce soient des discours d'amour
si est-ce que ma pretente, ny proget ne s'adresse aux follatres; ains
faire voir à la jeunesse le degast, la ruine et malheur qui luy advient
si elle suit ses desirs volages et lascifs'.[21] His apology for the disjunc
tion between his erotic subject-matter ('des discours d'amour') an

---

[21] 'And although at first sight it may seem as though these are discourses of love, never
theless my intention and purpose is not to address myself to fools but to show young peopl
the disaster, ruination and wretchedness which will come to them if they follow their flight
and lascivious desires.' François de Belleforest and Pierre Boaistuau, *Histoires Tragiques* (Pari
1565; quoted from the 1568 edn.), vol. ii, sig. A3ᵛ.

s purpose ('proget') identifies one of the ways in which Bandello's
ovels might be construed as misleading: the sentence recognizes a
plit between the *seeming* of the novels, their 'prime face', and their
intended didactic function, and this disjunction demands that his read-
rs must possess considerable critical maturity if they are to interpret
1em correctly. Yet if the novels are indeed addressed to 'la jeunesse'
1en their readership can hardly be expected to possess such maturity.
ainter's embellishment of the passage makes the paradox more
1arked:

nd although by the first face and view, some of these may seeme to intreat of
1lawfull Love, and the foule practises of the same, yet being throughly reade
1d well considered, both old and yonge may learne how to avoyde the
1ine, overthrow, inconvenience and displeasure, that lascivious desire and
anton wil doth bring to their suters and pursuers. (i. 5)

ainter fears that his novels will seem to recount not merely 'discours
'amour' but stories of 'unlawfull Love' and its 'foule practises', and
1is impression can only be dispelled by the novels 'being throughly
:ade and well considered'; a failure to do so may place his book
eyond the legal pale, and so precipitate its readers into political as
ell as moral 'ruine'. Painter's passage is meant to lead naturally into
1e statement that follows it, that the collection's diverse narratives fit
1to a simple scheme of 'good examples, the best to be followed, and
1e worst to be avoyded'. Instead it asserts their complexity as strongly
s Ascham could have done, and confirms that their interpretation as
;ood examples' is no simple feat of readership.

Lyly's Euphues, with his penchant for excess and his sensual tastes, is
1e epitome of Belleforest's 'follatres'; but Naples clearly makes fewer
laims for itself as a source of moral instruction than the *Histoires tragi-
ues*. The architecture of Naples parodically inverts the claims Painter
1ade for his palace; its 'walles and windowes' show it to be the
Tabernacle of *Venus*' instead of a mnemonic mansion, and the texts
7ith which it is associated constitute a far more dangerous and baffling
1iscellany. The Neapolitan court seems to justify all the accusations to
7hich Painter feared his collection might be subjected: it is 'more
1eete for an *Atheyst*, then for one of *Athens*, for *Ovid* then for *Aristotle*,
 or a gracelesse lover then for a godly lyver: more fitter for *Paris* then
or *Hector*, and meeter for *Flora* then *Diana*' (i. 185). The list combines
succession of contrasting names and concepts in such a way as to
mphasize the attractiveness of the court as much as its corruption;

but it also makes it next to impossible to distinguish between the two
The charge of atheism is clearly a serious one—Ascham brought i
against his Italianate Englishmen—but the personalities associate
with Naples grow progressively more appealing as the catalogu
unfolds: the erotic philosopher Ovid, the godless lover who follow
Ovidian precepts, Paris who rejected Athene in favour of Venus
and finally Flora, whose cornucopian fertility would seem to have a
much to recommend it as the sterile chastity of the moon goddess
And the uses to which texts are put at Naples are just as bewildering
varied as the texts themselves. The Italians who visit Euphues i
his lodgings exploit his discourse for a diversity of purposes, both ben
evolent and malign: they include 'as well the Spider to sucke poyson
of his fine wyt, as the Bee to gather hunny, as well the Drone, as th
Dove, the Foxe as the Lambe, as well *Damocles* to betraye hym, a
*Damon* to bee true to hym' (i. 186). The last of these examples—
that of Damon—warns of the political dangers of the variety of inter
pretations to which a sophisticated text like *The Anatomy of Wit* migh
be subject. It alludes to the story of Damon and Pithias, whose adven
tures had been dramatized by Richard Edwards in the 1560s, an
whose influence runs through Lyly's narrative like a vein of ore, emer
ging periodically in half-buried allusions which are only to b
unearthed by the informed and sharp-eyed reader, the 'anatomical
reader of the dedication. In Edwards's play the stranger Damon i
arrested while on holiday in Syracuse and accused of espionage b
cunning informers, who are able to twist his innocent expressions o
a tourist's curiosity by maliciously reporting them out of context
until they sound like the meticulous observations of an enemy
agent.[22] Damon is condemned to death, and only saved from exe
cution at the eleventh hour by the intervention of his best frien
Pithias, whom he later saves in his turn; and the young men's willing
ness to die for one another moves the tyrant Dionysius so much tha
he finally drops all charges against them both. Euphues at Naples find
himself in the position of Damon at Syracuse, subjected to the mal
evolent scrutiny of hostile observers, but unlike Damon he reject
both the qualities and the alliances that might protect him from th

---

[22] See *Chief Pre-Shakespearean Dramas*, ed. J. Q. Adams (London: George Harrap, n.d.)
571–608. The self-appointed chief of counter-espionage in Edwards's play is the philosophe
Aristippus, mentioned by Lyly a few lines after his reference to Damon ('Hee coulde easil
discerne . . . the faith of *Lælius*, from the flattery of *Aristippus*', i. 186). Euphues foolishl
commends Aristippus as 'courtely' in his answer to Eubulus (i. 190).

harge of espionage. The friendship he forges with Philautus is compared at the outset to the infrangible bond between Damon and
ithias (i. 198), but he breaks the bond almost as soon as it is forged,
nd he treats the wise old counsellor Eubulus, whose name recalls that
f the counsel for the defence at Damon's trial, with supercilious con-
empt. Euphues is justifiably proud of his own powers of reading and
manipulating the language of others, but his isolation at Naples com-
ines with his narcissistic singularity to blind him to the fact that he
imself constitutes a text to be read by equally cunning readers—the
ifters' of the epistle—and that their malicious readings might con-
rue him not merely as an obnoxious adolescent but as an 'intollerable
ouble ... to the common weale' (i. 186).

The perilous complexity of the act of reading is still more brilliantly
nvoked by the comparison of Euphues' Italian visitors to parasitic
nsects. 'There frequented to his lodging and mansion house as well
he Spider to sucke poyson, of his fine wyt, as the Bee to gather
unny', the narrator explains, and the sentence inaugurates a bewil-
ering series of variations on the theme of the spider and the bee
hich runs throughout the *Anatomy*, and which provides a running
ommentary on the ways in which a seemingly harmless text may
e exploited by the devious. The bee crops up repeatedly in Eliza-
ethan prefaces as a metaphor for the reader's capacity to derive
nstruction from a rewarding narrative. Painter, for instance, explains
hat he has included in his collection a diversity of novelistic speci-
nens of virtue and vice, to the end 'that ech Sexe and Kinde may
ike out like the Bee, of ech Floure, Honny, to store and furnishe
ith delightes their well disposed myndes' (ii. 301).[23] Characteristic-
ly, Gascoigne complicates Painter's analogy by adding the example
f the spider to that of the bee: 'although in deede out of everie floure
he industrious Bee may gather Honie, yet by proofe the Spider there-
ut also sucks mischeevous poyson' (i. 6); in the context of *The Posies*,
hat is, a text can never hope to control the readings of its miscella-
eous recipients. But Lyly takes the difficulties involved in controlling
he act of reading further still, by conflating the actions of the spider
nd the bee until they are practically indistinguishable. On its first
ccurrence, the proposition that some of Euphues' guests resemble

[23] On Classical and Renaissance uses of the bee metaphor, see A. E. B. Coldiron, 'Wat-
on's *Hekatompathia* and Renaissance Lyric Tradition', *Translation and Literature*, vol. v, pt. 1
996), 3–25, esp. 10–13. See also Rosalie Colie, '*My Ecchoing Song': Andrew Marvell's Poetry
Criticism* (Princeton: Princeton University Press, 1970), 174–5.

spiders while others resemble bees seems relatively simple to explain
the spiders aim to harm him, the bees to do him good. But within
few pages these analogies have lost their simplicity. In responding t
the wise advice of Eubulus, Euphues claims to have caught him i
the act of appropriating the 'honey' of the young man's wit for h
own ends: 'They that use to steale honny, burne hemlocke t
smoke the Bees from their hives, and it may bee, that to get som
advauntage of mee, you have used these smokie argumentes' (
194); and this misrepresentation of the old man's intentions sugges
that Euphues' rhetorical honey and the clever insect that produces
are more poisonous commodities than they might at first appea
Lucilla confirms the fact when she uses the analogy of the bee to sup
port her decision to break off her engagement to Philautus: 'the Be
that gathereth Honny out of the weede, when she espyeth the fair
flower flyeth to the sweetest' (i. 206); and later she transforms it int
an illustration of duplicity: 'the Bee that hath honny in hir mouth
hath a sting in hir tayle' (i. 224), a statement which is as applicab]
to herself as it is to Euphues. Lucilla's exploitation of the most exemp
lary of insects as an incitement to corruption lends added resonance t
her father's subsequent comparison of her to an unproductive dron
(i. 230). Meanwhile Philautus too has come to recognize that h
treacherous friend Euphues unites the qualities of the bee with the sp
der's venom: he resembles 'the humble Bee which having sucke
honny out of the faire flower doth leave it and loath it, or the Spide
which in the finest webbe doth hang the fairest Fly' (i. 234). The ana
logy of the bee is only restored to its traditional function in the corres
pondence that closes the narrative, when the reformed Euphue
enjoins Botonio to 'Learne of the Bee as wel to gather Honny o
the weede as the flowre, and out of farre countries to live, as wel a
in thine owne' (i. 314). Under the combined onslaughts of men
and women's wit, the industrious insect temporarily misplaces i
identity—it is rendered successively fickle, duplicitous, aggressive
and unproductive, and in the process the conventional injunction t
read texts for profit is perverted into an excuse for opportunisti
profiteering. And once again, the implications of this transformatio
are wider than they might seem at first. In addition to serving as a
example of readerly productivity, the bee was also a well-know
emblem for the citizen of an ideal state.[24] The corruption of the citi

---

[24] See Elyot, *The Governor*, 7–8.

zen implies the corruption of the system; and it was not until he published his second volume, *Euphues and his England*, that Lyly furnished
his readers with a model for the way the newly complex symbol of the
bee might be adapted to the sophisticated needs of a contemporary
monarchy.

Thus the parody of a conventional title-page which heralds the
young wit's entry into Neapolitan society also announces his entry
into a world of literary exempla which can either be used as old-fashioned incitements to good conduct or rifled as an inexhaustible source
of innovative notions. The tension between these two uses of exemplary texts is encapsulated in the first two extended speeches in the narrative: the advice given to Euphues by 'an olde Gentleman in *Naples*',
Eubulus, and the young man's reply. Eubulus' admonition is the most
eloquent appeal for temperance in the book. As such, the 'simple'
reader could regard it as the doctrinal centre of Lyly's text, and this
reading seems to be confirmed by Euphues' repetition of the old
man's advice 'as I can remember worde for worde' at the end of his
pedagogic pamphlet, the *Ephoebus* (i. 286). But a closer anatomy of
the speech shows it to be inexorably undermined by the reading
Euphues gives it, and hence to have little value as a model of persuasive oratory in the sophisticated context of *The Anatomy of Wit*.

Eubulus begins by acknowledging the distance between himself and
Euphues which the young man's status as a foreigner creates. The old
man has no 'authoritie' with which to confront the boy, either in a
political or a literary sense, and must rely instead on trust alone to
establish a simplicity of understanding between them. 'My good will
in giving you good counsaile should induce you to beleeve mee', he
insists, 'and my hoarie haires (ambassadors of experience) enforce you
to...followe my meaninge' (i. 187). By this means he comically
insinuates the difficulty involved in communicating with a stranger
by investing his 'hoarie haires' with ambassadorial status as if he is
involved in difficult diplomatic negotiations with a foreign power.
Despite this difficulty the old man goes on to express a 'meaninge'
which is as clear as it is well intentioned. He compares Euphues to
an unfinished work of art, the 'expresse and lively Image of gentle
bloude', a sculpture which is not yet much more than an idea in the
mind of the artist: 'As...the yron beeinge hotte receyveth any forme
with the stroake of the Hammer, and keepeth it beeinge colde for
ever, so the tender witte of a childe if with diligence it bee instructed
in youth, wyll with industrye use those qualities in hys age' (i. 187).

Like Elyot and Ascham, Eubulus sees the schoolmaster's vigorou fashioning of his pupil's intellect as a means to a specific end: the crea- tion of a finished product fixed for ever in the attitude of docile con- formity which the state demands of its citizens. He would like the finished image of Euphues to resemble the functional art with which Painter and Fenton identified their collections, and he describes the boy as fertile territory which needs to be carefully prepared for culti- vation: farmers 'sowe Hempe before Wheate, a grayne that . . . maketh the soyle more apte for corne', while gardeners 'mixe Hisoppe wyth Time as ayders the one to the growth of the other' (i. 187). In Eubu- lus' eyes the public weal consists of a mixture of disparate elements working in solidarity together; but here his context in Lyly's text begins to complicate his argument. He finishes his series of examples of fruitful mixtures with an allusion to clever painters, who resemble disciplinarian parents in that 'to make the Picture more amiable' they 'caste a blacke grounde for their white woorke, that is, they [mix] threates wyth faire lookes' (i. 187–8). Clearly this is a different, sim- pler, kind of painter from the one described in the epistle, who was equally willing to use a 'black ground' for a 'white counterfeit', but who took as his subject a Venus who looked 'most *amyable*, when she sate close by Vulcanus' (i. 181, my emphasis). Eubulus seems in fact to have strayed from a traditional work of Elizabethan fiction into a new, Italianate milieu in which the word 'amiable' seldom has the innocent meaning the old man would wish to give it.[25]

Unaware of the unfamiliar environment into which he has wan- dered, Eubulus continues to invite Euphues to contemplate works of art in the traditional didactic mould: the painting of an '*Epicure* sleeping with meate in his mouthe', whose 'monsterous' appearance encourages his youthful spectators to 'eschewe the meanes of the like excesse' (i. 188), and the sculpture of a blind young man who is being murdered and robbed by a figure who might have been plucked from one of Pettie's misogynistic fictions, a 'woman so exquisite, that in some mennes judgement *Pigmalions* Image was not halfe so excel- lent' (i. 188). Each of these works of art is clearly calculated to deter the spectator from sensual over-indulgence; and Eubulus ends by

[25] An Elizabethan reader might well have fancied that Eubulus had wandered into *Euphues* from an older text. Besides his appearance as a wise but ineffectual counsellor in Edwards's *Damon and Pithias*, Eubulus had played an equally ineffectual part in Sackville and Norton's *Gorboduc* (1561–2) and in Gascoigne's *The Glasse of Governement* (in both these plays his advice was ignored by its recipients, with calamitous consequences).

xhorting Euphues to 'use' Naples as a still more potent exemplary
rtefact: 'Heere, yea, heere *Euphues*, maiste thou see not the carved
isarde of a lewde woman, but the incarnate visage of a lascivious
vanton, not the shaddowe of love, but the substaunce of luste' (i.
89). His oration closes with a series of balanced clauses designed to
onvey the temperate middle way recommended by Elyot: 'Bee mer-
ye but with modestie, be sober but not to sulloume, bee valiaunt but
iot too venterous' (i. 189), and with an injunction reminiscent of
hose in *The Governor* and *The Scholemaster* to use words according
o their consensually accepted significations: 'use pastime as the
voorde importeth, to passe the tyme in honest recreation' (i. 190).
"he last phrase contains an echo of a yet older tradition of instructive
rt, since Honest Recreation is a character in Redford's moral inter-
ide *Wit and Science*, the virtue who revives the unfortunate protagon-
it after he has been killed by the giant Tediousness. In invoking her,
iubulus puts the finishing touch to his credentials as the champion of
raditional forms of fiction.

Euphues' reply to Eubulus delineates a novel, sophisticated form of
erbal art which is openly antagonistic to older art-forms. The narrator
lescribes how he 'beganne to shape ... an aunswere' (i. 190), as if
reating his own sculpture to rival the didactic images evoked by
iubulus. The principal characteristic of this new form of art is its
iarcissism: it celebrates not the virtues of a model citizen but the
ntellectual and imaginative life of the artist's mind, and instead of
einforcing social institutions it demolishes them. Euphues founds his
peech not on reason but on sophistry, the witty corruption of logical
ules. Gosson's *Schoole of Abuse* defines the art of logic as 'a rule, by
vhich wee mighte ... confirme our owne reasons, and confute the al-
egations of our adversaryes, the end beeing trueth, which once fished
ut by the hard encounter of eithers Argumentes ... both partes should
ie satisfyed and strive no more' (*Markets of Bawdrie*, 102–3). From the
ieginning of his speech it is evident that Euphues is the kind of logician
Gosson was later to attack, more interested in brilliantly and entertain-
ngly confirming his own reasons than in achieving any kind of con-
ensus. Lyly has told us that, when he abandoned Athens, Euphues
eft the rule of reason' (i. 185), and the boy effectively confirms that
ie is wedded to sophistry by denying it before he begins his defence.[26]

---

[26] It is tempting to see in Lyly's reference to 'the rule of reason' an allusion to the treatise
n logic published by Thomas Wilson in 1551, *The Rule of Reason*. In 1573 the idiosyncratic
ogician Ralph Lever associated logic with wit in the title of another treatise, *The Arte of*

'I meane not to cavill with you as one lovinge sophistrye', he announces, since this would 'bring my talke into the suspition o fraude' (i. 190). But despite his rejection of cavilling (the word Gossor uses to describe the abuse of logic at the English universities) he fill his speech with what any university-trained reader would recognize as logical fallacies, ranging from *antistrophon* (as when he adapts Eubulus' examples to his own ends) to *ad hominem* attacks (as when he mocks Eubulus for his 'melting brayne', i. 191). His abuse of logic culminates in a series of hypothetical propositions whose consequents do not follow from their antecedents—'If Nature be of strength or force what availeth discipline or nurture? If of none, what helpeth Nature? (i. 192)—which he then pronounces to be 'knowne evidently and graunted to be true'. This last and most blatant fallacy exposes his superficial understanding of the nature of Gosson's 'trueth'; he has demonstrated nothing, and has no more business affirming that he has done so than one of Sidney's poets. As he said it would, his 'sophistrye' brings his talk 'into the suspition of fraude', the obverse of the virtue of amity with which Eubulus opened his address. Elyot defines fraud as the sophistication which undermines the verbal 'simplicity' on which every social contract is based, 'an evil deceit, craftily imagined and devised, which under a colour of truth and simplicity endamageth him that nothing mistrusteth' (169), and, while this description seems too severe to be applied to Euphues' serio-comic reply to Eubulus, it describes perfectly the increasingly monstrous series of betrayals into which Euphues' imaginative 'caveling' draws him as Philautus later recognizes when he accuses him of practising 'fraude of the hearte' (i. 233).

In the course of his defence Euphues changes the shape of the old man's argument as freely as he 'shapes' his own. Eubulus presented himself as society's spokesman, supporting his precepts with social examples like those of the husbandmen and gardeners who work for the benefit of the public weal, and the civic art produced by the Persians and Parthians. Euphues' argument denies the possibility of there being any single spokesman for the confused collection of disparate personalities which is a society. He assumes that, far from speaking

*Reason, Rightly Termed, Witcraft.* For readers familiar with Wilson's and Lever's texts, Lyly' allusion might have alerted them to keep their logical wits about them as they followed the adventures of Lyly's witty hero. For an account of the different forms of sophistry available to Elizabethan logicians, see Sister Miriam Joseph, *Rhetoric in Shakespeare's Time* (New York Harcourt, Brace & World, 1962), 365–74.

ɔr the commonwealth, Eubulus is a private subject speaking out of
ɪalice, who has founded his argument either on groundless gossip
r on his own idiosyncratic opinions ('eyther you gave too muche
redite to the report of others, or to much lybertie to your owne
ɪdgement', i. 190), and that in admonishing Euphues he has gratuit-
usly insulted both the youth and his parents ('you convince my
arents of peevishnesse, in making me a wanton, and me of leaudnesse
ɪ rejectinge correction', i. 190). Having reduced Eubulus' argument
ɔ the level of personal insult, Euphues goes on to suggest that *all* phi-
ɔsophical systems are merely manifestations of the plurality of human
pinion, a plurality which makes it practically impossible to achieve
ɪe consensus necessary for a stable state:

ɔ many men so many mindes, that may seeme in your eye odious, which in
ɪ others eye may be gratious. *Aristippus* a Philosopher, yet who more courtly? *Diogenes* a Philosopher, yet who more carterly? Who more popular then
*Plato*, retayning alwayes good company? Who more envious then *Tymon*,
ɪenouncing all humaine societie? Who so severe as the *Stoyckes*, which lyke
ɔockes were moved with no melody? Who so secure as the *Epicures* which
ɪallowed in all kinde of licentiousnesse? (i. 190)

ɔor Euphues, as for the narrator of Pettie's *Petite Pallace*, there is no
entral system of thought, only a series of antagonistic 'mindes'
ɪhich are governed less by reason than by the senses ('your eye . . .
ɪ others eye'). Social conduct becomes a matter not of general con-
ɛnt but of private inclination: 'the nature of the man disposeth that
ɔnsent of the manners' (i. 191). In addition, according to Euphues
ach of the philosophers he mentions was notable for espousing his
ɔwn brand of excess (Plato *always* keeps good company, Timon
ɛnounces *all* society). He has already accused Eubulus of succumbing
ɔ a particularly malicious form of extremism (the old man gave '*too*
*ɪuche* credite' to others and '*to much* lybertie' to his own opinion),
ɪnd he proceeds to place the kind of excess to which his own inclina-
ɪon draws him at the opposite extreme to that of Eubulus. He does so
ɔy adopting as his argument the proposition that it is impossible 'that
ɪature may *any waies* be altered by education' (i. 191, my emphasis).
ɪt the same time he reduces the old man's argument to the equally
xtreme proposition that nature has no 'force' at all: 'And can you
ɛee so unnaturall, whome dame Nature hath nourished and brought
ɪpp so many yeares, to repine as it were agaynst Nature?' (i. 191).
ɔld age and youth subsist in a state of perpetual conflict, 'we in all

pointes contrary unto you, and ye in all pointes unlike unto us' (i
193). And the assertion that Nature may not 'any waies be altered'
either by education or by the communicative arts which are the
basis of education, makes it impossible that this particular generation
gap can ever be bridged.

Euphues is in fact espousing a new method of interpreting experience—or rather, of reading the text of the *Anatomy* which masquerades as experience. For Eubulus as for the traditionalists there is only
one set of legitimate responses to any given text—like North he
opened his speech with a request that his audience invest him with
the status of an undisputed authority. For Euphues, on the other
hand, the act of reading is a far more flexible and creative process.
He argues that the same texts will produce a variety of alternative
responses in their various readers, and that 'althoughe to you they
breede more sorrowe and care, then solace and comforte, bicause of
your crabbed age: yet to mee they bring more comforte and joy
then care and griefe . . . bicause of my youthfull gentlenes' (i. 192).
The difference between these two readings is not a matter of right
and wrong interpretations, but a difference in taste produced by a disparity in age—although Euphues, by alluding to his own 'youthful
gentlenes', claims to be the more sympathetic, expert, and creative
reader, the 'gentle reader' addressed by Painter and subsequent Elizabethan authors including Lyly himself, capable of deriving mellifluous
'comforte and joy' from even a morally suspect publication. As a result
the moralistic response to pleasure represented by Eubulus becomes
nothing but a manifestation of 'crabbed age', which seeks (like the
old men in Castiglione's second book) to reduce all readers' response
to its own desiccated condition.

Euphues' view of the aims of the traditionalists is by no means
unperceptive. Fenton defined the project of his collection as that of
making young men 'old . . . in experience and wisdom', and Euphues
accuses Eubulus of harbouring the same ambition, but converts it from
an altruistic desire to disseminate virtue and learning to a bid for absolute power prompted by envy: 'Eyther you would have all men olde
as you are, or els you have quite forgotten that you your selfe were
young, or ever knew young dayes' (i. 192). According to Euphues,
Eubulus' cantankerous rendition of the city of Naples is designed to
transform what the young man takes to be a promising field in
which to exercise the delightful variety of his leisure interests—'my
youthly and lusty affections, my sportes and pleasures, my pastimes,

(i. 192)—into a less attractive kind of text, a repository of repellent examples: the old man wishes to make Naples a 'canckred storehouse of all strife, a common stewes for all strumpettes, the sinke of shame, and the very nurse of all sin' (i. 193). This is not a reflection of Eubulus' moral judgement of the Neapolitans, Euphues implies, so much as a symptom of the monotonously uninventive forms of didactic art that appeal to him. Nevertheless, for argument's sake the boy is willing temporarily to accept this version of Naples as an example of unmitigated vice, in order to stress his own superiority as a reader of the urban experience—though he continues to insist on the fictional status of the city he is accepting, since he agrees only to 'suppose that which I never will beleeve'. Confronted with the moral cesspit of the old man's Naples, Euphues depicts himself as a heroic reader like the one in Milton's *Areopagitica*, who can enter the most dangerous literary territory without yielding to temptation:

shall it therfore follow of necessitie that all that are woed of love, should be wedded to lust...? No, no, it is the disposition of the thought that altereth the nature of the thing. The Sun shineth uppon the dungehill, and is not corrupted, the Diamond lyeth in the fire, and is not consumed... a perfecte wit is never bewitched with leaudenesse, neyther entised with lasciviosnesse. (i. 193)

Like Eubulus, Euphues asserts that the character of Naples matters less than his response to it: but where Eubulus had indicated that his reaction ought to be one of repugnance, we are already aware that Euphues has responded to the city with unalloyed delight. As soon as he passes through the city gates he plunges himself into Neapolitan 'sportes and pleasures'; so that if Naples is indeed the 'sinke of shame' the old man says it is, then Euphues is well and truly sunk.

The end of Euphues' speech confirms that he perceives the dispute as no more than a competition between outmoded and fashionable forms of verbal artistry. He assures Eubulus that 'you shal assone catch a Hare with a Taber, as you shal perswade youth, with your aged and overworn eloquence, to such severitie of lyfe, which as yet her was never *Stoycke* so strict... but would rather allow it in wordes then follow it in workes, rather talke of it then try it' (i. 193–4). The old man's speech is a comically crude form of music, the rattling of a morris-dancer's tabor, and as such it is the antithesis of the Orphic music practised by the true poet or rhetorician, of which Euphues had earlier set himself up as an expert critic ('Hee coulde easily

discerne *Appollos* Musicke, from *Pan* his Pype', i. 186). For Euphues
traditional didactic art is so morally simplistic and has so little vitality
that it is merely an abstract theory, drably prescriptive words with no
hope of being converted into works. In fact, even the words Eubulus
speaks have no intrinsic meaning: 'though your reasons seem inwardly
to your selfe somewhat substantial, yet beyng well wayed without
they be shadowes without substaunce, and weake without force' (i.
194). Eubulus had tried to persuade him to employ words in their
socially accepted senses; but Euphues adopts for his own ends the
very words which Eubulus had urged him to use with greatest circumspection. Where the old man urged him to 'use pastime as the woorde
importeth, to passe the tyme in honest recreation', Euphues uses the
words 'pastime' and 'honest recreation' to indicate the very activitie
the old man discommends. He defends 'my *pastimes*, my common
dalyaunce' (i. 192) and accuses Eubulus of accounting 'all *honest recrea
tion* meere folly' (i. 194, my emphases); and once again his subversion
of his interlocutor's well-meant injunctions involves a witty reference
to the inevitable supplanting of old-fashioned forms of fiction by more
modern and complex texts. At about the time of the *Anatomy*'s publication, Francis Merbury published a new version of Redford's *Wit
and Science* called *The Marriage of Wit and Wisdom*, in which Wit was
subjected to still more abject humiliations than he had been in the
earlier interlude. Merbury's chief innovation is to introduce a male
vice called Idleness, who is vastly more skilful in the art of rhetorical
improvisation than the inexperienced protagonist: 'I am of that condi-
tion | That I can change into all colours like a chameleon.'[27] One of
the vice's chameleon changes is to adopt the name of the virtue
Honest Recreation from Redford's play, and to convince the unfortunate Wit that the sensual pleasures he invites him to share represent a
legitimate diversion from the rigours of intellectual labour. Euphues
has duped himself like Merbury's Wit into believing that the term
'honest recreation' encompasses forbidden pleasures as well as legal
ones, so that it is rather for him than for Eubulus that words have
become deceptive, interchangeable, 'shadowes without substaunce'.
His parting shot effectively confesses this:

Seeing therefore it is labour lost for mee to perswade you, and winde vaynely
wasted for you to exhort me, heere I founde you, and heere I leave you, having neither bought nor solde with you, but chaunged ware for ware, if you

[27] *English Moral Interludes*, ed. Wickham, 191.

have taken lyttle pleasure in my reply, sure I am that by your counsaile I have reaped lesse profit. (i. 194)

Once again the speech echoes the title-page of Painter's *Palace of Pleasure*, but this time it is only to divorce the rhetorical art of Euphues once and for all from any claim to reproduce the crude coupling of pleasure and profit by which the traditionalists hoped to justify their miscellanies. Euphues has severed himself from the constraints of didacticism, and has liberated his discourse to be as innovative and as delightful as he pleases. In the process he has precipitated both his reader and his author into a subtle and dangerous literary universe.

Just as Euphues undermines Eubulus' central example of the city of Naples, so he undermines his use of shorter illustrative *exempla*. For Eubulus there should be only one agreed function for any given analogy—and he asks Euphues to consent to this at the beginning of his speech where he tells him to 'followe my meaninge' (i. 187). Euphues, however, is equally eager to attach new meanings to Eubulus' examples. He tells him, 'as you have ensamples to confirme your pretence, so I have most evident and infallyble argumentes to serve for my purpose' (i. 191); but since he has already claimed that Eubulus argued 'uppon no proofe', his equation of his own 'argumentes' with Eubulus' 'ensamples' suggests that he is merely accepting the premisses laid down by the old man as if they were the rules of a parlour game. This impression is reinforced by the ludic ingenuity with which he adapts his opponent's similitudes to his own uses. Where Eubulus emphasizes the malleability of clay ('The Potter fashioneth his claye when it is softe', i. 187), Euphues stresses the variety of forms it can assume ('there is framed of the selfe same clay as well the tile to keepe out water as the potte to containe lycour', i. 190). Where Eubulus points out that iron must be worked when hot, and argues that the youthful mind like iron should be given form while it is still workable, Euphues uses iron first to prove that the essential nature of a thing cannot be altered ('Though yron be made softe with fyre it returneth to his hardnes', i. 191) and then to insult his would-be counsellor: 'your example of the hotte and harde yron, sheweth in you but colde and weake disposition' (i. 191). By now it is clear that Euphues regards *exempla* not as 'evident and infallyble argumentes' but as indications of the condition of their users' mental powers: the analogies of Eubulus, for instance, furnish proof of his encroaching senility: 'The similytude you rehearse of the waxe, argueth your waxinge and melting brayne' (i. 191). By contrast, the exuberant abundance of Euphues' examples shows off the capaciousness of his memory and the breadth of his reading, which he emphasizes with a string of synonyms: 'Infinite and innumerable were the examples I coulde alleadge and declare to confirme the force of Nature, and confute these your vayne and false forgeries, were not the repetition of them needelesse having shewed sufficient, or bootelesse seeinge those alleadged will not perswade you'. Euphues may be a more imaginative storyteller than Eubulus, since his 'stories of beasts, fowls and fishes' are infinite and innumerable, but he has robbed literature of its power of influencing its readers, and made it both needless and bootless, both unnecessary and unrewarding.

For the most part the young man poaches his examples from the well-stocked reservoirs of natural history. His Nature is no transcendent organizing deity—she does not even wield the precariously constructive powers she possesses in Spenser's Mutability cantos or Lyly's court comedy *The Woman in the Moone*. Instead she remains the irascible potentate who proved herself 'impatient of comparisons' at the beginning of the book. Euphues' Nature is out of control, like Gosson's pagan gods; the frenetically fertile producer of 'infinite and innumerable examples' whose very abundance makes them meaningless; the insane antithesis of the neat alternative creation fashioned by Sidney's poets. And she dominates his speech from start to finish. Eubulus has used a few analogies from natural history, but he has been careful to select examples with a direct bearing on human interests —the beech that burns in the grate faster than the oak, the cultivated fruit devoured by the voracious caterpillar (i. 189). Euphues' reply, by contrast, is choked with a riotous profusion of flora and fauna, ranging from the familiar, such as the Aesopian fox and mouse, to the bewilderingly strange: exotic specimens such as a traveller might find in distant lands, or rather—as Sidney pointed out—such as a reader might discover in books about such travels: the 'mounting' palm tree, the leopard, the chameleon with its capacious guts, the bird Trochilus which 'lyveth by the mouth of the Crocodile and is not spoyled'. North's *The Moral Philosophie of Doni* represented Nature as an orderly treasury of mnemonics in which each animal had its appointed place and its proper interpretation. Euphues' Nature, by contrast, is bursting with surprises. Her bird-life cultivates deceptions as assiduously as human beings ('The Birde *Taurus* hath a great voyce, but a small body', i. 194), and her stones do not remain conveniently and proverbially cold but stubbornly insist on generating heat ('the stone *Abeston* being once made hotte will never be made colde', i. 191). Euphues has, in fact, combined two antagonistic forms of fiction: on the one hand the fable, the prototype of the instructive narrative, in which, as Thomas Wilson tells us, 'brute beastes minister greate occasion of right good matter, considering many of them have shewed unto us the paterns and Images of divers vertues';[28] on the other the travellers' tales which had become a byword for malicious falsehoods (in his *Dialogue against the Fever Pestilence* of 1564 William Bullein gave his archetypal mendacious traveller the name of Mendax). The 'safe' tradition of animal fables has been complicated and rendered duplicitous by its association with exotic and semi-fictitious creatures from outside the fabular tradition, who are used exclusively to illuminate the inconsistency of experience, the unreliability of the senses. These outrageous birds, beasts, and minerals swarm across Lyly's pages like the grotesques that swarm over Elizabethan tapestries and wall-paintings, and they conspire to prevent us from believing that the behaviour of things can ever be given or constant. Defending the constancy of women to an audience which includes the inconstant Lucilla, Euphues invokes 'the stone of *Sicilia*, the which the more it is beaten, the harder it is' (i. 204)—a reaction to blows quite contrary to the behaviour of traditional stones. Later he alludes to two more unusual stones as he considers the possibility that Lucilla will reject his suit: 'O my *Lucilla*, if thy hearte, be made of that stone which may be mollyfied onely with bloud, woulde I had sipped of that river in *Caria* which tourneth those that drincke of it to stones' (i. 210). The absurd alternative Nature that yields these eccentric minerals waxes still crazier when Lucilla starts to participate in the game of hunt the exotica. When Euphues finally summons up courage to communicate his feelings to her, she answers with a battery of extraordinary stones and plants:

I feare me thou hast the stone *Continens* about thee, which is named of the contrarye, that thoughe thou pretende faithe in thy words, thou devisest fraude in thy heart . . . And what for that? Though thou have eaten the seedes of Rockatte, which breede incontinencie, yet have I chewed the leafe Cresse which mainteineth modestie. Though thou beare in thy bosome the hearbe *Araxa* most noisome to virginitie, yet have I the stone that groweth in the mounte *Tmolus*, the upholder of chastitie. (i. 222)

---

[28] *The Arte of Rhetorique* (1560), sig. N$^v$.

These are not so much examples as exhibits in a geological and botanical freak-show. Lyly's readers have been plunged into a literary wilderness more trackless than Gascoigne's, with little hope of finding their way back to the orderly garden-miscellanies of Painter and Fenton from which they have been expelled. Even Philautus eventually recognizes Euphues' affinity not with any conventional creature but with 'the fish *Scolopidus* in the floud Araris' which 'at the waxing of the Moone is as white as the driven snow, and at the wayning as blacke as the burnt coale' (i. 232); Euphues has accomplished the final triumph of sophistry, which is to turn white into black, and thus to alter the very essences of things.[29] Lyly seems in fact to use his similitudes with a full awareness of the objections Sidney was later to raise against them. 'Now for similitudes in certain printed discourses', Sidney complains in the *Apology*, 'I think all herbarists, all stories of beasts, fowls, and fishes are rifled up, that they come in multitudes to wait upon our conceits' (139). Sidney objects to these 'similitudes' as a 'surfeit to the ears', since a similitude cannot prove anything to a 'contrary disputer' but can only elaborate on a theme to which the 'willing hearer' has already acquiesced. With the exception of the scriptural address delivered by the reformed Euphues to the inarticulate Atheos, none of the speeches in the *Anatomy* convinces anyone of anything when they are not predisposed to be converted, whether by the eloquence of others or by their own. The speakers in Lyly's narrative, then, are entirely self-absorbed, and this is how Sidney diagnoses those who over-indulge in similes: 'which, who doth generally use, any man may see doth dance to his own music, and so be noted by the audience more careful to speak curiously than to speak truly' (139).[30]

Fabular animals too have been infected by the complexity of the more exotic exempla whose menagerie they share. In reply to

[29] Among innumerable instances of the Renaissance commonplace that the sophister can turn white into black and so confound his interlocutors' understanding of right and wrong, what is and what is not, one might cite Lancaster's words to Mortimer the younger in Marlowe's *Edward II*: 'Can this be true, 'twas good to banish him? | And is this true, to call him home again? | Such reasons make white black, and dark night day.' *Christopher Marlowe: Complete Plays and Poems*, ed. E. D. Pendry and J. C. Maxwell (London: J. M. Dent, 1976), 138 (i. iv. 245–7).

[30] Another passage from *An Apology for Poetry* seems peculiarly applicable to *The Anatomy of Wit*: 'So is that honey-flowing matron eloquence apparelled, or rather disguised, in a courtesan-like painted affectation: one time with so far-fetched words, they may seem monsters, but must seem strangers, to any poor Englishman' (138; see also my Conclusion below). Euphues the stranger certainly gives the animals in his bestiary some far-fetched names. The notes to Croll's edition give an account of some of his sources.

Euphues' declaration of love Lucilla feigns the outrage of the conventional literary virgin, alluding to the Aesopian saying that 'When the Foxe preacheth the Geese perishe' (i. 220); but where the traditionalist might see the proverb as a commonplace objection to devious speech, it turns out to be as applicable to Lucilla as to Euphues. She herself is engaged in 'preaching' about the excellence of virginity when she fully intends to abandon it, and he is being talked into the position of the goose. She makes the same use of the fable of the wolf who 'weareth a faire face to devoure the Lambe' (i. 223); again it looks as though Euphues is the sophisticated predator and she his prey, but we soon learn that she has adopted the wolf as her own emblem. When she eventually abandons Euphues for another man (called Curio, like one of the bestial curiosities he resembles) she tells Euphues that 'if brute beastes give us ensamples' then she should imitate the wolf, who 'chooseth him for hir make, that hath or doth endure most travaile for hir sake' (i. 239). At this point Euphues suddenly realizes that she has undergone the Circean metamorphosis which is usually reserved for the traveller rather than his seducer; he tells her that 'in that you bringe in the example of a beast to confirme your folly, you shew therein your beastly disposition, which is readie to followe suche beastlinesse' (i. 240). The fable seems finally to have transformed the mind which has subjected it to so many curious transformations.[31]

### 4. SMALL HOPE OF AMENDMENT

Lyly's Euphues lives in a land of shadows, a forest of analogies where the play of light and dark makes it impossible to distinguish the solid

---

[31] *A Mirror for Magistrates* offers an intriguing insight into the problems of interpretation to which Euphues' selection of unfamiliar examples from natural history might give rise. The tragedy of George, Duke of Clarence, attributed in successive editions of the *Mirror* to William Baldwin, contains an extended discussion of animal fables and their vulnerability to misreadings. The duke explains that the traditional fable plainly delineates the characters of men through the use of familiar bestial analogies: '*By knowen beastes* thus truth doth playne declare | What men they be, of whom she speakes before' (228, my emphasis). But he goes on to complain that in recent times unscrupulous readers have tended to manipulate the examples of beasts to their own ends—especially by applying fables to the heraldic beasts of noble families: 'And thus there grewe of a mistaken truth, | An arte so false, as made the true suspect: | Wherof hath cum much mischiefe, more the ruth, | That errours should our mindes so much infect' (229). Euphues' use of 'unnatural natural history' might be taken to constitute a branch of this false art—as might Baldwin's own use of cats. See *The Mirror for Magistrates*, ed. Campbell, 227–30.

from the ghostly, the real from the imagined. His response to Eubulus can be read as a systematic disengagement of words and phrases from their referents, a reduction of language to an exercise in shadow-boxing, the effect of which is triumphantly to quash the old man's conviction that it is not only possible but necessary to achieve a consensus about signs and their meanings. For Eubulus, Naples offers a perfect example of the way the sign that is a work of art—whether verbal or visual—should be applied to the 'real' world to which it refers. 'Heere *Euphues*', he admonishes, 'maiste thou see not the carved visarde of a lewde woman, but the incarnate visage of a lascivious wanton, not the shaddowe of love, but the substaunce of luste' (i. 189). For the well-taught observer the city can only incarnate one meaning, a real-life enactment of the dangers represented by the instructive statue erected by the Parthians, the image of a beautiful woman who robs and knifes the young man she sleeps with. For Euphues, on the other hand, Naples has no essence, no uncontested application. It can either be taken for an infinitely varied repository of experiential clutter, from which bits and pieces can be plucked at random and fitted together in any shape that pleases the artist's eye; or else for a blank space on which its visitors are free to inscribe their private versions of urban life. Eubulus' version corresponds to nothing in the young man's experience; while it is 'inwardly to [himself] somewhat substantial', to Euphues it is nothing but 'shadowes without substaunce', a geriatric doodle. By virtue of their different ages the disputants effectively occupy different cities as well as different historical epochs, and no grand narrative exists that can join their disparate histories together.

For the rest of the first half of the *Anatomy*, Euphues treats his experiences as so much malleable clay, available to be moulded by rival artists into their own editions of Pygmalion's animated sculpture. Euphues is the most self-satisfied Pygmalion of them all, in love with the refined productions of his own imagination; at one stage he even acknowledges his connection with the Ovidian sculptor, assuring Lucilla that 'though *Proteus* transforme himselfe into every shape, yet *Pygmalion* retaineth his olde forme ... thoughe others seeme counterfaite in their deedes, yet *Lucilla* perswade your selfe that *Euphues* will bee alwayes curraunt in his dealinges' (i. 219). But Lyly's Pygmalion is in a far more ticklish situation than his precursors in the texts of Ovid or of Pettie. Eubulus compared the murderous Parthian statue to Pygmalion's image, so that if Euphues is the mythical sculptor and Lucilla his image, then she is the one who is likely to prove 'counterfaite'—indeed, the word implies as much, since it is the term used in the epistle to describe the portrait of the loose woman, Helen. In the world of the *Anatomy* the sophisticated artefact is invariably connected with disaster—Helen's 'looseness' provoked a war—and Lucilla is the subtlest of Lyly's artefacts. The 'forme' to whom Pygmalion remains true is herself endlessly protean; she is an acolyte of Euphues' riotous Nature, as well as the Neapolitan 'substaunce of lust' from Eubulus' oration, who possesses the 'incarnate visage of a lascivious wanton', and who can transform her admirers as completely as the most seditious of Ascham's Italian fictions. For all the young man's parading of his cosmopolitan sophistication—'if I be in *Crete*, I can lye, if in *Greece* I can shift, if in *Italy* I can court it' (i. 186)—it is in Italy that he learns that the more complex the work of art, the more strenuously it resists control, whether by its interpreters or by the cosmopolitan artist.

Euphues confirms his metamorphosis into a perverse Pygmalion when he 'writes' the first of his Neapolitan fictions, the story of his friendship with Philautus. He quickly transforms Philautus into a statue of himself, a narcissistic revision of Elyot's description of amity. Before Euphues even conceives the notion of such a friendship, Lyly loosens its foundations by telling us that the 'rypest wittes' only associate with those who resemble them, so as to prop up their own private fantasies: 'one flattereth an other in hys owne folly, and layeth cushions under the elbowe of his fellowe, when he seeth him take a nappe with fancie' (i. 195). When it comes, Euphues' and Philautus' exercise in mutual ego-boosting takes its place, in Euphues' mind, in an imaginary anthology of fictional friendships, among which he lists the celebrated alliances of Damon and Pithias, Pylades and Orestes, and Titus and Gisippus (i. 198). The behaviour of Euphues and Philautus bears the closest resemblance to that of Titus and Gisippus, who studied, dined, and lived together, and who finally 'together so increased in doctrine, that within a few years, few in Athens might be compared unto them' (*The Governor*, 136); but Lyly's friends are a good deal less exemplary. After holding a banquet to celebrate their newly formed alliance they dance all afternoon, and from then on Lyly tells us that 'they used not onely one boord, but one bedde, one booke (if so be it they thought not one to many)' (i. 199). Unlike traditional ideal friendships their relationship consists entirely of pleasure, with little or no instruction thrown in. In *The Governor* Elyot tells us that amity:

is a blessed and stable connection of sundry wills, making of two persons one in having and suffering. And therefore a friend is properly named of philosophers an other I. For that in them is but one mind and one possession and the which more is, a man more rejoiceth at his friend's good fortune than at his own. (134)

Euphues too describes Philautus as 'at all times an other I', but then exposes the narcissistic grounds for the comparison by transforming him into a sculptural self-portrait: he is 'in all places the expresse Image of mine own person' (i. 197). His vision of amity is one of perfect mutual trust based on perfect communication, but the sole beneficiary of this trust would seem to be Euphues, since his friend gives everything and gets nothing in return: 'whom thou maist make partner of all thy secrets without suspition of fraude . . . who will accompt thy bale his bane, thy mishap his misery, the pricking of thy finger, the percing of his heart' (i. 197).

Above all, their attachment is an airy verbal construct with nothing to substantiate its professions of unshakeable loyalty. Instead, the young men found their liking for one another on the stylishness with which they express it. 'Sithens a long discourse argueth folly, and delicate words incurre the suspition of flattery, I am determined to use neither of them' (i. 198), announces Euphues, and Philautus is so impressed by his authoritative handling of the plain 'Attic' style that he struggles at once to reproduce his technique: 'Friend *Euphues* . . . I dare neither use a long processe, neither loving speach, least unwittingly I should cause you to convince me of those thinges, which you have alredy condemned' (i. 198).[32] Philautus goes on to express the hope that 'my shorte answere wil worke as great an effect in you, as your few words did in me'; but Euphues considers effective discourse to be his own exclusive prerogative, and the series of amiable propositions and admiring responses which initiated the boys' companionship quickly degenerates into a surreptitious campaign on the part of Euphues to demonstrate the superiority of his creative intellect to that of his former friend. Once Euphues has fallen in love with Lucilla, the earlier fiction of the ideal friendship he has so carefully forged with Philautus assumes the status of a rival narrative, which must be aborted if his newly conceived romantic novel is to

---

[32] For a discussion of the 'Attic' style and Lyly's connection with it, see George Williamson, *The Senecan Amble: A Study of Prose Form from Bacon to Collier* (London: Faber & Faber, 1951), chs. 1–4.

flourish. When Philautus introduces him to Lucilla, he conceives of the introduction as a challenge to his critical accomplishments: 'Did *Philautus* accompt *Euphues* to simple to decypher beautie, or supersticious not to desire it?' (i. 210). And as if to prove the extent of his critical subtlety he proceeds to rewrite some of the most consensually simple texts in the canon of Classical literature to support his burgeoning plan to act on his desire. In Euphues' alternative canon, Lucretia the emblem of chastity becomes grotesquely marginal, a 'Monster in the desartes' (i. 211), and Penelope the essence of constancy succumbs at last to her suitors' advances: she 'woulde bee wearie to unweave that in the nyght, shee spunne in the daye, if *Ulysses* had not come home the sooner' (i. 211). These Pettie-like revisions of Classical texts pave the way for his corrupt variations on Italian narratives of friendship and forbidden love. In solitude he determines to 'unfolde my secrete love, to my secrete friende' (i. 210), and at this point it is not clear whether the 'secrete friende' is his male companion, the sharer of his secrets, or his projected female lover, to whom his desire is still a secret. The reader's confusion is compounded when Philautus enters and Euphues begins what looks like a complete confession of his love, like that of Titus to Gisippus; but at the last minute he substitutes the name of Livia, the one virtuous woman in the narrative, for that of Lucilla. His fake confession is full of allusions to evasive strategies, both military and civilian; he talks of his desire as an internal battle which can be won only by 'pollicie' (i. 212), of his relationship with Livia as a game of chess, and of the need to 'cloak' his intentions and to 'walke circumspectly' if he is to bring his courtship to fruition (i. 213). Once again Philautus eagerly swallows his account of his mental state, enthusiastically declaring his willingness to participate in Euphues' plot by filling Ferardo's 'olde heade' with 'new fables' so as to give his friend access to his supposed mistress (i. 214). Euphues' narrative, then, is an elaborate trap, a Silenic receptacle not for the secrets of collective wisdom that Golding and Rainolde detected in Classical fictions but for the cunningly concealed agendas that are the stock-in-trade of the Renaissance spy. As well as liberating Euphues' rhetoric from the constraints of didacticism, the boy's detachment of word from referent discharges him from the constraints of loyalty, and qualifies him admirably for a fraudulent career as a double agent.

If the rhetoric of Euphues resembles the complex interplay of dancing shadows, then the shadows they recall are not those of solid objects but the insubstantial kind Lyly invokes in the prologue of his play *Campaspe*, 'Agrippa his shadowes, who in the moment they were seene, were of any shape one woulde conceive' (ii. 316).[33] Philautus first introduces Euphues to Lucilla as his 'shadowe' as though the two boys have become extensions of one another's bodies; but when Lucilla playfully objects to the presence of an extra guest at dinner, Euphues insists that his darkness may prove useful to her, and indicates the kind of usefulness he means with a sexual quibble: 'Fayre Lady seing the shade doth often shilde your beautie from the parching Sunne... by so much the more you ought to lyke it, by how much the more you use to lye in it' (i. 200–1). A little later he returns to Philautus' metaphor in order to change its meaning again, and this time the shadow has become a disguise, a mask: 'As *Philautus* brought me for his shadowe the last supper, so will I use him as my shadow til I have gayned his Saint' (i. 209). Euphues' shadows can clearly be 'of any shape one woulde conceive', and they change shape continually. His speeches too slide evasively from one position to another, with each seemingly solid statement opening up to reveal an antithetical conclusion. In a speech he delivers after supper at Lucilla's, for instance, he shifts by a progression of fallacies from the conventional insistence that women dismiss their bodies as inverted Sileni ('Doth not experience teach us that in the most curious Sepulchre are enclosed rotten bones?' i. 202) to an exhortation to exploit their bodies to the full while they are able: 'If you will be cherished when you be olde, be curteous while you be young, if you looke for comfort in your hoary haires, be not coye when you have your golden lockes' (i. 203). Generic boundaries dissolve before the onslaught of his sophistry; *memento mori* merges with *carpe diem*; a sermon becomes a seduction; so that each rhetorical sculpture Euphues fashions in his capacity as Pygmalion seems to take on a life of its own, and then to keep on changing, unfolding to disclose new and unexpected linguistic configurations. It is only fitting, then, that when he comes to justify his treachery to Philautus in a letter,

---

[33] The prologue alludes to Cornelius Agrippa and his fascination with animated statues or shadows. In his treatise *Of the Vanitie and Uncertaintie of Artes and Sciences* Agrippa mentions the magicians who believe that 'with divers constellations of Starres rightly observed by distaunce of time ... and by the consent of heavenly sprites, an image maie receave the sprite of life, and understanding' (sig. Q). It is tempting to speculate that the moving images to which Pettie compares Pygmalion's image might be of the same kind. For a discussion of the use of the word 'shadow' in Elizabethan references to the visual arts, see Gent, *Picture and Poetry 1560–1620*, 19.

Euphues should describe his adventures as a revision of the most shifty canonical text of them all, the *Metamorphoses*: 'Did not *Jupiter* transforme himselfe into the shape of *Amphitrio* to imbrace *Alcmœna*? Into the forme of a Swan to enjoye *Læda*? Into a Bull to beguyle *Io*? Into a showre of golde to winne *Danae*?' (i. 236). Euphues' new version of Ovid's text has detached itself once and for all from the moral commentaries that gave it authority in the humanist schoolroom. Instead these modern fables serve only to demonstrate that 'anye impietie may lawfully be committed in love, which is lawlesse', and extend the effects of their lawlessness from the world of literature to the state of Naples.

But even as Euphues constructs his own set of innovative stories to mock the more simplistic 'new fables' of Philautus and the 'aged and overworn eloquence' of Eubulus, Lucilla is laying the groundwork for a still more sophisticated set of metamorphoses, a still more shifty kind of discourse. She begins to show her superior mastery of euphuistic sophistry as soon as Euphues has finished his after-dinner speech on the ephemeral nature of the female body. At this point, enchanted by his own eloquence, Euphues offers to fashion a rhetorical destruction (as Richard Rainolde called it) of any proposition his audience cares to advance. Lucilla immediately proposes that he refute the charge that 'Women are to be wonne with every winde' (i. 203), and Euphues recognizes that he has been 'taken napping', forced to develop a thesis he had not expected to defend and to narrate a 'tale' which is not of his devising (i. 204). Twice his efforts to elaborate on Lucilla's theme come to grief: first when he finds himself arguing that women are incorruptible and realizes half-way through that this argument acts against his interests as a would-be seducer, and later when he endeavours to give a 'lively substance' to the 'shadow' of his encomium of women (i. 216)—that is, to supply evidence to support it—only to lose himself in a crescendo of hyperboles which threaten to overwhelm his efforts to control them: 'I am entred into so large a fielde, that I shall sooner want time then proofe, and so cloye you wyth varietie of prayses that I feare mee I am lyke to infect women with pride' (i. 217). By this stage Euphues' attempts to build a spontaneous palace of pleasure which will surpass Pettie's extemporary *Petite Pallace* in the 'varietie' it contains seem to be running into serious difficulties. When he finally finds the opportunity to tell Lucilla that he loves her, his speech is rendered awkward and unconvincing by his efforts to prove himself *innocent* of 'subtiltie'—to deny the sophistication that he has so carefully cultivated up to this point; and he falls back on effusive offers of service which can hardly claim to be either witty or innovative, since they recall the effusions of melancholy knights confronted by their lovers in traditional courtly literature. For all his hubristic confidence in his abilities as an improviser, Euphues is simply not equal to the challenge posed by Lucilla's unexpected proposition.

Lucilla, on the other hand, is completely at home with the subtle rhetoric of lawlessness. Her reply to Euphues' profession of devotion is a masterpiece of duplicity, the most luxuriantly slippery speech in the *Anatomy*, as the narrator seems to recognize in the admiring précis with which he prefaces the discourse:

wisely did she cast this in hir head, that if she should yeelde at the first assault he woulde thinke hir a lyght huswife, if she should reject him scornefully a very haggard, minding therefore that he shoulde neyther take holde of his promise, neyther unkindenesse of hir precisenesse, she fedde him indifferently, with hope and dispayre, reason and affection, lyfe and death. (i. 219–20)

Lucilla treads an exquisitely fine line between acceptance and rejection, between posing as an innocent simpleton ('commonly we poore wenches are deluded through lyght beliefe', i. 220) and parading her incomparable sophistication ('I did at the firste entraunce discerne thy love but yet dissemble it'—something which Euphues markedly failed to do—'yet coulde hee not perceive hir willinge any way to lende hym a friendly looke', i. 200). At the same time she swings giddyingly between a half-accusing, half-admiring acknowledgement of Euphues' sophistication ('These subtill shiftes, these paynted practises (if I were to be wonne) woulde soone weane mee from the teate of *Vesta*, to the toyes of *Venus*', i. 221) and a subtle defence of his simplicity ('what greater triall can I have of thy simplicitie and truth, then thine owne requeste which desireth a triall', i. 224). By the end of the speech it remains as uncertain as it was at the beginning whether she is claiming to admire simplicity more than subtlety, or whether she claims to be subtle or simple herself.[34] But whatever her claims, her skills in elusive disputation cannot be disputed. In the course of her reply she has undergone an astonishing transition from the stance of a latter-day Lucretia to the qualified acceptance of an illicit lover, from a settled preference for one kind

---

[34] Her passing reference to 'the teate of Vesta', implying as it does that her version of Vesta is not a virgin, suggests perhaps that she is inclined to half-conceal her subtlety.

of text (she will use 'for lovers Sonettes, Davids Psalmes', i. 224) to the prospective acceptance of another ('whensoever I shall love any I will not forget thee'). Euphues is left hopelessly perplexed by this virtuoso rhetorical display, reduced (as Gascoigne's F.J. was by Elinor) 'into a great quandarie and as it were a colde shivering, to heare this newe kinde of kindenesse, such sweete meate, such sower sauce, such faire wordes, such faint promises' (i. 224). Lucilla, like her lover, is engaged in formulating a 'newe kinde' of language, one that resists all conventional terms of classification; a rhetoric that can be given two contradictory readings by proponents of simplicity and proponents of wit, like Lyly's duplicitous *Anatomy* itself. In the process she has beaten Euphues at his own game. If Euphues' fake confession was riddled with double meanings—encouraging Philautus to engage in deceitful practices as a cloak for his own deception of Philautus—Lucilla's response to Euphues goes one better, and deceives the deceiver's deceiver. Euphues can only marvel at the 'true loves knotte wrought of chaungeable silke' she has given him, and rack his brains for a means of imitating her virtuosity: 'I am devisinge howe I mighte have my coulours chaungeable also, that they mighte agree' (i. 225).

It would seem that in the *Anatomy*, as in *The Deceyte of Women*, Baldwin's *Beware the Cat*, Gascoigne's *Adventures*, and Pettie's *Petite Pallace*, women are the supreme exponents of the arts of policy, the mistresses of rhetorical manipulation, the most inscrutable of domestic agents. And in the misogynistic literature of the 1570s, women are also the most deceptive of Sileni. 'A cooling Carde for Philautus' recommends that they be subjected to the most hostile and invasive form of scrutiny in order to demonstrate their Silenic natures: 'Looke in their closets, and there shalt thou finde an Apoticaries shoppe of sweet confections, a Surgions boxe of sundrye salves, a Pedlars packe of new fangles' (i. 255). Even the term that describes them is duplicitously Silenic, as Euphues decides after Lucilla has left him. It can be unpacked to reveal two meanings: either that women are perfect companions for men—that they are 'as we men'—or that they are the most deadly of friendly enemies, that they represent 'woe unto men, by their falshood, gelousie, inconstancie' (i. 241). Their difference from men, which marks them out for Euphues as a malevolent alternative life-form, is signalled like so much else in the *Anatomy* by a series of analogies half-hidden in the text. At the beginning of the narrative the narrator compares Euphues to 'the fleetest fishe' in the sea—that is, the dolphin—whose rapidity cannot protect it from swallowing 'the delicatest bayte' (i. 185). Later Lucilla compares women to the 'fleete *Dolphin*' which can be caught by playing seductive music and the similitude is as applicable to the speedy Euphues as it is to Lucilla herself (i. 223). More so, in fact; because when Lucilla leaves Euphues for Curio, her abandoned lover decides that she is the most fugitive fish of all, the only one that cannot be fished for: 'in my minde if you bee a fishe you are either an Ele which as soone as one hath holde of hir taile, will slippe out of his hand, or else a Mynnowe which will be nibbling at every baite but never biting' (i. 239). In this way Lyly both pays homage to and improves on the metaphor that closed *The Adventures of Master F.J.*, in which F.J. compares Elinor to a fisherman who demands, and fails to get, exclusive rights to fish in the ocean.[35] Lyly's Lucilla, by contrast, can claim that the ocean of sexuality and the lawless rhetoric that feeds it are her element, and that she has absolute freedom of movement within these mesmerizing and uncharted waters.

The representation of women as the ultimate exponents of duplicit-ous rhetoric is, of course, one of the many manifestations of Eliza-bethan anti-feminism. But there might be another reason for putting the cleverest sophistries into the mouths of women, and that is to pro-tect the male exponents of politic discourse from the charge that Lodge brought against Gosson: the charge of endorsing what they claim to condemn. By giving the most powerful and cunning ex-amples of subtle discourse to the disempowered—by attributing the greatest political astuteness to those who, with a few notable excep-tions, have no active part to play in Renaissance politics—the men who champion wit proclaim the fact that their sophisticated texts pose no real threat to the security of the public weal. This is the strat-egy adopted by Gascoigne in his satire *The Steele Glas*, where he represents the satirist as a woman, or else as a tongueless hermaphro-dite—for Gascoigne the difference is minimal.[36] By cutting himself off from the wily destructiveness of women, Lyly's Euphues announces that he is not so wily or destructive himself, and that his skills may be reclaimed by the state despite their apparent lawlessness, because they are finally dependent on the institutions—both political and educational—that fashioned them. In Elizabethan fiction women

[35] The song in which the metaphor occurs is the most anthologized of Gascoigne's lyrics, 'And if I did what then?', *An Anthology of Elizabethan Prose Fiction*, 79.

[36] 'I n'am a man, as some do thinke I am, | (Laugh not good Lord) I am in dede a dame, | Or at the least, a right *Hermaphrodite*...'(ii. 144).

too are finally dependent on the men who rule the patriarchy, and this dependence is reinforced by the conditions under which Lucilla dies—'in great beggerie in the streets' (i. 312). The dazzling inventiveness of Euphues' and Lucilla's styles was too dangerously anarchic—and too contagious, as its many imitators demonstrate—to be left untamed at the end of the book. Its poisonous properties needed an antidote, its wildness needed a cage, and Lyly was prudent enough to supply his text with both. He tamed Lucilla by killing her off; and he decontaminated Euphues by converting him into the voice of moral probity, and allowing him to write a didactic appendix to his own adventures which is as long and elaborate as the adventures themselves.

The conversion of Euphues is announced by the triumphant reinstatement of the traditional moral commentary. Abruptly he decides that examples need to be tied to their agreed applications, and informs Lucilla with the zeal of a young apostate that the analogies she uses have a legitimate function: 'these are set down that we viewing their incontinencie, should flye the like impudencie, not follow the like excesse' (i. 240). Lucilla, meanwhile, succumbs to an appalling fate before she dies: that of being fixed for all eternity as one of the consensually simple examples which she has so cleverly eluded in the course of her career. In the act of transferring her affections from Euphues to Curio, she is suddenly struck by an insight into the way her action will be read by future generations:

I have chosen one (I must needs confesse) neither to be compared to *Philautus* in wealth, nor to thee in wit, neither in birth to the worst of you both, I thinck God gave it me for a just plague, for renouncing *Philautus*, and choosing thee, and sithens I am an ensample to all women of lightnesse, I am lyke also to be a myrrour to them all of unhappinesse, which ill lucke I must take by so much the more patiently, by howe much the more I acknowledge my selfe to have deserved it worthely. (i. 238–9)

Like Euphues she has returned to the territory of *The Palace of Pleasure*, and of the literary tradition in which fiction is an instructive mirror, a collection of 'ensamples' to delight and indoctrinate its placid readers, where every manifestation of female independence must be suppressed, and where wayward women are subjected to barbaric and humiliating forms of punishment. At this point Lucilla foreshadows the tragic situation of Shakespeare's Cressida, who struggles vainly to avoid being fixed in the exemplary mould to which she has been

consigned by the audience before the play begins: a mould which she
summarizes in the middle of the play in the hackneyed phrase 'As false
as Cressid' (III. ii. 192).

For the most part, Lyly's Lucilla is associated not with Cressida, the
most ubiquitous instance of the fickle woman in the 1570s, but with
the more politically devastating career of Helen, whose abduction
initiated a series of events that ended in the fall of Troy. A portrait
of Helen opened the epistle; and Helen, with her patroness Venus,
quickly becomes one of the dominant emblems of the book, evoking
the inevitable and disastrous intrusion of desire into the world of politics. The opening of the book concerns itself with Paris's attraction to
Helen rather than with Helen herself. We learn that he called the scar
on her chin '*cos amoris*, the Whetstone of love' (i. 184), and that he
would have felt at home in Naples (it is 'more fitter for *Paris* then *Hector*', i. 185); Euphues later uses the example of Paris to support his
decision to betray Philautus (i. 210). Only towards the end of his
career does Lucilla become openly associated with Helen, after the
male characters have decided that her beauty is a Silenic trap. Philautus
first makes the connection in a letter in which he reproves Euphues
for his treachery and warns him of the emptiness of his victory: 'I
know that *Menelaus* for his tenne yeares warre endured ten yeares
woe, that after all his strife he wan but a Strumpet' (i. 234). Immediately afterwards Lucilla herself embraces the parallel: 'As for chaun-
ging', she tells Euphues, 'did not *Helen* the pearle of Greece, thy
countriwoman first take *Menelaus*, then *Theseus*, and last of all *Paris*?'
(i. 239). Lucilla's adoption of Helen as her tutelary spirit, and her
reminder that Helen, like Euphues, was Greek, lends urgency to the
young man's task of dissociating himself from his former mistress,
especially since Philautus has earlier compared him to the treacherous
Sinon, who persuaded the Trojans to bring the wooden horse into
Troy, while he himself has repeatedly acknowledged his resemblance
to Ulysses, one of the devisers of the horse. The wooden horse might
be described as the most destructive Silenus of all, the perfect symbol,
as Gosson pointed out, of the infiltration of English culture by corrupt
Italian customs. Having demonstrated wit's potential for performing
similar acts of infiltration, it was evidently in Lyly's as well as in
Euphues' interests to show that wit could also be turned against the
infiltrators. The boy tells Lucilla that Helen of Greece was 'my coun-
triewoman borne, but thine by profession', and so disengages himself
from the reputation of the Greeks for shiftiness which he has eagerly

embraced till now. But Helen is not so easily dismissed as a simple example of female faithlessness. Unlike Cressida, her status as an example is not fixed; she is a topic for controversy, as she remains in Shakespeare's play. On the one hand she is the bane of Troy, on the other she is the 'face that launched a thousand ships'; her beauty competes with her looseness for attention, as Apelles' painting warned in the dedication. And at the end of the *Anatomy* this competition still awaits its resolution, both with regard to Helen and with regard to her Italian descendant, Lucilla. In one of his last letters of advice the reformed Euphues warns Philautus to beware of transforming the recently dead Lucilla into an example as equivocal as Helen's: 'Thou sayest that for beautie she was the *Helen of Greece*, and I durste sweare that for beastlines she might be the Monster of *Italy*' (i. 312). Lucilla's capacity for generating alternative readings remains as potent after her death as it was in her lifetime; the sophisticated discourse of the first half of the *Anatomy* cannot be unwritten by the moral treatises of the second, and the monstrous alternative schoolhouse constructed by wit continues to contend with the humanist curriculum throughout the texts of Euphues' reformation.

An Aschamite might recognize in these treatises a careful imitation of the imitation theory propounded in *The Scholemaster*. Just as in the first half of his career Euphues experiences the perils incurred by quick wits in the first half of Ascham's text, so in the second he produces, one after another, examples of the different kinds of imitation which Ascham recommends as the ground of all learning in the second book of his treatise. 'A cooling Carde for Philautus and all fond lovers' is a loose prose adaptation of Ovid's *Remedia Amoris*, and so exemplifies Ascham's *metaphrasis*, which he defines as to 'take some notable place out of a good Poete, and turn the same sens into meter, or into other wordes in Prose' (243). It is also a translation, although of necessity not the double translation from Latin into English and back again to Latin that Ascham assigns to his scholars. Euphues' recapitulation of Eubulus' advice at the end of *Euphues and his Ephoebus* (i. 286) illustrates both *epitome* and *paraphrasis* (which Ascham defines as 'in two sundrie places, to expresse one matter, with diverse wordes', 252). The *Atheos* both paraphrases and epitomizes the Bible, while countering Ascham's most serious objection to Italian influence, that it encourages atheism. Finally the *Ephoebus* enacts Ascham's theory of *imitatio*, both by describing the sequence of imitations by which a child's character is fashioned, and by itself closely following the model of Plutarch's *Moralia*. Lyly's use of Plutarch, whose success in educating the emperor Trajan was celebrated in one of Painter's novels, provides a happy epilogue to Eubulus' seemingly futile effort to educate the unregenerate Euphues.

But of course Lyly's imitation of Ascham is not a simple one. Ascham gives his readers no assurance that the practice of nurturing a fondness for the Classics will prevent a pupil's nature from asserting itself; and quick wits continue to disrupt his curriculum in the second book of *The Scholemaster* as they did in the first. They are clearly the 'readie speakers' Ascham mentions in the second book, who 'having their heades over full of matter, be like pennes over full of inke which will soner blotte than make any faire letter at all' (263–4). In the same way, the rhetorical excesses of Euphues' quick wit are just as evident in the treatises of his reformation as they were in his erotic adventures. Indeed, we might expect as much from the shaky premise on which he bases his sudden conversion: the assumption that if one woman proves untrustworthy then all must be corrupt.[37] Euphues has been converted to moral orthodoxy, but he has not been converted to coherence. The first of his treatises in particular—'A cooling Carde for Philautus'—is a tissue of wilful absurdities. It represents yet another of Euphues' attempts to rewrite the canon of Classical literature, like his earlier revisions of the stories of Lucretia and Penelope. It begins, as Ovid's poem does, by making exaggerated claims for its own effectiveness: 'If *Phillis* were now to take counsayle, shee would not be so foolish to hang hirselfe, neyther *Dido* so fonde to dye for *Aeneas*' (i 248). But the 'cooling Carde' fails to deliver a convincing alternative version of the stories of these celebrated suicides. Euphues says that he wrote it to avoid being idle; and the question of what exactly constitutes 'honest recreation', the fruitful occupation of leisure time, fills these final pamphlets, and never finds a satisfactory answer. Like Ovid, Euphues suggests that idleness is the most deadly of intellectual diseases: 'the man beeing idle the minde is apte to all uncleannesses' (i 251); yet he himself, in his leisure moments, has found his mind infected with thoughts of love, even if he claims to be interested only in stamping it out; and love quickly proves itself resistant to

---

[37] 'I had thought that women had bene as we men, that is true, faithfull, zealous, constant, but I perceive they be rather woe unto men, by their falshood, gelousie, inconstancie (i. 241). F.J. commits the same logical error at the end of the *Adventures*, when, as France points out, he is 'content to condemn a number unknown for the transgression of one too well known' (78).

every form of inoculation. Each antidote he proposes is followed by another which presupposes the failure of the one that precedes it. He takes Philautus on a whirlwind tour of the liberal arts, and seems to presume that he will prove quite incapable of applying himself to any single branch of study: 'Bende thy minde to the lawe . . . If lawe seeme loathsome unto thee, search the secretes of Phisicke . . . If thou be so nice that thou canst no waye brooke the practise of Phisicke . . . conferre all thy study all thy time, all thy treasure to the attayning of the sacred and sincere knowledge of divinitie' (i. 251–2). And all of Euphues' efforts to dissuade his recalcitrant reader from desire lead only to the conclusion that Philautus will be caught at last, and that he will fall in love before he has completed even one of the recommended courses. The pamphlet ends with the suggestion that he try duplicity as a last defence against desire: the same duplicity that brought about the perplexities of the *Anatomy*'s first half (he must be 'subtill to deceive these tame Serpents', as Euphues was, and pretend to love more than one woman, as Euphues did, i. 255). The 'cooling Carde' finally lapses into bathos, with the advice that the lovelorn Philautus should avoid being alone in case he should be driven to suicide—the suicide which Euphues promised to avert when he said he would rewrite the tale of Phyllis (i. 248). Philautus is left on the brink of self-destruction; in the meantime, Euphues' recommendation of divinity as a feeble alternative to sexual obsession hardly strengthens his readers' confidence in the educational system he goes on to delineate.

*Euphues and his Ephoebus* presents another of the elusive ideals that bedevil sixteenth-century texts: this time the portrait of the ideal student. Euphues has to build up this ideal from scratch, assembling his model pupil piece by piece from conception through birth to boyhood—and the first part of the *Anatomy* shows how necessary this is, since the fully formed wit would seem impossible to win to learning by the kind of verbal instruction that the *Ephoebus* represents. Yet the construction of Ephoebus turns out to be an abortive project, since we learn towards the end of the treatise that the universities where his education must be completed share the corruption of Naples. Ephoebus is an ideal without a context, who can inhabit only a fictional society: 'I hope that if ever *Platoes* common weale shall flourish, that my *Ephoebus* shall be a Citizen, that if *Aristotle* finde any happye man it will bee my childe, if *Tullye* confesse anye to bee an absolute Orator, it will be my young youth' (i. 283–4). In other words, Ephoebus has no

future. Even without resorting to that den of vice, the university, h
will find himself lost in a labyrinth of learning which is as convolute
as one of Gascoigne's: 'Hee that seeketh the depth of knowledge is a
it were in a *Laborinth*, in which the farther he goeth, the farther he i
from the end' (i. 289). And Euphues presumes that learning as well a
idleness will end by generating the literature of love: 'Heereof it com
meth that such vayne ditties, such idle sonnets, suche inticinge songes
are sette foorth to the gaze of the worlde and griefe of the godlye' (i
287). Desire and learning, the body and the mind, are hopelessly inter
twined—and equally fertile: we narrowly escape the pleasure of read
ing three volumes of Euphues' lectures before he changes his mind
The consequences of love and learning, too, are the same: 'I wa
determined to write notes of Philosophy', Euphues tells us, 'whicl
had bene to feede you fat wyth follye' (i. 189). It would seem tha
Ascham's schoolhouse and the school of prodigality have finall
merged, despite all the efforts of the pedagogues. Certainly Gosson
who wrote his *Schoole of Abuse* the year after the publication of th
*Anatomy*, believed that the one had taken over rather than demolishe
the other.

   Euphues' next solution to the problem of finding the ideal dis
course is as impractical as all the rest. The best of textbooks for th
study of language, he contends, is the Bible; it teaches the 'true an
perfect phrase', the rhetorical skills that cannot be corrupted. Accord
ingly Euphues abandons the less perfect phrases of euphuism and pro
duces in *Euphues and Atheos* a stream of scriptural quotations, whicl
(rather to the reader's surprise) succeeds in converting an atheist
The atheist, who is aptly named Atheos, puts an end to his religiou
agnosticism and to Euphues' fanatical tirade by hastily changing hi
name to Theophilus. But the words of the Bible are hardly the rhet
orical tools best suited to the needs of an Elizabethan state; and
Euphues seems to acknowledge as much when he returns to secula
stylistic ornament in the letters that follow the *Atheos*. Each of thes
letters takes European society one step further away from the idea
state where Ephoebus could have taken up residence. In the first we
learn that Philautus has returned to his old ways in Naples, untouche
by his friend's advice. In the next Euphues encourages an old man to
seek consolation for his daughter's death by freeing himself from th
complications of existence. In the third he congratulates Botonio fo
having been exiled from Naples; and the letters to and from Livi
paint a picture of a Neapolitan court where 'ther is no heed taken o

a commaundement' and where 'there is small hope to be looked for of amendement' (i. 321). It would seem that Euphues' destruction of Ferardo's household is symptomatic of a general malaise which permeates European culture; an unease that will only find a measure of resolution when it dissociates itself from the unruly fictions that people *The Anatomy of Wit*.

# 6

# The Resolution of *Euphues*

## 1. CONSTRUCTING ENGLAND

*Euphues: The Anatomy of Wit* is an uneasy volume, ready at any moment to fly apart at the seams. The book's volatile character is signalled by the picture Euphues draws in his final letters of a desperate Emperor trying to hold together a disintegrating court, of an Empress whose works of legislation are constantly getting mangled by her courtiers, of a Neapolitan society from which it is better to be exiled. The culture inhabited by Lyly's English readers is not exempt from the process of corruption, as the analysis of England's universities which Lyly added to later editions is at pains to confirm: Athens may not be Oxford, but Oxford shares its vices, and these are the vices of Naples.[1] If the *Anatomy of Wit* is Lyly's satire on the private lives of the ruling classes, implying that all the abuses which Ascham ascribed to Italian fiction are no more than accurate representations of the depravities that infest the upper echelons of European society, *Euphues and his England* (1580) contains his sometimes ironic version of the ideal public weal, an English Utopia, protected from foreign infiltration by a wealth of 'safe' native fictions, and described in a text which is capable of absorbing the sophistication of Italian forms of narrative without being destabilized by their ideological contents. If the *Anatomy* is destructive, then *Euphues and his England* is ebulliently constructive, and its combination of metamorphic fluidity and rigorous orderliness is again evident both in the smallest details of the book's composition and in the handsome architectural design of the work as a whole.

Instrumental in forming both the style and the stability of *Euphues and his England* is what might be called the 'harmonious' euphuism

[1] The letter is reproduced in *Works*, i. 324–6.

the parison in which one element complements and supports the other, in contrast to the destructive euphuism that topples every structure in *The Anatomy of Wit*. The differences between the two styles can be summarized by comparing two sentences which Lyly places close to the beginning of each volume. At the opening of the second, he announces his intention of interspersing the moral commentaries of Euphues with the sexual misadventures of Philautus, in words that recall Painter's apologies for the variegated blooms in his literary garden: 'And although some shall thinke it impertinent to the historie, they shall not finde it repugnant, no more then in one nosegay to set two flowers, or in one counterfaite two coulours, which bringeth more delight, then disliking' (ii. 14). The sentence bears a superficial resemblance to one that occurs near the beginning of the *Anatomy*: 'And true it is that some men write and most men beleeve, that in all perfecte shapes, a blemmish bringeth rather a liking every way to the eyes, then a loathing any waye to the mind' (i. 184). But the differences between the passages are essential. The sentence from the *Anatomy* begins by exposing the lack of consensus in the statement 'true it is' with which it opens ('some men write and most men beleeve'—the phrase encompasses the possibility of dissent); it goes on to note that many readers have a tendency to privilege the senses over the intellect, the eyes over the mind. The sentence from the second volume, by contrast, never specifies which aspects of the ensuing text its various readers will find most pleasurable. The intellectual reader will discover as much sweetness in Lyly's fiction as the sensualist, and the mixture of flowers in this textual nosegay hides none of the threatening implications of the perfect shape that sports a blemish—Lyly never suggests that the mixture he presents could ever generate 'loathing'. Philautus' love-affairs and Euphues' didacticism possess precisely the same value; neither is privileged at the other's expense.

    The same implied consensus is evoked in the epistle to the ladies: 'One hand washeth an other, but they both wash the face, one foote goeth by an other, but they both carrye the body, *Euphues* and *Philautus* praise one an other, but they both extoll woemen' (ii. 9). A sense of reconciliation dominates the narrative. Opposites are always being harmoniously combined, by a newly benevolent Nature as well as by human co-operation. As Euphues tells Philautus, 'Daunger and delight growe both uppon one stalke ... white and blacke are commonly in one border' (ii. 14), and later we learn that 'out of one and the self-same roote, commeth as well the wilde Olyve, as the sweete, and . . . the Palme *Persian* Fig tree, beareth as well Apples, as Figs' (ii. 22). Any disagreements in the stories arise from efforts to drive things apart by violence or by cunning, as in the story of Fidus and Iffida, where Fidus complains that Iffida will not allow him 'to joyne three flowers in one Nosegay, but to chuse one, or els to leave all' (ii. 72). A woman named Frauncis summarizes the mutual solidarity by which Lyly's England flourishes, when she gives the unruly force of love a quasi-geometrical structure:

There must in every triangle be three lines, the first beginneth, the second augmenteth, the third concludeth it a figure. So in love three vertues, affection which draweth the heart, secrecie which increaseth the hope, constancie which finish the worke: without any of these lynes there can be no triangle, without any of these vertues, no love. (ii. 177)

She tells Philautus, who is disgruntled after failing to initiate a destructive love-affair like the one between Euphues and Lucilla, that in love 'to be secreate and not constant, or constant and not secret, were to builde a house of morter without stones, or a wall of stones without morter' (ii. 176–7). *Euphues and his England* is the solid literary building which sets itself up in opposition to the *Anatomy*'s disintegrating works of urban architecture. Only at one crucial moment do the destructive euphuisms and the wild fallacies they encourage threaten to disturb its harmony, and then they have little disruptive force.

In its preliminary epistles the book stresses its playful but responsible participation in the society to which it addresses itself. Instead of being a passive recipient of the text, the reader is as much involved in writing the book as the author himself. In the dedicatory epistle Lyly explains that his first work had been a self-portrait, and that he had hesitated to produce a second volume for fear of falling into the trap of narcissism. If he had produced a more sympathetic version of Euphues in the sequel he might have been charged with flattering himself, 'as Narcissus did, who only was in love with his own face' (ii. 3). But in fact the book claims to have avoided narcissism from its inception. It was written at the request of an admiring public which had 'praised mine olde worke, and urged me to make a new' (ii. 3), and it addresses itself with jovial inclusiveness to every category of reader (the picture of Euphues, the narrator announces, 'I yeeld a common all to view', ii. 4), again in contrast to the *Anatomy*, which addresses itself to an imaginary intellectual élite made up of those few 'gentlemen readers' who are capable of appreciating its subtlety

he three epistles to *Euphues and his England* establish, not the shady
machinations behind its printing, as Gascoigne's and Pettie's epistles
did, but its partnership with three distinct sections of English society:
the aristocracy, the gentry, and the women of both classes; and Lyly
places himself in the class of tradesmen, which caters for the needs
of all three groups. The first epistle reverses the traditional claim for
fiction, that it will educate its readers, and insists instead that Lyly's
two books are ungainly children, wholly dependent both for protection and for education on their benevolent readerly foster-parents.
The *Anatomy* he 'sent to a noble man to nurse, who with great love
brought him up' (ii. 4), and the Earl of Oxford must perform the
same office, integrating *Euphues and his England* into the English
society which it describes, 'that in his infancie he may be kepte by
your good care from fals, and in his youth by your great countenaunce
shielded from blowes' (ii. 4). The epistle to 'the Ladies and Gentlewomen of England' begins with a story about the woman artist Arachne, who is engaged in weaving a tapestry as colourfully diverse as
the text Lyly is engaged in producing; and ends by asking its women
readers to assist him in tailoring his text to their tastes by altering it as
they alter their gowns. The third epistle requests the gentlemen readers to complete the process of writing that Lyly has begun—'Faultes
scaped in the Printing, correcte with your pennes' (ii. 12)—and so
reminds them of the general invitation to collaborate in the book's
production which is displayed as a motto on the title-page: 'Com-
mend it, or amend it' (ii. 1).

Women had been peripheral as readers of the *Anatomy*. Men only
were addressed in the preliminary epistle; a brief message to the chaste
matrons and virtuous maidens of Italy was added, seemingly as an
afterthought, to temper the misogyny of the 'cooling Carde for Philautus'; and Euphues' encomium on women described them as a
superfluous element in creation, disposed by the circumstances of
their formation to excess, since God made them after Adam had
already attained to his full perfection. Accordingly women furnished
Euphues with material both for his most extravagant hyperboles and
for his most virulent invectives. The 'cooling Carde' recommends
that men dissociate themselves from women's company, and Euphues
ends the book as a hermit. By contrast, in *Euphues and his England*
women take a central role both as readers and as participants in the
action. At the centre of the text are two ideal women on whom its stability depends: the one casting an oblique light on the other, like the

multiple portraits of Elizabeth I that interpenetrate *The Faerie Queene*.
The description of the idealized Englishwoman Camilla skilfully
inverts the portrait of Lucilla in the *Anatomy of Wit*. In place of th
destructive, Circean metamorphoses effected by her predecessor—
who transformed her lovers and herself to beasts—Camilla's 'rare qua
lyties, caused so straunge events, that the wise wer allured to vanitie
and the wantons to vertue, much lyke the river in *Arabia*, which turn
eth golde to drosse, and durt to silver' (ii. 85). The metamorphoses sh
effects are ambiguous enough, but not damaging; in a work with
nosegay as its emblem the product of complexity is only delight
Where the uniqueness of Lucilla's beauty demolished other women'
pretensions to attractiveness, Camilla, like most of the characters i
the book apart from Euphues himself, is part of a wider community
'such a one she was, as almost they all are that serve so noble a Prince
(ii. 85). Her qualities are an extension of the woman she serves, Eliza
beth I, who rules the state as a living confirmation of the politica
effectiveness which Pettie's Alexius ascribed to women. Under th
aegis of Elizabeth, men and women in the narrative attain to the con
dition of easy amity which they achieved in Edmund Tilney's narra
tive *The Flower of Friendshippe*, where guests agreed and disagreed o
the subject of marriage under the courteous, moderating eye o
Lady Julia. Indeed, *Euphues and his England* resembles among othe
things a complex set of variations on Tilney's popular little fiction
where Erasmus, Vives, and others participated in the kind of 'pleasaunt and profitable' conversational exchanges which 'were used i
the courts of Italie, and . . . are practised at this day in the Englis
court' (*Flower of Friendshippe*, 102). After a long delay, Castiglione'
Urbino (to which Tilney pays tribute) has found a worthy nativ
equivalent, united by its own chain of love and presided over by
mutually complementary succession of duchesses.

The qualities which Lyly ascribes to women are also the element
from which he fashions his narrative. Wit, for example, shifts from
its long-term habitation among Ascham's unruly youths and become
a predominantly female characteristic. We learn of Camilla that 'he
wit wold commonly taunt without despite, but not without disport
(ii. 84), so that she assumes the status of an updated Honest Recreation—a figure who was notably absent from the earlier volume
Iffida considers wit to constitute the most powerful weapon i
women's closely guarded armoury: 'It is wit that allureth, whe
every word shal have his weight, when nothing shal proceed, but i

shal either savour of a sharpe conceipt, or a secret conclusion' (ii. 60). The 'secret conclusions' of women's wit still lead men to confusion, but the confusions for the most part are benign ones, since what is concealed in *Euphues and his England*—the secrets kept by Camilla, Iffida, Frauncis, and the women of the English court—are the secrets that sustain the English idyll. Euphues tells Philautus that the inhabitants of England are 'politic', but goes on to explain that theirs is the cunning of integrity, aimed at protecting the body of the public weal against the disease of foreign infiltration. And the women of England practise the same sophisticated form of self-defence in the context of their private lives.

The first volume took the painful process of anatomizing as its presiding metaphor, in which the helpless bodies of passive subjects are violated without their consent, their internal organs laid open to the public gaze in a savage investigative operation which culminates in the rifling of women's closets in the 'cooling Carde for Philautus'. *Euphues and his England*, by contrast, is principally concerned with the preservation of privacy, and as a result transfers its attention from the body to the clothes that conceal the body from view. Lyly announces this sudden change of focus in the first epistle, where he confesses that 'whereas I had thought to shew the cunning of a Chirurgeon by mine Anatomy with a knife, I must play the Tayler on the shoppe boorde with a paire of sheeres' (ii. 7). The transition from the surgery to the tailor's shop proves a brilliantly successful venture, since the fashions which betrayed the secrets of their wearers in the first book (like Helen's head-dress in the dedication) spontaneously transform themselves into an expression of tactful imaginative exuberance in the second. *Euphues and his England* resembles, in fact, a shopping expedition in a glitzy market, where phrases as well as garments are displayed for the delectation of prospective customers, and where men as well as women are subjected to the shopper's delighted scrutiny. Iffida tells her lover Fidus that he is fashioning his courtship of her as if it were a modish dress: 'A Phrase now there is which belongeth to your Shoppe boorde, that is, to make love, and when I shall heare of what fashion it is made, if I like the pattern, you shall cut me a partlet' (ii. 68). And in the epistle to the ladies the text itself becomes a fashion accessory, a harmlessly flamboyant item of headwear to compete with Helen's treacherous veil: 'There is nothing lyghter then a feather, yet is it sette a loft in a woemans hatte, nothing lighter then haire, yet is it most frisled in a Ladies head, so that I am in good hope, though their be nothing of lesse accounte then *Euphue*: yet he shall be marked with Ladies eyes, and lyked somtimes in thei eares' (ii. 10). Women's fashions, like their wits, conceal as much a they reveal. The insides of their rings hide posies and critical judge ments which are inaccessible to men (ii. 10), their gowns are altere to hide the mistakes of their tailors, and the women of England i 'Euphues Glasse for Europe' use their 'ritch apparell' to baffle th intrusive gazes of lecherous courtiers (ii. 199). In this way wome: make the discreetest of contributions to the organization of Lyly's uto pian state, operating like undercover agents to counter the prodig: tendencies to which all men in the book are subject. And the boo: performs a similar function: not advertizing its utility, as convention: Elizabethan texts felt the need to do (indeed, it parades its own luxur ious uselessness in the famous remark that '*Euphues* had rather lye shu in a Ladyes casket, then open in a Schollers studie', ii. 9), but propos ing instead that the Silenic privacy of a lady's casket plays an essenti: role in conserving the nation's identity, a role as essential as the lan guage of power inscribed in Elizabeth's wardrobe. Meanwhile, Lyl shares the magpie creativity of the English gentlemen, whose on extravagance consists in the pleasure they take in imitating an assort ment of continental designers, 'nowe using the French fashion, now the Spanish, then the Morisco gowne, then one thing, then anothei (ii. 194). Lyly too is happy to cobble together his text from bits an pieces, including 'the Taylors shreds' of other men's works (ii. 5) and, by constructing a coherent 'Livery' in this way, he demonstrate: still more skilfully than he did in the *Anatomy*, his astonishing master of the art of innovative imitation.

*The Anatomy of Wit* advertised its own ephemeral nature by com paring itself to a nine-days' wonder. By comparing itself to a fashio: accessory, *Euphues and his England* proclaims both its flashy transienc and its participation in the 'constant . . . inconstancie' which is the dis tinguishing feature of the Englishman's attire (ii. 194). At one poir Euphues tells Philautus the story of an Italian who bought a hat onl to find that it had gone out of fashion the following day, whereupo: he 'hung it up in his studie' for a time, until 'viewing al sorts, al shape: [he] perceived at the last, his olde Hat againe come into the new fash ion' (ii. 96). The story recalls an observation Lyly made at the begin ning of *The Anatomy of Wit*, that 'a fashion is but a dayes wearing, an a booke but an howres reading' (i. 182): a sentence which involves th earlier volume in the disorderly version of time favoured by the unre generate Euphues, a version in which events follow one another with anarchic randomness, ungoverned by any providential plan, and must be responded to with a succession of brilliant improvisations on the part of the witty subject if he or she is to keep them under partial control. In *Euphues and his England* time loses none of its vigorous unpredictability; it is never allowed to become the drearily repetitive cycle of events to which it was reduced in *The Dial of Princes*, the *Tragicall Discourses*, or Gosson's *Ephemerides of Phialo*, where the most fleeting of incidents was relentlessly incorporated into the ponderous machinery of Providence. Instead its dizzying metamorphoses are rendered endlessly productive. Nothing is wasted: '*Adams* olde Apron, must make *Eve* a new Kirtle' (ii. 96), the scraps rejected by the tailor make up a new suit, broken friendships are put back together again, and the evanescent rhetoric of courtship ends in marriage—although never quite the kind of marriage the rhetorician expects. Throughout Lyly's plays, the supernatural powers that rule the lives of mortals share the condition of being 'constant in inconstancie'—a more sprightly variant of the dominant characteristic of Spenser's Nature, whose seemingly random alterations conceal the fact that she reigns 'eterne in mutabilitie'.[2] And in Lyly's utopian England, the inconstancy of the Englishman's constant changes of fashion conceals a controlled fertility of invention which finds its most satisfactory expression in the legitimate sexual practices of marriage. Just as the Italian finds himself unexpectedly restored to his headwear by the 'compass' of fashion, so Philautus at the end of the book discovers that two of his English friends have been secretly working their way towards marriage without his knowledge, in obedience to another kind of clock, the clock of the seasons: 'when as the corne whiche was greene in the blade, began to wax ripe in the eare, when the seede which I scarce thought to have taken roote, began to spring, when the love of *Surius* whiche hardly I would have gessed to have a blossome, shewed a budde' (ii. 218). One of the newly-weds tells him that their marriage has only seemed sudden to Philautus because of his habit of 'thinking the diall to stand stil, bicause you cannot perceive it to move' (ii. 219); the sentence seems

---

[2] In Lyly's *Gallathea* Fortune is described as 'constant in nothing but inconstancie' (I. i. 19-20, ii. 432), while his Endimion launches into a lengthy disquisition on the paradoxical constancy of the inconstant object of his devotion: 'O fayre *Cynthia*, why doe others terme thee unconstant, whom I have ever founde unmovable? Injurious tyme, corrupt manners, unkind men, who finding a constancy not to be matched in my sweete Mistris, have christned her with the name of wavering, waxing, and waning' (*Endimion*, I. i. 30-1, iii. 32). See also *The Faerie Queene*, III. vi. 47 and VII. vii. 58.

to mock the futile efforts of texts like *The Dial of Princes* to fix the con
duct of their youthful readers in a state of iconic moral immobility
Where earlier witty fictions of the decade concentrated on the anar
chic formlessness of history, the second *Euphues* book succeeds i
retaining a sense of time's ungovernable skittishness—which render
the art of improvisation as necessary as it was in the works of Gas
coigne—while simultaneously restoring the notion that time, lik
clothing, follows a coherent pattern, the same pattern that ensure
that the seasons follow one another in their duly appointed order
although never quite in the way you think they ought.

*Euphues and his England* might in fact be said to have achieved th
condition of legitimate fertility to which all Elizabethan fiction pur
portedly aspired. At one point Euphues and Philautus engage in
friendly dialogue on the subject of love and sex, which seems wittil
to encapsulate Lyly's new doctrine of the function of fiction.[3] Like
disciple of Guevara's narrowly prescriptive Marcus Aurelius, Euphue
insists that sex is an unnecessary complication in any relationshi
between the sexes, and so continues to develop the often absurdly the
oretical conception of human behaviour he espouses throughout th
volume: disengaging words from action, theory from practice, in
way that suggests he has learned very little from his adventures i
the previous book. Meanwhile Philautus asserts that love withou
sex would make it 'as pleasaunt to behold fruit, as to eate them, o
to see fayre bread, as to tast it' (ii. 157). Euphues replies with a parod
of the idealistic advice dispensed by moralists, in a phrase that echoe
the eleventh history of *A Petite Pallace of Pettie his Pleasure*: 'I have rea
of many, and some I know, betweene whom there was as ferven
affection as might be, that never desired any thing, but sweete talke
(ii. 159). The link with Pettie is confirmed by the example Euphue
uses to support his contention: '*Pigmalion* loved his Ivory Image
being enamoured onely with the sight' (ii. 159). In Pettie's collectio
Pygmalion came to represent the endless process of reshaping experi
ence by rhetoric to make it conform to the private fantasies of narcis
sistic wits, and one might suspect that Euphues is still engaged i
rewriting literature to force it into conformity with his own convic
tions. But Philautus reminds him of the end of Ovid's story, whe
Pygmalion's voyeuristic fantasies are given fleshly form, and he con

---

[3] On the open-ended nature of this debate, see Catherine Bates, *The Rhetoric of Courtsh*
(Cambridge: Cambridge University Press, 1992), 108–11.

cludes that, like Pettie's sculptor, 'I love the company of women well, yet to have them in lawfull Matrimony, I lyke much better' (ii. 158). Lyly's narrator endorses this view, but characteristically diminishes its pretensions to lawfulness by omitting all reference to marriage: 'I must needes conclude with *Philautus* . . . that the ende of love is the full fruition of the partie beloved, at all times and in all places' (ii. 160). The statement gleefully demolishes the admiring approbations of impracticable chastity with which collections like Fenton's are filled. Philautus' conclusion is the one that the narrative tends to confirm: the characters in *Euphues and his England* take marriage to be the social institution that most satisfactorily encompasses the reconciliation of diverse elements which the 'constructive' euphuisms enact on the level of syntax. Even the association of Euphues and Philautus is spoken of as a marriage. When their argument leads to a suspension of their friendship, Euphues agrees to resume relations after 'weighing with himselfe, that often in mariages, ther have fallen out braules, wher the chiefest love should be' (ii. 152). Euphues' epistle on matrimony which closes the book takes up this theme of endless disagreements which are endlessly resolved, both parodying and hinting at the possibility of the traditional happy ending.

For Lyly's England to work, the wild Nature of the *Anatomy* must be kept under tight restraint if she is not to resume her disruptive activities. Accordingly, the book is full of gardens: from the gardens in which his women readers 'gather flowers one by one' (ii. 8), to the garden in the epistle to the gentlemen readers, where women themselves are reduced to the status of vegetation, and where each female plant is adopted by some male passer-by, 'insomuch as there is no Weede almoste, but it is worne' (ii. 12); from Fidus' garden, a miniature model of the English public weal, to the 'garden of the worlde' which is London (ii. 82); from the garden where Fidus courts Iffida to the arbour where Philautus courts Camilla, and the garden of Lady Flavia, where three pairs of lovers engage in amicable disputations. These horticultural strongholds fragrantly avert the threat of moral disintegration which transforms all Gascoigne's gardens into wildernesses. They are other Edens, like the one in *The Flower of Friendshippe*, which resembles a 'terrestrial Paradise' inhabited by an Adam and Eve who give their blessing to the institution of marriage which is the subject of Tilney's book. Or, rather, they are gardens that fruitfully accommodate the consequences of the fall. The central garden in the *Anatomy* is the one described by Euphues in his hyperbolic encomium of women, where the first earthly marriage is marred by serpent. In *Euphues and his England* too the Garden of Eden is a mode for all gardens, a place where 'there was no pollycie, but playn dealyng' and where 'Affection was measured by faith, not by fancie (ii. 121). But the garden of England is a lovelier 'Paradise' still (ii 189), since it can safely integrate both policy and fancy into its care fully monitored flower-beds.

## 2. STORIES WITHIN STORIES

Lyly took as much trouble over the structure of *Euphues and his Eng land* as he did over the best of his plays. A remark by Frauncis (one o many comments on the practice of making fictions which are 'sowec ... lyke Strawberies' throughout the text) hints at the importance Lyl attached to the organization of a narrative: 'if I shoulde be so curiou to demaunde whether in a tale tolde to your Ladyes, disposition o invention be most convenient, I cannot thinke but you would judge them both expedient' (ii. 176).[4] And Lyly's own tale is as shapel as it is inventive. G. K. Hunter suggested that the first half of the *Anat omy* took as its model the five-act structure of a Terentian comedy, a did Sidney's *Old Arcadia*.[5] *Euphues and his England* can be seen as more ambitious experiment with the same structure, and in man ways a more successful one. The narrative can be divided into five dis tinct sections which correspond to the five Terentian acts. The first ac covers the voyage of Euphues and Philautus from Italy to England; th second describes their visit to the house of an old Englishman callec Fidus; the third gives an account of Philautus' abortive romanc with the exemplary Englishwoman, Camilla; the fourth comprises series of debates between men and women on the subject of love a the house of Lady Flavia. The last, which is announced by one o the few uses of theatrical vocabulary in Lyly's prose fiction ('return we to *Euphues*, who must play the last parte'), consists of Euphues description of England, with the queen at its centre, who preside over the dual marriages with which the story ends. Each section o act includes further narratives; and together the five acts and the storie they contain comprise an exhaustive demonstration of the differen

---

[4] The phrase 'sowed them heere or there, lyke Strawberies' occurs in Lyly's epistle to th ladies (ii. 8), and refers to the discourses of love which are scattered throughout the book [5] See Hunter, *John Lyly*, 57.

forms of prose narrative available to the Elizabethan storyteller which is unmatched in its controlled diversity by any of Lyly's contemporaries except Sidney.

Within this five-act structure, characters are constantly telling each other stories. When, on the ship bound for England, Euphues tells the tale of Callimachus, his story contains a further story told by the hermit Cassander to his profligate young nephew. In the second 'act', Fidus' autobiographical reminiscences contain two further stories; in the third, the mathematician Psellus to whom Philautus goes for a love-potion tells him a series of comic fables; and the three disputes about love which constitute the fourth 'act' are referred to as 'tales', each of which spills over into its neighbour—as at the point where Surius intervenes in the dispute between Flavia and Martius: 'The good Lady could not refraine from laughter, when she saw Surius so angry, who in the midst of his own tale, was troubled with hirs' (ii. 173). After the debate, Camilla finds herself entrammelled in a tale in which she had not meant to feature, and announces her entry into unfamiliar fictional territory with a bewildered soliloquy: 'She began in straunge tearmes to utter this straunge *tale*' (ii. 183, my emphasis). The fifth 'act' is a medley of interpenetrating fictions, which incorporates a literal palace of pleasure, the source of all 'safe' fictions, the court of Elizabeth, with which Painter took such pains to associate his earlier palace. *Euphues and his England* is in fact the most richly satisfying of Elizabethan story-collections, in which each story throws light on its neighbours and is itself illuminated by its context; and in which stories break out of their confines, spill into one another, and finally merge to develop a single overarching theme, the narrative of England presided over by the woman whom Puttenham called the 'most excellent Poet' of her time, Elizabeth I.[6]

Interwoven with the five major parts of the narrative and the stories they embrace are fleeting glimpses of additional narrative forms. After telling the tale of Callimachus on the ship to England, Euphues decides to regale his young companion with a lecture on contemporary Britain and its customs. In doing so he accidentally exposes his hopeless

---

[6] 'But you (Madame) my most Honored and Gracious: if I should seeme to offer you this my devise for a discipline and not a delight, I might well be reputed, of all others the most arrogant and injurious: your selfe being alreadie, of any that I know in our time, the most excellent Poet. Forsooth by your Princely purse favours and countenance, making in maner what ye list, the poore man rich, the lewd well learned, the coward couragious, and vile both noble and valiant.' *The Arte of English Poesie*, 2.

bookishness by basing his account on the pre-Christian observations of Julius Caesar—one of the writers Ascham recommended for his pupils' imitation. On Caesar's authority he asserts with confidence that 'All the *Brittaines* doe die them-selves with woad, which setteth a blewish coulour upon them' and that they 'weare their hayre long and shave al partes of their bodyes, saving the head and the upper lippe' (ii. 32), and his ignorance makes it conveniently necessary for the English people to complete his history lesson in their own words afterwards. A little later, Lyly parodies the fantastic stories traditionally told by travellers: 'what tempests they endured, what monstrous fishes were seene, how often they were in daunger of drowning, in feare of boording, how wearie, how sick, how angrie, it were tedious to write, for that whosoever hath either read of travailing, or himselfe used it, can sufficiently gesse what is to be sayd' (ii. 34). With comic abruptness the sentence dismisses an entire narrative genre in a few ironic phrases.[7] Already *Euphues and his England* is setting itself up as a new and different kind of narrative: one that concerns itself less with parroting the Classics or with listing improbable wonders than with matters of immediate topical interest to Elizabethan youngsters— who have perhaps been rendered 'some-what sleepy', like Philautus, while Euphues is showing off his knowledge of outmoded texts from the humanist curriculum (ii. 33).

In the second act, by contrast, a traditional genre which had been dismissed in the course of the *Anatomy* finds itself triumphantly reinstated. Fidus, the old Englishman who inhabits a diminutive commonwealth of a garden, grows testy when the strangers Euphues and Philautus seek, as he thinks, to 'undermine' his domestic security by enquiring too closely into English affairs of state (ii. 38). When with some difficulty Euphues has persuaded him that they are not spies by telling him a fable, he answers with another—'a *Caunterbury* tale, or a Fable in *Aesope*' (ii. 43)—which aims to define the prescribed limits both of curiosity and of fiction. The fable evokes a natural world which has its own inviolable hegemonic structure, like the world of the fables of Bidpai. The fox tells the wolf that the lion is not at

---

[7] In this it resembles a passage from More's *Utopia*, in which he dismisses travel narratives of the kind retailed by Sir John Mandeville, in favour of Hythloday's description of a well-governed state: 'But as for monsters, because they be no news, of them we were nothing inquisitive. For nothing is more easy to be found than be barking Scyllas, ravening Celænos, and Læstrygons, devourers of people, and suchlike great and incredible monsters. But to find citizens ruled by good and wholesome laws, that is an exceeding rare and hard thing' (18).

home; foolishly the wolf believes him and enters the lion's den, whereupon the lion seizes him and tells him that 'neither the wilines of the Fox, nor the wildnes of the Wolf, ought either to see, or to aske, whether the Lyon either sleepe or wake, bee at home or abroad, dead or alyve. For this is sufficient for you to know, that there is a Lyon, not where he is, or what he doth' (ii. 43). The wolf which had signalled Lucilla's 'wildnes'—she invoked it to justify her fickleness, and in the process showed her 'beastly disposition'—finds itself tamed at last by being readmitted into the familiar hierarchy of the Aesopian animal kingdom. Fidus' fable is a neat epitome of *Euphues and his England*, a Silenic container with a closely guarded secret at its core to which no enemy agent can have access: the mystery that sustains the power of Elizabeth. He produces a second explication of this mystery immediately after the first, when he tells Euphues the fable of the commonwealth of the bees, using his own hives as an illustration. The bees offer living evidence of the practicability of Plato's ideal state, which had been only a distant and unattainable fantasy in *Euphues and his Ephoebus*. Inspired by the example of their monarch they work together in harmonious co-operation:

in-somuch as thou wouldest thinke, that they were a kinde of people, a common wealth for *Plato*, where they all labour, all gather honny, flye all together in a swarme, eate in a swarm, and sleepe in a swarm, so neate and finely, that they abhorre nothing so much as uncleannes, drinking pure and cleere water, delighting in sweete and sound Musick, which if they heare but once out of tune, they flye out of sight: and therefore are they called the *Muses* byrds, bicause they folow not the sound so much as the consent. (ii. 44)

In the course of his description Fidus restores the poisonous insects of the *Anatomy* to their traditional status as the most productive of Nature's citizens, and reinstates Nature herself in her ancient role as the supreme artificer, whose meticulous craftsmanship provides the perfect pattern for the harmonious works of art which permeate Lyly's England.[8]

But Lyly's exploration of contemporary narrative forms does not stop with ancient history, travel literature, and the fable. When Philautus falls in love with Camilla, his fruitless desire for a woman beyond his reach precipitates him into a literary form which, thankfully, has been absent from the text till now: the narrative of abortive love, to which Gascoigne, Pettie, and Lyly himself had devoted so

[8] See Elyot, *The Governor*, 7-8.

many of their pages. The transition to a new kind of fiction is marked by a return to the kind of duplicitous discourse familiar from *The Anatomy of Wit*, littered with arcane analogies and ridiculous *non sequiturs*, like the soliloquy where Philautus considers the case for suicide, using one of the rare geological specimens that Euphues once exploited in such abundance: 'There is a stone in the floud of *Thracia*, that whosoever findeth it, is never after grieved, I would I had that stone in my mouth, or that my body were in that River' (ii. 90). The transition is also marked by a witty pastiche of Gosson's recent fiction, *The Ephemerides of Phialo*. As soon as he has fallen in love with Camilla, Philautus complains that Euphues belongs to a different, duller, literary genre than the one in which he wishes to become involved: Euphues is 'more likely to correct my follyes with counsaile, then to comfort me with any pretie conceit' (ii. 90). Having convinced himself that Euphues is his enemy, when he next meets him Philautus launches into a volley of abuse thinly disguised as admonition, as Philotimo did at the beginning of Gosson's narrative. Like Philotimo he sets himself up as a would-be moralist, and accuses Euphues of having fallen in love himself, undergoing in the process a change of literary colours: 'I see thou art come from thy booke to beastlines, from coting of the scriptures, to courting with Ladies, from *Paule* to *Ovid*, from the Prophets to Poets' (ii. 93). Euphues replies, of course, with another of his devastating rebuttals. He tells Philautus that he is being maliciously obtuse, that he is attempting to foist his own emotional turmoil on his friend, and that he resembles the legendary brigands Sciron and Procrustes who measured each passer-by on a bed of brass: 'if he wer to long for the bed, they cut off his legs for catching cold, it was no place for a longis, if to short they racked him at length, it was no pallet for a dwarfe' (ii. 97)—a painfully different attitude from the one Lyly ascribes to his readers in the epistles. And he accuses Philautus of having been corrupted by his taste for Italian fictions. He has spent more time with '*Reynaldo* thy countryman' than with his self-appointed pedagogue (ii. 97). The alert Elizabethan reader might have detected in the reference to Reynaldo an allusion to George Whetstone's recent narrative 'Rinaldo and Giletta' in *The Rocke of Regard*, whose protagonist is Italian.[9] This companionship with literary pseudo-Italians has blinded Philautus to the merits of

---

[9] See *The Rocke of Regard*, 42–90. 'Rinaldo and Giletta' is an imitation of *The Adventures of Master F.J.*. But it is a far less risqué literary exercise than Gascoigne's, and the only monsters it contains are made of 'a sugred substance' (44).

an English text which Euphues finds more congenial: 'Hast thou not read since thy comming into *England* a pretie discourse of one *Phialo*, concerning the rebuking of a friende?' (ii. 99). Lyly scatters his book with allusions of this kind to contemporary narrative—he christens his lady Frauncis, for instance, after Gascoigne's unfortunate heroine—and he alerts the reader to the pleasurable activity of spotting them in the dedicatory epistle, where he points out that he may seem here or there to 'gleane after an others Cart, for a few eares of corne' (ii. 5). But the text that results is decidedly Lyly's own, and Euphues' efforts to reproduce the persuasive magic of Gosson's pompous protagonist end in humiliating failure. In the irrepressibly fertile landscape of the *Euphues* books, romances are not so easily nipped in the bud.

Responses to the book's different narratives are as various as the narratives themselves, and the most accomplished storytellers carefully monitor the reactions of their listeners. Euphues' story in the first 'act' stresses the fact that the brothers Cassander differ radically from Eubulus in *The Anatomy of Wit* in that they are capable of predicting their listeners' reaction to their wise but arid counsel. Aware that young Callimachus will probably pay no attention to anything they say, they deliver their advice in striking and memorable forms which are designed to encourage him to profit by their words in retrospect when experience bears them out: the first Cassander leaves his advice in a money-box, the second couches it in the form of an autobiography. Lyly provides a comic illustration of the necessity for these elaborate persuasive measures in the way Philautus reacts to the story of the Cassanders. The young man's tastes incline more to 'an Eelegie in *Ovid*' than to an 'olde treatise of an auncient Hermitte' (ii. 14), so that while Euphues is telling the story he is too preoccupied with his own seasickness to show much interest in the moral. Later too, when Fidus and Euphues are happily engaged in exchanging their Aesopian fables, Philautus is 'more willing to eate, then to heare their tales' (ii. 47). But Lyly's volume caters for every literary preference, and Fidus goes on to tell a love-story, during which it is the learned Athenian's turn to fall asleep. On this occasion Philautus proves a model audience, who 'desired few parentheses or digressions or glosses, but the text, where he him-self, was coting in the margant'. Throughout *Euphues and his England* stories are as much a means of separating their audiences as of drawing them together: the literary tastes of Philautus and Euphues have nothing in common, and the multiple readings generated by the tales of love in the fourth 'act' throw their listeners into a state of barely restrained hostility. Perhaps the most dramatic instance of the hostility produced by conflicting readings occurs in the second 'act' when Fidus is courting Iffida. In a playful mood, Iffida tells the story of a gentleman in Siena who had three daughters, the first beautiful but foolish, the second witty but wanton, the third ugly but faithful; after describing each daughter in detail she asks Fidus which he would have chosen as his wife. Faced with a choice between 'three inconveniences' (ii. 63), Fidus selects the witty wanton, while asking Iffida to recognize the contingent nature of his selection. But, from this moment on, communication between Fidus and Iffida is vitiated by his choice, since Iffida interprets his every word as a gloss on her own narrative. She tells him, 'You tearme me fayre, and ther-in you flatter, wise and there-in you meane wittie, curteous which in other playne words, if you durst have uttered it, you would have named wanton' (ii. 64), and later she asks, 'am I the wittie wanton which you harped upon yester-night, that would alwayes give you a stinge in the heade?' (ii. 65). The problem of writing witty fiction—of producing texts which are intellectually demanding and deal with the pleasant subject of love, and yet at the same time manage to be consensually 'safe', to generate only constructive readings—is encapsulated in Fidus' dilemma, and it only achieves its resolution in the last 'act' of the book, in the medley of intersecting public narratives that comprise the portrait of Elizabeth.

Throughout the volume the problem of writing witty fiction is metaphorically connected with the labyrinth, the elaborate architectural trap in which F.J. lost himself, and which Whetstone's Rinaldo refused to enter.[10] Lyly summarizes the problem in the most labyrinthine section of the book, the third 'act', in which Philautus initiates his courtship of Camilla. Lyly introduces the episode with a passage signalling Philautus' entry into the maze of unauthorized desire. Love-stories, Lyly tells us, have been steadily increasing in complexity since the first romance of all, the tale of Adam and Eve:

[10] Although Whetstone's epistle describes the story as a 'laberynth of love' (*Rocke of Regard*, p. iii), Rinaldo and Giletta never embark on the kind of elaborate rhetorical exchange in which F.J. and Elinor embroiled themselves. When Giletta tells Rinaldo that 'since your wit serves you to flourish on every worde figuratively spoken, I will deliver the rest of my minde in more plaine speaches', Rinaldo obediently begins to court her in the plain style (52).

when *Adam* woed there was no pollycie, but playne dealyng, no colours but blacke and white. Affection was measured by faith, not by fancie: he was not curious, nor *Eve* cruell: he was not enamoured of hir beautie, nor she allured with his personage: and yet then was she the fairest woman in the worlde, and he the properest man. Since that time every Lover hath put too a lynke, and made of a Ring, a Chaine, and an odde Corner, and framed of a playne Alley, a crooked knot, and of *Venus* Temple, *Dedalus* Laborinth . . . A playne tale of faith you laugh at, a picked discourse of fancie, you mervayle at, condempning the simplicitie of truth, and preferring the singularitie of deceipt. (ii. 121)

The reader who has delighted in Gascoigne and Pettie prefers the subtle fiction which encourages duplicity to the simplicity that preserves commonwealths. Lyly's own *Anatomy* was the epitome of what he sees as contemporary taste, a chain of 'deceipt' with the same destructive potential as the chain-reaction of abuses which Gosson ascribes to poets. At the centre of its perplexities lurked the 'Monster of *Italie*' Lucilla, and its labyrinths were without egress, like the labyrinth of learning described at the end of the *Ephoebus*. The potential Ariadne of the text, Livia, was peripheral and ineffectual; and Theseus the conqueror of the Cretan maze was only noted for his treachery to Ariadne (i. 222). *Euphues and his England* is another kind of labyrinth, which combines the bonding properties of a ring (the circle of amity which draws its characters together) with the binding qualities of a chain (the sequence of interwoven narratives of which it is composed); the temple of Venus (love is its subject) with Daedalus' ingenious prison (its characters are always meeting unexpected complications). Each of its 'acts' contains another miniature labyrinth, a fiction with further fictions hidden inside it. But for all their ingenuity these mazes are benign ones, concealing not monsters like Gascoigne's Suspicion but helpful Ariadnes, witty men and women who use their intellectual gifts to guide young men out of the wanderings of unreason. Each of the fictions of *Euphues and his England* includes what Bacon calls a *Filum Labyrinthi*, a thread which will enable the protagonist to emerge unscathed from its complexities, despite the fact that they are often far more intricate than those of *The Anatomy of Wit*.[11] And each narrative is an alluring Silenus with

---

[11] Bacon wrote the *Filum Labyrinthi* to guide his readers through his plans for the Great Instauration, and thus to afford them safe conduct in the labyrinth of learning Euphues entered in *The Anatomy of Wit*. See *The Works of Francis Bacon*, ed. James Spedding, Robert Leslie Ellis, and Douglas Denon Heath, 14 vols. (London: Spottiswoode, 1857–74), iii. 496–504.

something still better inside it. The money-box which Cassander leaves to his son in the first 'act' contains an unexpected treasure, just as, in the last narrative of all, the exquisite Silenus of the court encloses the beauty and virtue of Lyly's idealized queen. Without succumbing to the constricting self-censorship of a Gosson, Lyly succeeds in achieving the impossible: an endlessly unfolding, endlessly inventive yet wholly legitimate work of prose fiction. In this text the metaphor of the labyrinth, which had come to represent the anxieties of Elizabethan writers about the complexity of contemporary emotional and political life, transforms itself into a cornucopian container—its folds embracing the friendliest of monsters.

The book begins with a series of nostalgically old-fashioned narratives, updated to conform to the new, sophisticated demands of an Elizabethan readership which had been subjected to Gascoigne's and Pettie's duplicitous literary education. In the story told by Euphues on the ship, the traditional structure of the story of the Prodigal Son, where a wise old man gives advice to a young one who promptly fails to follow it, attains the labyrinthine subtlety which is usually reserved for the 'piked discourse of fancie'. The dying Cassander wishes to dispense a few wise words to his son Callimachus; but he understands even before he opens his mouth that 'unbrideled youth, the more it is...by grave advise counselled, or due correction controlled, the sooner it falleth to confusion' (ii. 15). He therefore cuts short the speech he had prepared, like Eubulus, to deliver at length, and dies with some abruptness. Callimachus wastes no time in investigating the chest Cassander has left him, and finds to his fury that it contains only the continuation of the speech his father left unfinished. Enraged, like all quick-witted prodigals he sets out on his travels, only to encounter a further extension of his father in the person of Cassander's hermit brother, confusingly also named Cassander. The second Cassander inhabits another kind of chest, an eremitical cave (complete with a further container still—a cat asleep with a mouse in its ear— one of the more eccentric examples of the reconciliation of differences with which Lyly stocks his text). From this second chest, the cave, the second Cassander delivers a second set of precepts; but he first determines to 'make a Cosinne of his yong Nevew' (ii. 21)—the pun emphasizes the familial tenderness underlying the deception—by concealing his own identity and by presenting his advice in the form of yet another kind of container, this time an adventure-story. The story is autobiographical, and reveals the fact that the hermit is himself reformed Callimachus, who in his youth ignored all advice as Callimachus did, set out on his travels, suffered, and was made wise by his sufferings. The story presupposes that Callimachus will fail to apply it for his profit, as the old-fashioned Elizabethan narrative was meant to be applied. The hermit ends his tale by acknowledging the fact that had caused such grief in Gascoigne's and Pettie's fictions, that 'he that is young thinketh the olde man fond, and the olde knoweth the young man to be a foole' (ii. 26). As the hermit expected, Callimachus is not interested; instead he presents a cogent argument for the active life led by the wanderer Ulysses, sets out on his own travels, and returns suitably chastened, to find that the hermit has his financial inheritance waiting for him, to be issued to the reformed young man now that he has gained enough maturity to invest it with prudence. The series of Chinese boxes from which the story is constructed exempts each of its characters from blame; experience gained by travel is as dangerous as Ascham thought it, but Lyly has made it inevitable that experience will be sought, and finally desirable that it should be, since without it words will remain in the condition to which Euphues once reduced them, permanently divorced from action. In this story the generation gap is as wide as ever, but communications between the generations are finally restored. Advice and experience, like the other dualities in Lyly's second volume, are no longer antagonistic but complementary. Concealed in this labyrinthine narrative is not one monster but two, the brothers Cassander, who possessed such different inward qualities in youth that if their outward appearances had corresponded to their minds, the hermit says, 'I know not what *Dedalus* would have made a *Laborynth* for such Monsters' (ii. 22). But with the passing time the monsters have undergone a benign metamorphosis, their natures growing together, until at last they can conspire together in the benevolent 'cosenning' of their relative. The brothers bear a close family resemblance to the twins in the book's dedication, the 'blind whelp' and the 'monster' to which Lyly compares the *Euphues* volumes. Like the brothers, the books need outside intervention in the form of readerly collaboration before they can become productive, and, like the brothers, they play benevolent tricks on the youngsters who enter their fictive enclosures.

Lyly informs us that Fidus' narratives are as old-fashioned as that of the hermit. Certainly they are as labyrinthine, and the deceptions they involve are as good-natured. The hive of the bees is framed 'so artificially, that *Dedalus* could not with greater arte or excellencie, better

dispose the orders, measures, proportions, distinctions, joynts and cir
cles' (ii. 45). Here the labyrinth itself has suffered a sea-change
becoming a beautiful and orderly construction, whose complexit
preserves the harmonious proportions admired by Pietro Bembo
And Fidus' narrative of his tragic love-affair with Iffida is anothe
labyrinth which proves to possess an unexpected beauty. When h
first falls in love with Iffida he mournfully admits that he has lost hi
way: '*Thesius* had no neede of *Ariadnes* threed to finde the way int
the Laborinth, but to come out' (ii. 52); but Iffida herself turns ou
to be a benevolent Ariadne who shows him the way out of the com
plexities in which he gets entangled. After many misunderstanding
Fidus learns that her ambiguous name is another Silenic containe
concealing not the infidelity it hints at but her inward fidelity to he
absent lover Thirsus—the name suggests a faithful Theseus—t
whom she is secretly betrothed. The narrative is as witty and involve
as the best of Lyly's fictions, yet his narrator interposes an apology fo
its plainness: 'I trust you will not condempne my present tyme, wh
am enforced to singe after their plaine-songe, that was then used, an
will followe heare-after the Crotchetts that are in these dayes cun
ninglye handled' (ii. 57). The simplicity for which Lyly apologizes i
no lack of sophistication, but the fidelity which Fidus and Iffid
show to their respective lovers, and he expresses it in the musica
terms used first by Elyot and then by Gosson to signify good order.

In fact, Fidus' household nostalgically evokes the public wea
invented by Elyot. Elyot compared his public weal to a garden lik
that of Fidus; like Elyot, Fidus uses the analogy of bees to expres
the ideal political system (*The Governor*, 7–8); his name is the mascu
line form of Elyot's *fides*, the good faith on which his perfect stat
depended (172–9); and when Euphues and Philautus enter his hous
'they perceived a kinde of courtly Majestie in the minde of thei
host' (ii. 47), reminiscent of the majesty described by Elyot
which consists in 'honourable and sober demeanour, deliberate an
grave pronunciation, words clean and facile, void of rudeness an
dishonesty', and, above all, 'excellent temperance' (*The Governo*
100). The first two 'acts' of *Euphues and his England* constitute Lyly'
idiosyncratic threnody for passing literary forms, simpler (in his esti
mation) in every sense than the form he has invented for himself
the complex narrative in which he laments their passing.

Philautus is the next to enter the labyrinth of the love-story. As th
narrator has promised, his story uses the 'Crotchetts that are in these

dayes cunninglye handled', and as a result Philautus' labyrinth looks at first potentially disastrous. He begins by suffering a Circean metamorphosis, describing himself as 'the verye monster of Nature' and his love as a 'monstrous . . . desease' (ii. 113), and he concludes of the pains love has put him to that 'it were more meete to enclose them in a Laborinth, then to sette them on a Hill' (ii. 111). Like the Italian spies Ascham saw embodied in Italian fiction, he adopts the Machiavellian political vocabulary which Euphues used to justify his courtship of Lucilla: 'In the ruling of Empires there is required as great policie as prowes: in governing an Estate, close crueltie doth more good then open clemencie, for the obteining of a kingdome, as well mischiefe as mercy, is to be practised' (ii. 108).[12] The alternative state he plans to set up in competition with England is a tyranny more oppressive than Damon's Syracuse. But, like every other lover in the second *Euphues* book, he is granted a thread to get out by.

The auspices for his eventual emergence from his labyrinth are good even when he quarrels with Euphues, since Euphues uses the paradigms of exemplary friendships at the very moment when they part company: '*Titus* must lust after *Sempronia*, *Gisippus* must leave hir: *Damon* must goe take order for his lands, *Pithias* must tarry behinde, as a Pledge for his life' (ii. 102–3); in each case the friendship ended up stronger for the separation. In despair of obtaining Camilla, Philautus turns to another of his countrymen, the mathematician Psellus, for help of a necromantic kind.[13] But Psellus proves as unexpectedly benign as the other figures of mystery in the book, and aids him not by supplying him with a love-potion but by exposing the young man's unreasonableness through another piece of wittily disguised advice. In a series of descriptions of exotic minerals, Psellus transforms the fantastic natural history that enabled the unregenerate Euphues to baffle his rhetorical opponents into a series of comic logical conundrums, miracle cures each of which cancels out its own supposed effects. The mathematician offers Philautus an abundance of imaginary love-inducing products, such as the herb Carisium, which permits one to occupy the dreams of one's lover, but which is found 'in a Lake neere *Bœotia*, of which water who so drinketh, shall bee caught in

[12] For Machiavelli's discussion of cruelty see *The Prince*, trans. George Bull (Harmondsworth: Penguin, 1981), 65–6.

[13] C. S. Lewis mentions Cornelius Agrippa's interest in the Greek mathematician Psellus in *English Literature in the Sixteenth Century*, 9. As the allusion in *Campaspe* suggests, Lyly had an interest in Agrippa's writings (see above, Ch. 5, n. 33).

Love, but never finde the Hearbe: And if hee drincke not, the Hearbe is of no force' (ii. 115). At this stage Lyly has lapsed into self-parody, reducing his famously exotic analogies to an array of hallucinogenic drugs which have no function except to bend the user's mind.

Disabused by Psellus of his trust in enchantments, Philautus instead embarks on what Lyly characterizes as a typical modern romance, recalling F.J.'s convoluted adventures. He sends Camilla letters concealed in pomegranates and in works of Italian fiction; but her responses quickly disabuse him of the notion that she is an Elinor, or even an '*Italian* Lady' (ii. 129). Philautus sensibly re-emerges from his labyrinth as F.J. did not, by means of another string of letters to his erstwhile friend and mentor, this time conciliatory, and, with the complacency of one who knows he is always right, Euphues points out that withdrawal from desire is the safest course: '*Theseus* woulde not goe into the Laborinth without a threede that might shew him the way out, neither any wise man enter into the crooked corners of love, unlesse he knew by what meanes he might get out' (ii. 156). But he goes on to say, 'I have not forgotten one Mistres *Frauncis*'; and Philautus obediently turns his attentions to the Ariadne whom F.J. once abandoned, thus providing himself, as F.J. did not, with the possibility of finding an exit.

In the fourth act, the art of debate returns to the task with which it was occupied in *The Courtier*, the quest for a general consensus. Each of the topics discussed proposes that a divorce be made between elements which must remain unified if the English Utopia is to survive. Surius, Camilla's legitimate suitor, begins by asking what a man must do to win the affections of the woman he loves, and Camilla responds by planting a logical maze for him, from which he soon finds he is unable to extricate himself, despite his athletic efforts to 'leape over the hedge, which she set for to keep him in' (ii. 166). The fragile mutual understanding they have begun to forge seems to be jeopardized instead of strengthened by the exchange. Flavia proposes the question 'whether it be convenient for women to haunt such places where Gentlemen are, or for men to have accesse to Gentlewomen' (ii. 170), and almost involves herself in a quarrel with the lovesick Surius. Philautus asks Frauncis 'whether in love be more required secrecie, or constancy' (ii. 176); Frauncis rightly replies that the two qualities are inseparable; and all three disputes end with the men 'astonied' at the women's wit (ii. 179). But, as in each of the previous acts, the circumstances of this series of debates ensure that it will eventually find a resolution. The debates in the *Anatomy* had been nothing but wily attacks and counter-attacks, an exchange of 'ware for ware' which brought no profit to any of the rhetorical merchants (i. 194). But the last debate in the second volume has an impartial moderator, the regenerate Euphues, who draws all threads together in a series of unifying epigrams. With gnomic brusqueness he tells Surius and Camilla that 'love is to be grounded uppon Time, Reason, Favour and Vertue'; assures Flavia that it is 'requisite' men and women should meet, and that it is 'impossible but that they will meete'; and advises Philautus that 'constancie without secrecie availeth little, and secrecie without constancie profiteth lesse' (ii. 182). The stage has been cleared for the entry of the narrative's Hymen, Elizabeth I, who bars the peculiarly gentle confusion with which the volume has been filled.[14]

### 3. THE CENTRE OF THE LABYRINTH

Euphues leads his readers into the final section, *Euphues Glasse for Europe*, by way of a system of mirrors, a dazzling metaphorical entrance-lobby that signals his approach to the centre of all the book's eye- and brain-deceiving fictions. The epistle 'To the Ladyes and Gentlewomen of Italy' (ii. 189–90) is filled with allusions to different kinds of glass, from the tiny glass mirrors with which Elizabethan women decorated their fans to the glass necklaces that adorned their throats, from vanity-glasses for the inspection of the owner's face to spectacles for the scrutiny of other people's, from the wine-glasses that make a woman 'wanton' to the shards of broken glass which are all she has left when she puts a foot wrong. Every aspect of women's existence is dominated by this translucent and deceptive medium; so that the relationship between the female reader's shifting world and the textual mirror that follows—which contains the reflection of a perfect court, designed, as Euphues insists, to enable women to amend faults in their hearts as readily as they amend faults in their coiffures—is infinitely more difficult, more fraught with problems of perception, than the simple relationship between readers and prescriptive mirrors in conventional didactic texts. For Lyly, Gascoigne's distinction between the true steel glass and the flattering crystal one is a wholly inadequate metaphor for the multiple perspectives of contemporary court politics.

[14] See Hymen's speech in *As You Like It*, v. iv. 125.

Like the epistles that open the volume, this epistle does not aim to supplant but to supplement the pleasures of dressing up; by taking its admonitions to heart, Euphues claims, the women of Italy 'shall in short time be as much commended for vertue of the wise, as for beautie of the wanton' (ii. 190). He advocates not the naïve conformity urged by traditional moralists but a sophisticated union of pleasure and discipline which takes into account the material conditions of court life, where controlled wantonness is as necessary a component of courtly behaviour as are wariness and wisdom.[15] It is to this bewildering political hall of mirrors that the idealized women of Elizabeth's court respond, with their circumspect participation in potentially dangerous pastimes: 'conferring with courtiers yet warily: drinking of wine yet moderately, eating of delicats yet but their eare ful, listing to discourses of love but not without reasoning of learning' (ii. 200). *Euphues Glasse for Europe* records what might be called the feminization of late sixteenth-century politics. This is not to say that it depicts women as possessing more power than men—or much practical power at all. Instead it implies that the qualities that had been associated with women in sixteenth-century fiction were qualities essential for survival in early modern England: skill in improvisation; secrecy; evasiveness; the cultivation of sumptuous appearances; the discreet manipulation of men. And the supreme exponent of these skills is the woman at the centre of the mirror, the sun of England which can be seen only by viewing its reflection (ii. 211), Elizabeth I.

The queen inhabits a web of artefacts—fictions, paintings, statues, buildings—which combine to construct and protect her supremacy. Euphues describes her court, for instance, in terms that evoke the monkish romances condemned by Ascham, and in the process he gives them the delightful legitimacy that other forms of fiction have acquired in the course of the book. At first, Euphues explains, the beauty of the company that encompasses the queen was such that he believed 'in this island...some odd *Nigromancer* did inhabit'; but he quickly learns that 'the place where I stoode was no enchaunted castell, but a gallant court', a discovery which leads him to redefine the principle of beauty itself: '*There is no beautie but in England*' (ii. 200). In Euphues' England, 'beautie' is a carefully monitored union of the artistic representation of power and the actual power-structures of

---

[15] The best recent discussion of this aspect of Elizabethan court culture can be found in Bates, *The Rhetoric of Courtship*.

ιe state which this image reflects; and the care with which this union
monitored is implied by Euphues' indirect allusions to the royal pro-
lamation of 1563 regarding portraits of Elizabeth: 'Alexander... com-
ιaunded that none shoulde paint him but *Appelles,* none carve him
ut *Lysippus*' (ii. 204).[16] The proclamation made it illegal for portraits
f Elizabeth to be executed by any artist except the authorized few;
ut Lyly treats it not as an act of state censorship but as a challenge
ɔ his witty inventiveness. In a story that has no known source, he
xplains how the artist Parrhasius circumvented Alexander's com-
ιand by constructing 'a Table squared, everye waye twoo hundred
ɔote' (ii. 204) and presenting it to the Prince as the space in which
e would paint his portrait if it were legal to do so. The size of the
ame, he explains, is designed to express the vast imaginative possibi-
ties latent in the mere fact of undertaking to depict a Prince who
lans to conquer the world. This, incidentally, is the same Parrhasius
rho (in another story Lyly made up for his own purposes) drew the
ɔunterfeit of Helen at the beginning of the *Anatomy,* and so heralded
new and complex art which incorporates cunningly coded allusions
ɔ the nature of the subjects it portrays. Lyly's point would seem to be
ιat, despite its subtlety and the dangers it courts (of excess, of obscur-
y, of encouraging erotic adventure and adolescent rebellion), his
wn art is the medium best suited to representing the subtle, elusive,
angerous world of the court, and that his loyalty to the crown—the
;ood minde' Alexander detected in Parrhasius, the 'simplicity'
uphues claims for himself (ii. 214)—does not by any means necessi-
ιte a return to the prescriptive simplicity of conventional authorized
rriting. The tendency of euphuism to pander to tastes which demand
o heare finer speache then the language will allow' (i. 181) becomes,
ι *Euphues Glasse for Europe,* euphuism's greatest asset, since it is called
n to represent a political power which is beyond the expressive cap-
bilities of the finest speech. Euphues doubts 'whether our tongue
anne yeelde wordes to blase' Elizabeth's beauty (ii. 211), and adds
ιat the only satisfactory form in which her nature might be encom-
assed would be a language which conveyed several meanings at once,
ke the multiple echo 'in the gallerie of *Olympia,* where gyving forth
ne worde, I might heare seven' (ii. 214). Far from reproducing
lyot's strictures on fraud, Euphues here advocates the use of the

---

[16] For the proclamation regarding portraits, see *Calendar of State Papers, Domestic Series,*
ʻ47–1580, ed. Robert Lemon (London: Longman, Brown, Green, Longmans, & Roberts,
ʻ56), 232.

most fraudulent speech conceivable, a discourse of which ambiguity
or doubtfulness is the very essence. Elizabeth, of course, would have
no difficulty untangling this ambiguity, since Euphues presents her
as the ultimate wordmaster, familiar with all European languages
not just one—'fitter to teach others, then learne of anye, more able
to adde new rules, then to erre in the olde' (ii. 213). And the kind
of English which would seem to correspond most closely to this
ambiguous sevenfold language is euphuism, with its fertile puns, its
frequent excursions into the strange territory of analogies and anecdotes drawn from around the world, its lengthy but controlled periods, the echoes it awakens by assonance. The court Lyly depicts in
the *Glasse for Europe* is the wellspring of his idiosyncratic style, the centre that justifies and necessitates its cultivated eccentricity.

It is also the wellspring of complex narratives. Towards the end of
his encomium of Elizabeth Euphues expresses a mild anxiety 'that
being in this Laborinth, I maye sooner loose my selfe, then finde the
ende' (ii. 215); in doing so he draws the labyrinths of the book into the
protection of the Crown, and of the labyrinthine network of baffling
strategies that surrounds it. Euphues casts the English nobility closest
to the queen as characters from the subtlest of political narratives, a
version of the tale of Troy more intricate than Homer's. They combine the qualities of both sides in the Trojan war—the Greeks and
the Trojans—and their combined talents ensure that they constitute
the ultimate police network, a devastatingly efficient secret service
by which all plots are discovered, all attempts to topple the English
state suppressed. They are:

grave and wise Counsailors, whose foresight in peace warranteth saftie in
warre . . . how great their wisdom hath beene in all things, the twentie two
yeares peace doth both shew and prove. For what subtilty hath ther bin
wrought so closly, what privy attempts so craftily, what rebellions stirred up
so disorderly, but they have by policie bewrayed, prevented by wisdome
repressed by justice? What conspiracies abroad, what confederacies at
home, what injuries in anye place hath there beene contrived, the which
they have not eyther fore-seene before they could kindle, or quenched before
they could flame?

If anye wilye *Ulysses* should faine maddnesse, there was amonge them
alwayes some *Palamedes* to reveale him, if any *Thetis* went about to keepe
hir sonne from the doing of his countrey service, there was also a wise *Ulysses*
in the courte to bewraye it: If *Sinon* came with a smoothe tale to bringe in the
horse into *Troye*, there hath beene always some couragious *Laocoon* to

throwe his speare agaynst the bowelles, whiche beeing not bewitched with *Laocoon*, hath unfoulded that, which *Laocoon* suspected. (ii. 197)

By this unassailable system of counter-espionage, the endless 'bewrayals' which are the province of the quick wit are redeployed in Her Majesty's service; and the malicious secrets that lurked at the core of the sophisticated narratives of the preceding decade are unfolded and defused before they can demolish the Elizabethan hierarchy. Elizabeth is of course the catalyst of this process; she reconciles all factions and unifies all fictions in her person. Her ancestry ensures that 'the redde Rose and the white' are finally 'united and joyned together' (ii. 206) under her government; and the garden of her body which effects this most miraculous of reconciliations is the most extensive one of all, where Euphues cannot afford to 'lynger about one flower, when I have many to gather' (ii. 209). Finally in the Latin poem that ends the *Glasse* she anticipates the plot of George Peele's play *The Araygnement of Paris* by uniting all the diverse properties of the principal goddesses of Classical fiction—Juno, Minerva, and Venus—in herself, thus removing the cause of the Trojan war by becoming the undisputed winner of the golden apple that sparked it off.[17] The city of Troy, which kept collapsing in the course of the *Anatomy*, has been triumphantly reconstructed as Troynovant, the New Troy that was Elizabethan London. It is in her capacity as Juno, the goddess of marriage, that Elizabeth presides over the treatise that closes the book. She is not mentioned in the treatise—another admonitory letter from Euphues to Philautus, this time on the subject of matrimony—but she is present in the echo of her that the ideal marriage aspires to: 'Princes that are Musitians incite their people to use Instruments, husbands that are chast and godly, cause also their wives to imitate their goodnesse' (ii. 225). The musical allusions that have run alongside other forms of harmony throughout the text are present even in Euphues' sometimes sardonic commentary on conjugal life, and it is here that music too is finally traced to its princely source.

Lyly did not leave Elizabeth in her magical court, infinitely distanced, like all ideals, from the political and social realities which his interwoven fictions half-conceal. From the position of precarious

[17] At the end of Peele's play, Elizabeth receives the apple from the moon-goddess Cynthia. See *The Dramatic Works of George Peele*, 3 vols. (New Haven, Conn.: Yale University Press, 1970), vol. iii: *The Araygnement of Paris*, ed. R. Mark Benbow, 1–131.

strength which the success of the two *Euphues* books gave him, like the wolf in Fidus' fable he continued to penetrate more and more deeply into the lion's cave. His plays share the special relationship with their audiences which *Euphues and his England* established with its readership. The prologue to *Campaspe* urges its spectators to regard its effervescent fantasies as 'the daunsing of *Agrippa* his shadowes, who in the moment when they were seene, were of any shape one woulde conceive' (ii. 316). But the plays' susceptibility to the infinite interpretations of their courtly audience made them as dangerous as they were brilliant. His most lighthearted and fantastic productions show a constant alertness to this danger; in *Campaspe* one of Alexander's followers tells another, in a speech that echoes Gascoigne's tale of Philomene: 'Cease *Permenio*, least in speaking what becommeth thee not, thou feele what liketh thee not: truth is never without a scratcht face, whose tongue though it cannot be cut out yet it must be tied up' (ii. 41). In *Endimion* the sharp-tongued Semele finds herself silenced on pain of death, and in *Midas* the comic barber Motto, whose name betrays his love of gossip, almost falls victim to the same not-so-comic fate. The danger of unbridled discourse is intensified by the situations in which Lyly places his monarchs. Clitus' warning to Parmenio is occasioned by the devastation of the king's mind, and consequently of his state, by the anarchy of love; Sapho's princely mind is infiltrated by a similar potentially disastrous desire for one of her humblest subjects; and in *Endimion* Cynthia finds her state undermined by the destructive verbal magic wielded by the witch Dipsas. In Lyly's plays the 'triumph over all yll tongues' with which Pettie credits the queen in the *Civile Conversation* seems to be achieved only at the expense of considerable pains—and some violence.

The most disturbing metamorphosis to which Lyly subjects Elizabeth occurs in his comedy *The Woman in the Moone*. This is his only play in verse, and its title-page boasts that it was performed before the queen herself. Here the queen seems to have undergone a division into more than one person, as she does in *The Faerie Queene*. On the one hand she is the goddess Nature, reconciling with difficulty the warring forces of Discord and Concord. On the other she is irresistibly linked with Pandora, the bringer of gifts and the bringer of chaos, whom Nature creates, like one of Cornelius Agrippa's moving statues, by invoking the influence of the stars, and who continues throughout the play to be wrenched violently from one mood to another by the jealous planets who helped to form her.[18] Elizabeth was celebrated as Pandora several times by contemporary poets;[19] and the connection seems to be confirmed by the fact that Lyly's Pandora ends up by sharing the heavenly sphere which Elizabeth had taken for her own, the moon, with its traditional occupant, an unusually surly Cynthia. Whether or not *The Woman in the Moone* was intended as a satire on Elizabeth's volatile temperament, the Elizabethan delight in 'applying' plays could only make Lyly's extravagant theatrical games so close to the Lion's paws a risky occupation, and the inhibition of one of the companies he wrote for, the Paul's boys, helps to stress its riskiness.[20] After the inhibition Lyly's career did not prosper, as his acerbic petitions to the queen suggest. In the case of Lyly, Ascham's judgement seems to have been borne out, when he said of quick wits that among them 'few be found, in the end, either verie fortunate for them selves, or verie profitable to serve the common wealth' (190). Lyly may have found his wit more of a burden than a boon; after all, the many allusions to him as 'Euphues' by writers like Simon Forman and Gabriel Harvey constituted a rather dubious compliment.[21] One of his letters, addressed to his patron (and Ascham's before him) Lord Burleigh, shows him struggling to defend himself against an accusation whose nature we do not know, and finding his euphuisms frustratingly inadequate as a means of conveying the semblance of sincerity:

It may be manie things wil be objected, but that any thing can be proved I doubt, I know your Lordship will soone smell devises from simplicity, trueth from trecherie, factions from just servic [*sic*]. And god is my witnes, before whome I speak, and before whome for my speach I shall aunswer, that all

[18] Nature, like Agrippa's magicians, first creates a 'lifeless Image' and then declares 'life and soule I shall inspire from heaven' (see Ch. 5 n. 33).
[19] By Spenser, for instance, in *The Teares of the Muses*, and by Dekker in *Old Fortunatus*. See Spenser, *Works*, i. 171, and *The Dramatic Works of Thomas Dekker*, ed. Fredson Bowers, 4 vols. (Cambridge: University of Cambridge Press, 1953), i. 113.
[20] According to G. K. Hunter, the inhibition of the Paul's boys lasted from about 1590 to 1600. *John Lyly*, 78.
[21] Forman refers to Lyly as 'Ephues' when recounting the tale of 'the mayor's daughter of Bracly': Feuillerat, *John Lyly*, 274–5 n. Harvey refers to Lyly as a more redoubtable version of Euphues in his *Advertisement to Pappe-Hatchett*: 'all you, that tender the preservation of your good names, were best to please Pap-hatchet, and fee Euphues betimes, for fear lest he be moved, or some one of his apes hired, to make a play of you' (reproduced in Lyly, *Works*, i. 54 n). Nashe refers to him as Euphues in *Strange News*: 'the vaine which I have ... is of my own begetting, and cals no man father in England but my selfe, neyther *Euphues*, nor Tarlton, nor *Greene*'. Lyly, *Works*, i. 60 n.

my thoughtes concerning my Lord have byne ever reverent, and almost relli
gious . . . That your honnor rest persuaded of myne honest mynd, and m
Lady of my true servic, that all things may be tried to the uttermost, is m
desire, and the only reward I crave for my just, (I just I dare tearme it) servic
(i. 28).

The near loss of the clever balances of euphuism in the final sentence—the abandonment of alliteration and the careful repetition o
the word whose 'simplicity' he most needs to establish, 'just'—seem
to suggest how uncertain Lyly is that Burleigh *will* be capable of sorting 'trueth' from 'trecherie' in a case like his; the case of a servan
whose credentials are so very far from simple. The ideal public weal
of *The Governor*, of *Utopia*, and of *Euphues and his England*, in whicl
the policing of language is a fundamental principle of state policy
must have seemed peculiarly oppressive at the time Lyly wrote thi
letter.

# Conclusion
# Hideous Progeny

And if this chapter shall seem to any Quixotic and fantastical, let
them recollect that the generation who spoke and acted thus in
matters of love and honour were, nevertheless, practised and
valiant soldiers, and crafty politicians: that he who wrote the
Arcadia was at the same time, in spite of his youth, one of the
subtlest diplomatists of Europe; that the poet of the Faery
Queene was also the author of The State of Ireland; and if
they shall quote against me with a sneer Lilly's Euphues itself, I
shall only answer by asking—Have they ever read it?

(Charles Kingsley, *Westward Ho!*)

And now, once again, I bid my hideous progeny go forth and
prosper.

(Mary Shelley, *Frankenstein*)

As Gosson might have anticipated, the monstrous fictions of the 1570s
had many offspring, more than can ever be counted.[1] The volumes of
energetic prose produced by Greene and Lodge in the 1580s are only
the most self-conscious of their literary descendants; but it is also
tempting to see the distinguishing features of Gascoigne's, Pettie's,
and Lyly's textual progeny more or less distinctly reproduced in
the ambitious literary projects of more familiar writers. The erotic

[1] Catherine Bates discusses contemporary responses to *Euphues* in ' "A Large Occasion of
Discourse": John Lyly and the Art of Civil Conversation', *Review of English Studies*, NS 42
(1991), 469–86. See also Hunter, *John Lyly*, ch. 5.

A glance at the *OED* entry for 'euphuism' offers a fascinating insight into the periodic
resurgences of interest in Lyly since the 16th cent., from Blount's mid 17th cent. edition
of the plays to Pater's theory of euphuism in *Marius the Epicurean*, from Scott's portrayal of
the 'Euphuist' Sir Piercie Shafton in *The Monastery* to Kingsley's 'reply' to Scott in *Westward
Ho!*

narrative poems of Marlowe, Shakespeare, and Marston seem to ow
an unacknowledged debt to Pettie's Ovidian pyrotechnics, as well as to
Gascoigne's fable of Philomene in *The Steele Glas*. Elizabethan drama
too, may owe as much to the prose fictions of the 1570s as it does to
Painter's *Palace of Pleasure*. Marlowe's Dr Faustus is Euphues gon
mad, the university wit who refuses to seek employment in the servic
of the state, but who finds himself trapped instead in the schemes o
more powerful and seductive political operators: not merely enemie
of the state, but enemies of reason, of rhetorical resourcefulness, o
the human soul. If Euphues had been unlucky and if Naples had trea
ted him less mildly, it is easy to imagine him talking himself to death a
Faustus does in his play's last scene. Shakespeare's earliest comedy *Th*
*Two Gentlemen of Verona*, with its broken agreements and treacherou
friendships, is the play in which he is most clearly indebted to *Euphues*
but *Love's Labour's Lost*, *Measure for Measure*, and *Othello* may be equall
indebted in their different ways to the adventurous prose of the 1570s.
Once you start looking, the children of Gascoigne's F.J., of Pettie'
articulate heroines, and of Lyly's insufferable Euphues seem to throng
the pages of later sixteenth- and seventeenth-century poetry, prose
and drama. Nashe's unfortunate traveller Jack Wilton is, as his nam
suggests, a wilder and more wilful wit than Euphues, who gets on
of his gullible victims arrested for espionage before being thrown
into prison as a spy himself;[3] while wits and master improvisers dom
inate the comedies of Middleton and Jonson. Jonson and Nashe wer
both, like Gascoigne, victims of the censor, and it is not difficult to
imagine that Gascoigne and Lyly taught them some of the tricks o
the literary trade that enabled them to tread the satirical tightrope, pre
cariously poised between applause and a sudden fall, which stretche
itself throughout their fictions.[4]

---

[2] For Lyly's influence on *The Two Gentlemen of Verona* and *Love's Labour's Lost* see Hunte
*John Lyly*, ch. 6. The ducal spy in *Measure for Measure*, disguised as a Catholic confessor an
preoccupied with the sexual private lives of his subjects, has affinities with the secretive pro
tagonists of Elizabethan fiction, and Othello's willingness to populate his domestic environ
ment with monsters seems to hint at Shakespeare's familiarity with the labyrinthin
narratives of Fenton and Gascoigne.

[3] In Jack's first two adventures he accuses two followers of Henry VIII of espionage: h
first victim is a cider-salesman, his second a captain, who is 'turned on the toe'—that i
hanged—after Jack informs on him. Jack later finds himself imprisoned along with the Ea
of Surrey on a trumped-up charge of 'conspiracies against [the] state'. See *The Unfortuna*
*Traveller*, 259, 268–9, and 304.

[4] On the censorship of Jonson's plays see Dutton, *Mastering the Revels*, 10–14, 171–9. O
the censorship of the works of Nashe see Hutson, *Thomas Nashe in Context*, 1.

But a few important texts of the late 1570s and early 1580s offer more detailed perspectives on the shifty literary territory that prose fiction had helped to open up. One of these is Spenser's *The Shepheardes Calender*, his first publication and a book that many of his contemporaries regarded as the catalyst of a literary revolution.[5] The only reference in the text to a contemporary English poet outside the enchanted circle formed by Spenser, Sidney, and Harvey is a rather condescending mention of George Gascoigne: 'a wittie gentleman, and the very chefe of our late rymers, who, and if some partes of learning wanted not (albee it is well knowen he altogyther wanted not learning) no doubt would have attayned to the excellencye of those famous Poets' (113).[6] As one might have expected, Spenser's commentator E.K. was particularly interested in the fable of Philomene from Gascoigne's *The Steele Glas*, which bears a close resemblance to the satirical fables scattered through Spenser's text.[7] But *The Shepheardes Calender* shares the world inhabited by Gascoigne in other, subtler, ways. It shrouds itself in mystery, and advertises its own perplexing allusiveness, in a manner that recalls *The Adventures of Master F.J.*. Like Gascoigne's novel it incorporates a commentary, hints that the love-affair of its central character is designed to 'coloure and concele' a real relationship (42), and expresses a profound admiration for the 'novells' of Geoffrey Chaucer (22), who features in the text as the dead shepherd Tityrus (27). More interestingly, it develops the discussion about simplicity and subtlety in Elizabethan fiction that was the obsessive preoccupation of every writer in this book. Both *The Shepheardes Calender* and its commentary exhibit a profound anxiety about the act of producing fiction which would have been as familiar to Gascoigne as it was to Gosson. In Tityrus' day, Colin Clout explains to Hobbinol, fiction had a clearly defined function: it served as a means of alerting shepherds—or figures of authority—to the dangers that threatened their flocks or subjects (Tityrus would 'tell us

[5] E.K. was, of course, Spenser's most enthusiastic admirer; for his analysis of Spenser's contribution to contemporary letters see Spenser, *Works*, i. 3–9. William Webbe was another admirer; his *Discourse of English Poetrie* can be found in *Elizabethan Critical Essays*, ed. G. Gregory Smith, 2 vols. (Oxford: Oxford University Press, 1904), i. 226–302. For a discussion of the high hopes attending the publication of the *Shepheardes Calender*, see Richard Helgerson, *Self-Crowned Laureates: Spenser, Jonson, Milton, and the Literary System* (Berkeley, Ca.: University of California Press, 1983).

[6] All references to *The Shepheardes Calender* are taken from Spenser, *Works*, i. 1–121.

[7] The reference to Gascoigne occurs in E.K.'s gloss on the name Philomele in Spenser's text. Spenser, *Works*, i. 113.

mery tales to keepe us wake, | The while our sheepe about us safely
fedde', 63). In Colin's time, on the other hand, 'mery tales' have
acquired a more ambivalent status. *The Shepheardes Calender* opens
with an act of self-censorship on the part of the most talented poet
of his time, Colin himself, who breaks his pipe at the end of the January eglogue, and this is only the first of a number of instances where
shepherd–poets lapse into silence or obscurity in response to the hostility of their audiences. Colin's mistress seems to distrust his poetry as
much as she dislikes it: 'Shepheards devise she hateth as the snake, |
And laughes the songes, that *Colin Clout* doth make' (16). When in
September Diggon starts to talk too 'playnely' about the abuses con-
nived at by the English church, Hobbinol urges him to keep as
quiet as Colin, or at least to cover up his criticisms with an allegorical
veneer:

> Nowe, Diggon, I see thou speakest to plaine;
> Better it were a little to feyne,
> And cleanly cover that cannot be cured:
> Such ill, as is forced, mought nedes be endured. (90)

In October, Cuddie refuses to venture into the dangerous imaginative
heights occupied by religion and politics, and chooses instead to sing
'safely' for his own private pleasure and that of his friends (100). In
December Colin consigns his pipe to silence once again, so that the
text is framed with lamentations over a loss of poetic liberty which
may spring from more than personal causes.[8] Clearly poetry no longer
functions as a vehicle for simple and direct warnings to the great, as
Colin tells us it did in the time of Chaucer. Vigilance and fiction no
longer go hand in hand, and the shepherds must constantly remind
one another to keep an eye on their sheep as they tell each other stories.[9] The relationships between a tale, its teller, and its recipients have
become radically unsettled since the days when poet and politician

---

[8] In his youth, Colin tells us, he freely wandered 'the woodes and forest wide, | With-
outen dreade of Wolves to bene espyed' (115); and the use of 'espyed' might encourage
readers to associate these wolves with the cunning undercover agitators of the September
eglogue. The implication is that 'dreade' has entered his wanderings since, and that the
time when 'ylike to me was libertee and life' is long past (116).

[9] In the March eglogue Thomalin mentions the difficulty of keeping an eye on his sheep
while relating anecdotes ('thy seeing will not serve, | My sheepe for that may chaunce to
swerve, | And fall into some mischiefe', 31). In May Piers warns of the 'fondnesse' of
poets who celebrate the season 'With singing, and shouting, and jolly chere' while their
'flockes be unfedde' (47–8), and illustrates their irresponsibility with the fable of the fox
and the kid.

hared a common pastoral concern for the well-being of their English
ock.

In addition, fiction no longer has the persuasive force it once
ommanded; the fables shepherds tell each other provoke only
ontemptuous dismissal from their hearers. Cuddie tells Thenot,
fter he has listened to his fable of the oak and the briar, that he has
arrated 'a long tale, and little worth' (26); Palinode is equally un-
nterested in the story of the kid and the fox narrated by Piers in
May, and Morrell dismisses Thomalin's account of Catholic pastors
s 'a great deale of good matter ⏐ Lost for lacke of telling' (73).
Iven when a story finds a sympathetic audience, as when Diggon
ells Hobbinol about the clerical corruptions he has witnessed, its
ffectiveness remains debatable: 'all this long tale,' he sighs at last,
Nought easeth the care, that doth me forhaile' (93). The uselessness
f the shepherds' fictions stems partly from the divided condition of
astoral society—different shepherds espouse antagonistic ideological
ositions, and there is little indication that their differences can
ver be settled—and partly from the obscurity of the stories, which
Hobbinol considers to be a necessary authorial strategy given the hos-
le political environment in which they are told. E.K., on the other
and, who seems to be a dedicated Aschamite, traces the decline of
iction to the fact that it has been irremediably corrupted by unscru-
ulous practitioners. The Arthurian ladies of the lake—referred to
vithout a shadow of distaste by the poet—are for E.K. figments of
he corrupt imaginations of medieval monastic makers, 'fine fablers
nd lowd lyers... who tell many an unlawfull leasing' (44); while
he elfs and goblins of English fairy-tales are monstrous products of
he Italian mind, as he explains in a passage which fuses Ascham's
ttack on medieval Catholic literature with his assault on books
rom Italy:

he truth is, that there be no such thinges... but onely by a sort of bald Friers
nd knavish shavelings so feigned; which as in all other things, so in that,
oughte to nousell the comen people in ignorounce, least being once
cquainted with the truth of things, they woulde in tyme smell out the
ntruth of theyr... Massepenie religion. But the sooth is, that when all
taly was distraicte into the Factions of the Guelfes and the Gibelins, being
wo famous houses in Florence, the name began through their great mis-
hiefes and many outrages, to be so odious or rather dreadfull in the peoples
ares, that if theyr children at any time were frowarde and wanton, they
vould say to them that the Guelfe or the Gibeline came. Which words

nowe from them (as many thinge els) be come into our usage, and for Guelfe
and Gibelines, we say Elfes and Goblins.(65)

E.K. has evidently been reading Fenton as well as Ascham.[10]

The infiltration of the English mind by Catholic fictions has led in
its turn, Spenser's commentator suggests, to an insidious corruption of
the English language—against which Spenser's text militates by abandoning Italian, French, and Latin neologisms (the latter, presumably
imported by those Latin-speaking friars) in favour of the unsullied
English of Chaucer's time.[11] And the same insidious influences, it
would seem, have irreversibly devalued the notion of simplicity. In
much of the text simplicity is treated as a virtue: E.K. says Spenser
has cultivated a 'seemely simplycitie of handeling his matter, and fram-
ing his words' (3), he has sought to appeal to the 'simplicitie of common understanding' (13), and Christ himself was 'simple, as simple
shepe' (71). At the same time, simplicity is elsewhere a synonym for
gullibility: shepherds have 'simple' notions about the operations of
love, the kid who is tricked to his death by a fox is said to represent
'the simple sorte of the faythfull and true Christians' (58), and Catholic
undercover agents, like the fox, are able to impersonate simplicity
with terrifying ease.[12] 'Simple' fictions, then, like the traditional Aesopian fable, are no longer able to cope with the subtlety and duplicity of
contemporary life in England. The inadequacy of simple fictions is
hinted at in the September eglogue, the darkest and most anxious
poem in the calendar, where Diggon tells a version of Aesop's fable
about the wolf in sheep's clothing that suggests that elaborate fictions
are the stock-in-trade of Catholic moral assassins. The clerical wolves

---

[10] Fenton has many references to the 'civil dissensions among the nobility' which torment the 'crabbed climate' of Italy (*Bandello: Tragical Tales*, 62), although he does not discuss
the feud between the Guelphs and the Ghibellines. But his story of the Lord of Virle contains an allusion to Lord Talbot which may have suggested the link between Italian 'civil factions' and the English war-hero, whose name E.K. introduces into his gloss immediately
after the passage I have just cited (his 'noblesse bred such a terrour in the hearts of the
French, that oft times even great armies were defaicted and put to flyght at the onely hearing
of hys name', 65). In Fenton's story the Piedmontese protagonist meets and unhorses Talbot
'whose virtue made him so famous in those wars that the very remembrance of his name
procureth a terror to the stoutest Frenchman that this day liveth' (460).

[11] Still spoken, according to Richard Stanyhurst, in Elizabethan Ireland. For the suggestion that Spenser's 'Chaucerian' English derives from the English spoken in Ireland, see
Willy Maley, 'Spenser's Irish English: Language and Identity in Early Modern Ireland', *Studies in Philology*, 91 (1994), 417–31.

[12] The fox, as Piers explains, is the personification of 'craft, coloured with simplicitie'
(55).

that were eradicated from the English countryside in King Edgar's time have recently returned in force, more cunningly disguised than ever, capable of evading the sensitive noses of the shepherds' dogs, and even of imitating the shepherds' voices. These are wolves in shepherds' clothing, in other words, and their subtlety can be countered only by an equal subtlety on the part of the shepherds, who must 'Forstallen hem of their wilinesse' (93). The time of 'mery tales' is over; in the complex context of Elizabethan politics, it is time to adopt the dangerous course of taking on the Catholics at their own subtle literary games, and 'seeing all things accounted by their showes' (as Spenser puts it in his letter to Ralegh) to enter the field of ideological battle disguised as one of those dangerous Catholic fictions, a follower of King Arthur.[13]

If the connection between *The Shepheardes Calender* and the prose fiction of the 1570s seems a little tenuous, Lyly lent it weight when he produced his own version of the hymn to Eliza from the April eglogue in *Euphues and his England*.[14] But a stronger case can be made for the dialogue Sir Philip Sidney conducted with the texts discussed in this book. Sidney had owned a copy of Belleforest's novels since his childhood; Fenton dedicated the *Tragicall Discourses* to Sidney's mother; Stephen Gosson dedicated both *The Schoole of Abuse* and *The Ephemerides of Phialo* to Sidney himself, and *An Apology for Poetry* contains a famous reference to the stylistic excesses of euphuism.[15] Like Gascoigne and Lyly, in much of his writing Sidney represents the modern maker of fictions as a truant schoolboy, a malcontent, a lawbreaker, perhaps even a spy; and recent scholarship has argued that his writing registers an acute consciousness of the activities of the Elizabethan censors, as all practitioners of poetry needed to do after the suppression of Gascoigne's miscellanies.[16] *An Apology for Poetry* has little that is complimentary to say about contemporary fiction; the only recent English poetic texts it selects for praise are Surrey's poems, *Gorboduc*, *A Mirror for Magistrates*, and *The*

---

[13] For Spenser's letter to Ralegh see *The Faerie Queene*, 711–13.

[14] See Hunter, *John Lyly*, 47 and 355 n.

[15] For Sidney's ownership of Belleforest's novels, see Katherine Duncan-Jones, *Sir Philip Sidney: Courtier Poet* (London: Hamish Hamilton, 1991), 30. For allusions to euphuism in *An Apology for Poetry*, see above, Ch. 5, s. 3.

[16] See Annabel Patterson, *Censorship and Interpretation* (Madison, Wisc.: University of Wisconsin Press, 1984), ch. 1. See also Hadfield, *Literature, Politics and National Identity*, ch. 5. For a discussion of Sidney's associations with espionage, see Archer, *Sovereignty and Intelligence*, ch. 2.

*Shepheardes Calender*. But Sidney confesses himself to share in the general debility of imaginative writing in England—to be 'sick among the rest' (140); and it might be argued that his acknowledgement of his participation in the 'common infection' is more than just a courteously self-deprecating gesture. Instead he may be signalling his awareness of the idea of fiction as a treacherous act, a medium for expressing points of view distasteful to the authorities, which had been so cleverly developed by writers of prose fiction in the previous decade.

*An Apology for Poetry* divides itself into two parts, the first of which is a serious defence of the art of imaginative writing as the biblical King David and other ancient authors practised it: that is, as the most forceful method of instruction available to 'degenerate souls' (104). But the second part marks the gulf that has opened up between the theory of poetry and its current practice, between the school of heroic virtue which is what fiction ought to be and the playground of youthful minds and bodies it has become. The theory of poetry Sidney propounds in the first part seems to advocate the 'simple' discourse championed by Gosson, and lays a similar emphasis on the necessity of fusing word with action. The 'golden world' of ideal poetry delivers instructions that are plain enough to banish readerly confusion, and the examples it presents to its recipients are utterly straightforward: 'if the poet do his part aright, he will show you in Tantalus, Atreus, and such like, nothing that is not to be shunned; in Cyrus, Aeneas, Ulysses, each thing to be followed' (110). But this sentence begins with one of those pregnant 'ifs' which fill the first part of the *Apology*, making it speculative, contingent, inconclusive. The conditional imparts to the simple fables of Tantalus and Ulysses the status of conjecture—Sidney gives us no assurance that the poet *will* invariably 'do his part aright'—and so relegates such fables to the dream-world of the ideal. And as the *Apology* proceeds, the probability that poetic practice will ever again conform to this idealized simplicity grows ever more remote. Throughout the treatise, Sidney's poet is as dangerously liberated from convention as Gosson could have feared: he generates his fictions without respect for regulations or restrictions, 'freely ranging only within the zodiac of his own wit' (100), and his 'high flying liberty of conceit' (99) finally exposes him (and, by implication, the reader he draws after him) to the danger of self-destruction. In the second part of the treatise Sidney discusses the state of the poetic art in England, and shows it to bear little relation to the safe simplicity of the 'golden world' he has imaginatively constructed in the first. The poet's 'high flying' becomes a potentially disastrous tendency to excess, reminiscent of the suicidal high spirits of Ovid's Icarus; and Sidney makes the association with Icarus explicit when he proposes that each practising poet be accompanied by his own self-appointed flying instructor: 'yet confess I that as the fertilest ground must be manured, so must the highest-flying wit have a Daedalus to guide him' (132). This 'Daedalus' should teach the young poet the mastery of technique—the rules of 'Art, Imitation, and Exercise' (133)—but his course of instruction proves as unsuccessful as that of the original Daedalus; Sidney says of English poets that 'these, neither artificial rules nor imitative patterns, we much cumber ourselves withal' (133). For moralizers of Ovid, those who ignore their Daedaluses doom themselves to the fall that killed his son, and Sidney's discussion of contemporary fiction implies that other poets share the English writer's suicidal disregard for rules.

The crucial transition between the theory of the ideal poetry with its 'golden world' and the actual productions of the poets comes at the point when sexual desire intrudes on Sidney's text. Having dismissed one by one all the objections to imaginative writing ranged against it by the 'poet-haters', Sidney ends with the one abuse of fiction whose validity he is willing to concede; that is, 'how much it abuseth men's wit, training it to sinfulness and lustful love: for indeed that is the principal, if not the only, abuse I can hear alleged' (125). Far from refuting the accusation, he chooses to accept it as an accurate summary of current literary fashions:

Grant, I say, whatsoever they will have granted, that not only love, but lust, but vanity, but (if they list) scurrility, possesseth many leaves of the poets' books; yet think I, when this is granted, they will find their sentence may with good manners put the last words foremost, and not say that Poetry abuseth man's wit, but that man's wit abuseth Poetry.(125)

The concession to the poet-haters is made wittily enough, but for a sceptical, Gossonian reader it could be said to have demolished at a single blow the entire defence of poetry that Sidney has so carefully mounted in the first half of the treatise. The part of the mind that resists the effects of the original fall—the rational and imaginative part Sidney has earlier characterized as the 'erected wit' (101), from whose microcosmic zodiac the poet plucks his simple and potent speaking pictures—turns out to be the very same wit that is most capable of abusing poetry, of transforming it from the '*eikastike*, which some learned have defined, "figuring forth good things", to be *phantastike*, which doth contrariwise infect the fancy with unworthy objects' (125). The consequences of this transformation are as potentially disastrous in Sidney's text as they were in Gosson's, since poetry 'being abused, by the reason of his sweet charming force...can do more hurt than any other army of words'(125). Like Castiglione's perfect courtier, Sidney's poetic golden world is itself a fiction which exists only in certain ancient texts, or within the speculative confines of his treatise. The contemporary practices of poetry are as unruly and as potentially calamitous as a military rebellion.

In fact in the *Old Arcadia* the poet acts as the rebel's accomplice, the secret agent in borrowed apparel who prepares the ground for insurrection or foreign invasion. The book begins in a dispassionate style which avoids the intrusive use of rhetorical ornament as it mimics the stability of the Arcadian state. It opens with a sentence made up of balanced clauses that recalls the opening sentence of *The Anatomy of Wit*: 'Arcadia among all the provinces of Greece was ever had in singular reputation, partly for the sweetness of the air and other natural benefits, but principally for the moderate and well tempered minds of the people' (4). The Arcadians practise a rational poetry reminiscent of the art that produces the 'golden world' in the *Apology*: 'the very shepherds themselves had their fancies opened to so high conceits as the most learned of other nations have been long time content both to borrow their names and imitate their cunning' (4). But an excessive regard for one of the functions of poetry mentioned in the *Apology*—its power of prophecy—persuades the head of state to abandon his responsibilities and withdraw into the country, reversing as he does so the effect that a poetic text ought to have on its readers, which is to stir them to right action. The ruler's withdrawal plunges his country into political chaos, and at the same time leaves his subjects at the mercy of a new and more disruptive kind of poetry. Once Basilius, like Gosson's Jupiter, has removed his guiding hand from the framework of government, the organized discourse that preserved the stability of the state collapses into incoherence, as his counsellor Philanax recognizes when he submits to his master's 'dukely sophistry' (8).

At this point the foreign princes Pyrocles and Musidorus enter the narrative. Like Ascham's Italianate Englishmen or Lyly's Euphues (and like Sidney himself in the 1570s), they are travelling to complete their

education; again, like Euphues or the Italianate Englishman, they succumb to the allure of love, and as a result import political ruin into the
country they have infiltrated. Pyrocles is the first to succumb to love's
unreason, and to poetry. He claims to have been drawn to the groves
frequented by the woman he loves because of the botanical and architectural treasures they enclose; but his irrational discourse quickly
undermines his pretensions to intellectual detachment: 'Do you not
see how everything conspires together to make this place a heavenly
dwelling? Do you not see the grass, how in colour they excel the
emeralds, everyone striving to pass his fellow—and yet they are all
kept at equal height?' (14). Pyrocles' pathetic fallacies lead as inexorably as they do in Gosson's criticism to much more serious fallacies:
to lies and betrayals, rapes, disguises, secret plots, and midnight poi-
sonings. Love for Pyrocles compels Musidorus to abandon his own
logical arguments in sympathy: he closes his attempts to dissuade his
friend from his destructive pursuit of desire ('how sharp-witted you
are to hurt yourself!', 21) by encouraging him in the excesses to
which he is already committed. He gives Pyrocles 'three absolute
commandments: the first, that you increase not your evil with further
griefs; the second, that you love Philoclea with all the powers of your
mind; and the last commandment shall be that you command me to
do you what service I can towards attaining of your desires' (23).
With his last commandment Musidorus relinquishes the authority
that his age gives him over Pyrocles, and with this, the second abandonment of responsibility in the text, the unreason of love finally
'possesseth the leaves' of Sidney's book. The narrative, which has
been plain and unmetaphorical up to this point, suddenly takes on
Pyrocles' stylistic eccentricities. The narrator abruptly announces his
intention to collude with the young man's deceptions by referring
to him by the new name of Cleophila, which Pyrocles has adopted
to suit his Amazonian disguise: 'I myself feel such compassion of his
passion that I find even part of his fear lest his name should be uttered
before fit time were for it' (25). By the end of the first book the narrative is as full of pathetic fallacies and Ovidian metamorphoses,
rampant beasts and impossible passions, as any Italian or English story-
collection. And by the end of the fourth book Arcadia stands on the
verge of civil war, as a direct result of the princes' erotic machinations.

Pyrocles' decision to disguise himself as an Amazon marks him out
as a tricky ambassador from Fenton's, Painter's, and Pettie's Amazonian republics, where the structures of patriarchal power are inverted

and the traditional occupants of domestic space take over the throne
of monarchs. Like Gascoigne and Lyly, Sidney depicts his heroes as
spies, and makes his narrator complicit with their subterfuges. Like
Ascham, Lyly, and Gosson he portrays the disruption of a nation by
dangerous fictions from beyond its boundaries, the penetration of
civilized culture by the passion and violence of the wilderness.[17]
And like all the most sophisticated writers of the 1570s he compares
the movements of his characters to the gropings of baffled wanderers
who have embroiled themselves in the bowels of an emotional labyrinth. At the centre of the *Old Arcadia* is a cave that recalls the gloomy
rock inhabited by Gascoigne's Suspicion. In it Pyrocles encounters
another form of suspicion—sexual jealousy—in the form of Gynecia,
a married woman whom he cannot love, but whom he agrees to court
(as Euphues courted Livia) in order to distract attention from the
secret object of his desire. The darkness of the cave reproduces the
confusion generated by the princes as they pursue their private agendas—a confusion that threatens to spill out of its strategic enclosure
and overwhelm all the efforts of counsellors and legislators to impose
order on the motions of the mind. Sidney's friend Fulke Greville
described the *Arcadia* as a collection of 'moral images and examples,
as directing threads, to guide every man through the confused labyrinth of his own desires and life';[18] but both versions of the text—the
*Old Arcadia* and the *New*—seem to have the opposite effect: they
merely replicate the labyrinth's contortions.

   The trial to which the princes are subjected at the end of the *Old
Arcadia*—like wayward young authors interrogated by the censors—
confirms the text's resistance to the reimposition of order, rule, and
authority. When replying to the accusations of the prosecutor Philanax, Pyrocles seems to be on the verge of clarifying everything that

---

[17] Sometimes in an unexpected way. An interesting example is the song sung by Sidney's
pastoral alter-ego Philisides in the third eclogues (221–5). The song tells of an orderly paradise inhabited by the animals before the advent of humanity, where lions lie down with
lambs and every beast is a vegetarian. Desirous of a king, the beasts ask Jove to give them
one, and each offers one of its physical attributes to construct him from. Unfortunately
the human being that results bears a close resemblance to the monstrously slippery composite
beast to which Ascham compares the Italianate Englishman, and his subtle power-games
quickly reduce the animals' Edenic wilderness to the tormented likeness of a sophisticated
16th-cent. state. The story, with its wonderful evocation of the always increasing complexity
of contemporary politics, seems to echo Lyly's account of the way narratives and lovemaking
have become more complex since the time of Adam.

[18] *The Prose Works of Fulke Greville, Lord Brooke*, ed. John Gouws (Oxford: Clarendon
Press, 1986), 134.

has been obscure in the foregoing narrative; he offers to give an honest account of the labyrinthine events that have taken place, and having delivered his account he assures the judge Euarchus: 'Here have you the thread to guide you in the labyrinth this man of his tongue hath made so monstrous' (340). But what Pyrocles claims to be an honest explanation of his actions is in fact another of his blinds, a web of falsehoods spun (like his Amazonian garments) to obscure his name and origin. In this new version of events he gives himself and Musidorus new histories and new pseudonyms, and Euarchus does not learn their true identities until after he has passed judgement against them. The fictions of Sidney's protagonists come closer to killing them than any of the complex narratives devised by the heroes and heroines of the 1570s; the princes are saved from execution only by an improbable last-minute intervention by Providence. But rebellion, civil war, and assassination also lurked at the edges of earlier English fictions. Baldwin's cats held their criminal trials on the rooftops of London where the dismembered bodies of rebels were displayed; F.J. played his word-games on the site of the northern rebellion; Euphues could be said to have killed the governor of Naples (Lucilla's father), and Pettie's revisions of Classical texts hover at the intersection between domestic conflict and armed struggle.[19] The relative impunity afforded him by his aristocratic status gave Sidney the opportunity to carry the word-games of his predecessors to their terrifying conclusion: to convert their petty treasons to high treason.[20] Sidney's *New Arcadia*—the revised and expanded version of the *Old*—might, as Greville speculates, have led its readers as well as its characters to safety; but in its unfinished state it merely leaves them hopelessly entangled. And *Astrophil and Stella* does so too, beginning as it does

[19] It is worth mentioning that the most influential English prose fiction of the 16th cent., More's *Utopia*, also takes place, at least in part, on the site of a rebellion. Raphael's one visit to England was made 'not long after the insurrection that the western Englishmen made against their king, which by their own miserable and pitiful slaughter was suppressed and ended' (21). This lends some urgency to the discussion of legal and economic reforms that dominates the first book.

[20] There can be no better illustration of Sidney's relative impunity than the response of the Elizabethan authorities to his attack on Elizabeth I's prospective marriage to the Duc d'Alençon. In 1579 a Puritan gentleman called John Stubbs wrote and published a pamphlet against the proposed marriage. In the same year Sidney wrote a *Letter to Queen Elizabeth Touching her Marriage with Monsieur*, which argued against the marriage as vehemently as Stubbs did, and which achieved a wide circulation in manuscript. Both writers may well have written at the instigation of Sir Francis Walsingham. Stubbs had his right hand struck off for inciting the public to sedition. Sidney merely withdrew from court to let things simmer down. See Duncan-Jones, *Sir Philip Sidney: Courtier Poet*, 160–5.

with a truant scholar who dismisses his teachers and throws away hi
books, and ending with his failure to commit himself to a profitabl
career.[21]

The reputation of Sidney's *Old Arcadia* has enjoyed a renaissance i
the last few years. But after a little time spent in their company, it i
easy to develop an equally high regard for the other writers of earl
Elizabethan prose fiction mentioned in this book. It is easy to lik
and even to admire their achievements almost as much as they seen
to demand, with their dazzling displays of verbal fireworks and thei
flattering invitations to take an active part in their devious literar
enterprises. It is tempting to match one's wit to theirs, to find onesel
falling into the posture of easy gamesmanship they adopt in their pre
liminary epistles, and to lose sight of their failures: the longueurs, th
excesses, and the lapses of taste of which they are sometimes guilty.

But it is well worth taking the time to get to know them. To ignor
their work is to miss out on a vital phase in the development of Eliza
bethan culture. Their brilliantly witty narratives may have helped t
teach their readers to engage in the sophisticated acts of readin
which were a prerequisite for the astonishing burst of literary creativ
ity that characterized the 1580s and 1590s. Their obsession with th
fluctuations of contemporary fashion—with the skills of improvisatio
and close observation essential for survival in the volatile world of Eli
zabethan public and private life—associates them with the emergenc
of new attitudes to the studies of science and of politics. And their flir
tations with many different kinds of controversy helped to transforr
prose fiction into what, at its best, it has remained ever since:
space available to be exploited for the investigation of what must b
left unsaid in official documents—versions of history which the officia
historiographers are unable or unwilling to record. They found chink
in the defences of the censors that later writers were able to widen
contradictions in current ideologies that opened the possibility o
new political and philosophical perceptions, and a variety of nev
rhetorical tricks and tools that expanded the capabilities of the Englisl
language far beyond the limits set by their predecessors. And ther
remains a very great deal more to be said about them. Recent discus-

---

[21] Sidney's decision to 'look in his heart, and write' in the first sonnet might be taken a
the action of a truant prodigal; and in the penultimate sonnet he asks for 'respite' from hi
love in order to commit himself to some 'great cause'. But the last line of the sonnet, and th
last sonnet in the sequence, give little indication that his desire has granted him a vacation
See *Sir Philip Sidney*, ed. Katherine Duncan-Jones, 153 and 211.

sions of Elizabethan prose fiction have been lively but few, and it continues to be excluded from the bulk of commentaries on the English Renaissance, left to nurse its scandalous secrets in an eccentric wilderness of its own making.

Some of these secrets have already begun to leak out into the open. Among other things, Elizabethan prose fiction has been found to offer a partial answer to a question which has preoccupied many scholars in the past decade: the question of how women first came to enter the field of print at a time when economic and political power was being ever more stringently denied them.[22] The prose narratives of the 1560s and 1570s often address themselves to women, and their fictitious heroines are more eloquent and more politically adept than any of the women in contemporary drama. Fenton's scheming Amazons, Baldwin's quasi-matriarchal cats, Gascoigne's elusive female conspirators, Pettie's unfortunate wives, and Lyly's articulate gentlewomen struggle to establish secret miniature commonwealths of their own within the compass of their domestic enclosures, and some of them even succeed, at least for a little while. These narratives exempt themselves, for a space, from the usual rules which govern the power-relations between the sexes. So it is hardly surprising that a few women writers of the sixteenth and early seventeenth centuries should have produced texts which testify to their interest in the new Elizabethan fictions. In the early 1570s Isabella Whitney wrote an autobiographical miscellany which bears a marked resemblance to Gascoigne's quick-witted mixtures of verse and prose. At the end of the decade Margaret Tyler published a translation of a prose romance, which explicitly presents itself as a response to fictions addressed by men to a female readership.[23] In the 1580s Jane Anger published a fierce rebuttal of the misogyny of Lyly's *Euphues*, and in the early years of the following century Lady Mary Wroth took up the challenge thrown down by Gascoigne, Lyly, and Sidney when she printed the first volume of her prose epic, *The Countesse of Montgomeries Urania* (1620)—for which she, like Gascoigne, quickly found herself in trouble with the censors.[24] The Amazons eventually founded a powerful

---

[22] A question which is asked by Caroline Lucas in *Writing for Women* and by Lorna Hutson in *The Usurer's Daughter*.

[23] Isabella Whitney and Margaret Tyler are discussed in Hutson, *The Usurer's Daughter*, 122–8 and 91–8 respectively.

[24] For *Jane Anger her Protection for Women*, see *The Women's Sharp Revenge*, ed. Simon Shepherd (London: Fourth Estate, 1985), 29–51. For a brief account of Wroth's *Urania*, see Salzman, *English Prose Fiction 1558–1700*, 138–44.

literary republic of their own, despite the consistent efforts of the academy to devalue and forget their works. And the early Elizabethan writers of prose fiction may have helped to prepare the ground for its foundation.

There are many reasons why texts get devalued and forgotten, and it is often a laborious task to recover or to reconstruct them. The writers of the self-consciously ephemeral narratives of the 1570s were well aware of this; but their monsters, labyrinths, incompetent spies, and treacherous lovers are still available to be liberated from their pages whenever we care to seek them out.

# Bibliography

PRIMARY SOURCES

AGRIPPA, HENRIE CORNELIUS, *Of the Vanitie and Uncertaintie of Artes and Sciences*, trans. James San[d]ford (1569).

ANGER, JANE, *Jane Anger her Protection for Women*, in *The Women's Sharp Revenge*, ed. Simon Shepherd (London: Fourth Estate, 1985), 29–51.

ASCHAM, ROGER, *Roger Ascham: English Works*, ed. W. A. Wright (Cambridge: Cambridge University Press, 1904).

BACON, SIR FRANCIS, *The Advancement of Learning and The New Atlantis*, ed. Arthur Johnston (Oxford: Clarendon Press, 1986).

—— *The Wisedome of the Ancients*, trans. Sir Arthur Gorges (1619).

—— *The Works of Francis Bacon*, ed. J. Spedding, R. L. Ellis, and D. D. Heath, 14 vols. (London: Spottiswoode, 1857–74).

BALDWIN, WILLIAM, *Beware the Cat* [1570]: *The First English Novel*, ed. William Ringler, Jr., and Michael Flachmann (San Marino, Ca.: Huntington Library, 1988).

—— *The Mirror for Magistrates* (first surviving edn.: 1559), ed. Lily B. Campbell (Cambridge: Cambridge University Press, 1938).

—— *Treatise of Morall Phylosophie* (1548); publ. as *The Sayings of the Wise; or, Food for Thought. A Book of Moral Wisdome, Gathered from the Ancient Philosophers*, ed. Edward Arber (London: privately printed, 1907).

BANDELLO, MATTEO, *Tutte le Opere di Matteo Bandello*, ed. Francesco Flora, 2 vols. (Verona: Mondadori, 1942).

BELLEFOREST, FRANÇOIS DE, *The French Bandello: A Selection. The Original Texts of Four of Belleforest's Histoires Tragiques Translated by Geoffrey Fenton and William Painter, Anno 1567*, ed. Frank S. Hook (Columbia, Oh.: University of Missouri Press, 1948).

——and BOAISTUAU, PIERRE DE, *Premier et Second Thomes des Histoires Tragiques* (Paris, 1565; edn. cited 1568).

BOCCACCIO, GIOVANNI, *The Decameron*, trans. G. H. McWilliam (Harmondsworth: Penguin, 1972).

—— *Early English Versions of the Tales of Guiscardo and Ghismonda and Titus and Gisippus from the Decameron*, ed. Herbert G. Wright (London: Early English Text Society, 1937).

BROOKE, ARTHUR, *The Tragicall Historye of Romeus and Juliet* (1562), in William Shakespeare, *Romeo and Juliet*, ed. G. Blakemore Evans, The New Cambridge Shakespeare (Cambridge: Cambridge University Press, 1984), 213–47.

BROWNE, THOMAS (trans.), *A Ritch Storehouse or Treasurie for Nobilitye* (1570).

BULLEIN, WILLIAM, *A Dialogue Against the Fever Pestilence* (1564), ed
    Mark W. Bullen and A. H. Bullen (London: Early English Text Society
    1888).

BURTON, ROBERT, *The Anatomy of Melancholy* (1621), introd. Holbrook
    Jackson, 3 vols. (London: J. M. Dent 1932).

*Calendar of State Papers, Domestic Series, 1547–1580*, ed. Robert Lemon (Lon
    don: Longman, Brown, Green, Longmans, & Roberts, 1856).

CASTIGLIONE, BALDASSARE, *The Book of the Courtier* (1528), trans. Si
    Thomas Hoby (1561), ed. W. H. D. Rouse (London: J. M. Dent 1928).

*Certain Sermons or Homilies Appointed to be Read in Churches in the Time*
    *Queen Elizabeth of Famous Memory*, ed. John Griffiths (London: SPCK
    1864).

CHAUCER, GEOFFREY, *The Works of Geoffrey Chaucer*, ed. F. N. Robinson
    (Oxford: Oxford University Press, 1966).

CICERO, *De Oratore*, trans. E. W. Sutton, in *Cicero in Twenty-eight Volume*
    (London: Heinemann, and Cambridge, Mass.: Harvard University Press
    1967), vols. iii. and iv.

COX, LEONARD, *The Art or Crafte of Rhetoryke* (1532).

*The Deceyte of Women* (*c.*1520).

DEKKER, THOMAS, *The Dramatic Works of Thomas Dekker*, ed. Fredso
    Bowers, 4 vols. (Cambridge: Cambridge University Press, 1953).

EDWARDS, RICHARD, *Damon and Pithias* (1566), in *Chief Pre-Shakespearea*
    *Dramas*, ed. J. Q. Adams (London George Harrap, n.d.), 571–608.

ELYOT, SIR THOMAS, *The Book Called The Governor*, (1531) ed. S. E. Lehm
    berg (London: J. M. Dent 1962).

—— *The Dictionary of Syr Thomas Eliot* (1538); rev. and enlarged as *Bibliothec*
    *Eliotae* (1542).

—— *Four Political Treatises by Sir Thomas Elyot*, introd. Lillian Gottesman
    (Gainesville, Fla.: Scholars' Facsimiles and Reprints, 1967).

*English Mystery Plays*, ed. Peter Happé (Harmondsworth: Penguin, 1975).

ERASMUS, DESIDERIUS, *Collected Works of Erasmus* (Toronto: Toronto
    University Press, 1974–    ).

—— *Erasmus on his Times*, ed. Margaret Mann Phillips (Cambridge: Cam
    bridge University Press, 1967).

—— *The Essential Erasmus*, trans. John P. Dolan (New York: Mentor
    1964).

FENTON, GEOFFREY, *Certaine Tragicall Discourses* (1567); publ. as *Bandello*
    *Tragical Tales*, ed. Hugh Harris, introd. Robert Langton Douglas (London
    Routledge, 1924).

—— *A Discourse of the Civile Warres and Late Troubles in Fraunce* (1570).

—— *The Historie of Guicciardin, Conteining the Warres of Italie and Other Parte*
    (1579).

FLEMING, ABRAHAM, *A Panoplie of Epistles* (1576).

GASCOIGNE, GEORGE, *The Adventures of Master F.J.* (1573), in *An Anthology of Elizabethan Prose Fiction*, ed. Paul Salzman (Oxford: Oxford University Press, 1987), 1–81.

—— *The Complete Works of George Gascoigne*, ed. John W. Cunliffe, 2 vols. (Cambridge: Cambridge University Press, 1907).

—— *A Hundreth Sundrie Flowres* (1573), ed. C. T. Prouty (Columbia: University of Missouri Press, 1942).

*Gesta Romanorum*, trans. Charles Swan (Toronto: General Publishing, and London: Constable, 1959).

GOLDING, ARTHUR (trans.), *The Fyrst Fower Bookes of P. Ovidius Nasos Worke, intituled Metamorphosis* (1565); complete trans. publ. as *The .xv. Bookes of P. Ovidius Naso, entytuled Metamorphosis* (1567).

GOSSON, STEPHEN, *The Ephemerides of Phialo* (1579).

—— *Markets of Bawdrie: The Dramatic Criticism of Stephen Gosson*, ed. Arthur F. Kinney (Salzburg: University of Salzburg, 1974).

GRANGE, JOHN, *The Golden Aphroditis* (1577).

GREENE, ROBERT, *The Life and Complete Works in Prose and Verse of Robert Greene*, ed. Alexander B. Grosart, 15 vols. (London: Hazell, Watson & Viney, 1881–6).

GREVILLE, FULKE, *The Prose Works of Fulke Greville, Lord Brooke*, ed. John Gouws (Oxford: Clarendon Press, 1986).

HARVEY, GABRIEL, *The Works of Gabriel Harvey*, ed. Alexander B. Grosart, 3 vols. (London: Hazell, Watson & Viney, 1884).

HAWES, STEPHEN, *The Works of Stephen Hawes*, introd. Frank J. Spang (Delmar, NY: Scholars' Facsimiles and Reprints, 1975).

HERBERT, GEORGE, *The English Poems of George Herbert*, ed. C. A. Patrides (London: J. M. Dent 1974).

H[OWELL], T[HOMAS], *A Fable of Ovid treting of Narcissus* (1560).

*The Image of Idleness* (1556); publ. as 'The First English Epistolary Novel: *The Image of Idleness*. Text, Introduction and Notes', ed. Michael Flachmann, *Studies in Philology*, 87 (1990), 1–74.

*Irish Historical Documents 1172–1922*, ed. T. C. Curtis and R. B. McDowell (London: Methuen, 1943).

KINGSLEY, CHARLES, *Westward Ho!* (London: Walter Scott, n.d.)

LEVER, RALPH, *The Arte of Reason, Rightly Termed, Witcraft* (1573).

LIVY, *Livy*, ed. G. P. Goold, trans. B. O. Foster *et al.*, Loeb Classical Library, 14 vols. (Cambridge, Mass.: Harvard University Press, and London: William Heinemann, 1984).

LODGE, THOMAS, *The Defence of Poetry* (1579), in *Elizabethan Critical Essays*, ed. G. Gregory Smith, 2 vols. (Oxford: Oxford University Press, 1904), i. 61–86.

LYLY, JOHN, *The Complete Works of John Lyly*, ed. R. W. Bond, 3 vols. (Oxford: Clarendon Press, 1902).

LYLY, JOHN, *Euphues: The Anatomy of Wit (1578) and Euphues and his Eng*
*land* (1580), ed. M. W. Croll and H. Clemons (London: Routledge, 1916).

MACHIAVELLI, NICCOLÒ, *The Prince* (1514), trans. George Bull (Harmondsworth: Penguin, 1981).

MACILMAINE, R., *The Logike of P. Ramus* (1574).

MARLOWE, CHRISTOPHER, *Complete Plays and Poems*, ed. E. D. Pendry
and J. C. Maxwell (London: J. M. Dent 1976).

MERBURY, FRANCIS, *The Marriage of Wit and Wisdom* (first publ. before
1579), in *English Moral Interludes*, ed. Glynne Wickham (London: J. M.
Dent 1976), 163–94.

MORE, SIR THOMAS, *Utopia* (1516), trans. Ralph Robinson (1551), introd.
Richard Marius (London: J. M. Dent, 1985).

NASHE, THOMAS, *The Unfortunate Traveller and Other Works*, ed. J. B. Steane
(Harmondsworth: Penguin, 1972).

*A New and Pleasaunt Enterlude intituled The Mariage of Witte and Science* (*c.*1569)

NORTH, THOMAS, *The Dial of Princes* (1557; repr. with additions, 1568).

—— (trans.), *The Morall Philosophie of Doni* [1570]: *The Earliest English Version*
*of the Fables of Bidpai*, ed. J. Jacobs (London: David Nutt, 1888).

NORTHBROOKE, JOHN, *Spiritus est Vicarius Christi in Terra: A Treatise*
*wherein Dicing, Dauncing, Vaine Playes or Enterludes, with Other Idle Pastimes*
*. . . are Reproved* (1577).

PAINTER, WILLIAM, *The Palace of Pleasure* (1566–7), ed. Joseph Jacobs, 3
vols. (London: David Nutt, 1890).

PEACHAM, HENRY, *The Garden of Eloquence* (1577).

PEELE, GEORGE, *The Dramatic Works of George Peele*, ed. R. Mark Benbow et
al., 3 vols. (New Haven, Conn.: Yale University Press, 1970).

PETTIE, GEORGE, *A Petite Palace of Pettie his Pleasure* (1576), abridged and ed.
I. Gollancz, 2 vols. (London: Chatto & Windus, 1908).

—— *A Petite Pallace of Pettie his Pleasure* (1576), ed. Herbert Hartman (London: Oxford University Press, 1938).

—— and YOUNG, BARTHOLOMEW, *The Civile Conversation of M. Steeven*
*Guazzo* (1581), ed. Charles Whibley, 2 vols. (London: Constable, 1925).

PIZAN, CHRISTINE DE, *The Book of the City of Ladies* (1404–5; first trans.
1529), trans. Earl Jeffrey Richards (London: Pan, 1983).

PLATO, *The Republic*, trans. Paul Shorey, 2 vols. (London: William Heinemann, and New York: G. P. Puttnam's Sons, 1930).

PLUTARCH, *Plutarch's Moralia*, ed. E. H. Warmington, 15 vols. (London: William Heinemann, and Cambridge, Mass.: Harvard University Press, 1968).

P[UTTENHAM], G[EORGE], *The Arte of English Poesie* (1589), facsimile edn.
(Menston: Scolar Press, 1968).

RABELAIS, FRANÇOIS, *The Lives, Heroic Deeds and Sayings of Gargantua and*
*his Son Pantagruel* (1653–94), trans. Sir Thomas Urquhart and Peter Le
Motteux (London: Chatto & Windus, 1921).

RAINOLDE, RICHARD, *A Booke Called The Foundacion of Rhetorike* (1563).

RAINOLDES, JOHN, *Oratio in Laudem Artis Poeticae*, ed. William Ringler, trans. Walter Allen Jr. (Princeton: Princeton University Press, 1940).

R. B., *A New Tragicall Comedie of Apius and Virginia*, in *Tudor Interludes*, ed. Peter Happé (Harmondsworth: Penguin, 1975), 152–70.

REDFORD, JOHN, *Wit and Science* (1531–4), in *Tudor Interludes*, ed. Peter Happé (Harmondsworth: Penguin, 1975), 181–219.

SCOTT, SIR WALTER, *The Monastery* (London: Adam & Charles Black, 1898).

*Select Statutes and Constitutional Documents Illustrative of the Reigns of Elizabeth and James I*, ed. E. W. Prothero (Oxford: Clarendon Press, 1913).

SHAKESPEARE, WILLIAM, *The Riverside Shakespeare*, ed. G. Blakemore Evans (Boston: Houghton Mifflin, 1974).

SHELLEY, MARY, *Frankenstein* (1818), ed. Paddy Lyons (London: J. M. Dent, 1992).

SHERRY, RICHARD, *A Treatise of Schemes and Tropes* (1550).

SIDNEY, SIR PHILIP, *An Apology for Poetry* (1580–5), ed. Geoffrey Shepherd (London: Nelson, 1965).

—— *The Old Arcadia* (completed 1580), ed. Katherine Duncan-Jones (Oxford: Oxford University Press, 1985).

—— *Sir Philip Sidney*, ed. Katherine Duncan-Jones (Oxford: Oxford University Press, 1989).

SMITH, SIR THOMAS (?), *A Discourse of the Common Weal of this Realm of England*, ed. Elizabeth Lamond (Cambridge: Cambridge University Press, 1893).

SPENSER, EDMUND, *The Faerie Queene*, ed. A. C. Hamilton (London: Longman, 1980).

—— *The Complete Poetical Works of Edmund Spenser*, 3 vols. (Oxford: Clarendon Press, 1909–10), vol. i, *Minor Poems*, ed. Ernest de Selincourt.

TACITUS, *Tacitus in Five Volumes*, trans. Clifford H. Moore and J. Jackson (Cambridge, Mass.: Harvard University Press, 1931).

TILNEY, EDMUND, *The Flower of Friendship* [1568]: *A Renaissance Dialogue Contesting Marriage*, ed. Valerie Wayne (Ithaca, NY: Cornell University Press, 1992).

*A Transcript of the Registers of the Company of Stationers of London 1554–1640*, 3 vols., ed. Edward Arber (London: privately printed, 1875–94).

*Tudor Interludes*, Ed. Peter Happé (Harmondsworth: Penguin, 1975).

TURBERVILLE, GEORGE, *Tragical Tales* (1576).

VICARY, THOMAS, *The Anatomie of the Bodie of a Man* (first publ. 1548; reissued 1577), ed. F. J. Furnivall and Percy Furnivall (London: N. Trübner 1888).

WEBBE, WILLIAM, *A Discourse of English Poetrie* (1586), in *Elizabethan Critical Essays*, ed. G. Gregory Smith, 2 vols. (Oxford: Oxford University Press, 1904), i. 226–302.

WHETSTONE, GEORGE, *The Rocke of Regard* (1576), ed. J. P. Collier (n.p.: Collier's Reprints, 1870).

WILDE, OSCAR, *The Picture of Dorian Gray*, introd. Peter Ackroyd (Harmondsworth: Penguin, 1985).

WILSON, THOMAS, *The Arte of Rhetorique* (first publ. 1553; rev. edn. 1560).
—— *The Rule of Reason, Conteinyng the Arte of Logique* (1551).


SECONDARY SOURCES


ALTMAN, JOEL B., *The Tudor Play of Mind* (Berkeley, Ca.: University of California Press, 1978).

ARCHER, JOHN MICHAEL, *Sovereignty and Intelligence: Spying and Court Culture in the English Renaissance* (Stanford, Ca.: Stanford University Press, 1993).

BAKHTIN, MIKHAIL, *Rabelais and his World*, trans. Helen Iswolsky (Cambridge, Mass.: MIT Press, 1968).

BALDICK, CHRIS, *In Frankenstein's Shadow: Myth, Monstrosity, and Nineteenth-Century Writing* (Oxford: Clarendon Press, 1987).

BALDWIN, T. W., *William Shakespere's Small Latine and Lesse Greeke* (Urbana, Ill.: University of Illinois Press, 1944).

BALDWIN SMITH, LUCY, *Treason in Tudor England* (London: Jonathan Cape, 1986).

BARBOUR, REID, *Deciphering Elizabethan Fiction* (London Associated University Presses, 1993).

—— 'Recent Studies in Elizabethan Prose Fiction', *English Literary Renaissance*, 25 (1995), 248–76.

BARISH, JONAS A., 'The Prose Style of John Lyly', *ELH* 23 (1956), 14–35.

BARTON, ANNE, *Ben Jonson, Dramatist* (Cambridge: Cambridge University Press, 1984).

BATES, CATHERINE, '"A Large Occasion of Discourse": John Lyly and the Art of Civil Conversation', *Review of English Studies*, NS 42 (1991), 469–86.

—— *The Rhetoric of Courtship* (Cambridge: Cambridge University Press, 1992).

BENNETT, H. S., *English Books and Readers 1558–1603* (Cambridge: Cambridge University Press, 1965).

BINNS, JAMES W., 'Henry Dethick in Praise 1of Poetry: The First Appearance in Print of an Elizabethan Treatise', *Library*, 30 (1975), 199–216.

BONAHUE, EDWARD T., '"I Know the Place and the Persons": The Play of Textual Frames in Baldwin's *Beware the Cat'*, *Studies in Philology*, 91 (1994), 283–300.

BOSSY, JOHN, *Giordano Bruno and the Embassy Affair* (New Heaven: Yale University Press, 1991).

BRAMMALL, KATHRYN M., 'Monstrous Metamorphosis: Nature, Morality, and the Rhetoric of Monstrosity in Tudor England', *The Sixteenth Century Journal*, 27 (1996), 3–21.

BRENNAN, GILLIAN, 'Patriotism, Language and Power: English Translations of the Bible, 1520–1580', *History Workshop Journal*, 27 (1989), 18–36.

BUSH, DOUGLAS, '*The Petite Pallace of Pettie his Pleasure*', *JEGP* 27 (1928), 166–9.

CASSIRER, ERNST, *The Platonic Renaissance in England* (London: Nelson, 1932 and 1953).

CAVE, TERENCE, *The Cornucopian Text: Problems of Writing in the French Renaissance* (Oxford: Clarendon Press, 1979).

CHAMBERS, E. K., *The Medieval Stage*, 2 vols. (Oxford: Oxford University Press, 1903).

CLEMENTS, ROBERT J., and GIBALDI, JOSEPH, *Anatomy of the Novella: The European Tale Collection from Boccaccio and Chaucer to Cervantes* (New York: New York University Press, 1977).

COLDIRON, A. E. B., 'Watson's *Hekatompathia* and Renaissance Lyric Tradition', *Translation and Literature*, vol. v, pt. 1 (1996), 3–25.

COLIE, ROSALIE, '*My Ecchoing Song': Andrew Marvell's Poetry of Criticism* (Princeton: Princeton University Press, 1970).

CRANE, WILLIAM G., *Wit and Rhetoric in the Renaissance: The Formal Basis of Elizabethan Prose Style* (New York: Columbia University Press, 1937; repr. Gloucester, Mass.: Peter Smith, 1964).

CREWE, JONATHAN V., *Trials of Authorship*, (Berkeley, Ca.: University of California Press, 1990).

CURTIS, MARK H., *Oxford and Cambridge in Transition, 1558–1642* (Oxford: Clarendon Press, 1959).

DAVIS, WALTER R., *Idea and Act in Elizabethan Fiction* (Princeton, NJ: Princeton University Press, 1969).

DEWAR, MARY, 'The Authorship of the "Discourse of the Commonweal"', *Economic History Review*, 2nd ser. 19 (1966), 388–400.

DONAWERTH, JANE, *Shakespeare and the Sixteenth-Century Study of Language* (Urbana, Ill.: University of Illinois Press, 1984).

*Dictionary of Literary Biography*, cxxxvi: *Sixteenth-Century British Nondramatic Writers*, ed. David A. Richardson (Detroit, Mich.: Bruccoli Clark Layman, 1994).

DUNCAN-JONES, KATHERINE, *Sir Philip Sidney: Courtier Poet* (London: Hamish Hamilton, 1991).

DUTTON, RICHARD, *Mastering the Revels: The Regulation and Censorship of English Renaissance Drama* (Basingstoke: Macmillan, 1991).

ELLIS, P. BERRESFORD, *The Cornish Language and its Literature* (London: Routledge & Kegan Paul, 1974).

FEUILLERAT, ALBERT, *John Lyly: Contribution à l'histoire de la Renaissance en Angleterre* (Cambridge: Cambridge University Press, 1910).

FIELER. FRANK B., 'Gascoigne's Use of Courtly Love Conventions in *Master F.J.*', *Studies in Short Fiction*, 1 (1963), 26–32.

FUMERTON, PATRICIA, '"Secret" Arts: Elizabethan Miniatures and Sonnets', in Stephen Greenblatt (ed.), *Representing the English Renaissance*, (Berkeley, Ca.: University of California Press, 1988), 93–133.

GENT, LUCY, *Picture and Poetry 1560–1620* (Leamington Spa: James Hall, 1981).

GOHLKE, MADELON, 'Reading *Euphues*', *Criticism*, 19 (1977), 103–17.

GREENBLATT, STEPHEN, *Renaissance Self-fashioning* (Chicago, Ill.: University of Chicago Press, 1980).

HADFIELD, ANDREW, *Literature, Politics and National Identity* (Cambridge: Cambridge University Press, 1994).

HAMILTON, A. C., 'Elizabethan Romance: the Example of Prose Fiction', *ELH* 49 (1982), 287–99.

——— 'Elizabethan Prose Fiction and Some Trends in Recent Criticism', *Renaissance Quarterly*, 37 (1984), 21–33.

HELGERSON, RICHARD, *The Elizabethan Prodigals* (Berkeley, Ca.: University of California Press, 1976).

——— *Self-Crowned Laureates: Spenser, Jonson, Milton, and the Literary System* (Berkeley, Ca.: University of California Press, 1983).

HOUPPERT, JOSEPH W., *John Lyly* (Boston, Mass.: G. K. Hall, 1975).

HOWELL, W. S., *Logic and Rhetoric in England 1500–1700* (Princeton, NJ: Princeton University Press, 1956).

HUNTER, G. K., *John Lyly: The Humanist as Courtier* (London: Routledge & Kegan Paul, 1962).

HUNTER, PAUL J., '"News and New Things": Contemporaneity and the Early English Novel', *Critical Inquiry* 14 (1988), 492–513.

HUTSON, LORNA, *Thomas Nashe in Context* (Oxford: Clarendon Press, 1989).

——— 'Fortunate Travellers: Reading for the Plot in Sixteenth-Century England', *Representations*, 41 (1993), 83–103.

——— *The Usurer's Daughter: Male Friendship and Fictions of Women in Sixteenth-Century England*, (London: Routledge, 1994).

JEFFERY, VIOLET M., *John Lyly and the Italian Renaissance* (Paris: Champion, 1929).

JOHNSON, RONALD C., *George Gascoigne* (New York: Twayne, 1972).

JOSEPH, SISTER MIRIAM, *Shakespeare's Use of the Arts of Language* (New York: Columbia University Press, 1947).

—— *Rhetoric in Shakespeare's Time* (New York: Harcourt, Brace & World, 1962).

KING, JOHN N., *English Reformation Literature: The Tudor Origins of the Protestant Tradition* (Princeton, NJ: Princeton University Press, 1982).

—— 'Spenser's *Shepheardes Calender* and Protestant Pastoral Satire', in Barbara Kiefer Lewalski (ed.), *Renaissance Genres: Essays on Theory, History, and Interpretation*, (Cambridge, Mass.: Harvard University Press, 1986), 369–98.

KING, WALTER N., 'John Lyly and Elizabethan Rhetoric', *Studies in Philology*, 52 (1955), 149–61.

KINNEY, ARTHUR F., *Humanist Poetics: Thought, Rhetoric, and Fiction in Sixteenth-Century England* (Amherst, Mass.: University of Massachusetts Press, 1986).

LANHAM, RICHARD A., 'Narrative Structure in Gascoigne's *F.J.*', *Studies in Short Fiction*, 4 (1966), 42–50.

LEVAO, RONALD, *Renaissance Minds and their Fictions: Cusanus, Sidney, Shakespeare* (Berkeley, Ca.: University of California Press, 1985).

LEWALSKI, BARBARA KIEFER (ed.), *Renaissance Genres: Essays on Theory, History, and Interpretation* (Cambridge, Mass.: Harvard University Press, 1986).

LEWIS, C. S., *English Literature in the Sixteenth Century Excluding Drama* (Oxford: Oxford University Press, 1954).

LUCAS, CAROLINE, *Writing for Women: The Example of Woman as Reader in Elizabethan Romance* (Milton Keynes: Open University Press, 1989).

MCCABE, RICHARD A., 'Wit, Eloquence and Wisdom in *Euphues*', *Studies in Philology*, 81 (1984), 299–324.

MCCOY, RICHARD C., 'Gascoigne's *Poëmata castrata*: The Wages of Courtly Success', *Criticism*, 27 (1985), 29–55.

MCGRATH, LYNETTE, 'George Gascoigne's Moral Satire: The Didactic Use of Convention in *The Adventures Passed by Master F.J.*', *JEGP*, 70 (1971), 432–50.

MAJOR, JOHN N., *Sir Thomas Elyot and Renaissance Humanism* (Lincoln, Nebr.: University of Nebraska Press, 1964).

MALEY, WILLY, 'Spenser's Irish English: Language and Identity in Early Modern Ireland', *Studies in Philology*, 91 (1994), 417–31.

MARGOLIES, DAVID, *Novel and Society in Elizabethan England* (London: Croom Helm, 1985).

MOODY, T. W., MARTIN, F. X., and BYRNE, F. J. (eds.), *A New History of Ireland*, 9 vols. (Oxford: Clarendon Press, 1976–87).

MUELLER, JANEL M., *The Native Tongue and the Word: Developments in English Prose Style, 1380–1580* (Chicago, Ill.: University of Chicago Press, 1984).

NELSON, WILLIAM, *Fact or Fiction: The Dilemma of the Renaissance Storyteller* (Cambridge, Mass.: Harvard University Press, 1973).

NICHOLL, CHARLES, *The Reckoning* (London: Picador, 1993).

PARKER, ROBERT W., 'Terentian Structure and Sidney's Original *Arcadia*', in Arthur F. Kinney *et al.* (eds.), *Sidney in Retrospect* (Amherst, Mass.: University of Massachusetts Press, 1987), 151–68.

PARRISH, PAUL A., 'The Multiple Perspectives of Gascoigne's *The Adventures of Master F. J.*', *Studies in Short Fiction*, 10 (1973), 82–4.

PATTERSON, ANNABEL, *Censorship and Interpretation: The Conditions of Writing and Reading in Early Modern England* (Madison, Wisc.: University of Wisconsin Press, 1984).

—— *Fables of Power: Aesopian Writing and Political History* (Durham, NC: Duke University Press, 1991).

—— 'Censorship and the 1587 "Holinshed's" Chronicles', in Paul Hyland and Neil Sammuells (Eds.), *Writing and Censorship in Britain* (London: Routledge, 1992), 23–35.

PINCOMBE, MICHAEL, 'The Date of *The Image of Idleness*', *Notes and Queries*, 239 (ns 41/1) (1994), 24.

PROUTY, C. T., *George Gascoigne: Elizabethan Courtier, Soldier, and Poet* (New York: Columbia, 1942).

PRUVOST, RENÉ, *Matteo Bandello and Elizabethan Fiction* (Paris: H. Champion, 1937).

READ, CONYERS, *Mr Secretary Walsingham and the Policy of Queen Elizabeth*, 3 vols. (Oxford: Clarendon Press, 1925).

RINGLER, WILLIAM, 'The Immediate Source of Euphuism', *PMLA*, 53(1938), 678–86.

RODAX, YVONNE, *The Real and the Ideal in the Novella* (Chapel Hill, NC: University of North Carolina Press, 1968).

ROHR PHILMUS, M. R., 'Gascoigne's Fable of the Artist as a Young Man', *JEGP*, 73 (1974), 13–31.

ROWE, GEORGE R., Jr, 'Interpretation, Sixteenth-Century Readers, and George Gascoigne's *Master F.J.*', *ELH*, 48 (1981), 271–89.

RUSSELL, CONRAD, *The Crisis of Parliaments* (Oxford: Oxford University Press, 1977).

RYAN, LAWRENCE V., *Roger Ascham* (Stanford, Ca.: Stanford University Press, 1963).

SALZMAN, PAUL, *English Prose Fiction 1558–1700* (Oxford: Oxford University Press, 1985).

SCHLAUCH, MARGARET M., *Antecedents of the English Novel 1400–1600* (Warsaw: PWN, and London: Oxford University Press, 1963).

—— 'English Short Fiction in the Fifteenth and Sixteenth Centuries', *Studies in Short Fiction*, 3 (1966), 393–434.

SCRAGG, LEAH, *The Metamorphosis of Gallathea: A Study in Creative Adaptation* (Washington, DC: University Press of America, 1982).

SIEGEL, PAUL N., 'A New Source for *Othello*?', *PMLA*, 75 (Sept. 1960), 480.

SMITH, ALAN G. R., *The Emergence of a Nation State: The Commonwealth of England 1529–1660* (London: Longman, 1984).

STAUB, SUSAN C., ' "According to my Source": Fictionality in *The Adventures of Master F. J.'*, *Studies in Philology*, 87 (1990), 111–19.

STEINBERG, THEODORE, 'The Anatomy of *Euphues*', *Studies in English Literature*, 17 (1977), 27–38.

STEPHANSON, RAYMOND, 'John Lyly's Prose Fiction: Irony, Humour and Anti-Humanism', *English Literary Renaissance*, 11 (1981), 3–21.

STREITBERGER, W. R., *Edmond Tyllney: Master of the Revels and Censor of Plays* (New York: AMS Press, 1986).

SWART, J., 'Lyly and Pettie', *English Studies*, 23 (1941), 9–18.

TAYLOR, BARRY, *Vagrant Writing: Social and Semiotic Disorders in the English Renaissance* (New York: Harvester Wheatsheaf, 1991).

THOMAS, KEITH, *Religion and the Decline of Magic* (Harmondsworth: Penguin, 1978).

TROUSDALE, MARION, *Shakespeare and the Rhetoricians* (London: Scolar Press, 1982).

WARNEKE, SARA, 'A Taste for Newfangledness: The Destructive Potential of Novelty in Early Modern England', *The Sixteenth Century Journal*, 26 (1995), 881–96.

WILLIAMS, GORDON, 'Gascoigne's *Master F. J.* and the Development of the Novel', *Trivium*, 10 (1975), 137–50.

WILLIAMSON, GEORGE, *The Senecan Amble: A Study of Prose Form from Bacon to Collier* (London: Faber & Faber, 1951).

WILSON, KENNETH JAY, 'Ascham's *Toxophilus* and the Rules of Art', *Renaissance Quarterly*, 1 (1976), 30–51.

—— *Incomplete Fictions: The Formation of English Renaissance Dialogue* (Washington, DC: Catholic University of America Press, 1985).

YATES, FRANCES A., *Giordano Bruno and the Hermetic Tradition* (London: Routledge & Kegan Paul, 1964).

—— *The Art of Memory* (Harmondsworth: Peregrine, 1969).

# Index

Bold figures denote main references.

Achilles 15n.
Adam 65, 89n., 160, 257, 261, 263, 270–1, 296n.
adventures 115–16, 129–31
Aeneas 292
Aesop 3n., 47, 71, 75, 124, 266–7, 290
Agrippa, Henry Cornelius 2, 242, 275n., 282
Alcibiades 202–3
Alcmene 243
Aldgate 79
Alexander 91–2, 204–6, 279, 282
Amazons 86–7, **90–3**, 100, 110–11, 159, 194, 295, 299–300
Amphitryon 243
Anger, Jane 299
Ansley, Brian 86n.
Apelles 204–5, 249, 279
Apollo 173, 232
Arachne 257
Archer, John Michael 10n., 291n.
Aretino, Pietro 47n.
Ariadne 197, 271, 274, 276
Ariosto, Lodovico 33, 118, 138–9
Aristippus 222n., 229
Aristotle 5, 55, 73, 116, 221, 251
Arthur, King 291
Ascham, Roger **2–7**, 8, 20, 26, **40–55**, 57–8, 60, 85, 105, 109, 140, 151, 155, 161–2, 201, 209, 212, 226–7, 254, 266, 273, 275, 278, 283, 289–90, 294, 296
  *The Scholemaster* **2–7**, 24, **40–52**, 62, 66, 80, 93–5, 101, 103, 107, 111–12, 121–2, 125, 162, 168–9, **214–22**, 227, 249–50, 283
  *Toxophilus* 47
atheism 7, 156, 221–2, 236, 249, 252
Athene 203, 222, 281
Athens 28, 209, 211, 221, 227, 254
Atreus 292
'Attic' style 240
Augustine, St 115–16
Aulus Gellius 88
Aurelius, Marcus 32–3, 65, 171, 262

Babel 23, 77
Bacon, Sir Francis 45–6, 67, 74

*The Advancement of Learning* 45
*Filum Labyrinthi* 271
*The Wisedome of the Ancients* 74n.
Baldick, Chris 100n.
Baldwin, T. W. 17n.
Baldwin, William 20, **75–84**, 152, 159, 185
  *Beware the Cat* 20, **75–82**, 112, 134, 152, 159, 185, 237n., 245, 297, 299
  *A Mirror for Magistrates* 75, 83–4, 91, 99, 143n., 237n., 291
  *A Treatise of Morall Phylosophie* 73
Baldwin Smith, Lucy 9n.
Bandello, Matteo 8, **85–113**, 158, 164–5, 190, 220–1
Barbour, Reid 19n.
Barish, Jonas A. 200n.
Bartello 8
Barton, Anne 25n.
Bates, Catherine 262n., 278n., 285n.
Bedlam 100
bees 15n., 88, **222–5**, 267, **273–4**
Belleforest, François de 85–6, 88n., 91–2n., 97–8, 220–1, 291
Bembo, Pietro 103
  *see also* Castiglione, Baldassare, *The Courtier*
Beverley, Peter 90
Bible 23, 47, 99, 153n., 195, 252
Bidpai 71–2, 77, 124, 266
  *see also* North, Thomas, *The Morall Philosophie of Doni*
Binns, James W. 56n.
Bliss, Alan 78n.
Blount, Edward 285n.
Boaistuau, Pierre de 85n., 220n.
Boccaccio, Giovanni 8, 29, 34, 40, 47, 111n.
  *De Genealogia Deorum* 2n.
  *The Decameron* 21, 26–7, 34
  *Filocolo* 40
Bonahue, Edward T. 76
Bond, James 9
Bond, R. W. 14n., 199n.
Bossy, John 10n.
Brammall, Kathryn M. 101n.
Brennan, Gillian 79n.
Brooke, Arthur 93–5, 195n.
Browne, Thomas 17n.